WEDDED TO THE ROCKS

ALSO BY CHRIS PARK

Swaledale and Richmond: the story of a dale

God: real or imagined?

Francis: Life and lessons

Oxford Dictionary of Environment and Conservation

The Environment: Principles and Applications

Sacred Worlds: an Introduction to Geography and Religion

Caring for Creation

Tropical Rainforests

Environmental Hazards

Acid Rain: Rhetoric and Reality

Chernobyl: The Long Shadow

WEDDED TO THE ROCKS

The Life and Work of
Adam Sedgwick (1785-1873)

Chris Park

*"I am wedded to the rocks, and Mount Sorrel ... is
my present mistress. By the way she is a little coy and
hard-hearted, and refuses to tell me her pedigree, and to
introduce me to her old relations."*

Published by Chris Park [chris@chris-park.com]

Printed by CreateSpace, An Amazon.com Company

Available from Amazon.com, CreateSpace.com, and other retail outlets

Contents

For Penny, my rock, my sunshine,
and my companion on the journey

Acknowledgements

During the writing of this book I have greatly enjoyed and benefitted from time spent discussing it with my two Lancaster "coffee-mates", philosopher Vernon Pratt and listener David Barnett, and from the support and encouragement of my great friend historian Michael Seymour. Any mistakes and misrepresentations are mine and mine alone.

Introduction

This is a book I'd hoped to find and read, but ended up having to write myself. I quickly discovered that no popular biography of Adam Sedgwick has yet been written, so I took on the task myself. Colin Speakman's *Adam Sedgwick. Geologist and Dalesman, 1785-1873. A biography in twelve themes* (1982) is very readable and informative, but the sub-title underlines the book's selective coverage, and it has long been out of print.

I was drawn to Adam Sedgwick mainly out of intellectual curiosity. I was fascinated by the man himself, one of Britain's most prominent early geologists, widely regarded as the father of modern geology. He lived and worked at a critical time in the development of the subject, the tipping point between 'Biblical geology' and modern 'scientific geology', when ideas about the age and formation of the earth, and about how species evolve, were being hotly debated. He had strong views and was not afraid of expressing them. He mixed with the great and the good of Victorian society, including William Wordsworth, David Livingstone, and Prince Albert.

Without in any way wanting to suggest that I am made of the same stuff as Sedgwick, I soon discovered that we have some important things in common – like him I am a "son of the dales", and an environmental scientist, with a strong Christian faith. Personal affinity made him an intriguing subject to try to capture, although it is clearly important that we view Adam in context – historically, geographically, and culturally – and not judge him by the standards and expectations of today.

The task of writing a biography about someone two centuries after they lived was made possible because Adam left a very clear paper trail through his adult years. This includes a range of contemporary reports and accounts of his geological work in publications of the Geological Society of London and reports of annual meetings of the British Association. A complete list of his publications is given in Appendix 2. We also have an obituary and several contemporary articles in *The Times*, appreciations of his work in geological journals, and mentions of him in biographies of other leading scientists of the day (including Charles Darwin).

As far as we know Adam never kept a diary, but like many of his contemporaries he was a very keen letter writer. Through exchanging letters, he kept in touch with members of his family and close friends, discussed geological matters with other scientists, shared news and views with fellow churchmen, and engaged in many heated exchanges with people whose views he disagreed with or who did not share his views.

It was not uncommon for prominent people in the early nineteenth century to be immortalised in a *Life and Letters* book compiled by those who knew them and had an interest in promoting their legacy. Thankfully this is the case with Adam Sedgwick. Two academics who knew him and worked with him – John Willis Clark (Fellow of Trinity College and Superintendent of the Cambridge University Museum of Zoology and Comparative Anatomy) and Thomas McKenny Hughes (Professorial Fellow of Clare College and Woodwardian Professor of Geology after Sedgwick) – collected together a huge number of Adam's letters and compiled the two-volume *The Life and Letters of the Reverend Adam Sedgwick*. The Cambridge University Press published the books in 1890 and they provide a very useful source of information about his life, work, thoughts, hopes and dreams, much of it in his own words.

The collection of letters is useful but not without some serious limitations. The editors invited anyone they could think of to lend them any letters from Sedgwick they had kept, and the collection is made up largely of the letters he sent rather than ones he received. Not everyone would have kept every letter they received from Adam; some recipients may have been reluctant to lend them; and the editors doubtless either didn't know or couldn't contact every single person Adam wrote to.

It would also be wrong to assume that the letters cover everything Adam found interesting or everything he did or thought. Gaps in coverage are inevitable and, as lawyers say, "absence of evidence is not evidence of absence"; just because something isn't mentioned does not mean it didn't happen. One of the most curious things on which *Life and Letters* is stubbornly silent is the 1851 Great Exhibition of London, that was one of the most significant and high profile national events during Adam's lifetime and it was organised by Prince Albert, with whom Adam enjoyed

2

a close working relationship. Yet the only mention it gets is "visits to the Crystal Palace".

Adam never wrote the letters with the expectation that people other than his intended recipients might end up reading them, particularly so long after the event. He was not drafting his biography in bite-sized chunks, consciously or unconsciously, and we must exercise caution in reading between the lines of what he said and didn't say. His language is inevitably of its day, particularly in his many letters to family members and close friends. He reads like a typical Victorian gentleman, both in the words he uses and the sentiments he expresses, which can come across to modern readers as rather gushing and over-sentimental.

Adam Sedgwick also speaks to us through two books he wrote on radically different themes – *A Discourse on the Studies of the University* (1833) and *A Memorial by the Trustees of Cowgill Chapel* (1868). As well as discussing the themes given in the titles these books offer valuable insights into his thoughts, experiences, concerns and priorities.

This is his story, so I have tried wherever possible to let him speak for himself, which is why I have included so many direct quotations from his letters and papers. To allow the text to flow smoothly, and reduce the risk of making the book too heavily academic, I have avoided the temptation to use footnotes. Unless otherwise mentioned in the text, all quotations are from *Life and Letters*.

Adam might not have wanted a biography to be written. I have several reasons for saying this – he was driven by a strong desire to do what was right, not by personal ambition; he urged his nieces in letters not to think too highly of themselves, to be modest in all they did and not to think of themselves as better than anyone else; in April 1840 Adam wrote to his niece Isabella urging her to "continue to be single-hearted, and humble, and charitable in the true and Christian sense. And God forbid that you should ever learn to think too well of yourself, and too ill of those about you."

Biographers can always be accused of putting their subject on a pedestal or portraying him or her in soft focus. I have tried hard to avoid this biography becoming hagiography, and treating my subject with undue reverence. My aim has been to give a coherent account of his life and work, consistent with the known facts.

PART ONE. DALES MAN

"He was a most primitive man – of the solid ancient rock of humanity. He appears like a great boulder stone of granite, such as he describes, transported from Shap Fell over the hills of Yorkshire, dropped here in our lowland country, and here fixed for life; primitive in his name, Adam; primitive in his nature; in his noble rugged simplicity; a dalesman of the north; primitive in his love of all ancient good things and ways; primitive in his love of nature, and of his native rock from which he was hewn; primitive in his loyalty to truth, and hatred of everything false and mean; a heart, if ever there was one, that 'turned upon the poles of truth.'"

Professor Selwyn, posthumous tribute to Adam Sedgwick (March 1873)

1. Adam O'th' Parsons

His childhood was passed amongst the hearty, straightforward
dalesmen, and he was a general favourite with them all.
Thomas McKenny Hughes (1883)

"Give you joy, Sir, give you joy! a fine boy, Sir, as like you Sir, as one
pea is to another." The year is 1785 and it would turn out to be a momen-
tous one in a variety of ways. The *Daily Universal Register* (later
renamed *The Times*) was first published at the start of the year. Air travel
began that year, when two men crossed the English Channel in a hot air
balloon. The factory system was also born that year, when James Watts'
steam engine was adapted to drive looms in a cotton factory. It was the
year in which science started to seriously challenge the received wisdom
of a Biblical interpretation of the world around us, when geologist James
Hutton proposed to the Royal Society of Edinburgh the theory of Uniformitarianism (that we'll learn more about in Chapter 10).

The man being asked to "give joy" is the Reverend Richard Sedgwick, Vicar of Dent in north-west Yorkshire. The "fine boy", just born, is
his third child, to whom he and his wife Margaret would give the name
Adam.

A heavy storm raged over the lower part of Dentdale, in the West
Riding of Yorkshire, through the night of Monday the 21st of March,
causing deep snowdrifts to pile up and almost cut off the village of Dent.
Reverend Sedgwick sat anxiously by the fire in the little back parlour of
the Vicarage while his wife was upstairs giving birth. John Dawson, a
doctor who had struggled to get there through the deep snow blocking the
rough mountain track from Sedbergh, five miles to the northwest, was
attending her. There were complications with the birth, so a local woman
called Margaret Burton – the "wise woman of the village", who had no
training but great experience as a midwife – was sent for.

Between them Margaret and John managed to deliver the baby boy
safely. At about 2 am early the next morning the midwife carried baby
Adam carefully downstairs in her apron and presented him to his father.
Relieved, Richard looked closely at his new son for a moment or two,
then kissed him.

Adam Sedgwick had a rather unpromising start in life and, but for the skill and dedication of John Dawson and Margaret Burton, he might well not have lived long, if at all.

Childhood

Young Adam, who the villagers of Dent often referred to as Adam O'th' Parsons, had a reputation as a bright and serious boy.

We only catch glimpses of his childhood through *Life and Letters*. He had a stable and happy home life in the Parsonage at Dent, where his father Richard. As he described in a letter to Lady Augusta Stanley in July 1865, "Here I spent my childhood and my early boyhood, when my father and mother and my three sisters and three brothers were all living in this old house. Our home was humble; but we were a merry crew; and we were rich in health, and rich in brotherly love."

By all accounts, as a child Adam was "active and merry, fond of play, and given to tearing his books rather than reading them." But his attention was captured when he was five years old, when his godfather – Mr. Parker, then Master of the Dent Grammar School – gave him a new and nicely-bound spelling book, which he treasured and quickly learnt to read. Three years later, when Adam was eight, Mr. Parker took him riding on horseback to visit friends near Carlisle. Adam really enjoyed the freedom and the sights, greatly impressed his godfather with his powers of observation, and often looked back fondly on his first expedition.

From a very early age Adam loved the call of the wild and the freedom he had to explore the hills and dales around Dentdale. Thomas McKenny Hughes (1883), who co-edited *Life and Letters*, describes how "he delighted in every kind of sport and out-door exercises, and he had always a quick eye for anything curious and unusual, which he might come across in his scrambles amongst the crags and fells which surrounded the valley." His native fells and moors were his playground but also his classroom, where he learned to fish, shoot, and poach by moonlight, and he hunted for and collected rocks and fossils. There's no doubting the impact these early years would have on his adult life, when he was at his happiest out and about studying rocks and fossils, and trying to make sense of the world around him.

Dent Grammar School

Like his father Richard, Adam and at least two of his three brothers (John and Richard) attended the local Grammar School in Dent. Adam was taught there between the ages of 8 and 16 (1793-1801).

1. Adam O'th' Parsons

As Adam described in *Memorial* (1868), looking back in old age, "for more than two centuries the Grammar School has had a very healthy influence upon the education and manners of the valley. The leading statesmen's sons attended the Grammar School, and acquired a smattering of classical learning ...". The school was not just for "the leading statesmen's sons", though, because it also taught the sons of local parishioners. Neither did it just teach "a smattering of classical learning", because as well as basic Latin the boys were taught writing and reading, and probably some mathematics too.

Adam also tells us that the school broadened its syllabus after he was there; "it had large English classes, in which writing and arithmetic were taught to young persons of both sexes: and there were also itinerant Masters ... who visited certain Schools, in a regular cycle, and were chiefly employed in teaching writing, arithmetic in all its branches, and the principles of surveying."

Typically, in such Grammar Schools, the local Vicar would sometimes have to serve as schoolmaster as well as parish priest. This happened during Adam's time at the school, when his father was urged by the Governors to take over as Master after Mr. Parker left, "with one or more under-masters to assist him. After some hesitation he consented, and taught his own boys along with his other scholars."

Youth

As the editors of *Life and Letters* (1890a) point out, "about Adam's progress [at school] tradition is silent". But they conclude that he must at least have worked hard because in later years "his knowledge of Greek and Latin was superior to that of most men as distinguished in mathematics as himself".

They have more to say about Adam's character as a youth, noting that "he did not give any special promise of future intellectual power, but he was remarkable ... for a frank, genial disposition; he was full of fun and high spirits; he delighted in rambling over the fells and climbing the hills which bound his native dale; his powers of observation were great; and he had a plentiful share of sound practical common-sense. He was also distinguished for undeviating truthfulness in all that he said and did. Among his brothers and sisters and school-fellows, if Adam said a thing was so, there was no further question about the matter."

Adam himself tells us that his love of the outdoors continued through his teenage years. In 1873 he wrote to John Salter, his assistant in the Geology Museum at Cambridge, "I almost lived out of doors ... at fourteen years old I was trusted with a gun, and coursed over the heathy moors the whole autumn day. I believe I was a tolerably good shot. I was a fisherman too at this age, and was particularly careful to obtain the exact feathers which were considered the most killing flies for trout, grayling, etc. Nor ... was I quite free from the crime of poaching [rabbits, hares, and pheasants]."

In the same letter, Adam told Salter that he "did not quite forget the rocks and the fossils. One of my early employments on a half-holiday when nutting [collecting nuts] in Dent woods, was, as I well remember, collecting the conspicuous fossils of the mountain-limestone on either side of the valley. It was not till many years afterwards that I understood its structure, but these early rambles no doubt aided to establish a taste for out-door observations."

Sedbergh School

After Dent Grammar School, at the age of sixteen Adam moved to Sedbergh School, a few miles west of Dent. He spent three years there, between 1801 and 1803. Sedbergh is now a fee-paying independent school, but in his day it was free, having been founded as a Chantry School in 1525 by Roger Lupton (Provost of Eton), who endowed it with land.

Although it was not far from home, Adam was a boarder, like almost all of the boys who studied there. He boarded along with three other boys at a farmhouse near Winder, just north of Sedbergh, owned by Edmund Foster, a Quaker whose family were close friends with his. Adam wrote that "we were treated with infinite kindness by the family, and our happy freedom made us the envy of our schoolfellows". It suited him that "half [term] holidays were generally spent in fishing in the Rawthey or the Lune, or in rambles over the mountains."

The post of Master of Sedbergh School was in the gift of St John's College, Cambridge, and in Adam's day it was held by Rev William Stevens. Adam described Stevens as "an excellent scholar, and a good domestic and social man", although discipline was not high on his list of priorities and the number of boys on the roll often fell below ten. As a result, the school struggled under his leadership, although Adam's father Richard was confident enough in Stevens' abilities to send all of his sons to Sedbergh. Despite Stevens' limited success as Master of Sedbergh, many of his pupils went on to study at Cambridge, and to have successful careers after graduating.

Adam made two good friends at Sedbergh who he kept in contact with for many years afterwards. His best friend William Ainger was a year older than him. They remained close as students at Cambridge, rarely met afterwards, but kept in contact via letters. After graduating, Ainger was ordained and held various church posts before becoming Principal of the Theological College at St Bees (near Whitehaven on the west coast of the Lake District), and a Canon of Chester Cathedral. Adam nursed his old friend as he died after a short illness in 1840. Afterwards he collected subscriptions for a monument to Ainger to be erected in St Bees in 1842, and fulfilled Ainger's wish for him to serve as guardian to his daughters.

Adam's other good friend at Sedbergh was Miles Bland who became a Fellow of St John's College in Cambridge, where he and Adam (then at Trinity College) probably met regularly. Their friendship appears to have waned after Bland left the university in 1823 and accepted the post of Vicar of Lilley in Hertfordshire.

After Stevens died in 1819 Adam and Miles Bland "raised ... a large sum of money for the benefit of his widow and children, for whom he had neglected to make any provision."

John Dawson

John Dawson (1734-1820) was the son of a poor statesmen in Garsdale, near Dentdale. The family could not afford a formal education for him. and he worked as a shepherd on the hills until his early twenties. But he had a great appetite for learning and was largely self-taught, begging or borrowing books from local families. Adam would later describe him as belonging to "the very highest order of intellectual greatness".

As a young adult, Dawson supplemented his meagre income by teaching mathematics to local boys, including Adam's father Richard. Although he was probably never formally a member of staff at Sedbergh, many of the boys' successes were credited to him because he privately coached and tutored the brighter ones, particularly in mathematics.

He later trained as a physician and surgeon, and worked as a doctor in the area around Sedbergh. Both reasons together explain why Adam's father called him to be present at Adam's birth.

But Dawson's heart lay more in mathematics than in medicine and in 1790, at the age of 56, he gave up his medical practice and devoted himself fully to teaching mathematics, at which he was a genius. Among his many other achievements, he developed the so-called Lunar Theory, demonstrating that it was possible to work out the distance between the earth and the sun by observing the orbit of Venus. James Cook confirmed this method during his voyage to Tahiti in 1768.

John became a gifted teacher with a national reputation. Adam described how "Cambridge undergraduates flocked to him every summer" for extra tuition in maths during their long summer vacations, and how "between 1781 and 1794 he counted eight Senior Wranglers [first class honours graduates] among his pupils."

John and Adam crossed paths several times, starting with Adam's birth. When Adam was a teenager at Sedbergh, John tutored him in mathematics. He also offered his father Richard advice on which Cambridge College might best suit Adam, and subsequently helped Adam prepare for the admissions process. By this time John was seventy years old and, as Adam put it, "his intellect was then as grand as it had ever been, but his memory had begun to fail."

Dawson died in September 1820, aged 86, and was buried in the churchyard at Sedbergh Church. A few years later a monument was erected to his memory inside the church by some of his former pupils, who noted on a marble tablet how he was "Distinguished by his profound knowledge of mathematics, beloved for his amiable simplicity of character, and revered for his exemplary discharge of every moral and religious duty."

2. Meet the Sedgwicks

---

*It may still, I hope, please God to spare him to our family for some
years.*
Adam Sedgwick, on his elderly and frail father (letter, 1820)

Adam Sedgwick was born into a family that had deep roots in Dentdale.
His ancestors can be traced directly back at least as far as the early sixteenth century.

Surname

Adam explained the origin of the family name in a letter to a distant relative in Connecticut in New England in February 1837. As he understood
it, he said, his ancestors – indeed, "every family in this island [with] the
name of Sedgwick" – were people from Germany or Denmark who settled in the mountainous border area of Lancashire, Yorkshire, and
Westmoreland, and originally spelled their surname as Siggeswick, according to "parish records that go back to the reign of Henry VII."

The earliest record is of Thomas Sidgwick (around 1520-1588) of
Banklands and Gibbs Hall, Kirkthwaite in Dent. The direct line continues
through his eldest son Leonard Sidgwick (around 1560-1646) of Banklands, and his son Thomas Sidgwick (around 1605-1663), also of
Banklands.

The spelling of the surname then changes to Sedgwick. Thomas's
son Leonard Sedgwick (1635-1687) is followed by John Sedgwick (1672-
1752), a tanner of Gibbs Hall, then Thomas Sedgwick (1705-1782), also a
tanner of Gibbs Hall. Thomas was Adam's grandfather, and he had three
sons. The first (John) lived less than a week, and the second was Richard
Sedgwick (1736-1828), who in turn was Adam's father. The third, a tal-
low chandler of Leithbank in Dent, also called John, was born two years
after Richard.

The head of each of these seven generations of Sedgwicks was born
in Dent and married a woman from Dent or the surrounding area. Most
found their final resting places in Dent churchyard.

13

Parents

Richard Sedgwick (1736-1828)

Richard Sedgwick was born in Dent in March 1736, the seventh generation of Sedgwicks to live in the dale. He was educated at Dent Grammar
School until the age of fifteen, then at Sedbergh School, before being tutored in mathematics by the brilliant young John Dawson of Garsdale –
the same John Dawson who would later be present at Adam's birth.

In 1754, at the age of eighteen, Richard headed south to Cambridge
to study at St Catharine's Hall (renamed St Catherine's College in 1860).
There he was a sizar – a scholarship student who received financial assistance towards the cost of his lodging, meals and fees. He graduated in
1760 with the degree of Bachelor of Arts, coming seventh in the second
class of the Mathematical Tripos (degree scheme).

Richard was ordained deacon in March 1760, and priest that December. Between 1761 and 1768 he served as Curate at Amwell, Hoddesdon
in Hertfordshire. He also worked as Assistant Master in Hoddesdon
School, a boarding school run by Rev Dr James Bennet, "a gentleman of
some distinction in the literary world". In 1766 Richard married Bennet's
daughter Catherine (1741-1768).

Two years later, in February 1768, he was licensed as Chaplain (effectively Vicar) of St Andrew's, the parish church in Dent. The post was
offered to him by the church's patrons, twenty-four of the leading yeo-
men farmers in Dentdale who were known locally as 'statesmen' (who
we'll learn more about in Chapter 3). They chose well, because Rev
Richard Sedgwick served as much-loved Vicar there for more than five
decades, retiring in May 1822. Richard also served for a short time as
Master of Dent Grammar School.

Richard's first year in Dent was blighted by the death of his young
wife Catherine in July 1768. She died giving birth to a girl whose name is
unknown, but who died aged nine in June 1777. Catherine is buried at
Dent. Richard remarried in September 1781; his second wife was a distant cousin called Margaret Sturges, daughter of Adam Sturges of Dent.

Adam was extremely proud of his father and often wrote about him
in letters to family and friends. He admired "his public character, his
management of the parish, and his influence in the dale". He described in
his book *Memorial* (1868) (of which more in Chapter 17) how his father
"loved his flock", who in return "loved my Father, because by birth he
was one of themselves, and because of his kindness and purity of life.
They were proud of him too, because he was a graduate of the University

of Cambridge, and had been living in good literary society some years before he fixed his home in Dent."

Adam was proud of "the influence he had over the minds of his flock [that] rested on his humble teaching of Gospel truth; the cheerful simplicity of his life; and his readiness, at every turn and difficulty, to be in true Christian love an adviser and a peace-maker."

Richard's influence extended far beyond the walls of the church, and he was well known and much appreciated for organising sports competitions between local parishes, which he believed "promoted health, temperance, and good social temper", although the rivalry would sometimes get rather savage. Adam tells us in *Memorial* that "matches at leaping, foot-racing, wrestling, and football, were all in fashion among the Dalesmen. But the victory of the football match was regarded as the crowning glory of the rural festival."

Increasing blindness restricted Richard's last twenty years of life, but he accepted it with grace. In 1829, shortly after his father died, Adam wrote that he had been "a very happy old man, and over and over again said that his blindness was a blessing, as it made him more religious and more fit to die." Richard took on a curate to oversee the church services, but he knew the services by heart and often helped with them. He led some Burial Services himself, meeting the mourners at the gate of the churchyard and walking ahead of them into the church, on the arm of one of his sons or a friend.

Richard resigned as Vicar of Dent in May 1822, at the age of 86, after serving faithfully for 54 years. As he moved out of the Parsonage his son John moved in, having being appointed to succeed him as Vicar. As if to keep 'the family business' going, John's son Richard (1827-1885) would later take over as Vicar of Dent, and live in the Parsonage with his own family.

On his retirement, Richard moved to Flintergill, a small house around the corner from the Parsonage in Dent, to live with and be cared for by his eldest son Thomas and daughter Margaret. His solid Christian faith meant he had no fear of death and, as Adam put it, "the feebleness of age seemed to give strength to his faith in the promises of the Gospel." Adam wrote affectionately of how his sister Margaret "watched and supported for years the dear old man with the tender care that becomes a Christian daughter; and her own character became exalted and purified by the long task of love which Providence had given her."

That "long task of love" was to last six years, until Richard died in the Parsonage in Dent in May 1828 at the age of 92, having lived in Dent for more than sixty years. Adam was then 43. Richard was buried in Dent churchyard, and the following year a monument was erected in his memory inside Dent Church. Adam wrote the inscription for it, that tells of how "He lived among his flock for fifty-four years, revered as their pastor and loved as their brother."

Margaret Sedgwick (1752-1820)
Margaret became Richard's second wife when they married in September 1781. They had nearly forty years together and were blessed with seven children, of which Adam was the third.

Perhaps surprisingly, Adam reveals little about his mother in the many letters he wrote to family and friends. In one of the few references to her, he describes how "I rejoice to say that she possessed her self-possession almost to the moment of her death, and expressed her entire resignation to the will of God." Margaret died in Dent in October 1820, after an illness of a week, and was buried in the churchyard. Adam learnt of his mother's death while he was engaged in geological fieldwork on the Isle of Wight, and he went to Dent as quickly as he could. He later wrote "I should have been very thankful had it pleased God to have allowed me to arrive in time to receive my poor mother's last blessing; but that melancholy satisfaction was denied me."

Brothers and sisters
Adam was part of a large family – he had six brothers and sisters, three of whom presented him with a total of five nephews, four nieces and one step-niece. Strikingly, of Richard and Margaret's first four children, three (including Adam) never married and none gave their parents any grandchildren.

Margaret (1782-1855)
Richard and Margaret's first child was born in Dent in 1782. Like her mother and paternal grandmother, she was named Margaret. She was three years older than Adam, and she spent much of her adult life caring for her ageing father, like many daughters were expected to do in those days.

Eight years after her father died, Margaret married the Rev John Mason (Vicar of Bothamsall in Nottinghamshire and chaplain to the Duke of Newcastle) a distant cousin in June 1839. She was 57 years old, and Adam attended the wedding in Dent. There were no children, and within four years Margaret was widowed when John Mason died in October 1844.

Margaret survived her husband by eleven years. After he died she returned to Dent where she lived until her own death in January 1856, at the age of 74. She passed her final days peacefully, living back in the Vicarage she had been born in back in 1782, being cared for by her brother John (then Vicar of Dent) and his wife Jane.

She had inherited from her father a deep and strong faith. In her final weeks, with her strength failing fast, she kept insisting, "I think this will be my last service in the church in which my father used to teach me, and in which I have so long been permitted to hold communion with my Maker." She wanted people to keep reading to her the 17th chapter of John's Gospel, which describes (in the words of the King James version she would have had) how Jesus prayed for his disciples, reminding them that "this is eternal life, that they may know You, the only true God, and Jesus Christ whom You have sent."

Two days before she died, she is reported to have said "I am ready to die, when it is God's will to call me away, but I should like to live a little longer because you are so sorry to part with me." She died peacefully with her niece Isabella at her bedside. Adam later described her then as "calm, sensible, humble, and most thankful", uttering the words "O Father, receive my soul for Jesus' sake" before "she fell asleep as quietly as does a little child on its mother's breast." She was buried five days later in Dent churchyard, with her four brothers, sister-in-law Jane, niece Isabella, and two nephews at the graveside.

As had happened with his mother in 1820, and would happen with his sister Isabel three years later, Adam had hoped but failed to reach Dent before Margaret took her final breath.

The Sunday following Margaret's funeral Adam preached at the church in Dent. He spoke from John chapter 17, explaining to the congregation that he "had fixed on that chapter because my sister's soul had rested in it. It is delightful to preach to country people, but in this instance the task was not an easy one for me."

Margaret was, by all accounts, a very hard-working, humble, kind-hearted and courageous woman. She was very generous to people in need, grateful to those who helped her, and did much good work in and around the parish. As we shall see in Chapter 17, she played a key role with her mother Jane (Adam's sister-in-law) in the founding and building of Cowgill Chapel in 1814, further up Dentdale, and in developing the school that was attached to it.

Thomas (1783-1873)
Richard and Margaret's second child Thomas was born in Dent in August 1783, 14 months after Margaret and two years before Adam. Adam tells us nothing about him in his letters. Thomas is believed to have spent his whole life in Dent and never married, but we have no record of what he did or how he spent his time. He died in Seedsgill Cottage (now Seeds Gill House) in Dent in September 1873, aged 90. He is buried in the churchyard.

Adam (1785-1873)
Adam was the third child, born in March 1785. He never married and spent his whole adult life living in Trinity College at the University of Cambridge. Although he wrote that Dentdale was "the land of my birth; … the home of my boyhood, and … the home of my heart", he died in his adopted home of Trinity College in January 1873, aged 87. He is buried in the College Chapel, and (as we'll see in Chapter 20) is commemorated in inscriptions there, in Norwich Cathedral, and in Dent parish church.

Isabel (1787-1823)
In February 1787 Richard and Margaret presented the 2-year old Adam with a sister who they named Isabel. Although a third sister, Ann, came along two years later, Isabel – who he refers to in some letters as Bell – was always Adam's favourite, and he described her as his "chosen friend and companion". Like two of her three older siblings, she never married and had no children.

Like almost all the rest of the family, she was born in Dent, lived in Dent, and died in Dent. She died in January 1823, aged 35 years, after a brief illness and rapid decline, and is buried in Dent churchyard.

Adam described in one letter how Isabel "was blessed with a quiet and affectionate temper which greatly endeared her to every one of us; and during her painful illness she exhibited a humble resignation to the will of God; bearing with patience her afflictions here, in the Christian hope of being received with favour by her Maker in a place where there is neither sorrow nor suffering."

Isabel's death was a big blow to the family. Her father Richard was 86 years old when his second daughter died, but Adam wrote of how he bore the "affliction with that patience we all expected from him." Adam's sister-in-law Jane (wife of his younger brother John) was in the final stages of pregnancy when it happened, and was so shocked by Isabel's death that she gave birth early to a daughter; mother and child survived the ordeal. Adam wrote "The young one is to have the name of Margaret Isabella after my mother and sister, and I hope to take upon me the duties of sponsor before my return to Cambridge."

Adam and Isabel had been very close, and he missed her terribly for the rest of his days. This is clearly borne out in a letter he wrote in 1849, twenty-six years after Isabel's death, to a lady who had just lost her own sister; he told her "I can feel for your great sorrow. I once lost a sister, the dearest of all my sisters, and the darling companion of all my early years. … We had our little squabbles about our toys when children; but after we reached our teens I think I never heard so much as a word from her lips that was not spoken in kindness. Her death was a grievous blow to me, and I never visit my native hills without being reminded of her at every turn."

Ann (1789-1862)
Adam was four years old when his third and youngest sister, Ann, was born in Dent in June 1789. We hear little about her in his letters. In September 1820, at the age of 31, she married William Westall (1781-1850), an English landscape artist of the picturesque school, with a growing reputation, who travelled widely and was one of the first artists to work in Australia. William and Ann had four sons – William (1821-1901), Thomas (1823-??), Robert (1825-??) and Richard (1827-??). Ann's husband William died in London in January 1850, and she died twelve years later in Dent.

John (1791-1859)
Richard and Margaret's fifth child was a son, John, born in Dent in October 1791. He was six years younger than Adam but they were close and Adam wrote to him regularly, describing his travels in Britain and Europe.

John followed in the footsteps of his father and two older brothers. After Sedbergh School he went to Cambridge University as a sizar student in December 1808, the first in his family to be admitted to St John's College. He won a scholarship in 1813, and graduated with the degree of Bachelor of Arts in 1815, without obtaining Honours. In 1817 he was awarded a Master of Arts. Like his father and two older brothers, he became a Clerk in Holy Orders after graduating, being ordained deacon in May 1815 and priest in June the following year.

After a period as curate of Stowe in Lincolnshire, in 1822 he succeeded his father Richard as Vicar of Dent, serving there for 37 years before dying in post in February 1859. Between them, his father and he held the post of Vicar of Dent for a total of 91 years, back-to-back. John also served his community as a Magistrate.

In April 1822 he married a local lady, Jane Davoran (1788-1865), a niece of General Brownrigg of Broadlands, Dent, at Painswick in Gloucestershire. We'll learn more about Jane in Chapter 17 when we look at the foundation and development of Cowgill Chapel. In *Memorial*, Adam wrote of how Jane, "personally devoted the best efforts of her life [to that project]. Year after year she worked on in good hope; and her pious work had its blessing."

Over the next six years John and Jane had five children – Margaret Isabella (1823-1911), Emma (1825-1840), Anne (1826-1827), Richard (1827-1911), Jane Ann (1829-1833). Adam's first niece (Isabella) and only nephew (Richard) from this part of the family play more important roles in his life story than the other three.

In his letters Adam always refers to Margaret Isabella simply as Isabella. She was born in Dent in February 1823, the day after Adam's sister Bell had died, by which time he was 38 years old. The 1881 census lists Margaret Isabella Sedgwick living at Thorns Hall in Sedbergh with her niece Maribel Sedgwick and nephew Adam Sedgwick. Isabella died in February 1911 at Thorns Hall, aged 88, and is buried at Dent.

One-year old Isabella was presented with a younger sister, Emma, in December 1824. Sadly, Emma only lived sixteen years, and died in February 1840. Another sister, Anne, was born in Dent in April 1826 but died within ten months.

John and Jane's fourth child and only son, Richard, was born in Dent in August 1827. Richard kept the pattern going that his grandfather, father, and older uncle had established – school in Sedbergh followed by Cambridge and ordination. He was admitted to Trinity College, uncle Adam's *alma mater* and adopted home, in May 1846, and graduated with the degree of Bachelor of Arts in 1850 and Master of Arts in 1853. After being ordained deacon in 1850 and priest in 1851, he served as Vicar of St Martin's-at-Oak & St Giles in Norwich from 1851 to 1859, before being chosen unanimously by the 'statesmen' to succeed his father as Vicar of Dent in 1859. In November 1852 he married Mary Jane Woodhouse, daughter of John Woodhouse of Bolton-le-Moors in Lancashire, and they had eight children. Richard served as Vicar of Dent for 25 years, up to 1885, bringing the family total to 116 unbroken years over three generations. Mary died in January 1891 at Guildford in Surrey, and Richard died at York in 1911 aged 84.

John and Jane's fifth and final child was a daughter, Jane Anne. She was born in Dent in January 1829 but died in June 1833 at the age of four years and four months.

Adam's brother, John Sedgwick, died at Dent in February 1859 after suffering from an undisclosed painful illness for some months. He is buried in the churchyard in Dent. His widow Jane and daughter Isabella then moved out of the Parsonage to allow the new Vicar, her son Richard, to move in with his family. They went to live in "a cottage on the outskirts of the village", which Adam said he was pleased about because it gave him "two homes in Dent" to visit, the Parsonage and the cottage. The 1861 census lists Jane and Isabella living at Langcliffe in Yorkshire. Jane died in November 1865, aged 77, and is buried at Dent.

James (1794-1869)

Adam's fourth brother, James – Richard and Margaret's seventh child – was born in Dent in November 1794. He was nine years younger than Adam but followed a similar path to his grandfather and brothers Adam, Richard and John – school at Sedbergh followed by Cambridge University. He was admitted a sizar student in St John's College in September 1812, won a scholarship in 1816, and graduated with the degree of Bachelor of Arts in 1817 and Master of Arts in 1821. He might have had high hopes of following in the footsteps of his older brother Adam, but he was not a diligent student; he graduated sixth in the third class of the Mathematics Tripos, and later failed the Fellowship Examination.

Like his father and three older brothers, James became a "man of the cloth". He was ordained deacon in March 1818 and priest that September, and served as curate of Freshwater on the Isle of Wight (1823-1839), and curate of Downham Market in Norfolk (1839-1840), before being appointed Vicar of Scalby, near Scarborough in Yorkshire, between 1840 and 1869.

James married three times. His first wife was Sophia Corton of Southampton, who he married in May 1834; she died in 1835. In 1838 he married Catherine Hicks, a widow from Freshwater, but we know nothing about her fate. In 1867 he married Amelia Alice Hawksley, who survived him. There is no mention of any biological children to John, but he left behind a step-daughter called Fanny (Hicks) who Adam would grow very fond of. James died in post in August 1869, having served just under three decades as Vicar of Scalby.

Nieces

Adam grew very close to two of his brother's children – his brother John's daughter Isabella, and his brother James' step-daughter Fanny – and they deserve special mention because they played an increasingly important role in Adam's final years.

He never married and had no children of his own, but he loved being in the company of children and ladies of any age, and he more or less adopted them as surrogate children of his own, with their parents' full knowledge and blessing.

Such behaviour might raise eyebrows today, but in Victorian times it was quite common for young ladies to dedicate themselves to the care of their elderly and frail relatives, it was regarded as the highest form of Christian duty for them to sacrifice their own needs and happiness for the benefit of others, particularly close family members with little or no alternative means of support.

Isabella Sedgwick

Isabella was the daughter of Adam's brother John. When her sister Anne died in April 1840 Adam wrote to her mother Jane suggesting that, if Isabella were without a home, "she shall live with me, and I will love her as much as if I were her father." Later that month he pursued the matter further, advising Jane that "she shall work hard with me, but it shall be a work of goodwill. For example, while I am at morning service in the Cathedral she may be taking a music lesson, if she likes, of one of the best masters in England. We will walk together, and drive out together, and perhaps I may procure a pony for her to accompany me on horseback. She will see much good society, and I trust she will improve in health, spirits, and information."

Adam took his self-appointed responsibilities towards Isabella very seriously, and his letters to her over her adult years often include advice and guidance on her personal development. The best example is a letter he wrote to her in April 1840, when she was 23 years old, in which he tells her "I do trust you will go on improving in knowledge and in goodness, and that you will become a well-informed woman; but I trust also that you will continue to be single-hearted, and humble, and charitable in the true and Christian sense. And God forbid that you should ever learn to think too well of yourself, and too ill of those about you. But I will not fear this. Simplicity, humility, and charity are a woman's best graces." He urged her to take seriously "the daily duties that are before you, such as helping your mother in her household duties, visiting and comforting your neighbours in distress, attending to the Sunday school", to "get into habits of strong exercise", to "strive ... day by day and hour by hour to improve your understanding, and to add to your knowledge" and to be "regular and systematic in your studies", particularly of the Bible, ancient history and "books of poetry in general."

In the first volume of *Life and Letters*, Clark and Hughes (1890a) point out that "Sedgwick's affection for his sister [Isabella] was trans-ferred, so to speak, to the child-niece whose birth coincided with her death, and who became, as she grew up, his chosen friend and indispen-sable companion." This closeness can be seen in a letter Adam sent to her in December 1865, when he was 80 and she was 42, in which he writes "Sometimes I think of you as my darling child, sometimes as my beloved companion and Christian friend, the comfort and solace of my old age."

There is no mention in *Life and Letters* of Isabella marrying. She died childless in February 1911 in Sedbergh, and is buried at Dent.

Fanny Hicks
Fanny was the step-daughter of Adam's brother John, daughter of John's second wife Catherine. She was born in 1828 but, after her mother died in 1838, Adam began to write to her regularly, as he did with Isabella. He also developed a strong attachment to her, through her teenage years and beyond.

He often wrote in terms that would cause raised eyebrows today. For example, in a letter he sent her in May 1842, when he was 57 and she was 14, he told her he was struggling with his "old enemy the rheumatic gout" which made him "so sour-faced and ill-tempered, and abominably cross, and so hate myself, that I do not think you would now, if you saw me, give me one corner of your heart, or a single kiss. You might just as well kiss an old decayed thistle, which would leave its prickles sticking to your lips."

He also took a keen interest in Fanny's personal development, as he did with Isabella, and he frequently offered her unsolicited advice. For example, in a letter he sent in October 1840, he urges her to "improve ... [and] cultivate [her mind] by systematically committing to memory some beautiful short passage in prose or verse every day of your life", not to "be slovenly either in your person or habits", never to "leave your pocket-handkerchief about; keep all your books and things in their right places". He also reminds her "when you are working at anything ... do it heartily. Avoid dawdling ... Be punctual in all your engagements. ... we have no right to waste God's gifts by dawdling and other bad habits.'"

As with Isabella, there is no mention of Fanny every marrying or having children, and she often spent time caring for Adam in his later years, particularly in Norwich. We have no record of when or where she died.

3. Dentdale

His University claimed his life's labour; but though removed for the greater part of his life from his beloved birth-place, his love for it was always fresh, and he ever revisited it with increasing affection.
Memorial tablet to Adam Sedgwick in Dent Parish Church

Adam Sedgwick loved Dent, and insisted that his heart belonged to Dentdale. Although he spent his whole adult life living away, in Cambridge and Norwich, he returned frequently to Dent to visit family and friends, and enjoy the slower pace of life, lack of work responsibilities and the freedom to roam the hills and take the air. It was his bolthole and his second home.

Life and Letters allows us to hear Adam's thoughts on many things. His *Memorial* (1868) is equally valuable as a source, because in it he speaks to us in his own words about the place he knew and loved better than anywhere else. He paints a vivid picture of Dent town and dale, which he knew intimately, and he looks back nostalgically on its more prosperous past.

Location and character
Dentdale lies sixteen miles east of Kendal and five miles south east of Sedbergh. Historically, it was part of the West Riding of Yorkshire, but in 1974 it was incorporated into the new county of Cumbria when that was formed from combining Westmorland and Cumberland. The dale is also part of the Yorkshire Dales National Park, that was created in 1954 and extended in 2016.

This is true dales country, dominated by the high hills – Middleton Fell, Aye Gill Pike, Baugh Fell, Great Knoutberry Hill (Widdale Fell), Blea Moor, Whernside, Great Coum and Gragareth – and sweeping open moorland that enclose scattered farms and homesteads. The dale is about twelve miles long and up to two miles wide. It contains a few small villages, and the only town is Dent. In 1837 Thomas Moule pointed out that "when viewed from the higher grounds it presents a scene of rural beauty"; that remains true today.

The valley is isolated and relatively secluded, and throughout history this has helped to shelter it from the strong currents of social, economic and technological change that have swept across England. That same seclusion is now one of the dale's greatest assets. Today it attracts a large number of walkers, day-trippers, photographers and artists eager to experience its peace and tranquility.

The main settlement in the dale is the small tight-knit village of Dent, which was often referred to in Adam's day as DentTown. Lake District poet Hartley Coleridge wrote a poem about it in about 1825: "There is a town, of little note or praise, Narrow and winding are its rattling streets, Where cart with cart in cumbrous conflict meets, Hard straining up or backing down the ways."

Though small and "of little note or praise", Dent was then and remains today full of character – with narrow cobbled streets, white-washed houses, two inns, the parish church, a few tiny shops, an old stone bridge over Flinter Gill, and a village green that is tucked away behind the centre of the village. The distinctive wooden galleries on the side or front of many of the houses, reached by outside stairs, where the hand-knitters used to sit while they spun the wool and knitted, have long since gone.

History

The Romans arrived in the north of England around 50 A.D. but no trace of them has been found in Dentdale. The first settlers to leave their mark in the dale were Norse Vikings from Ireland and the Isle of Man; they arrived in about 956 A.D., settled peacefully, and build scattered farms in upland sites, many of which are still occupied today.

The Norman Conquest in 1066 saw much of England divided up into large estates and given to friends and supporters of William. Roger of Poitou was given what is today the Cumbria region. Throughout the Middle Ages (5th to 15th centuries) the Manor of Dent was owned by the FitzHugh family of Ravensworth Castle in North Yorkshire. The first church was built in Dent in the twelfth century. It was then a small village but quickly grew as a centre with a market and annual fairs.

During the Wars of the Roses (1455-1487) the men of Dentdale supported the House of York, which ultimately lost, and the dale was severely damaged by its neighbours and laid waste after the war.

Dentdale recovered and in Elizabethan times (1558-1603) there was enough local business to keep three corn mills busy – Gawthrop Mill on the River Dee, Over Mill in Deepdale, and Nether Mill near Kirk Bridge. Problems were caused by shortage of water and flood damage but, when a new mill was built further downstream at Rash, the existing millers objected and the matter was settled in a court-case. Further legal disputes over the mills followed in early Stuart times (1603-1714), when the manor was Crown property, culminating in a major case in 1698 after a fifth mill was built when the existing four were struggling to survive because little corn was being grown locally and much was imported.

Prosperity

In many ways, the late seventeenth century was the "golden age" for Dentdale. Adam Sedgwick pointed out in a letter to a relative in Connecticut in February 1837 that, "from the Reformation to the latter half of the last [18th] century, our border country enjoyed great prosperity."

Butter and cheese were produced locally and sold in surrounding markets. Adam points out in *Memorial* (1868) how "the valley was well known for its exports of butter; which … was highly salted and packed in [wooden barrels called] firkins." This in turn encouraged some local men to become coopers (wooden barrel-makers), an industry that "flourished [in the dale] for several generations." Recall (from Chapter 2) that some of Adam's distant ancestors had been coopers, making good use of the trees growing on their own land. There was also a tradition in the dale of breeding Galloway ponies, strong horses that were highly valued by drovers and carters.

During the eighteenth century employment and income were boosted in Dentdale by the working of minerals and coal. The rocks beneath the dale (that geologists now call the Yoredale Series) comprise a series of nearly horizontal beds of limestone, sandstone, and shale, with in some places thin beds of coal, all capped by Millstone Grit, a coarse gritstone. The lowest of the five groups of limestones contains beds of black marble. Marble has long been quarried and worked, and a bed of coal from within the highest limestone layer (the Upper Scar Limestone) was worked commercially for domestic use.

Wool and knitting

From the late sixteenth century onwards the economy of Dentdale grew increasingly dependent on a knitting industry, supported by the area's extensive hill pastures and common grazing for local sheep.

Much of the wool produced in the dale was exported, but some was retained for domestic use. Adam explains in *Memorial* (1868) how the local wool industry evolved from being hand-carded then spun into a very coarse thread, to the preparation of finer material by wool-combing and, by the beginning of the eighteenth century, the manufacture and export of the finest quality yarn stockings. Machines were introduced later that could spin worsted, and by the 1760s hand-knit knit worsted stockings "were the great articles of export from the Northern Dales", particularly during 'The Seven Years War' (1756-1763) when demand for them from the British Army was particularly high.

Local people hand-knitted home-produced wool and imported dressed wool into stockings and gloves, that were sold locally and further afield. Adam describes how "now and then an adventurous 'statesman' rode up to London on his own stout nag to do business with the drapers of Cheapside."

Prosperity in the dale peaked at the turn of the nineteenth century, partly as a result of the Napoleonic Wars (1799-1815) when agricultural prices were high and there was strong demand for knitted goods. By then water-powered mills were producing woollen yarn on an industrial scale, but many local people continued to make a living in the cottage industries of hand-knitting and weaving.

In his book *The Doctor* (1834), Lakeland poet Robert Southey called the hand-knitters "the terrible knitters of Dent", and William Howitt also used the phrase in his *Rural Life of England* (1838). The expression, de-scribing the great speed at which they knitted not the quality of their work, stuck. Hand-knitting was a source of much-needed income for the poor, and almost all of the local men, women and children knitted. Much of the wool came from their own sheep and was spun locally, either by individuals, or in the woollen mill built near Cowgill. As we'll see, the knitters often sat and knitted together in groups in each other's houses. But they also knitted on their own, using any moment of 'spare' time – when out walking to visit family and friends in scattered farms, as they drove the cattle to and from the fields, as they walked to market and back, while they were doing daily tasks such as churning the butter or wrapping cheeses, and apparently even during church services until the Vicar told them off.

The slave trade
Between the seventeenth and early nineteenth centuries at least two fami-lies in Dentdale were directly involved in the lucrative slave trade. The so-called "Triangular Trade" involved three legs – ships loaded with manufactured goods made in Britain sailed from Whitehaven to West Africa; there they were exchanged for slaves, who were carried on the "Middle Passage" from West Africa to the West Indies or southern states

of North America; on the voyage back to Whitehaven from the West Indies the cargo was mainly tobacco, sugar and rum.

The most successful and prominent local family were the Sills who lived in West House (now Whernside Manor), that is likely to have been built with the profits from slavery. Edmund Sill, his brother John, and Miles Mason all invested in slave ships. The Sill family also owned a sugar plantation called Providence in Jamaica, that depended heavily on slave labour and generated great wealth for the family. They owned up to 180 slaves, some of whom were brought to West House to work as their servants.

Adam writes in *Memorial* (1868) of how his father regarded the slave trade "as a foul national sin, which (however deep its roots might be struck into the policy of the State) every man, who believed in the over-ruling Providence of God, was bound, by all lawful means within his reach, to root out and trample underfoot."

Although his father Richard and brother John preached sermons in Dent church against slavery, a pair of marble wall tablets to members of the Sill family can be seen in the north aisle of Dent church, one to John Sill "of Providence in the Island of Jamaica", who died in 1774. Adam and his father and brother campaigned for the abolition of the slave trade, and they and others in Dentdale supported William Wilberforce who achieved the abolition of slavery in Britain in 1807.

Decline

The population of Dentdale peaked in the early years of the nineteenth century. That marked a turning point in the fortunes of the dale, because economic decline was already setting in. By then levels of poverty were growing and many people started to migrate away from the dale.

Most of the farms had by then been mortgaged and sold, but many former owners continued to occupy them as tenants. Many land-holdings were too small to be economically viable at a time of high rents and low agricultural prices. Free trade and the import of grain promoted deeper agricultural depression and the end of mixed farming. Some families were reluctant to move away and desperate to supplement their meagre incomes, so they took to swopping produce and labour in a local cashless economy. That trend became more challenging as demand for hand-knitted goods declined in response to the growing availability of cheaper machine-made woven and knitted goods. Most people still lived off the land and barely scraped by.

But the local economy was boosted a bit by the development of the Stone House marble works, that provided work for some men right through the nineteenth century. Other men were employed for a period in building the drystone walls when the local common land was enclosed in 1859. The construction of the Settle to Carlisle railway line across the top of the dale between 1869 and 1876 also boosted employment and the local economy, although most of the 'navvies' were itinerant workers who lived in shanty towns and moved on to the next project when the current one was completed. The construction projects turned out to be mixed blessings. Enclosure deprived local land-less people of common land on which they could graze their cattle and sheep, making it more difficult for them to remain self-sufficient. The arrival of the railway led to the end of local quarrying and coal mining, further reducing local employment and incomes.

By the end of the 1860s, towards the end of Adam's life, emigration of families out of the dale had eased the pressure. Although the local economy was showing signs of recovery, it would never again reach the levels of prosperity it had enjoyed during the eighteenth and early nineteenth centuries.

Statesmen

In late medieval times a distinctive type of yeoman farmer had emerged in and around the Lake District, who held and cultivated a small estate and was known locally as a 'statesman' (probably from "estate man"). There were twenty-four of these freeholders, who had the right to hold land and pass it on to their descendants, but not the right to own it. They remained tenants of the Lord of the Manor, and had a duty to provide men to fight against invading Scottish armies and rampaging Border Reivers, as and when required.

The Manor of Dent passed from the FitzHughs of Ravensworth to the Parr family through marriage, and in about 1574 it passed to the Crown. In 1629 it was bought by Sir Allan Apsley, and during the Commonwealth (1649-1660) it was owned by a man called Parsons. In 1670 Charles II granted the Manor of Dent back to Apsley, who sold it to a group of tenants, to keep "in Trust for the Tenants generally". A small number of trustees tried to hold on to ownership of the land for themselves, but after a legal dispute all the tenants – the 'statesmen' – won the right to purchase the freehold (ownership) of the land they were holding and pass it on to their successors.

3. Dentdale

In *The English Counties Delineated* (1837) Thomas Moule described how, within living memory, each statesman had lived on his freehold, which included a garden and an orchard. Their houses were "rude [simple] structures" with a distinctive architectural style – 2 or 3 families lived together, one occupying each floor, and each house had an external stone staircase and long wooden gallery where people sat outside weaving and knitting woollen goods. By the mid-1830s most of the galleries were "rapidly falling into decay".

Thirty years later, in *Memorial* (1868), Adam described how things had changed, noting that "The estates were small; but each of them gave a right to large tracts of mountain pasturage; and each 'statesman' had his flock and his herd. A rented farm was once a rare exception to the general rule: but now nearly the whole dale, from end to end, is in the occupation of farmers with very small capital, and living at a high rack-rent."

Memories of the statesmen of past times are preserved in the box pews in St Andrews Church in Dent, that date from the seventeenth century and were the family pews of the '24 Sidesmen'.

Recall (from Chapter 2) that it was the statesmen who elected the Vicar of Dent, so the fact that they chose Adam's father, brother and nephew to serve for more than a century back-to-back shows how well respected and embedded the Sedgwicks were in local society at that time. It's not known whether any of Adam's ancestors or close family were statesmen.

Life in Dentdale

In *Memorial* (1868) Adam describes the people of the dale fondly and nostalgically, noting that "with the exception of certain festive seasons, their habits were simple, primitive and economical".

School

There had been a school in Dent from medieval times until 1560, but in 1604 a Grammar School (originally called the 'Free Grammar School of King James, Dent') was founded through the generosity of local benefactors who donated rent from land and farms to support it. The school was for boys only, and it was run by a headmaster who would usually be the Vicar of Dent. Adam's father Richard had a spell multi-tasking in this way, when Adam was a youngster. Itinerant masters would often visit schools like this one on a regular circuit, teaching writing, arithmetic and surveying. The boys also learned Latin and Greek grammar. Adam's father, Adam and his brothers John and Richard were all pupils at the school, up to the age of about fifteen.

The Grammar School closed in 1897, after the governors had struggled to compete with the cheaper schooling provided at the 'National' elementary schools for boys and girls, that opened in Dent in 1845 and in Cowgill in 1866. The Grammar School building, in the corner of the churchyard, was long abandoned and derelict, but has been restored and converted into flats.

Girls were taught in the so-called dame schools or knitting schools. These were private elementary schools, taught by women, often in their own home, and the emphasis was on teaching the girls to read and to knit. Adam writes, in *Memorial* (1868), of how "all the women with very rare exceptions learned to read; and the upper Statesmen's daughters could write and keep family accounts. They had their *Bibles*, and certain good old-fashioned *Books of Devotion*; and they had their *Cookery Books*; and they were often well read in ballad poetry, and in one or two of De Foe's novels. And some of the younger and more refined of the Statesmen's daughters would form a little clique, where they met – during certain years of last century – and wept over Richardson's novels."

Parents who had ambitions for their sons to progress on to university – in England the choice then was between Oxford and Cambridge; in Ireland there was only Dublin; and in Scotland there were St Andrews, Glasgow, Aberdeen and Edinburgh – would often employ private tutors, usually on a part-time basis, to tutor, coach and prepare them, most commonly in mathematics. John Dawson, who we met (in Chapter 1) in the Vicarage in Dent on the night Adam was born, was a tutor as well as a medical man, and he tutored Adam's father Richard, Adam, and his brothers Richard and John (as we saw in Chapter 2).

Church and chapel

In Adam's day, as it had been for centuries, the parish church in Dent was at the centre of religious life in Dentdale.

St Andrew's was established in the twelfth century, but little of the original Norman building remains other than three western bays and an Early English (1180-1275) doorway in the Early Gothic style, which has been blocked in. The church was largely rebuilt in 1417, in the Perpendicular style (c1350-c1550), and it was restored in 1590 and again in 1787, when the clerestory (upper windows just below the roof) and tower were rebuilt.

Further restoration was carried out in 1889, and the upper section of the three-deck Jacobean pulpit (1614) is still in use. The floor around the altar is paved with black and grey marble, quarried in Dentdale, which contains many fossils. The pews of the 24 sidesmen or 'statesmen' have been preserved on the south side of the aisle.

The church also contains brass plaques in memory of Adam's father Richard, Adam himself, and his brother John, and three windows in the south aisle commemorate the Sedgwicks. Near the church, on Main Street, is a huge block of Shap granite with a water fountain in it, a simple but striking memorial to Adam Sedgwick, the best-known 'son of Dent'.

A second Church of England church was built in Dentdale in 1838, by Adam's sister Margaret and sister-in-law Jane further north along the dale at Cowgill. As we'll see in Chapter 18, Adam laid the foundation stone for it in June 1837. Although it was established as an Anglican church, Adam notes that "men of different communions [denominations] had subscribed to the cost of building" it, on the site of a non-conformist chapel, in the Early English style. Originally called Cowgill Chapel, it was also known as Kirkthwaite Chapel, and is now St John the Evangelist. The story of this daughter church to St Andrew's is recorded in Adam Sedgwick's (1868) *A Memorial to Cowgill Chapel*.

Many of the old statesmen in upper Dentdale were respected Quakers, members of the Society of Friends. This should come as no surprise given that Brigflatts – the birthplace of Quakerism after George Fox preached there in 1652 – is only a few miles away to the west, near Sedbergh. Adam spoke highly of the Quakers and wrote of what "excellent men they were, and well informed in matters of common life; lovers of religious liberty; of great practical benevolence, and of pure moral conduct; and they were among the foremost in all good measures of rural administration." The Quakers built Meeting Houses at the Laning (1701-1834), a mile or two west of Dent, and at Yea Leat (1701-c1910), east of Dent, near Cowgill, where they also built a school in about 1880.

Non-conformism was strong across the Yorkshire Dales and many poor people were drawn to the chapels rather than the church, which was more the domain of the better-off. Benjamin Ingham broke away from the Wesley brothers' Methodist movement in the 1730s, preached extensively in Yorkshire and Lancashire, and formed many 'societies' (practically independent churches that regarded Ingham as their head). An Inghamite chapel was opened in Dentdale in 1754, but in the 1860s its members switched allegiance to Robert Sandeman, who disagreed with and broke away from Ingham. By the 1780s the chapel had been abandoned after the congregation merged with the local Methodists.

During the early nineteenth century, a number of non-conformist chapels had been established in Dentdale, including Zion Congregational Chapel at Flintergill, which opened in 1834.

The different branches of Methodism were well-represented by a Wesleyan Methodist Chapel (opened 1834) and a Primitive Methodist Chapel (1841-1934), both at the Laning; Deepdale Methodist Chapel (opened 1889); Dent Head Wesleyan Methodist Chapel (1856-1876); and Dent Foot Methodist Chapel (dates unknown).

There is no mention of any Roman Catholic church or chapel in Dentdale in Adam Sedgwick's *Memorial* (1868). There is none in the dale today, although a Roman Catholic service is held each Sunday in St Andrew's, the Church of England parish church five miles away in Sedbergh.

Houses

In Adam's day most people in Dent lived in small houses packed tightly together, with simple furnishings and basic facilities. Most farming families lived in scattered farmsteads, where the traditional longhouse (with animals housed at one end and people at the other) was the norm.

The only domestic architecture that Adam describes in *Memorial* (1868) is that of the grander house of a typical statesman. He writes that it "had seldom more than two floors, and the upper floor did not extend to the wall where was the chief fire-place, but was wainscoted off [lined with wooden panelling] from it. ... a part of the ground-floor, near the fire-place, was open to the rafters; ... It was in this space, chiefly under the open rafters, that the families assembled in the evening. ... About the end of the 17th century grates and regular flues began to be erected; but during Dent's greatest prosperity, they formed the exception and not the rule."

He does offer a glimpse inside the ground floor of a typical small house in the town, where local people would meet together in the evenings to knit. In his words, "First there was a blazing fire in a recess of the wall; which in early times was composed of turf and great logs of wood. From one side of the fire-place ran a bench, with a strong and sometimes ornamentally carved back, called a *lang settle*. On the other side of the fire-place was the Patriarch's wooden and well carved arm-chair; and near the chair was the *sconce* adorned with crockery. Not far off was commonly seen a well-carved cupboard, or cabinet, marked with some date that fell within a period of fifty years after the restoration of Charles the Second; and fixed to the beams of the upper floor was a row of cupboards, called the *Cat-malison* (the cat's curse), because from its position it was secure from poor grimalkin's [cat's] paw. One or two small tables, together with chairs or benches, gave seats to all the party there assembled. Rude [simple] though the room appeared, there was in it no sign of want. It had many signs of rural comfort: for under the rafters were suspended bunches of herbs for cookery, hams sometimes for export, flitches [sides] of bacon, legs of beef, and other articles salted for domestic use."

Clothing and fashion

For the many people of limited means in the dale, clothing was inevitably simple, plain, usually well-worn, and of the "make-do-and-mend" variety. Looking back to his childhood, Adam wrote in *Memorial* (1868) of how he remembered that "many of the old-fashioned dresses, seen on a holiday, were the signs of poverty rather than of pride. The coats were threadbare, and worn by men who had seen better days. The looped broadbrim [hat] was seen, but as a sign of mourning ... But there were many exceptions to these mournful signs of decay. There still remained many Dalesmen with old fashioned dresses, and with cheerful, prosperous looks, among the Sunday congregations at Dent; but the ancient fashions were wearing fast away."

More prosperous families could afford newer, better quality and more fashionable clothing, particularly the men who valued having a highly visible sign of their earthly success. Adam writes that "The dress of the upper Statesman's wife and daughters was perhaps less costly than that of the men who affected fashion; and according to modern taste we should call it stiff and ugly to the last degree; as was the fashion of the day. There was one exception however, both as to cost and beauty: for the Statesman's wife often appeared at Church in the winter season in a splendid long cloak of the finest scarlet cloth, having a hood lined with coloured silk. This dress was very becoming, and very costly; but it was carefully preserved; and so it might pass down from mother to daughter. Fortunately, no genius in female decoration ... seemed to have brought patches and hoops into vulgar use (as in the preposterous modern case of crinoline)." Clearly, in matters of ladies' fashion, Adam Sedgwick was an unreconstructed traditionalist at heart.

Wigs and embroidered coats were still commonly worn by men when Adam was a child, and he thought his father's well-dressed and well powdered Sunday wig "one of the most beautiful sights in the world."

Social life

Adam was born into the dale at a time of major social and economic change. He was keen to record in *Memorial* (1868) "the domestic state and habits of our countrymen, before their old social isolation had been so much broken in upon by the improved roads and rapid movements of modern times", which he looked upon very much as a mixed blessing.

One hallmark of the Dentdale folk was their very sociable nature. In this largely self-contained and self-sufficient cultural backwater, the local people met together regularly to sit and gossip, share pastimes and festivities, and simply enjoy each other's company. It was an effective way of building a sense of belonging and a spirit of community, both of which would be eroded during Adam's lifetime.

Adam describes how "the festivities of Christmas, and other holiday seasons, were kept up among our countrymen with long sustained and sometimes I fear intemperate activity. They had their Morris dances; their rapier dances; and their mask dances." He looked down on these sorts of pursuits through Puritan eyes, and was not sorry that they had largely died out by the time he was born. With a certain amount of relish, he explains how "these grotesque and barbarous usages of a former age disappeared a considerable time before the end of the last century. I believe I saw the end of them full eighty years since, while I was in my nurse's arms."

Adam looked back with pride on the part his father Richard had played in organising sports matches, particularly football and [Cumbrian] wrestling, between local parish teams. They were popular with players and spectators, and helped bring local people together, but he does note that "the robust games" were not always played with the right spirit.

For many centuries, Dent had been famous for its Galloway ponies, and before Adam's time horse-racing was popular to do and watch; there was a race-course in Dent that "had its celebrity". But, again looking at the world around him through Puritan eyes, he was pleased to see it go. He writes "I believe I saw, in my very early boyhood, the last race ever run upon the old Course. Since then, the old ground has been so cut up and changed, that, happily, it would be impossible to re-open it as a race-course were the old taste to come to life again."

Adam reserved his most serious criticism for the traditional country sport of cock-fighting, a blood sport in which two roosters ("gamecocks") are placed in a ring and forced to fight to the death for the amusement and pleasure of onlookers, which had long been popular in the Yorkshire dales. He described it as "among the vulgar sports of England ... [a] vile and cruel sport" and bemoaned the fact that "men of character joined in it without compunction ... I have been present during some of these matches as a looker-on in my early days ... and I have witnessed their fruits; which were reaped in gambling quarrels, drunken riots, and bellowings of blasphemy. Thank God, they have gone from sight; and will never again, I trust, defile the light of day. So far as Dent is concerned, this form of cruel sport died away in the unhappy years that closed the last century."

Local customs
A number of traditional local customs had also played important roles in the social life of Dentdale before Adam's time and were on the decline or had died out not long before he was born in 1785.

'Lating râ'
One effective way of maintaining a stable community in Dent Town in this isolated dale at that time was the formation of what we would now call "self-help groups", in which near-neighbours looked out for each other and helped look after each other. As Adam describes them, "a number of houses within certain distances of one another were said to be in the *lating râ* (the seeking row), and formed a kind of social compact. In joy or sorrow they were expected to attend and to give help and comfort."

'Crying-out'
One local custom that continued at least through Adam's childhood was the *Crying-out*, celebrating the birth of a new child in the town or hamlet.

He describes how "before the birth of a new inhabitant of the hamlet, all the women of mature life within the *lating râ* had been on the tip-toe of joyful expectation: and the news of the first wailing (the *Crying-out*, as called in the tongue of Dent) – the sign of coming life – ran through the home-circle like the fiery cross of the Highlanders: and were it night or day, calm sunshine or howling storm, away ran the matrons to the house of promise: and there with cordials and creature comforts, and blessings, and gossip, and happy omens, and with no fear of coming evil (for the women of the valley were lively ...) they waited till the infant Statesman was brought into this world of joy and sorrow - inasmuch publicity as if he were the heir to the throne of an Empire."

There is no record of whether Adam's birth in the Parsonage was celebrated in this traditional way.

'Lyke-Wake'

There were also local customs for dealing with death and in the conduct of funerals, which had died out before Adam wrote *Memorial* in 1868.

In many parts of the country wakes were held, in which a group of people gathered to watch over the body of a dead person through the night before they were buried, usually as a celebration to mark the passing of the person's soul. Adam writes of how local people "kept a watch in the house, with burning lights in the room of death. This passed under the name of the *Lyke-Wake*: but the custom had become very rare, and I believe entirely went out before the end of the last [eighteenth] century ...". The name Lyke-Wake comes from Late Middle English, "lyke" meaning body and "wake" meaning vigil.

Dentdale also had a custom in which many local people were "bidden [invited] to the funeral" at which "there was a peculiar refreshment called the *arval*, offered even at a poor man's funeral, before they went with the coffin to the church." The term *arval* apparently comes from a body of ancient Roman priests who presided over an annual fertility festival held every May. Food and drink were also offered after the burial to those who had been invited. Adam describes how, "if the mourning family belonged to the better class of Statesmen, those who had been bidden to the funeral had a dinner provided at one of the inns, which the immediate mourners did not attend. ... It may be better now to conduct a funeral with more quiet simplicity."

'Ganging A Sitting'

One particularly popular and colourful local tradition was the knitting party, locally called a *sitting*. Adam points out that "the knitters of Dent had the reputation of being lively gossips; and they worked together in little clusters - not in din and confinement like that of a modern manufactory [factory]."

When they went *ganging a sitting*, groups of women from several houses met together in the evening in one of their houses, in rotation. They gathered to knit together but at the same time exchange gossip, tell stories, read extracts from well-loved books, and sing songs like sea-shanties. This helped pass the time, but it also encouraged them to knit at great speed (hence "the terrible knitters of Dent").

3. Dentdale

During the summer they would sit outside, on the stairs and wooden galleries in front of the house; during the winter they sat inside. It is said that they often sat in the dark, with candles snuffed out to preserve wax and keep costs down, though the blazing logs in the hearth gave light as well as heat during the long, dark winter months. We looked earlier at Adam's description of the layout and furniture of a typical room in which the women knitted.

Adam also describes in some detail, in *Memorial* (1868), how a typical knitting session would unfold – "They took their seats; and then began the work of the evening; and with a speed that cheated the eye they went on with their respective tasks. Beautiful gloves were thrown off complete; and worsted stockings made good progress. There was no dreary deafening noise of machinery; but there was the merry heart-cheering sound of the human tongue. No one could foretell the current of the evening's talk. They had their ghost tales; and their love tales; and their battles of jests and riddles; and their ancient songs of enormous length, yet heard by ears that were never weary. Each in turn was to play its part, according to the humour of the *Sitting*. Or by way of change, some lassie who was bright and *renable* [talkative] was asked to read for the amusement of the party. She would sit down; and, apparently without interrupting her work by more than a single stitch, would begin to read – for example, a chapter of *Robinson Crusoe*. In a moment the confusion of sounds ceased: and no sound was heard but the reader's voice, and the click of the knitting needles, while she herself went on knitting: and she would turn over the leaves [pages] before her ... hardly losing a second at each successive leaf, till the chapter was done."

Adam reports that "the custom [of *Ganging a sitting*] prevailed, though with diminished frequency, during the early years I spent in Dent."

Adam's reflections, regrets, and perspective
Adam spent most of his adult life in Cambridge, but he was frequently drawn back to Dentdale to visit family and friends, attend funerals, rest and recuperate after spells of illness, and sometimes to carry out geological fieldwork. This gave him a particular perspective on how the dale and its people were changing over the course of his life. He was seeing a series of snapshots through time, rather than a continuously moving image, so he was probably more aware than many of those who lived there permanently of the direction and pace of change.

Adam had many regrets about what had been lost in Dent during his own lifetime, as the dale had become more accessible. Its traditional industries had changed forever and many had declined. Many people had emigrated not only out of the dale but out of the country, seeking better and brighter futures for themselves and their families.

He wrote in *Memorial by the Trustees of Cowgill Chapel* (1868) of how – "I regret the loss of some old trees that covered its nakedness; and most of all the two ancient trees that adorned the Churchyard, and were cut down by hands which had no right to touch a twig of them. I regret the loss of the grotesque and rude, but picturesque old galleries, which once gave a character to the streets; and in some parts of them almost shut out the sight of the sky from those who travelled along the pavement. For rude as were the galleries, they once formed a highway of communication to a dense and industrious rural population which lived on flats or single floors. And the galleries that ran before the successive doors, were at all seasons places of free air; and in the summer season were places of mirth and glee, and active, happy industry. For there might be heard the buzz of the spinning-wheel, and the hum and the songs of those who were carrying on the labours of the day; and the merry jests and greetings sent down to those who were passing through the streets. Some of the galleries were gone before the days of my earliest memory, and all of them were hastening to decay. Not a trace of them is now left. The progress of machinery undermined the profitable industry of Dent, which, in its best days, had no mechanical help beyond the needle, the hand-card, or the cottage spinning-wheel. I still regret the loss within the village streets of those grotesque outward signs of a peculiar industry which was honourable to my countrymen; but has now left hardly a remnant of its former life. I regret [the loss of] its old market-cross, and the stir and bustle of its market-days. I regret [the loss of] its signboards dangling across the streets; which though sometimes marking spots of boisterous revelry, were at the same time the tokens of a rural opulence. Most of all do I regret [the loss of] the noble trees which were the pride and ornament of so many of the ancient 'statesmen's' houses throughout the valley. Nearly all the old forest-trees are gone: but the valley is still very beautiful, from the continual growth of young wood which springs up, self-planted, from the gills and hedgerows."

He had already starting commenting on the changes three decades earlier, in a letter to a relative in Connecticut in February 1837, in which he wrote "The changes of manners, and the progress of machinery, destroyed, root and branch, this source of rural wealth; and a dismal change has now taken place in the social and moral aspect of the land of [our] fathers. It is now a very poor country, a great portion of the old yeomanry (provincially called 'statesmen') has been swept away. Most of the family estates (some of which had descended from father to son for three hundred years) have been sold to strangers. The evil has, I hope, reached its crisis, and the country may improve, but it seems morally impossible that it should ever again assume the happy Arcadian character which it had before the changes that undermined its whole social system."

Adam acknowledged that it was not all bad news; some things had changed for the better. As he looked back from 1868, towards the end of his life, he conceded that "Emigration has relieved the burden of the five Hamlets. Education has made good progress. Roads are greatly improved. Railroads are touching the extremities of the valley, and are greatly benefiting the farmers of our Dale. We are not now so isolated in England as we once were. The markets are reviving; and again there is hope and cheerfulness among my countrymen."

4. Profile of the Man

A man of vigour intellect, impressive character, and engaging per-sonality, of liberal sympathies in politics, and, on the whole, of generous proclivities in academical matters ...
Posthumous description of Adam Sedgwick in *The Times* (19 June 1890)

This book focuses on Adam's achievements, but before we look at those it makes sense to look at what he was like as an adult. This will help us better understand why he did the things he did, the way he did, and why he behaved and reacted as he did.

Unless otherwise stated, the source of all quotes in this chapter is *Life and Letters* (1890), using his own words from his letters and comments made by the editors, Clark and Hughes.

Attachment to Dentdale

As we saw in Chapter 1, Adam was born in Dent and spent his childhood and youth there. It was a familiar environment and a safe place, that contained all he needed in life during his early years. Young Adam showed no particular interest in leaving the dale; Clark and Hughes tell us that, "keenly as Adam admired new scenes and fresh objects of interest, we do not hear that he was fired with any special ambition to leave his native dale, and try his fortune in the great world beyond it."

But his education and career took him away to Cambridge. He probably felt that he had to leave Dentdale in order to prove himself to himself and to his family, particularly his father, and to gain some financial independence. Adam wrote in *Memorial* (1868) "The brightest days of my early manhood were those in which during successive years (after fighting hard battles of the brain [at Cambridge University], whereby I won, under God's blessing, a position of independence) I was permitted to return to my native valley, again to receive the blessing of my parents ...".

Although he was deeply grateful for all that Cambridge offered him, Adam looked back fondly on the dale and its people for the rest of his days. He was always eager to return to Dentdale to spend time with family and friends, and enjoy the slower pace of life, the escape from work pressures, and the opportunities to roam the hills in peace and quiet.

Clark and Hughes – both Cambridge men, so perhaps not entirely objective – point out that "when he had tasted the sweets of University life, he was apt to find Dent somewhat dull; and in middle life he had other objects of interest, and perhaps thought less of his home than of those who lived there." Nonetheless, in *Memorial* Adam lamented that, although he had left Dent half a century earlier, "yet my love for the valley and its mountains, and its honest warm-hearted inhabitants, has not become cold." He added "whenever I have revisited the hills and dales of my native country, and heard the cheerful greetings of my old friends and countrymen, I have felt a new swell of emotion …".

His attachment to Dentdale was strong, deep-seated, and enduring. It's difficult to judge how much the attachment was to the place and how much to the people, but even after the death of his parents and some of his siblings, he remained eager to spend time there.

We've already seen (in Chapter 3) how Adam always looked upon Dentdale as "the home of my heart", and it's clear that absence from the dale really did make his heart grow fonder. In June 1870 he wrote in a letter to a Miss Duncan of how, when he was recovering from a serious attack of bronchitis, "my spirits and senses were alive again, and I longed to be in Dent, which I had not visited for two years. I really felt a home sickness (what the doctors, I think, call a *nostalgia*) with painful intensity."

Return visits to Dentdale offered him very effective and highly valued opportunities to recharge his physical, mental and emotional batteries. The "home sickness", that he thought might be called "nostalgia", was a core part of his character. The Welsh have a word for the sentiment – *hiraeth*. The word does not translate directly into English, but it means a yearning or longing tinged with sadness.

The pull of Dentdale was so strong that Adam was prepared to put up with great inconvenience during his travels back there from Cambridge, in all weathers. For example, he wrote to his friend Ainger in February 1812 of how he had had to sit on the outside of the coach, fully exposed to the weather, noting "I had fortified myself with a box-coat of huge dimensions and impenetrable thickness, so that, notwithstanding a keen north wind and hard frost, I found little inconvenience from the weather." On another occasion, in February 1836, when travelling back to Dent through sleet and heavy wind on a dark night, after the coach had been blown off the rough country track onto its side, he helped to push it back upright then walked in front of it for seven miles, carrying a lamp to light the way, "with a hairy cap on my head, and a boa [scarf] about my neck, all bespattered with sleet and snow, and looking like an old grizzly watchman."

Adam's journeys to and from Dent were made much easier, quicker and more comfortable with the arrival of the railway, initially in Kendal. He wrote to his niece Fanny Hicks in October 1847 of how he took the post-coach over the snow-covered fells from Dent to Kendal, where he caught a train south to London: "At a quarter past two I entered the express train, and at twenty minutes before eleven I was safely set down at Euston Square! What a charming change since I was an undergraduate, when I used to be two nights out on my way from home to Cambridge …"

Adam paid his last visit to Dentdale in June 1870, three years before he died. He was then 85 years old, the visit was short, and he was unable to walk without help. He returned to his college rooms in Cambridge straight afterwards.

Health
Adam's adult years were blighted by health problems. He had a weak constitution and often suffered from poor health. *The Times*, in a posthumous review of *Life and Letters* published in July 1890, pointed out that "His health was not strong. He lacked the 'good gizzard' he pronounced needful for 'hard grinding'." *Life and Letters* is in some ways a catalogue of the various illnesses, complaints and accidents that befell Adam. Given his health record, it's a wonder he lived as long as he did; he died in 1873 at the age of 88.

There is no mention in either *Life and Letters* or *Memorial* of any health problems before the age of twenty-eight, but after that they started to take a toll on him.

The turning point came in 1813, when he suffered a breakdown in his health following a river trip. It might have been a nervous breakdown, but that is nowhere stated explicitly. It knocked him out of action for some months, during which he recuperated by taking a walking holiday in his beloved Dentdale. He never fully recovered from the breakdown, but he was determined not to let it stop him from pursuing the academic career he by then felt drawn to.

Three years earlier, in 1810, he had been awarded a Fellowship in Trinity College, which gave him a degree of financial security and independence, but it came at a heavy cost. The workload was heavy and never-ending. He enjoyed the intellectual side of the work, but often found it draining and demanding. As an undergraduate he had studied mathematics and had proved very proficient in it, but his academic interests were changing, and at the same time his levels of anxiety and stress were increasing. His teaching duties (leading tutorials, not delivering lectures) were heavily focused on mathematics, but he felt that his students had little interest or motivation in learning, which ground him down further. By that time he was also finding life as a Fellow, living full-time in college and surrounded by other male Fellows and teaching only male students, an increasingly lonely experience, and he missed the convivial company of friends he had studied with but had since graduated and left Cambridge.

All in all, life in college was creating for him a 'perfect storm' of stresses and strains, and so it is quite possible that this, coupled with his weak constitution, caused the breakdown.

But Adam was also plagued through his adult years with more routine ailments, particularly rheumatic gout, bronchitis, and inflammation of the eyes. He also had more than his fair share of colds and influenza.

His ability to work and walk was at times seriously constrained by gout, which stalked him regularly. Clark and Hughes report that in late 1833 "Sedgwick's exertions to entertain the [natural] philosophers [i.e. scientists] brought on a fit of the gout" which they called his "close companion". A recurrence of the gout between March and late June 1846 forced Adam to spend time at the spa in Harrogate, where the "sweet waters … offended my nostrils, and did no good to my hands and feet."

The gout seriously affected his wellbeing and restricted what he could do, as he described in a letter to Miss Kate Malcolm in May 1869: "I am penetrated, at this season, by gout. It prevents all kindly emotions; makes me sour and selfish; incapable of labour, yet never at rest; dull as ditch-water, yet abominably irritable and waspish; incapable of continued thought bent to any good purpose; my memory refusing to do its hourly duty, yet stored with gloomy, worthless images; my moral sense perverted."

Adam was also laid low in his college rooms with a bout of influenza during 1837; a particularly heavy cold in late 1853, during which he never left his rooms for 29 days; serious attacks of bronchitis in early 1854 and for seven months between October 1854 and May 1855, and a particularly serious attack in January 1870 from which he never fully recovered, and which flared up again that June.

4. Profile of the Man

Some of Adam's health problems were self-inflicted, because he was prone to accidents. He was a keen horseman and an experienced rider, but sometimes he came to grief. In 1837, for example, his horse fell on him, damaging his knee and deeply bruising and grazing his face. On Christmas Eve 1849, his horse fell on him again, this time on frozen ground, breaking his arm just below the shoulder, and making it impossible for him to work (on a revised edition of *Discourse*) for many weeks.

He didn't always need a horse to cause accidents. In May 1849, he fell over a window sill at his cathedral house in Norwich, confining him to bed for two weeks and stopping him from walking or riding for a whole month. In July 1868, he twisted his knee badly while scrambling up a steep cliff in the hills around Dentdale, again keeping him "prisoner for many months".

Adam often had to spend time resting after being laid low with one health problem or another. He much preferred to do that in Dentdale, of which he wrote in 1846 "what noble scenery! Such scenes not merely delight the senses, but minister food to the heart and understanding." When it wasn't possible for him to retreat to the bosom of his family in Dent, he took time to recuperate either in his rooms in Trinity College, Cambridge, or his cathedral house in Norwich.

He occasionally visited a spa to "take the waters". This was a popular and fashionable thing to do in Victorian times, and it was believed to be an effective 'cure' for any number of conditions and ailments. Charles Darwin retreated to a spa in Ilkley when his *Origin of Species* was published in 1859, partly to escape the attention it was guaranteed to bring him. Adam is first recorded spending time towards the end of April 1839 at the Spa in Cheltenham, where "the waters agreed with him, and he was soon able to report some slight improvement." We have already seen him in the spa in Harrogate in 1846; he had an extended stay in one in Wiesbaden in Germany in 1844, seeking a water cure for the gout, and a short stay at a spa in Bath in 1870.

Sadly, for Adam, the breakdown he experienced in 1813 left him frail for the rest of his days. This, coupled with a relentlessly heavy workload through most of his adult life, commonly flagging spirits, and bouts of anxiety (caused in part by his determination to stand his ground in some very high profile geological debates and disputes), meant he often had to endure long spells of fatigue. These laid him low, made it difficult if not impossible for him to work, and often left him feeling isolated and lonely. In a letter he sent to fellow geologist Roderick Murchison in June 1833, for example, Adam describes the knock-out effect of "a fresh attack of illness that put an end to all work", noting that "during the last seven or eight weeks I have been under a strange mental obscuration, unable to do a stitch of work requiring thought or attention."

As his career progressed he was drawn into a variety of high-profile projects in Cambridge, Norwich and London, that we'll explore in later chapters. But his workload was often heavy and relentless, and matters were made worse by time lost through illness and the need for long spells of recuperation. To take just one example, during 1851, as Clark and Hughes put it, "Sedgwick, whether well or ill, was compelled to lead what he once happily described as 'a shuttlecock existence.' His duties as [University] Commissioner (Chapter 8) frequently took him to London, and compelled him to pass long and weary days in Downing Street; while his position as Prince Albert's Secretary (at Cambridge, Chapter 9) entailed upon him numerous social engagements which he enjoyed while they lasted, but which occupied his time and over-taxed his strength."

All the while, he was still working more-or-less full-time at Cambridge (Chapters 6 and 7), and part-time in Norwich Cathedral (Chapter 17). As a result, they note, "he was beginning to feel his years, and, had he not been an unthrifty economist of his powers and his time, he would have sought repose rather than fresh employment." In late October that year Adam wrote to his niece Isabella, complaining "I have too much on my hands for an old man ... Rest for a winter – absolute rest – spent perhaps abroad, might set me on my legs again. Wherever I go I am bothered." There were no sabbaticals for academics in those days!

An ability to say "no" to some of the endless stream of requests to do things would have helped him, but he didn't have it. The ability to organize his time better, rather than being "an unthrifty economist of his powers and his time", would also have been useful, but here again he didn't really take care of himself as much or as well as he doubtless should have done.

The almost inevitable end result was one over-worked, over-stressed, over-tired, but highly dedicated man, determined to cram as much as possible into his time on earth. He never married and appears to have had few close friends of either sex, who might have taken him under their wing and tried to encourage him to take better care of himself.

As a result, Adam showed regular and recurring signs of stress and anxiety. Whilst his condition was never diagnosed or described in terms of mental health, the evidence points in that direction. For example, he advised his friend Ingle by letter in February 1843, that his doctor, Dr Haviland, "thinks my malady chiefly nervous." Three months later he advised his friend Brodie by letter that "To my friends I show my best face: but by myself I am often oppressed with miserable spirits, and with the consciousness of doing so little of what I ought to do ...". Eight years later, in June 1851, he wrote to his brother John that "Sometimes I think that this long-continued nervous and gouty worry will end in positive insanity, or perhaps paralysis. But God forbid! I am at present pressed by too much work. And how seldom have I any time to work for myself." It is easy to wonder to what extent some of Adam's health problems might have been at least partly psychosomatic in origin and nature.

Adam never hesitated to seek advice from doctors about his conditions and medication for them. In 1839 he wrote to the wife of the eminent geologist Charles Lyell, describing how his "daily bread is made of calomel [mercury chloride, then given to release the body of impurities] and colchicum [a type of crocus, then used to treat gout]; and ... they have given me every day a stew in her caldron. It would melt your heart, could you see me sitting for half an hour each day in brimstone vapour at a temperature of 110°C!". In November 1853, after "a determination of blood to the head", and given that "he ought to have abstained from all mental and bodily exertion, but rest was out of the question", he was treated in Cambridge with "copious applications of leeches", medicinal bloodsuckers then in popular therapeutic use for drawing blood. The following February he took ill in Norwich and was given "the doctor's orders to live on Sangrado physic [a natural plant, *Polygata seneca*, then commonly prescribed for respiratory problems such as pneumonia], and never to read, or write, or think about anything heavier than the froth of a modern novel." In February 1854 he was confined to bed in college with a heavy cold, where he spent his days "in drinking slops and sudorifics [drugs that cause sweating] enough to dissolve a block of granite. Mustard foot-baths and mustard chest cataplasms [poultices] were all in vain. So the doctor dabbed my throat and chest with a liniment [ointment] which gave me a kind of horrible red mange, and made me unfit for a civilized piggery."

Medication did not always work as Adam hoped. For example, after a "malady" [probably the gout] lasting five months during the winter of 1842-43, he had hoped to be prescribed colchicum but Dr Haviland "for the present forbids its use, as he thinks my malady chiefly nervous."

At times, he almost appears to revel in his poor health. For example, he wrote to Mrs Lyell in 1839 "all winter I have been a cross, crusty, crabbed, careworn, caitiff [coward]. In outer looks I am sour, and ill-favoured; ... I have been ashamed of my ill-looks, and have not called on any one ...". Clark and Hughes, who knew him personally, admit that Adam "allowed his ailments to occupy too large a space in his conversation and his letters", but in his defence, they point out that, "in judging him – and in taking stock of what he accomplished during his long life – it must be recollected that from 1813 to his death he could never count upon robust health for even a single day."

Adam's tendency to define himself in terms of ill-health, and indeed to wallow in it, even if some of it was self-inflicted, and his habit of seeking medication without always giving his body and mind adequate time to rest and recover after illness, taken together, sound like the behaviour of a hypochondriac, or at least point in that direction. That was the verdict of at least one distinguished medical man in Adam's day – Charles Darwin had once taken Adam to meet his father in Shrewsbury, where "he talked so much about his health and uncomfortable feelings that my father, who was a doctor, thought that he was a confirmed hypochondriac."

Character

Adam had a reputation for being straightforward and honest. A tribute by "one who knew him in the intimacy of everyday life", included in *Life and Letters*, speaks of him being "transparent and straightforward - the very soul of uprightness and honour – tender and affectionate – most generous and kind. He had a hatred of all duplicity and meanness. He was entirely unsuspicious of evil, unless it was forced upon his notice; and he expected and believed everyone to be as straightforward and truthful, as he was himself."

Clark and Hughes highlight other important aspects of Adam's character. They tell us, for example, about his good manners that "were distinguished by an old-fashioned stately courtesy". They write of his generosity, noting how he showed little interest in acquiring material possessions, and great willingness to share or give away what he had. Prominent lawyer and MP William Henry Maule praised Adam's "conscientiousness in the discharge of duties which might at first sight appear so incompatible as a Professorial Chair at Cambridge, and a Prebendal Stall [canon's post] at Norwich ...".

Adam was highly intelligent and had been since childhood, even though his application to his studies was often somewhat lacking while he was growing up, as we saw in Chapter 1.

He was also easily distracted from his work by social activities, political engagements, visits to Dent, and a myriad of other activities. *The Times* (29 July 1890) pointed out that "Sedgwick had too much joyous human nature in him to make a first-rate student", and geologist Charles Lyell, who knew him well, bemoaned the fact that "he has not the application necessary to make his splendid abilities tell in a work [book]. Besides, everyone leads him astray. A man should have some severity of character and be able to refuse invitations ..."

Company

We might view the adult Adam as a troubled soul who was only at peace in Dent and when out in the fresh air engaged in geological fieldwork, and who only enjoyed periodic spells of happiness, usually when in the company of close family. Whilst such a view is consistent with what he wrote about himself in letters to family and friends, it only tells half of the story.

There is no shortage of evidence that Adam was gregarious and fond of company, and by nature was outgoing and, if anything, slightly extrovert. He was certainly people-friendly. Clark and Hughes describe him as friendly and approachable, noting that "there was nothing forbidding about him". They also describe him as well-liked, noting that they "do not think any man was so beloved by his friends as he was."

For a person who spent much of his adult life on his own, Adam clearly had an outgoing personality and got on well with all kinds of people. As Clark and Hughes point out, his "geological tours gave him a wide and varied experience of mankind. With all sorts and conditions of men, quarrymen, miners, fishermen, smugglers, shepherds, artisans, grooms, inn-keepers, clergy of all denominations, squires, noblemen he was equally communicative, and soon became equally popular." He was also comfortable mixing with 'the great and the good', including royalty (as we shall see in Chapter 9), politicians (Chapter 8), and members of the Royal Society and other leading scientists of the day.

Adam was also very sociable and hospitable, and led a very active social life. Clark and Hughes tell us that "high spirits had been granted to him in no stinted measure". He loved good company and "was a diner and giver of dinners ... and a lover of hospitality". As a young man he loved dancing, and throughout his adult years he loved good food and fine wine. He also loved the company of ladies, children and young people. By all accounts he was an engaging conversationalist, not short of jokes, and easy to chat with, although his plain-speaking style and colourful language might not always have gone down well. Clark and Hughes describe how "it was impossible to resist the infection of that boisterous laugh; that cheerful geniality; that persistence in looking at the bright side of things ..."

Clark and Hughes add that "he sometimes grumbled at the number of invitations he was obliged to accept; but society, especially the society of ladies and young people, was quite essential to his happiness. If it did not come to him, he sought it out. He paid calls; he constantly appeared, without special invitation, at the tea-tables of intimate friends; he got up [arranged] parties in his own rooms; and took his young friends to any show that happened to be passing through Cambridge. No dinner-party was thought to be complete without 'old Sedge' – as he was usually called – to brighten it up, and keep everybody in good humour ...". His social life slowed down as he grew older; he told his niece Fanny Hicks in 1856 "I avoid all dinner-parties; but I have generally a tea and coffee party at my own rooms after Sunday evening chapel."

Adam was also an engaging story-teller, always on the lookout for tall tales to tell. Clark and Hughes report that "he had unrivalled powers as a raconteur, and when he could be started on one of his well-known stories, there was a dead silence till he had finished." They note that "his return to Cambridge, after a summer's [geological] excursion, was eagerly looked forward to by his friends, for the sake of the budget of fresh stories with which he was certain to regale them."

We are fortunate that Adam was also a prolific writer of letters to family, friends and acquaintances. But he often felt weighed down by the responsibility of replying to the enormous number of letters that had arrived while he was away on his travels, visiting Dentdale, doing geology fieldwork, and attending meetings.

The price of having a gregarious nature was loneliness when people stopped visiting him or stopped inviting him to join them, particularly when poor health made it impossible for him to visit other people and keep in close contact with them. His loneliness grew stronger as Adam grew older, particularly as he was still living on his own most of the time.

At different times in his life Adam enjoyed the company of a dog. The first one we hear of was "an excellent greyhound" he acquired in February 1818 while on a visit to family in Dent. He mentioned it in a letter to his good friend Ainger, to whom he writes "You may depend on it that dogs are the best company a man can have with him in the country." We hear nothing for three decades, until 1839, when Adam, then aged 54, returns from a geology trip to Germany with him a pair of Pomeranian Spitzhunds, which he called Max and Shindy. Max died young but Shindy lived a long and happy life with Adam at Cambridge and

Norwich. Apparently, he sometimes gave her puppies to friends as gifts. Writing to Miss Kate Malcolm in December 1844 about life in his cathedral house in Norwich, Adam told her "I meet my servants at eight, and we have morning prayers by candle light … they are my only live companions, except my dog …".

In 1845 Adam was told off by William Whewell, the Master of Trinity College, where he was based in Cambridge, for keeping the dog in college. Whewell wrote to him advising "Your frequent appearance at the College Courts [grounds] accompanied by a dog is inconsistent both with [the College] Rules and with the [University] Statutes", although their friendship survived this incident. Two years later we read that Miss Malcolm's brother had given Adam a "Chinese dog" called Zoe, which was "born at the kennel of Windsor Castle".

Women and marriage
Adam grew up surrounded by women, particularly in his close family – his mother Margaret, older sister Margaret and younger sister Isabella, to whom he was very close but who died young, unmarried and childless (as we saw in Chapter 2). Throughout his adult life, he was very happy in the company of girls of all ages and of ladies of all social classes, and he always displayed old-fashioned courtesy in female company. In old age he relied heavily on two of his nieces (Isabella and Fanny) for companionship and practical assistance.

Yet he sometimes expressed some rather odd views on ladies in general, certainly by today's standards and sensitivities. For example, he wrote in a letter to a Miss Gerard in March 1854 (when he was 69 years old) of how "ever since I was fifteen … all young ladies have been to me a most amazing puzzle." He ended a letter to his colleague John Herschel in April 1848 with the expression "My kindest regards to your best rib", referencing the Biblical story of how God made Eve from one of Adam's ribs.

Adam was familiar with the sight of women in his classes at the University and his public lectures in Norwich and elsewhere. Through most of his career ladies were not admitted to Cambridge as students, but ladies from the town were allowed to attend lectures. Describing a lecture he gave to the Norwich Society of Naturalists in January 1844, he wrote "I think I had a class of nearly 300, and more than half the number were of the softer sex – at least they wore the outer symbols of womankind – but whether their stockings were blue I know not from ocular proof."

'Blue stockings' was an expression commonly used in those days to describe educated, intelligent women.

But Adam still appears to have regarded ladies in lectures as curious creatures, because his letter continues "I have heard it said that a good woman might have her stockings as blue as you like, only she ought to have petticoats long enough to cover them." This hints at a belief that women should not display their intelligence but keep it hidden from sight.

When Cambridge voted to admit female students in 1865, Adam wrote to his friend Ainger confessing "I was in the minority. I think the plan will be a mere stepping-way to the puffing of second-rate forward chits and 'bloomers.' I hope, however, now that the Grace [proposal] is carried, that I was mistaken."

Given Adam's attitudes to women, it is little surprise that he remained a confirmed bachelor. He was not alone in this, safely sheltered as he was in the closed male-dominated world of the Oxbridge colleges of his time, where there were no female students or academics, with a separatist lifestyle more akin to a monastery than a modern seat of learning.

Adam's attitude towards women doubtless coloured views on marriage in his letters to friends and family. He acknowledged the sanctity of marriage, writing to his friend Arthur Stanley in December 1863 that "marriage was the most solemn contract which could be made between God's children, that it had His most holy sanction, and that husband and wife were to be sharers in the sorrows of life, as well as in its joys."

He recognised the happiness and comfort that marriage was clearly offering to members of his close family, and in one letter he urged some young ladies he knew to "steer into the haven of marriage". He wrote as a 23-year-old to his friend Ainger in 1808 "I wish some blooming damsel could contrive to kindle a flame in my breast, for then I might stand some chance of keeping up a proper degree of animal heat ..."

On the other hand, he sometimes paints marriage as a trap or a burden. In that same letter he told Ainger that "marriage may be all well enough when a man is on his last legs, but you may depend on it that to be linked to a wife is to be linked to misery." He reprised the theme in a letter to Ainger four years later, in which he describes an unmarried clergyman in Macclesfield he knew well who "was not tormented by that bane of domestic happiness a wife", which meant that when he visited him they could "keep up the conversation till two or three o'clock in the morning".

No matter what his views were on the question of marriage, his career choice ruled it out as an option for him personally. As we shall see in

4. Profile of the Man

Chapter 7, if he married he would have had to give up his post as Professor of Geology, which he regarded as his primary calling in life. As he wrote to the wife of fellow geologist Roderick Murchison on August 1833, "I am wedded to the rocks, and Mount Sorrel [in Leicestershire] ... is my present mistress. By the way she is a little coy and hard-hearted, and refuses to tell me her pedigree, and to introduce me to her old relations."

He accepted bachelorhood as the price of his calling, but not without some regrets. Congratulating Ainger on the birth of his first child in April 1821, he added "my own destinies were ... fixed at the font, and I already feel myself fast sinking in the mire of celibacy." In March 1845 he wrote to his niece Isabella, to whom he was by then very close, telling her "I have now given up all thoughts of marriage; and it is high time, is it not? But, do you know, it is a very hard thing for a man to give up, even at my own time of life ...".

Life and Letters contains a letter Adam sent to Isabella seven years later, in November 1852, when he was 67 years old, which shows something of the inner turmoil he sometimes felt about the life he had missed out on. He wrote "Had I not been born about 40 years too soon I would have made love to you [courted you] in such an ardent manner that you would surely have been melted, and I should have carried you in my arms to the altar-rails ... A wheezing old man makes, however, but a sorry bridegroom, and, besides, you are my niece, and therefore within the prohibited degrees ..."

Although he never married, as Adam grew older "he particularly enjoyed the companionship of young women", as Colin Speakman (1982) put it, "treating them with a tenderness and consideration not all that common among elderly bachelors, particularly those of an academic persuasion. Many of his most characteristically generous and lively letters were to his nieces or other young ladies of his acquaintance, and it is not too fanciful to suggest that the remarkable bond between the two Isabellas of his life influenced this."

Adam also loved the company of children and young people. At the age of 71 he wrote to a colleague "I love children and I love young people, there is a charm about them which is cheering to a rickety old fellow like myself."

Like many Victorian men and women, in his later years Adam depended increasingly on his nieces Isabella and Fanny for companionship and practical assistance.

Interests
Whilst Adam committed his adult years to his work in geology, he did find time to pursue other interests too.

As a youth, he very much enjoyed traditional country sports including fishing and shooting game birds, but when he was promoted to Professor of Geology at Cambridge his sporting days were over, and he gave away his guns and his hunting dogs. His interest in horse-riding continued throughout his life, although as we have already seen he had some accidents and incidents on – or rather, off – his horse. He loved being in the open air, and in good weather was fond of walking in the countryside around Dent, Cambridge or Norwich, ideally with a close friend. As he once described himself, "Like my ancient namesake, I was meant to delve in the open air, and often have I done so, and always have been the better for it."

Adam had intellectual interests too, beyond his geology. He was particularly interested in philosophy and theology. As Clark and Hughes put it "was fond of metaphysical and moral speculations", as becomes clear in his *Discourse on the Studies of the University of Cambridge* (that we'll look at in Chapter 8). William Whewell, Master of Trinity College, believed that if Adam's life had not "been absorbed in struggling with many of the most difficult problems of a difficult science," he would have been a great help to him while he was writing *The Philosophy of the Inductive Sciences*. He also had a strong desire to make science in general, and geology in particular, more accessible to the general public. As a result, he made time available to give public lectures on geology in Norwich, and at the annual meetings of the British Association that were held in different towns and cities around the country.

Adam's interests stretched to public affairs and (as we'll see in Chapter 8) he was very active in local and at times national politics. In his younger days he was a liberal, a member of the Whig Party, active in the affairs of his college and University, and he worked hard for his party in Cambridge and Yorkshire. As he grew older he became more conservative and described himself as a "stiff-backed Tory". Adam was also an ardent royalist and nationalist; he wrote in 1867 "I wished the old elements of King, Lords, and Commons to keep their well-balanced places in the adjustment and conservation of our nation's liberties." He actively supported William Wilberforce and his campaign against slavery, which led to the abolition of slavery in Britain in 1807. He also campaigned against the Penal Laws that sought to uphold the establishment of the Church of England against Protestant nonconformists and Catholicism.

56

As Clark and Hughes put it, "to the end of his life he watched public affairs, both at home and abroad, with unabated zeal; and his letters ...
show how heartily he rejoiced over a national triumph, how bitterly he
mourned a national disaster."

Adam was a man of culture as well as action, as is clear from the
names that he dropped into his letters. He loved books, particularly older
literature, and read widely. He read travel books, biographies, novels,
poetry, theology books, and his favourite authors included Chaucer, Jonathan Swift, William Shakespeare, Daniel Defoe, and his contemporary
Walter Scott. Adam wrote to a church colleague in February 1847 of
how, after a spell of serious ill-health, "But for old Daniel de Foe I should
have died. I steadily read through eighteen volumes of his works, at the
rate of about a volume a day. What a wonderful genius he was, and unlike
any one else in our literary history."

In his letters he also mentions theatre, having seen on stage great ac-
tors including the Kemble family (John, Charles, Roger and Sarah), and
"the prince of clowns" Joseph Grimaldi. He liked opera and classical music, and saw performances by British opera singer Elizabeth Billington,
Italian singer Angelica Catalani, and Swedish singer Jenny Lind who
"sang like a lark, and ... was like angel". Amongst the men he heard were
English bass singer James Bartelman and tenor John Braham. In 1851 he
attended a performance of Handel's *Messiah* in London.

We read little about the visual arts in Adams' letters other than a
mention of visiting an exhibition at the Royal Academy in 1860. He did
not like Landseer's painting of the Highland Flood ("clever in many of its
details, but its colour is dismal"), but thought Millais' Black Brunswicker
"admirably painted, but ... as stiff as a poker", and had mixed views on
pre-Raphaelite Holman Hunt's painting of Christ discussing with the
Doctors in the Temple, describing it as " stiff, formal, but exquisitely
painted." He was clearly hard to please in the art department!

Faith and vocation
No profile of Adam's character would be complete without mention of
his Christian faith, which we will look at in more detail in Part Four.

As we saw in Chapter 2, he came from a family of church-men, and
was steeped in the teaching, traditions, values and expectations of the
Church of England. He had a strong and deep personal faith – this was
much more than just head knowledge – which never wavered even when
he found himself immersed in some serious and very public geological
controversies.

Although (as we shall see in Chapter 5) after graduating and being awarded a College Fellowship at Cambridge, he was ordained as a priest in the Church of England, he truly believed that his primary calling or vocation lay in geology rather than the church. Looking back on his life at the age of eighty-three, Adam wrote in *Memorial* (1868) "For more than three score years Cambridge has been my honoured resting-place, and here God has given me a life-long task amidst a succession of intellectual friends."

This sense of responding to a divine vocation in geology helps us understand why Adam wrote of himself being "wedded to the rocks", in much the same way as Catholic nuns have traditionally thought of themselves as "married to Jesus", as their primary focus and love above all else.

PART TWO. CAMBRIDGE MAN

"For more than three-score years Cambridge has been my honoured resting-place, and here God has given me a life-long task amidst a succession of intellectual friends. For Trinity College, ever since I passed under its great portal, for the first time, in the autumn of 1804, I have felt a deep and grateful sentiment of filial regard."
Adam Sedgwick (1868), in *Life and Letters* (1890)

5. Student Days

*More than one of Sedgwick's contemporaries has been heard to say
that when he first made his appearance in Trinity College he was thought
uncouth, and that some time elapsed before he was properly appreciated.*
Clark and Hughes (1890) *Life and Letters*

After his school days at Dent Grammar School and Sedbergh School, by
the autumn of 1803 the question arose of which university Adam should
progress on to. In those days, the choice in England was limited to Oxford or Cambridge, and further afield there was Dublin in Ireland and St
Andrews, Glasgow and Aberdeen in Scotland.

Trinity College Cambridge
Adam's father Richard had studied at Cambridge and he had fond memories of the place, so that was a natural choice for his bright and inquisitive
second son who was then approaching twenty. Richard had studied at St
Catherine's Hall (now College), but which college would be best for Adam? To help decide the matter, Richard gathered together two people
whose judgments he trusted – Rev William Stevens, the Master of Sedbergh School, and Rev D. Peacock, the Vicar of Sedbergh – for an
informed discussion of the options. Stevens had studied at St John's College and Peacock was a Fellow at Trinity College

St John's College had a lot going for it; most boys from Sedbergh
School were admitted there, because it had ten Scholarships and three
Fellowships "appropriated" to the School. Stevens strongly encouraged
Bland and Sedgwick – the two brightest boys of their year – to apply for
St John's, but Peacock saw things differently. His reasoning was clear
and fair; he was convinced that Bland was better than Adam at mathematics, and would always beat him in examinations, and then in the
competition to win one of the Sedbergh Fellowships at St John's. Richard
agreed with Peacock's logic and proposed his own college (St Catherine's), but in the end he decided upon Trinity for Adam.

In November 1803 Adam applied to and was accepted by Trinity
College. To help him prepare intellectually for the move, his father arranged for him to be tutored during the summer months of 1804 by John

Dawson (who we met in Chapter 4), who had tutored Richard himself 48 years earlier.

In October 1804 Adam entered Trinity College, Cambridge, which was to be his main home for the rest of his days.

Life within Cambridge University at that time was not spared from the shadow of possible invasion by the French, because of the French Wars (1793-1813). Clark and Hughes mention "the occupation of arming and drilling, which had penetrated even to the University". The economy was also seriously affected by the French Wars, with trade restricted if not totally paralysed, and the cost of many basic goods running very high. Reflecting the depressed state of the country, the number of families who could afford a university education for their sons fell dramatically. In 1804 only 128 young men applied to Cambridge, the smallest number for thirty years.

Early days
Adam's early days in Trinity College were not the most comfortable for him, because it took some time for his fellow students to understand him and appreciate him.

He must have felt like a fish out of water, certainly at the start of his time there, because he was so different from many of his peers. When he started at Cambridge he was a year or two older than many of them. Many of his peers would have spent years in boarding schools, but he had never lived away from home. Indeed, he had rarely spent a night away from the family home, or travelled out of Dentdale for more than a few days at a time. The furthest he had travelled before Cambridge was probably the fifty miles or so to Carlisle.

Growing up in Dentdale had suited him well, but it was a sheltered life and not ideal preparation for engaging with the wider world beyond. He had little contact with adults beyond his immediate family, and – as Clark and Hughes put it – "from the young men of his own age, whose ideas of amusement were confined to sport, wakes, and drinking-bouts, he could have learnt nothing but tastes and customs 'more honoured in the breach than the observance'." They add, rather pointedly, "that he never gave way to such himself, to any serious extent, is a proof either of his father's influence, or of his own strength of will."

Whilst Adam was "thought uncouth" in many ways, he also stood out in the crowd because he looked and behaved differently – "his dress, his manners, and his bearing would bespeak him a plain unsophisticated Dalesman." His strong Yorkshire accent, and plain speaking, must also have made him an easy target amongst his more prosperous, confident and opinionated peers.

Studies

Compared with universities today, students at Cambridge at the start of the nineteenth century had a very limited choice in what they studied. They had a choice between two triposes, or schemes of study – Classics or Mathematics.

Given the amount of time Adam had spent being tutored by John Dawson before he started at Cambridge, it is no surprise that he chose the Mathematics Tripos, which majored in Mathematics but also included some Classics – the study of which was in those days regarded as the highest form of intellectual activity.

His tutor at Trinity was the Rev Thomas Jones, who had graduated from Trinity with distinction as the top student ("Senior Wrangler") in 1779 and had been elected to a College Fellowship two years later. Clark and Hughes were clearly impressed by him; in *Life and Letters* they wrote "it would be difficult, if not impossible, to name any one man, who by force of personal character, vigour of intellect, and unwearied devotion to his duties, was enabled to effect a more enduring influence for good on the moral and intellectual life of his college." Adam valued his tutor's advice and instruction highly, and was greatly saddened when Jones died in July 1807.

Scholarship

We have already seen that Adam came from a family of modest means, and how this worked against him in his early days as a student in Trinity College. It also meant that he could not enjoy the active social life of most of his peers, or the extra comforts that made living in college more tolerable for many of them.

There was an added reason why Adam's financial situation made life difficult for him, and that was the impact it might have in curbing his academic ambitions. From the start of his time in Cambridge, he appears to have set his mind on working hard and aiming for a distinction in his degree. This was probably in part because he felt the need to prove himself to his family, but also because, under the college rules at that time, without a distinction, he would not have been allowed to apply for a College Fellowship, which he very much aspired to.

His hard work during the first two terms in Trinity was rewarded with a scholarship, won by success in a tough examination, which defined him as a 'sizar'. Sizars were bright but poor students, to whom the university gave financial support in return for doing chores in college during term time. We have no record of what chores Adam did, or what he thought about them, but he was clearly ready and willing to work his passage, and remained grateful to the university for helping him in this way.

Typhoid fever

Adam had just returned to Cambridge at the start of his second year in September 1805, when he suffered a serious attack of typhoid fever that nearly killed him. He was confined to his room in Trinity and the doctors who looked after him feared for the worse, but he pulled through. Ainger, his old school friend from Sedbergh, who was studying at a different college at Cambridge, "nursed him ... with unremitting diligence", and Adam used to say that he owed his life more to him than to his physicians.

Adam's recovery was slow, and he was unable to leave his rooms in college for at least four months. Looking back on that time more than six decades later (in 1871), he recalled "the early weeks of the year 1806, when I crawled out of my rooms, one bright sunny day (about February I think) after my long confinement from typhus fever. I had great difficulty in getting back. But then I was young, and my rate of recovery was astonishing. I am not strong now ...".

When he was fit enough to travel, in the summer of 1806 he returned to Dent to recharge his batteries, where amongst other things he spent time studying mathematics with John Dawson.

Examinations

It is worth pausing briefly to look at the ways in which students at Cambridge were examined in Adam's day, because it is so different from the experience of undergraduate students today.

As Clark and Hughes explain "The ordeal was in those days specially [sic] formidable, for a *viva voce* [oral] examination used to be held in the Hall [in College] in the presence of the Master, who sat in the centre of the dais [platform], with the Seniors [Senior Students] to his right and left ... The persons to be examined stood in front of this awe-inspiring assemblage, and questions were passed down the line from one to another by the presiding examiner, the Master occasionally interposing a word of praise or reproof – more frequently the latter. Men have been known to faint with apprehension even before it had come to their turn to be questioned. When the examination was over the names of those only were published whom the examiners thought specially [sic] worthy of commendation. A place in the first class was therefore a considerable distinction."

Although Adam found preparing for these examinations extremely stressful, he put time and effort into it and did his best. And his best turned out to be very good – at the end of his first year, in June 1805, his name appeared on the first-class list along with six others. To achieve that he must have been thoroughly well prepared in the classical subjects as well as in mathematics.

By the start of 1807 he was starting to prepare seriously for his final exams. He advised Ainger by letter in May that he was then getting down to some serious reading; he had just finished the first of three volumes of Isaac Newton's *Principia* (*Philosophiæ Naturalis Principia Mathematica*, in Latin, first published in 1687), and was about to start the second. His did admit, though, "in making an attempt, last night, upon the philosophy of sound, I got so completely fast, that after retiring to rest I was disturbed with the most horrid dreams you have the power of conceiving", adding that he intended to get up for the rest of the summer at 5 am each day to study.

The stakes were high, because unlike the system of continuous assessment over at least the final two years which is commonly used in degree schemes today "in those days the University required no proof of a student's proficiency until his third year", as Clark and Hughes put it.

A key part of the final examination at Cambridge in Adam's day involved each student having to take part in two *Acts* in the Lent (second) Term of the second year (early 1807) followed by two *Opponencies* in the Michaelmas (first) Term of the third year (late 1807). These took the form of gladiatorial contests in which students battled against each other to convince the adjudicator (*Moderator*) who was best.

Each student (*Respondent*) was given two weeks' notice of the summons to appear before the *Moderator* at the *Act*, where they were required to debate the truth of three 'Questions' (*Propositions*) against any three other students of the same year (*Opponents*) chosen by the Moderator. The first Question was usually drawn from Newton's *Principia*, and the second from another writer on Mathematics or Natural Philosophy (Science). The third was a Moral Question, drawn from the writings of philosophers such as John Locke (1632-1704), David Hume (1711-76), Joseph Butler (1692-1752), David Hartley (1705-57) or William Paley (1743-1805).

As Clark and Hughes explain, at that time it was not uncommon "during the fortnight's preparation for the *Respondent* to invite the *Opponents* to wine, or tea, or breakfast, in order to compare arguments, and generally to rehearse the performance."

On the appointed day, the *Respondent* was asked to read one of three essays they had prepared, in Latin, in answer to the three Questions. The three *Opponents* were then invited, in turn, to debate the essay with the *Respondent*; the first was required to raise three arguments against the essay, the second five, and the third three. After that the *Act* was opened up to a free debate, guided and controlled by the *Moderator*. Each *Act* lasted about two hours, of non-stop intellectual jousting. The proceedings were carried out entirely in Latin, and other students were allowed to sit and watch. After the *Respondent* and *Opponents* left the room, the *Moderator* awarded marks to the *Respondent* and the *Opponents*, and after all of the *Acts* had been completed the two Moderators agreed how many marks to award to each student (as *Respondent* and *Opponent)*, which determined that student's place on the final class list.

The other part of the final examination involved both a written test and an oral test (*viva voce*), which took place in the Senate House of the University. Adam took both tests in January 1808. The students' marks on both tests were collated, and a list "of those who had passed with the greatest merit" was published "on the pillars of the Senate House" and, as Clark and Hughes report, "men who were joined together in the same bracket [i.e. listed in the same class; the boundaries between classes being treated as watertight] had the opportunity of fighting the battle out under the direction of some Master of Arts appointed for the purpose." Quite what form "the battle" took is not recorded, but Adam Sedgwick emerged fifth in the first-class list – Fifth Wrangler in Cambridge parlance – on the list of successful candidates who were admitted to the degree of Bachelor of Arts.

Graduation

The Times wrote in a review of *Life and Letters* published in July 1890 that Adam Sedgwick's "undergraduate career was not particularly brilliant", which is curious given that this poor, hard-working, scholarship student came fifth in the whole University for mathematics in his year. He graduated with distinction, and was awarded the degree of Bachelor of Arts in 1808 and Master of Arts in 1811.

6. College Fellowship

"When I first arrived at Cambridge [in 1846], I found Professor Sedgwick, then Vice-Master of Trinity, the most popular and beloved man in the University, and his reputation for eloquence, and for devotion both to the University and to his clerical duties, as fully recognised as his scientific standing and labours."

Frederick McCoy, Geological Museum Assistant (1854)

In January 1808, shortly after completing his examinations in Cambridge, for which he had prepared hard and after which he was mentally and physically drained, Adam returned to the family home in Dent hoping to get some rest and clear his head.

That was Adam's default strategy for recharging his batteries but, on this occasion, he soon found himself wondering if he had done the right thing. He wrote to his friend Ainger in February "all the last week I have thought myself a fish out of water. I rise about 9 in the morning; come down stairs in all due form, and commence breakfast ... [but] no sooner have finished breakfast than I become miserable for want of employment. The weather is so bad that to walk is impossible. I have therefore nothing to do all morning but amuse myself with my own pleasant reflections, surrounded and perplexed with all the clamour of domestic music [noise]."

He experienced disappointment more than refreshment during this trip, so he cut it short and returned to Cambridge a month or so earlier than planned. Against his own expectations, Cambridge had captured his mind as well as feeding it, and he was eager to get back there and be among like-minded people. Like most students who have just completed their degrees, he was eager to get on with the next chapter of his life. Unbeknown to Adam at the time, and despite his love of Dentdale, Cambridge would be his base for the rest of his days.

Career planning

When Adam first went to Cambridge as a student he probably had no idea what he wanted to do in terms of a career. No doubt his father had visions of him following in the family business and becoming a clergyman, but we have few clues from Adam's letters about what he himself might have had in mind.

Apparently, his own wish was to train in law and become a barrister, like his friend Bickersteth was doing. It seemed to offer good prospects for Adam to better himself and give him financial independence, and it promised a better quality of life than his immediate family could enjoy back in Dent. His father's stipend as Vicar of Dent was small, even by comparison with many other church livings, so the family always had to scrape by.

Now that he had finished his own studies, Adam felt a responsibility to help support the family and not just look after himself. It was becoming clear that his father's general health was declining, and his eyesight was failing fast, but there was also the question of funding the education of his two younger brothers, John and James.

Much as he loved his close family, and had a strong attachment to Dent, Adam dreaded the prospect of having to return there to take over his father's teaching duties in Dent Grammar School when rather than if blindness made it impossible for him to continue. He made his position clear in a letter to Ainger in the summer of 1807, pointing out that the reports on his father's condition "produced such a depression in my spirits that I was prevented from reading; my sorrow, indeed, was in a good measure selfish ... for, if my Father's sight should continue to decline, a fixed residence in Dent must be my inevitable lot. This situation of all others I should dislike. Little as I have seen of the world, I have seen enough to find that to me no pleasures are to be found in illiterate solitude. These thoughts are to me too gloomy to dwell upon."

So Adam must have wrestled with the question of what career path he should try to pursue. He might have thought of a career that made direct use of the mathematics he had studied and proved good at but hardly enjoyed, perhaps in one of the new industrial enterprises that were then starting to emerge and show great promise, but we get no sense of that in *Life and Letters*.

Adam was fully aware of his father's ambition for him to become a clergyman, but he did not share it. As Clark and Hughes put it, "considering the poverty of his father's vicarage in the countryside and the prospect of returning there, he must have preferred a teaching position at the prestigious university, living in the old, historic, world-famous town of Cambridge."

As the rest of this book will show, Adam chose to follow an academic career at Cambridge University, where by then he felt at home, which offered him the sheltered but intellectually stimulating life of a don. The gateway to that career would be winning a Fellowship in Trinity College, from which he had just graduated.

Private Tutor (1808-10)
Then, as now, getting on the first step of the academic career ladder in Cambridge required more than just evidence of academic ability and promise. There were few openings and strong competition, and ambition had to be supported by persistence and self-belief.

Bright as Adam was, it would take him two attempts over two years to succeed in winning a Fellowship in Trinity. We saw in Chapter 5 how he had been prepared to work his passage as a scholarship student, and to his credit he carried this attitude into this quest for a Fellowship.

Recall (from Chapter 4) how Adam had benefited from John Dawson's teaching in mathematics, and how he looked on Dawson as a role model. Both experiences pointed Adam in the direction of working as a Private Tutor in maths, to support and teach young undergraduates in Cambridge who needed extra coaching and were willing to pay for it. The work was poorly paid so he led a "frugal life", but that was not a new experience for him and it was a cost he was prepared to bear.

We get a glimpse of what was involved in Clark and Hughes' account of Adam's first assignment. He returned to Cambridge from Dent in May 1808 and spent the summer months leading a "reading-party" of seven male students, tutoring them in mathematics. They stayed close to Cambridge, basing his "colony", as he called it, two miles downstream on the River Cam on a farm just outside the small village of Ditton. Adam and one student lodged at the farmhouse and the other students lodged nearby. By all accounts, Adam took his responsibilities seriously and worked the students hard. On one occasion, he turned down an invitation from his friend Ainger to join him on a day trip on the Broads near Whittlesea, and "the only amusement which he allowed himself was an occasional visit to the theatre at Sturbridge Fair." The party returned to Cambridge towards the end of October.

College Fellowship (1810)
Each year a small number of Fellowships fell vacant in Trinity College through the death or resignation of existing Fellows. New Fellows were selected by the Master and Senior Fellows, based on performance in an examination designed to test applicants' abilities in both mathematics and classics.

As one of the top students of his year, Adam thought he would stand a good chance of being selected for a Fellowship in 1809, when there were two vacancies. The competition that October was close fought, but he was beaten by two other applicants, one of whom had been third Wrangler and the other (a man called Clark) seventh Wrangler, while he had been fifth. Clark had performed worse than Adam in undergraduate exams in mathematics, and shown no real strength in classics, but he did extremely well in classics in the Fellowship examination. Adam saw which way the wind was blowing and recognised the need to improve his classical knowledge, so he worked hard on that to improve his prospects next time around.

There were four vacancies the following year, and Adam was selected to fill one of them. As a result, in 1816 he became a Fellow of Trinity College, which he and his family were very proud of. He had got onto that critically important first step on the academic career ladder, thanks to his hard work, commitment and persistence.

College Fellows in Adam's day were responsible for leading small tutorial groups within the college. They did no teaching at university level, and they were not allowed to marry.

Despite the hard work invested in gaining the position and, contrary to what he had imagined, Adam did not enjoy the work or find it fulfilling. His tutorial duties were in mathematics, and as Clark and Hughes point out, "he had never taken any deep interest in mathematics, or done any original work in them, and when it became necessary to teach them, merely for the sake of money, to young men of whom some probably approached their study with unwillingness as great as his own, he regarded both the subject and the pupils with feelings little short of detestation. He worked hard, and evidently did his duty conscientiously and thoroughly, but he was at heart profoundly dissatisfied with himself and his surroundings."

This was not a happy period for Adam. He carried out his teaching duties conscientiously but reluctantly. He could not hide his disappointment with the work, which shines through in letters he sent to family and friends. In one letter in 1810 be bemoaned the fact that "six of these blessed youths I have to feed [intellectually] each day". In the summer of 1811, after leading a maths reading-party at Bury St Edmunds, he wrote of how "five pupils and an empty purse interpose difficulties not easily got over". The following February he wrote to Ainger "Here I am grinding away with six pupils. Under such circumstances it is impossible to advance [career-wise] one step. But I am compelled by circumstances to undergo this drudgery. When I look back on what I have done since I was elected Fellow I cannot discover that I have made any proficiency whatever, or gained one new idea. This is miserable stagnation, but I thank God that I am not yet in the 'slough of despond'. I hope for better things."

Within a few years of becoming a College Fellow Adam clearly felt that he was treading water rather than making progress in his academic career. Teaching maths in college was becoming hard work and dull; leisure time was in short supply; his mind was not being challenged or stretched. Already, at this early stage in his career, we find him looking forward with eager anticipation to a future in which he will be able "to have done with the system altogether." His ambition remained undiminished, but he was starting to wonder how he could best move forward, and ideally upward.

Clark and Hughes capture something of this unhappy period in Adam's life, in his late twenties, describing how "the elasticity of youth had passed away, and had not yet been replaced by the cheerfulness of a man who is doing work which he enjoys contentedly and resolutely." He was on a treadmill, stuck in a rut, with no obvious way out.

He described his workload in a letter to Ainger in November 1817: "I am as usual employed two hours every morning in lecturing to the men of the first and second year, and every other day we are engaged about two hours and a half more in examining the men of the third year. We are besides employed at least three hours in the evening in looking over [marking] their papers."

Discontent and overwork took their toll on Adam's health. One of his friends wrote of him in 1810 "a man who is reduced two or three stone below his standard weight cannot be very well", and we've already seen (in Chapter 4) how he suffered a serious health breakdown in 1813, from which he never fully recovered. He fell ill again shortly after the start of the 1817-18 academic year, but ignored the advice of family and friends who urged him to resign from his teaching post and walk away from all the stress it was causing him. He returned to Cambridge after spending that summer in Dent, but quickly slid back into poor health.

Adam was nothing if not resolute, some would say stubborn. But shortly afterwards things were to change for the better for him when a highly suitable career opportunity opened up, as we'll see in Chapter 7.

Life in College
Although the teaching workload ground Adam down, the life of a College Fellow was not too onerous. The living conditions suited him fine, and in

many ways he grew increasingly institutionalised and felt safe in his sheltered life in the college within the prestigious "ivory tower".

The "rooms" he was allocated as a Fellow – which were to be his
home base for the rest of his days – were situated right at the heart of the
college buildings, in the Great Court, next to the Master's Lodge. They
were large and comfortably furnished, and included a bedroom, a tiny
kitchen with very basic facilities, and a formal dining room which Clark
and Hughes describe as "simply but comfortably furnished, with plenty of
chairs and sofas - and on the walls hung watercolour drawings of Dent,
Norwich, and the Lake District, a portrait of Mr. Dawson, and other memorials of his Yorkshire home". He also had a book-lined study with a
large table in the centre, where he spent most of his time. It was here that
he read, wrote, took tutorials, socialised with colleagues and received visitors. It was usually cluttered and piled high with books, papers and
letters, which he only tidied infrequently, and where he regularly mis-
placed important papers he was working on.

Living in College offered a very privileged but secluded life to the
Fellows who made Cambridge their home, many (including Adam) for
life. Adam had a "man" called John who served as butler and general factotum. In Adam's early days as a Fellow there were few newspapers
available, and they did not always arrive punctually. Letters to or from
Cambridge often took a long time to arrive. Communication with parts of
the country beyond Cambridge was slow and costly, and few people travelled far or often. Foreign travel was impossible during the wars on the
continent.

Life in College was sheltered socially, too. It was an almost totally
male environment. In those days, very few men in the University other
than Heads of College were married. The only female staff worked below
stairs, for example in the kitchens. It was also a rather inward-looking and
privileged environment. Heads of College often shunned non-University
people or non-church people, certainly within Cambridge, and – as Clark
and Hughes (both academics themselves) put it – other senior members
"thought themselves too important to associate with anybody whose degree was below that of a Doctor, or who had not achieved the dignified
position of a Professor." Fellows typically kept their distance from undergraduate students within the College, too, except when compelled to
be in their company while teaching or examining them.

One of the privileges of being an MA in the College was the right to
dine at High Table in Hall, which was strictly reserved for 'the great and
the good'. Here again Adam found the experience disappointing, noting

6. College Fellowship

in a letter to Grainger in 1811 that many of the MA men "are gloomy and discontented, many impertinent and pedantic; and a still greater number are so eaten up with vanity that they are continually attempting some part which they cannot support."

Somewhat cryptically, Clark and Hughes wrote of the sheltered life of College Fellows, "no wonder that those who had to endure a life which had all the dullness of a monastery without its austerity or its religious enthusiasm, should become soured, eccentric, selfish, if not intemperate and immoral."

Sub-Lecturer (1811-12)

Adam was appointed Sub-Lecturer in Trinity College towards the end of his second year as a Fellow, at the beginning of the Easter Term in 1812. This was a step up from Fellow, and it required him to take part in and help organize the College examinations.

The role put him in much closer contact with all of the undergraduates and tutors in College, and it enabled him to feel more involved in the life and work of the College. This in turn allowed him to see students through fresh eyes, and gave him a better understanding of their mind-set and behaviours.

He had agreed to serve as Moderator of the following year's examinations but was unable to do it after he suffered a serious health breakdown in May 1813 and had to return to Dent to rest and recover. According to Clark and Hughes, over the next two years he suffered from "listlessness and want of energy" and "felt indisposed for any intellectual exertion that was not absolutely indispensable." The breakdown was to throw a long shadow over the rest of his days; looking back on it five decades later, he wrote in a letter to Dr Hooker in 1864 "I have been liable to attacks of congestion ever since 1813 ... [and had become] unfit for sedentary labour after 1813."

Assistant Tutor (1815)

Despite his "want of energy" after the 1813 breakdown, within two years Adam was offered the post of Assistant Tutor in mathematics at Trinity College.

The post fell vacant after the Senior Tutor left to become Vicar of Kendal, one of many livings within the gift of Trinity College (as patron). The Master and Senior Fellows agreed to increase the number of tutors from two to three, because of the rising number of students who needed to be looked after. One of the existing Tutors was promoted to Senior

73

Tutor and two Assistant Tutors moved up to be Tutors, who then selected Adam to fill one of the vacancies as Assistant Tutor.

Clark and Hughes point out that, although the post would offer Adam "a congenial occupation with less wear and tear than private tuition" and might lead to a Tutorship, he weighed it up carefully before agreeing to accept it. He wrote to Grainger the following month to tell him that he had "accepted the office of mathematical lecturer under our new Tutors, and I was desirous of having some time to prepare for my duties. ... as for myself I am in better health than I have enjoyed for three years before."

Typhoid epidemic
1815 was to be an eventful year for Adam in more ways than one. A particularly severe epidemic of typhoid fever broke out in Cambridge just after Easter. The University initially thought it would escape the worst of it, but after several members died and other started to fall seriously ill, on the 3rd of May the Senate agreed to allow the undergraduate students to leave the city to seek sanctuary elsewhere. Most students and many staff – including Adam, who retreated to the safety of Dent – chose to evacuate, and the University more or less closed down until the epidemic had run its course.

Trip to Europe
Adam's life would also be affected by events in Europe. The French Wars between 1793 and 1815 had made travel around Europe difficult and dangerous, and not just for the wealthy young Englishmen enjoying their Grand Tour of France and Italy in search of art, culture, and the roots of Western civilization. The fighting ended and the First French Empire fell with the defeat of Napoleon at the Battle of Waterloo on the 18th of June 1815. Adam records in *Memorial* how he had the pleasure of bringing the news of Wellington's victory to Dent.

The second Treaty of Paris, which established peace between England and France, was signed in November 1815. After that travel restrictions were removed, opening up the continent to a whole new generation of travellers eager to see new sights, experience new things, and learn more about their foreign neighbours. Sedgwick shared those ambitions, and his interest grew when he started to receive interesting letters sent by friends who described their travels in exotic-sounding places – Bland had gone to Switzerland and Charles Musgrave to France. Musgrave wrote of the richness and beauty of the country, the relatively cheap cost of living, and the determination of the French to repair their reputation as well as infrastructure.

By early spring 1815 Adam had started to plan his first tour of France, and had started to learn French and to read French books by way of preparation. He had hoped to go that year, but his plans were set back by Napoleon's escape from Elba. Instead he spent much of the summer in Bury St Edmunds, reading theology books rather than French literature.

The trip was undertaken during the summer of 1816, when he spent four months travelling in France, Switzerland, part of Germany, and Holland. He travelled mostly by coach, which was slow and uncomfortable, but it opened up new horizons for him which he enjoyed greatly. He had planned to write a book about his travels after he returned, but the only record he left was a journal in which he wrote notes intermittently, which describe the places he went, the people he met, and the inns he stayed in.

He spent two weeks in Paris early in July, then travelled on to Switzerland where he the scenery impressed him greatly. He wrote "we proceeded in a voiture [horse-drawn carriage] to Martigny, through a valley infinitely more beautiful than anything my imagination had ever formed. Of the Alps I had formed a good general notion. … a man can imagine a mountain four times as high as any he has seen; but of that exquisite perfection of scenery which arises from contrast and combination, no one can have any perfect notion who has not been in Switzerland."

He visited Chamonix where, among other things, he was impressed by a walk on the Mer de Glace, a valley glacier where "everything is rude, barren, and desolate. … The lowest parts of these enormous glaciers appear to me by much the most interesting. One cannot form any perfect notion of the depth of the sea of ice, or of its general magnitude, but no one can see without astonishment huge blocks of ice, some of them coming down into the even fields, piled one upon another to the thickness of some hundred feet, and extending for many leagues in the channelled sides of the mountain. In the lower part of the glaciers large masses are continually rolling down the hill with a loud rumbling noise, which adds much to the effect produced by such savage scenery."

This direct encounter with a valley glacier was clearly a memorable experience for Adam, then in his pre-geology days as an Assistant Tutor in Trinity College. But it is curious that, decades later, by which time he was a well-known and very active Professor of Geology, he did not believe that surface deposits in Britain could possibly have been dropped by huge ice sheets, but insisted they must have been dropped by floating icebergs at sea (about which more in Chapter 11).

Adam returned to England via the Rhine, passing through Amsterdam and Antwerp, before stopping in Brussels to see for himself the field of Waterloo, then finally to Calais and across the Channel to Dover.

Career options

Three career paths were open to men in Adam's day who had been elected to a College Fellowship – they could leave "the ivory towers" and seek employment in the world outside; they could take Holy Orders and become a Vicar in a church of which the College was patron; or they could continue as a College Fellow. Each option had its pros and cons.

Men of ambition often moved out of the sheltered world of the University and sought fame and fortune in business and industry. Some left as soon as they had obtained their Fellowship, which offered social status, opened doors of opportunity, and gave certain bragging rights. Some graduates left for the outside world even before trying to secure a Fellowship.

Fellows who chose to remain in College were required to take Priest's Orders and be ordained into the Church of England. But not every Fellow who got ordained was offered a College "living" (the freehold of a church to which the College, as patron, owned the right to appoint clergy) partly because there were a fixed number of livings and vacancies did not arise very often. Many Fellows held on year after year, diligently performing their duties in College, in the hope of one day obtaining a College living "and for the marriage which in many cases depended on it", Clark and Hughes (1890a) point out rather poignantly, "till not only had he become unfit for active work in a parish, but his hopes of domestic happiness had too often ended, sometimes by mutual consent, sometimes in a sadder way, by the death of the intended wife."

Many Fellows gratefully accepted the offer of a living, sometimes in Cambridge close to their *alma mater* but often scattered across the length and breadth of England. The College livings were tenable with a Fellowship, so they provided the Fellow with additional income. They did not require the Fellow to live within the parish, so most continued to live in College. Neither did they require him to lead regular Sunday services; curates were appointed to take care of the routine duties, and the Vicar was only expected to appear and serve occasionally. As Clark and Hughes (1890a) emphasise, for most Fellows, "the fact that they were clergymen imposed upon them no duties, and effected no difference in their manners, habits, or language."

6. College Fellowship

As we will see in Chapter 16, Adam Sedgwick followed the traditional path of getting ordained (in 1817) and then following what today would be called a "portfolio career", holding appointments and receiving payments as a College Fellow, a University Professor, and a Vicar and Cathedral Canon.

Professor of Geology (1818)
Without doubt the best thing that ever happened to Adam, certainly from his point of view, was being promoted to Professor of Geology in 1818. He would hold and value the post for 42 years until he resigned in 1860, at the age of 75.

We will look at that in more detail in the next chapter, but for now simply note the importance of two factors other than naked ambition that encouraged him to put his name forward for that post,. The first was his strong desire to escape the drudgery of giving tutorials in mathematics to students who he often found lacking in interest and application, and the burden of a heavy workload within the College; it would be his means of escape from the treadmill existence he had endured for eight years.

The second factor was his own concern about his health. He was then 33 years old, had suffered numerous spells of serious ill-health, and – as Clark and Hughes put it – "fresh air and regular exercise became indispensable to him; and frequent attacks of ill-health warned him that he must seek for a profession which would keep him out of doors for several months in each year. This conviction, more than any other consideration, determined him to become a candidate for the Professorship of Geology in 1818."

Senior Proctor (1827)
In 1827 Adam, then Professor Sedgwick, was offered the post of Senior Proctor in Trinity College. He was strongly encouraged to accept it by the Master, Dr Christopher Wordsworth, youngest brother of poet William Wordsworth. The Proctor was (and is still today) responsibility for discipline among the students in the College. It was an elected post, tenable for one year.

Adam was widely viewed as the ideal man for the job, which required tact and firmness in equal measure and had the potential to be quite onerous. Clark and Hughes write of how "a certain amount of unruliness, not to say dissipation, had made itself apparent among the undergraduates, which could only be put an end to by severe measures carried out with discretion and strict impartiality. It was felt that Sedg-

77

wick, with his peculiar geniality, and known sympathy with the younger members of the University, had special qualifications for such a task. ... he fully justified the hopes that had been formed of him. He detected several evildoers, *flagrante delicto*, and had them removed from the University, without either losing his personal popularity, or imperilling the dignity of his office."

Vice Master of Trinity College (1845-62)

Adam grew in stature and reputation as he grew older and more experienced in the ways of College life. His leadership qualities were clear to those around him, both within the College and across the University. He probably had ambitions to one day be selected as Master of Trinity, but that was not to be.

He came close in October 1841 when the post fell vacant after the sudden retirement of Christopher Wordsworth. Apparently, he and George Peacock (Dean of Ely) were the front-runners to succeed Wordsworth, but their prospects were damaged by the intervention of Sir Robert Peel – a graduate of Christ Church College, and recently re-elected as Prime Minister – who supported Trinity Fellow and Tutor William Whewell, a fellow Conservative.

Whewell was a polymath, and 9 years younger than Sedgwick. He had been Professor of Mineralogy between 1828 and 1832, and Professor of Philosophy since 1838 (a post he held until 1855). Brilliant as he obviously was, he was in some ways a surprise choice for Master, and he felt the need to reach out with the hand of friendship to his more senior colleague Sedgwick. He wrote to Adam on the 19th of October, "At present I look with alarm at the thought of being placed in a position of rule over persons my seniors in standing, and my superiors, as I sincerely believe, in the qualities requisite for the government of the College; and I especially feel myself out of my being made superior in status to yourself." Adam wrote back graciously, telling the new Master "It is well for a man to think humbly of himself, but I assure you, that of all men living, you are by common consent thought most worthy of the high honour of ruling our great intellectual body ... As for myself, it will delight me to give you all the help I can. ... had I gained your present position I should have been out of my right place."

Sedgwick and Whewell had long enjoyed each other's company, although the friendship was seriously tested by the fallout in October 1845 over the matter of Adam keeping his dog in the College (as we saw in Chapter 4). Adam had close intellectual ties to Whewell, whose views on induction and truth clearly shaped Adam's approach to geology and evolution (as we'll see in Chapters 14 and 15).

William Whewell held the post of Master of Trinity College until his death in 1866, at the age of 72. Adam wrote warmly about him to fellow scientist Sir John Herschel, famous as the inventor of photography amongst other achievements, noting "He was not only my dear and honoured friend of full fifty years' standing, but he was the only *friend* at Cambridge who was associated in memory with the joyful days of my early and hard-working academic life. ... He was a great, generous, large-hearted, and good man, and during the short remnant of my life I shall not see again his like among the members of Trinity College."

Adam never became Master of Trinity College, but in July 1845 he was elected Vice-Master after the resignation of Thomas Thorp. He took the role seriously, and was a valued and popular senior member of the College. Adam was a cordial host, although he sometimes said that he had "company more than enough" in College, and longed for "a quiet domestic fireside with cheerful domestic talk."

He wrote to his niece Isabella at the end of December 1851 pointing out that "Ever since Trinity College was founded it has been the custom to welcome in the New Year by a merry party. I never eat supper, but, as Vice-Master, I must be present, and I expect five or six guests whom I have invited. A few minutes before twelve St Mary's [church] twelve bells strike off a merry peal. Exactly at twelve our butler walks in with a goblet of seasoned hot wine we call Bishop. 'Gentlemen, I wish you all a happy new year, and prosperity to Trinity College.' We then stand up and cheer, three times three, to the toast; after shaking hands we sit down again."

Adam loved entertaining distinguished guests in College. For example, in December 1857 he hosted a dinner in Trinity for the explorer and missionary David Livingstone, who he described as "a plain, single-minded, cheerful man – somewhat attenuated by years of toil, and a face tinged by the sun of Africa."

As Vice-Master he took a keen interest in the welfare of the Fellows in his College. For example, he wrote to Herschel's daughter Isabella in October 1857 that "on returning at the end of last week I found the College in turmoil – the Fellows hammering at a new constitution – all the juniors [Junior Fellows] mad for the repeal of the celibacy clause – all dreaming of loves, olive-branches, nursery-maids, toys, and trundling hoops etc. to decorate our old cloisters. Poor green-horns, they little think what troubles they are trying to bring upon themselves!"

The seniority of his post also allowed Adam to play a prominent role within the University. For example, he led campaigns to open Cambridge to non-Anglicans and to organize the academic programmes, which we will look at in Chapter 8. It also gave him an opportunity to meet and become close to Queen Victoria and her consort Prince Albert, as we shall see in Chapter 9.

Adam served as Vice-Master for 17 years, until September 1862. In his resignation letter to the Master (Whewell) he admitted "I know that I am unfit for the place", and insisted "considering the lingering infirmities of my head, I shall be much better ... without the responsibility of any official duties; and I shall consider it as personally kind to me, if you will declare my office vacant ...". He added "Now that I am working my way through the eighth year of my eighth decade, there is no shadow of hope that during the remnant of life, whatever it may be, I shall be better able to do my duties to the College than I have done them during the past years, while many infirmities of mind and body have been gathering round me."

7. Professor of Geology

"Geology has been a hard task-mistress, but she has paid me nobly in giving me health, which I had utterly lost before I put myself under her robust training."
Adam Sedgwick in a letter to Mrs Norton (August 1867)

Adam Sedgwick's career started to take off when he was appointed Professor of Geology at Cambridge in 1818, a post he would occupy for 42 years until he retired a few years before his death. He found the work interesting, and enjoyed the freedom it gave him to work outdoors. His sphere of influence expanded as he emerged from being a Fellow in a College to become more visible and audible as a man of science, with a wide circle of admirers and an international reputation.

In this chapter, we'll look at the nature of the job and what it involved, and consider why Adam thought himself suitable for it. We'll also look at how he set about becoming a professional geologist and one of Britain's leading scientists of his day.

In Part Three we'll explore the contributions he made to the emerging science of geology, and the controversies he sparked off through his work.

John Woodward (1665-1728)
Adam's geological career owes much to one of his academic forebears at Cambridge, a "gentleman of a good family" called John Woodward, who was born in Derbyshire in May 1665.

After leaving school at the age of sixteen, Woodward was apprenticed to a linen draper in London. He soon left that employment, then spent four years living with and being privately tutored in medicine by Dr Peter Barwick, physician to Charles II. Under the patronage of Sir Ralph Dutton of Sherborne, he began studying the earth's surface, from which grew an abiding interest in geology. In 1692, at the age of 27, he was appointed Professor of Physic [medicinal drugs] at Gresham College in London, which had been established in 1596 to give free educational lectures to the general public. He was elected a Fellow of the Royal Society the following year but was expelled in 1710, for "conduct unbecoming a gentleman" after publicly insulting Sir Hans Sloan, a prominent Fellow, at a meeting chaired by Sir Isaac Newton. The Archbishop of Canterbury created him a Doctor of Medicine in 1695, which was awarded by Cambridge University, and he was made a Fellow of the College of Physicians in 1702. He practiced as a physician but, by all accounts, was not a particularly good one.

After his interest had been captured by the rocks, and as Clark and Hughes put it, "in order to inform himself of the present condition of the earth, he travelled through the greatest part of England, enquiring [in his own words] 'for intelligence of all Places where the Entrails of the Earth were laid open, either by Nature' or by human activity." Everywhere he went he jotted down notes of what he saw in mines, down wells, in quarries, cliffs, natural outcrops and elsewhere. He recorded his observations and interpretations of them in a book with the rather wordy title *An Essay toward a Natural History of the Earth and Terrestrial Bodies, especially Minerals; as also of the Sea, Rivers, and Springs, with an Account of the Universal Deluge, and of the Effects that it had upon the Earth.* The book was first published in 1695, when he was 30 years old. It attracted much attention and gained him a good reputation. Woodward had hoped the book would be the first step towards a much larger volume, but that never happened.

Woodward's thinking (that we'll look at further in Chapter 10) was progressive in its day, but as science in general and geology in particular continued to develop in the decades after his book appeared, it was progressively overtaken by newer ideas, more substantial evidence, and better informed ways of explaining what was being observed or uncovered across the natural world. Within a hundred years, Clark and Hughes – the editors of Sedgwick's *Life and Letters* (1890) – refer to Woodward's "geological speculations ... [which] are in many parts absurd", and dismiss them as "geological romance".

But, to give due credit to Woodward, we can see in his writings very early examples of emerging scientific ideas within the study of rock layers and layering (stratigraphy) and the study of fossils (palaeontology). He was also ahead of his time in building, cataloguing and describing a large collection of specimens of rocks and fossils, and recording where he found them. This formed the nucleus of the Geological Museum at Cambridge that Adam Sedgwick inherited and developed further during his time as Professor of Geology.

7. Professor of Geology

Woodwardian Professorship

John Woodward never married. He died in his apartments at Gresham College in April 1728, at the age of sixty-three, and was buried in Westminster Abbey close to Isaac Newton.

Woodward's will, written eleven years before his death, instructed his executors to sell his "personal estate and effects", including a fine library of books and an extensive collection of antiquarian objects, and use the proceeds to buy land which would yield an annual rental income of a hundred and fifty pounds. That money was to be given to the University of Cambridge, who were to use two-thirds of it (£100) to employ a Lecturer in geology.

Terms and conditions

Woodward left very specific instructions about the terms and conditions of the appointment.

Woodward's executors would form the selection panel for the Lecturer post, but after they died the panel would comprise the Archbishop of Canterbury, the Diocesan Bishop, the Presidents of the Royal Society and the College of Physicians, the two members of Parliament who represented the University, and the entire membership of the Senate.

The selection criteria were just as specific. Woodward instructed that the Lecturer must be a bachelor and, if he subsequently married, "his election shall be thereby immediately made void, lest the care of a wife and children should take the Lecturer too much from study, and the care of the Lecture." Wherever possible, the Lecturer should be a layman not an ordained man, "not out of any disrespect to the clergy, for whom I have ever had a particular regard, but because there is in this kingdom better provision, and a much greater number of preferments, for the clergy than for men of learning among the laity."

Strict conditions were also attached to the post, particularly in terms of the commitment and availability of the Lecturer. Woodward instructed that he should not hold "any preferment, office, or post, whatever, that shall any ways so employ and take up his time as to interfere with his duty herein set forth, and in particular that shall require his attendance out of the University; if he accept such, his post is to become vacant." The Lecturer should not be absent from Cambridge for more than "two months in the year, and those to be in the long vacation in the summer."

The Lecturer, initially called the Woodwardian Lecturer and known today as the Woodwardian Chair of Geology, was required to undertake

83

two specific tasks in order to raise the profile of geology at Cambridge – give lectures, and maintain and build the rock collection.

Lectures
The teaching duties were not particularly onerous; the Lecturer was to "read at least four Lectures every year, at such times, and in such place of the said University, as the majority of the said electors shall appoint". The scope and content of the lectures were strictly proscribed – the Lecturer could select any "of the subjects treated of in my [Woodward's] *Natural History of the Earth*, my *Defence* of it against Dr Catnerarius, my *Discourse of Vegetation*, or my *State of Physick*".

The Lecturer had no say in whether the lectures should be given in English or Latin, that was to be decided by "the Chancellor [of the University], Vice-Chancellor, Provosts, and Masters of the several Colleges and Halls belonging to the … University." At least one of the lectures was to be printed and published each year, with the Lecturer free to choose which one or ones.

Rock collection
Woodward was proud of the collection of English rocks and fossils he stored in two wooden cabinets, and he left clear instructions about what the Lecturer should do with them. Copies of the catalogues of the collection were to be "reposited in the public Library of the … University, for greater security that the said Fossils be preserved with great care and faithfulness."

The fossils were to be "lodged and reposited in such proper room or apartment as shall be allotted by the … University." The Lecturer was to "have the care and custody of all the said Fossils and the catalogues of them"; he is to "live and reside in or near the said apartment so to be allotted for repositing the said Fossils", and to be "ready and attending in the room where they are reposited, from the hour of nine of the clock in the morning to eleven, and again from the hour of two in the afternoon till four, three days in every week (except during the two months in the long vacation, wherein he is allowed to be absent) to show the said Fossils, gratis, to all such curious and intelligent persons as shall desire a view of them for their information and instruction." Woodward was very protective of the fossils and insisted that the Lecturer should "be always present when they are shown, and take care that none be mutilated or lost."

As Clark and Hughes point out, "It is evident that Woodward's primary object in this foundation was the permanent commemoration of

7. Professor of Geology

himself and his researches without limitation of subject. Geology was not, in his eyes, more important than Medicine or Botany, provided his collections – the monument of his industry and sagacity [wisdom] - could be preserved, extended, and displayed to the public. ... [and provided the Lecturer] took the Woodwardian utterances on those subjects as his textbook ...".

Today we might call it a vanity project, but it provided the catalyst for lasting developments in geology, more significant and in ways that John Woodward could never have imagined.

Appointments
Despite Woodward's preference that the post of Lecturer be held by a layman, the first incumbent was an English clergyman called Conyers Middleton, from Richmond in North Yorkshire. He was appointed in 1731, at the age of 48, having arrived there by a rather round-about route. He graduated from Trinity College in 1703, was elected a Fellow in 1705, was ordained priest in 1708, worked as a librarian in the University Library, travelled widely, and collected antiquities. After his first wife Sarah died in 1731, he was appointed first Woodwardian Lecturer, and delivered an inaugural address in Latin, describing how a study of fossils would be useful in confirming the history of Noah's Flood. He resigned the chair in 1734, on his second marriage, to his cousin Mary. He subsequently married a third time, before dying in 1750 at the age of 67.

Middleton was succeeded by four more Lecturers before John Hailstone was appointed Woodwardian Professor in 1788, having been elected Fellow of Trinity College four years earlier. He studies geology for a year under Werner in Freiburg (who we will return to in Chapter 10) and never delivered any lectures, but he collected geological specimens and built up the museum. He held the post for thirty years, until in 1818 he married at the age of 58 and accepted the post of Vicar of Trumpington near Cambridge. He remained interested and active in geology and chemistry, was elected to the Linnaean Society in 1800 and to the Royal Society a year later, and was a founder member of the Geological Society of London. He died in 1847, aged 88.

Sedgwick's appointment
When news broke in Trinity College in the Lent term of 1818 that Hailstone was proposing to resign as Woodwardian Professor of Geology and "take himself a wife", Adam Sedgwick was one of a small number of Fellows who started thinking seriously about allowing their name to go

85

forward for election when the post fell vacant, ninety years after it had been endowed.

Adam spelt out his reasons for wanting the post in a letter to his old friend Ainger in March 1818. It would offer him some important benefits, including a much lighter teaching load and not in mathematics; he admitted that he was "most heartily sick" of the tutorial work that he had to do. It would offer him interesting opportunities and mental stimulation; he told Ainger "I am at this moment doing nothing. ... [even worse] I am gradually losing that little information I once had." It would allow him to work outdoors, offering him exercise, fresh air, opportunities to visit new places and meet new people, all beneficial to his mental health. It would allow him to dedicate himself to an academic career, even though he had been ordained just a year earlier. And it would create opportunities for him to rise in status and mix with the great and the good, within and beyond the College and University. He was well aware that there would be costs involved, too, particularly the requirement not to marry, and the relatively low pay provided for in the endowment – a stipend of £100 a year plus an annual allowance of £10 to cover the cost of fieldwork, experiments, purchase of specimens, and correspondence.

Ainger had known Adam for many years and they had remained close. Although he had some reservations about him accepting the post, he assured Adam "I really think the pursuit of mineralogy [most people then viewed geology as just collecting and arranging rock specimens] will suit you to a hair, as I take it for granted that it will sometimes lead you to pick up stones [work outside], as well as to arrange them in your lecture-room."

Competition

When the vacancy was formally announced only one man other than Adam Sedgwick showed any real commitment to trying to secure the post. Robert Wilson Evans was a Fellow and Assistant Tutor in Trinity College; he was well liked and held in high esteem in the College and across the University. A third candidate soon appeared in the shape of George Cornelius Gorham, who had graduated in 1809 with a better degree than Adam. Gorham was reported to have "been studying geology for a long time", although no firm evidence was offered to support the claim, which Adam responded to by acknowledging that although he himself then "knew absolutely nothing of geology", Gorham "knew a great deal – but it was all wrong!"

7. Professor of Geology

Having two Fellows from the same College competing for the same post was generally regarded as unfortunate, if not downright ungentlemanly, and Evans withdrew at an early stage.

In the election for the post, many more Fellows voted for Sedgwick than for Gorham, but he also attracted the votes of the great and the good within the University. Adam won convincingly and in 1818 was appointed the seventh Woodwardian Professor of Geology at Cambridge.

Ambitions

Looking back at the end his long career as Professor of Geology, three months before he died in 1873, Adam described the hopes he had and the objectives he had set himself when he took up the post 55 years earlier.

He wrote "There were three prominent hopes which possessed my heart in the earliest years of my Professorship. First, that I might be enabled to bring together a Collection worthy of the University, and illustrative of all the departments of the Science it was my duty to study and to teach. Secondly, that a Geological Museum might be built by the University, amply capable of containing its future Collections; and lastly, that I might bring together a Class of Students who would listen to my teaching, support me by their sympathy, and help me by the labour of their hands."

Building the rock collection and giving some lectures on geology were the primary tasks Woodward had specified, so Adam was simply reflecting back what he had been signed up to do. Interestingly, his three-fold manifesto says nothing about the parts of the job he would end up investing most time on and being best known for – field mapping, writing geological papers, and engaging in high profile geological controversies – which we will explore further in Part Three.

Starting geology

When he was elected Professor of Geology, Adam Sedgwick knew next to nothing about the subject and readily owned up to the fact. He was at best an enthusiastic amateur geologist, but he loved the great outdoors, walked through the countryside a great deal, and was a keen collector of fossils and bits of rock. As his colleague McKenny Hughes (1883) put it, he "had long been an intelligent observer of geological phenomena. As he wandered with his gun, or fishing rod, among the crags and up the streams of his native Yorkshire, he noticed the lie of the rocks and the occurrence of fossils."

Adam won the post on his personality, particularly his integrity and vigour, and on his general merits, rather than on any proven knowledge or expertise in the subject. But that was no handicap for professorial appointments at Oxford and Cambridge in those days; for example, Adam's colleague in Trinity College John Henslow was appointed Professor of Botany despite the fact that he had trained as a metallurgist not a botanist.

To be appointed Professor in today's leading research-intensive universities requires substantial evidence of appropriate specialist knowledge, experience, and expertise, but when Adam was appointed he lacked all three. As a student he had studied mathematics and classics, although he had attended a course of lectures on mineralogy and some lectures on chemistry, and read a few books on what was then known about geology. But up to that point his two main interests were mathematics and general literature, although he had read theology in preparation for his ordination the previous year. His scientific literacy was strictly limited, but he aimed "to promote [his] intellectual improvement" by learning on the job, rather like a self-directed apprenticeship.

Getting down to work
During the contest for the post, Adam is said to have admitted "Hitherto I have never turned a stone; henceforth I will leave no stone unturned."

He wasted no time in getting down to work as Professor of Geology, and took his responsibilities more seriously than many of his predecessors had done. He worked hard to get up to speed, and was eager to sit at the feet of some of the leading scientists of the day and learn from them about the state of geological understanding and the nature of geological controversies at that time. For example, he attended some lectures by Georges Cuvier (who we'll meet in Chapter 10), the "father of palaeontology" (the study of fossils), and was tutored in geological observation, description and mapping by John Henslow, the Cambridge mathematician and botanist who would many years later sponsor Charles Darwin for the post of naturalist on the *Beagle*.

Although it wasn't formally listed as part of his job description or a condition of the Woodwardian funding, geological mapping and observation in the field would be Adam's main preoccupation through his years as Professor of Geology. He was determined to see things for himself, and draw his own conclusions based on what he saw and what he knew, rather than just accepting other people's observations and interpretations.

As Clark and Hughes put it, "he was the last man in the world to take facts at second-hand, and therefore, so soon as the Easter Term

[1818] was over, he set out to use his eyes in the field. ... his object was to learn, not to instruct others." In a letter he wrote to Ainger in late October 1818, Adam describes a five-week trip to Derbyshire which began in early August, when he visited Matlock, "following the strata of the different rocks, collecting specimens, and driving into mines". He also visited the salt mines at Northwich in Cheshire, before heading off to visit his family in Dent.

For many decades after he started as Professor Adam looked forward to his annual field season, during which he set aside several months each summer "for the investigation of some definite group of rocks." Between 1819 and 1827, for example, he spent time on fieldwork in the west of England, Yorkshire, Durham, and the Lake District. For him it was detective work – intentional, pre-planned and highly structured – a far cry from wandering about the countryside looking at anything of interest that caught his eye. He would later write up what he had observed in the field in a series of academic papers, as we shall see in Chapter 11.

In Adam's early days as Professor his focus was very clearly on geological mapping. The question of Theories of the Earth, at that time a common preoccupation of other leading geologists across Europe (as we shall see in Chapter 10), does not surface in *Life and Letters* for more than a decade. As Clark and Hughes put it, rather obliquely, when he set forth on his geological career "there is no evidence that he had ever troubled his head with any cosmical speculations."

At this time, during Adam's intellectual honeymoon period, there is no hint of the raging controversies between religion and geology that would engage him from the 1840s onwards, to which we will return in Chapter 14.

Teaching geology
When he was appointed Professor, Adam promised to deliver public lectures "on some subjects connected with the Theory of the Earth", a key requirement of the post. He started doing so at Easter the following year (1819), after completing his first geological excursion, and continued to give the lecture series until 1870 when his declining health made it necessary to appoint a deputy to deliver them on his behalf. Apparently, he was fond of telling his students how many times he had given the lectures before he started each new course; the last course was his 52nd, almost without a break. He was then 85 years old.

He described a typical lecture course in a letter to his niece Fanny Hicks in November 1856: "I began my lectures the last week in October, and I hope to lecture four days a week till Friday the 12th of December. I have generally an hour's preparation for each lecture in mounting sections and wonderful pictures, etc., an hour for the lecture, and nearly a third hour in talk and explanation to the lads [students, all male]. The work fatigues me, but I like it ..."

Popularity

He was, by all accounts, a highly engaging lecturer and his lectures were extremely popular. As he told his students, "I cannot promise to teach you all geology, I can only fire your imaginations."

Eric Ashby and Mary Anderson (1969) stress that "in Cambridge Sedgwick was esteemed not because he had made discoveries but rather because he had made geology popular. His lectures, at the time of his appointment, formed no part of the degree course. Attendance at them was purely voluntary. Yet from the outset Sedgwick drew crowded classes [including colleagues and townspeople, as well as undergraduates] to hear him ...". They were attracted partly by the subject matter, at a time when geology was fashionable, but Adam's "very personal style and quality as a teacher" drew them in too.

Adam had great physical presence, being relatively tall, "not handsome ... but [with] powerful features ... together with a swarthy complexion and penetrating eyes." He spoke clearly and confidently, with a broad Yorkshire accent, and talked around his copious and well-prepared notes rather than simply reading them out. He brought his lectures to life by the effective use of "humour, anecdote, and reminiscence, and occasionally illuminated by passages of great eloquence, struck off in the heat of the moment." He inspired his listeners by sharing "something of his own consuming passion for his subject", which helped to make his lectures accessible and stimulating. His aim was to inspire new ways of thinking in his students. His approach was deliberately broad-brush, and he took great care to avoid burdening them with trivial details, looking on lectures as an introduction to the details to be found in textbooks.

Whilst most professors in his day would never have considered admitting ladies from town into their lectures, Adam broke with that tradition because, as Clark and Hughes point out, he believed that women "could make great contributions to natural history." We've already seen (in Chapter 4) that Adam had some curious attitudes about women, and these are echoed in a letter he sent to Miss Kate Malcolm in February 1848 in which he touches on the subject of women in lectures. He wrote "They believe, in their hearts, that geologists have dealings with the spirits of the lower world; yet [in] spite of this they came, and resolved to learn from me a little of my 'black art.' And … it is now no easy matter to find room for ladies, so monstrously do they puff themselves, out of all nature, in the mounting of their lower garments, so that they put my poor lecture-room quite in a bustle. Lest they should dazzle my young men, I placed them, with their backs to the light, on one side of my room." Regardless of where he made them sit, he firmly believed that they were a distraction to the "lads" in the class!

Lectures

We can get a feel for what Adam's lectures covered, as well as how he structured his material, because he published the syllabus for his students in the form of a book. *Syllabus of a Course of Lectures on Geology*.

The first *Syllabus* was published in 1821, and successive editions demonstrate how his knowledge, insight and understanding grew over the years. They also show his willingness to adapt his views and explanations to accommodate new findings in geology, by himself and other geologists he trusted. Adam believed in following the evidence wherever it leads to and, as Clark and Hughes tell us, "He professed to the audience his belief in the importance of open-mindedness, that they should be ready to accept new ideas and opinions without any prejudice." As an aside, this emphasis on open-mindedness is curiously paradoxical given how entrenched he later proved to be over the emerging ideas about the evolution of species, a theme to which we will return in Chapter 14.

There are some interesting differences between the first (1821) and second (1832) editions of his *Syllabus*. Both open with an introductory chapter that sketches out the history and development of Geology, clarifies the difference between Natural Philosophy and Natural History, summarizes earlier speculations and Theories of the Earth, and highlights the connections between Geology and Natural History.

In 1821 Adam emphasized the connections between Geology and Mineralogy, whereas in 1832 he stressed their separation. In 1821 he contrasted in some detail the different Theories of the Earth proposed by Abraham Werner and James Hutton, schools of thought now described respectively as Catastrophism and Uniformitarianism (of which more in Chapter 10). In 1832 he treats them very briefly as "Ancient Theories" and devotes much more space and attention to the "True mode of conducting geological speculations" [based on induction, that we'll look at in detail in Chapter 15], which rapidly became his own way of working.

Comparison of the two editions of *Syllabus* also shows how, over that nine-year period, Adam moved away from the theories of Werner (that we'll look at in Chapter 10), of which he was a strong supporter when he started work as Professor in 1818. In the 1821 edition, for example, one chapter is devoted to 'Transition Rocks', whereas in the 1832 edition the term 'Transition' is relegated to the end of a chapter, where he briefly sketches out "Origin of the term Transition – with what limitations it is applicable to the upper series – no clear line of separation between the two." In 1821 he describes the rocks from the Transition rocks upwards through the stratified rocks above, in ascending order; in 1832 he reversed the order, and describes them working down from the better known to the less well known. Clark and Hughes interpret this change as "showing that he now more fully realised the truth that the history of the earth must be deduced from a study of the operations of nature which we see going on around us at the present time."

Adam always paid close attention to the study of fossils, and we see this in Part II of his *Syllabus* that concludes with his thoughts on the "Importance of organic remains – in the identification of contemporaneous deposits – in determining the successive conditions of the earth". Clark and Hughes also point out that "He always carefully collected fossils, and referred them to the best authorities he could find on each special group for determination; but, while he appealed to palaeontological evidence whenever he could, he always maintained that the first thing was to get the rocks into the right order in the field."

Successive editions of Adam's *Syllabus* throw light on the importance he attached to particular themes within geology, and on some important ways in which his thinking evolved through time. But to get a sense of how he made those themes come alive in his teaching, we need to look inside one of his lectures and see how he linked material together into an engaging narrative that captured the interest and imagination of his audience. We can do that thanks to the inclusion in *Life and Letters* of Adam's own outline of a lecture he gave in Cambridge in December 1859. The lecture was structured in two parts, the first dealing with the history of the museum during his time as professor, and the second with a history of geological work and theories.

Part one is very autobiographical – it explains why Adam had applied for the Professorship, particularly when "I knew very little indeed of geology - just enough to know that it was a glorious and healthy field in which I might find ample enjoyment and better health". It describes how he built up the rock collection year by year and within about three years, by 1822, it had grown faster than the space in which it could be stored and displayed. He noted that it would take a further 24 years until the Geology Museum was finally built.

Adam also talked about the personal sacrifice involved in his work, noting that "Geology [was] a hard task-mistress, but paid me in health and happiness", and adding that "my Museum is in the place of wife and children; and my family are mute as the inhabitants of the water, and never scold me, nor ever express a want – and how few men of the Benedictine Order can say as much."

The second part of the lecture is an outline of the geological history of the earth, as then understood or being debated. It mentions Charles Lyell's Uniformitarian ideas, dismissing them as "not true, and based on a false analogy", and is critical of Hugh Miller's interpretation of the days of creation, noting "much truth here, but not exact truth, and I am bound to tell you truth so far as I know it". We'll look at the details of what these geologists were proposing in Chapter 10.

The lecture is also highly critical of the ideas then emerging about the evolution of species by natural selection, or as Adam referred to it, the "theory of development and transmutation", which Charles Darwin had championed in his book *On the Origin of Species*, published two years earlier (about which more in Chapter 14).

Adam continued to argue strongly against Darwin's ideas in subsequent lecture series. For example, in 1867 he "pointed out the proofs of wisdom and design through all nature, and its subordination to Law – enlarged on the folly of the Darwinian theory, and its inevitable tendency to rank materialism – and ... showed the manner in which natural science might be wedded to moral conclusions", as he wrote to his niece Isabella that December.

The following year, as Clark and Hughes inform us, Adam reviewed the evidence then available about whether humans were "a relatively recent appearance on the earth" (as he believed) or "of a far higher antiquity" (as Lyell believed), and concluded that "man is of a far higher antiquity than that which I have hitherto assigned to him", Adam told his students that "I shall always protest against that degrading hypothesis which attributes to man an origin derived from the lower animals", as Darwin had proposed.

Final lecture
We noted above that, after starting them in 1819, Adam continued to deliver his lectures on geology through most of the rest of his life. It was a

long farewell, because he mentions having given his last lectures in several letters spread across many years. He wrote as much to his niece Isabella in November 1861 – "I finished my lectures yesterday; and gave the last I shall ever give as Woodwardian Professor." Nearly ten years later, in October 1870, he wrote to Lady Augusta Stanley that if his health allowed he was about to start his 52nd "and undoubtedly my last" course of lectures, "a thought that should fill my heart with thankfulness; and there is sorrow too in the thought that it must be my last course." His lecturing days eventually drew to a close in 1871 when Professor John Morris was appointed to give the lecture series in his place.

Curating geology

Care of the geological collection in the Woodwardian Museum was one of Adam's main responsibilities as Professor. But for him that was part of the appeal of the post, and from the first days he was committed to collecting rock and fossil specimens by undertaking systematic tours in the British Isles and Europe, both on his own and with experienced geologists. Through this he became a very experienced field geologist, and it provided the material for his numerous geological papers that we will look at further in Chapters 11 to 13.

The collection grew rapidly in Adam's time. He collected many of the specimens himself in the field; others he bought either with his own money, university money, or funds solicited specifically for that purpose. With the help of others, he wrote and published catalogues of the collection, in order to share the information more widely among members of the growing geological community. One of the best known was a systematic description of the Palaeozoic fossils that was published in 1855.

Housing the collection

By 1830, within twelve years of his appointment, the collection was outgrowing the space made available for it. Most was housed in a group of wooden cabinets in Adam's cramped rooms, where there were also "ten or twelve packing-cases from Germany and other parts of the continent, as yet unopened". More storage space for the growing collection was created in 1833, when two rooms were made available within the Divinity School. While Adam was grateful for small mercies, he did complain that "this addition is by no means adequate for the reception of the present collection, much less for its proper exhibition, or for such augmentations as the present state of geological science requires."

7. Professor of Geology

Hopes were raised in 1835 when the university agreed to "solicit subscriptions" (invite donations) towards the cost of building "a new Library, with Museums and Lecture-Rooms beneath it", which held out the prospect of providing appropriate space for the geological collections. That same year there was great excitement when Adam managed to obtain for the collection "an almost complete skeleton of the extinct Elk (*Cervus thegaceros*) commonly called the Irish Elk", partly funded from the Woodwardian legacy.

A new wing had been built on the Library in 1839 and it included space for the Woodwardian Museum. The following February Adam met with the architect to finalise the fitting out of the Museum, and shortly afterwards an important collection of fossils was delivered from Germany. At last the collection had its own space, and Adam wasted no time in colonizing it. In 1841, after his annual cathedral "Residence" in Norwich on church business (of which more in Chapter 17) he rushed back to Cambridge "to superintend the removal of his Museum to its new quarters, and the unpacking of some forty cases."

Managing the collection

As the collection grew, and after it was first opened to the public in 1840, it was clear that Adam would require assistance in running it, to help identify, describe and display items, and to watch over it and guide people around it when it was open.

Over the years, a number of Museum Assistants were appointed which gave them almost unique experiences and skills working in the world's first dedicated Museum of Geology. It opened the door for many of them to subsequently develop distinguished careers and reputations of their own. The Sedgwick connection would also have made them highly employable.

The first Museum Assistant was David Thomas Ansted, who provided much needed help in the early days, when cases had to be unpacked, specimens sorted, and displays set up. Adam later described how their joint efforts brought the collection "into approximate order". Between 1840 and 1853 Ansted was Professor of Geology at King's College, London, and in 1844 he was made a Fellow of the Royal Society.

Next came John William Salter, who assisted Adam between 1842 and 1845 and accompanied him on geological excursions in Wales in 1842 and 1843. In 1846 Salter was appointed as palaeontologist in the Geological Survey of England and Wales, where he specialised in the Palaeozoic fossils of Wales and the border counties.

95

Salter was followed by Frederick (later Sir Frederick) McCoy who was Museum Assistant between 1846 and 1849. In 1850 he was appointed Professor of Geology at Queen's College (now University) Belfast, and four years later emigrated to Australia to take up the newly created post of Professor of Natural Science at the University of Melbourne, where he remained for the next 30 years. While based in Belfast, he returned to Cambridge during the spring and summer months each year to continue the work he had begun in describing the Palaeozoic fossils in the Museum, a *Descriptive Catalogue of the British Palaeozoic Fossils*. The University published the *Catalogue* in book form in 1855 as *A Synopsis of the Classification of the British Palaeozoic Rocks*, for which Adam wrote a detailed introduction.

The next known Assistant was Lucas Barrett, who Adam later described as "my friend, assistant, and fellow-workman in the museum". Barrett worked closely with Sedgwick from 1855 to 1859, when he left for Jamaica to take up the post of Director of the Geological Survey of the British West Indies.

Barrett was succeeded by Harry Govier Seeley, who after some years as Museum Assistant turned down offers of jobs at the British Museum and the Geological Survey of Britain to work on his own. In 1876 he was appointed Professor of Geology at King's College Cambridge, and from 1896 to 1905 was Professor of Geology and Mineralogy at Kings' College, London. He was elected Fellow of the Royal Society in 1879.

Under the terms of Woodward's legacy Sedgwick had overall responsibility for the development and management of the Museum and its collections, but the University also appointed several Inspectors who were required to visit the Museum annually to audit its financial accounts, inspect its records of purchases, view the collections on display, and offer advice on how best to develop and curate the collections. The annual inspections were rigorous and the inspectors had great authority, although Adam was doubtless exaggerating when he told his niece Fanny by letter in May 1842 "To-morrow is the annual audit of my accounts; and if I am reported a good boy, they may perhaps pay me my salary."

The inspections were social as well as managerial occasions; Adam told Fanny how "Dr Woodward ... was a sensible, good-living, man; and he ordered the Vice-Chancellor at the annual Woodwardian audit to give a good dinner, and to see that all his guests gladdened their hearts with the best French wines, such as burgundy, and claret, and champagne.

Sure enough, all this is in his Will, by which he bequeathed to us our Collection!"

Writing geology
Adam was a prolific writer of letters to family, friends and acquaintances, and many of the letters he sent and received are included in *Life and Letters*. These throw light on many things he did and what he thought and felt about them, which gives us fascinating glimpses of some important aspects of his life and work. Many of the letters throw light on his geology – the places he visited and the fieldwork he did, the observations he made, the ways in which he interpreted his findings, and his thoughts about and reactions to the work of other geologists. We'll make good use of this valuable source in Part Three.

Academic papers
After he was appointed Professor of Geology in 1818, Adam also wrote many academic papers. Between 1820 and 1854 he published more than 70 papers on geology; the most important ones are listed in Appendix 2.

That output sounds impressive, and it is. He could have written more but he struggled with writing up his work for three main reasons – he found academic writing a great chore; he was often reluctant to commit his ideas to print before doing more research; and he lacked focus, his mind and time often being distracted by many other things.

In his early days he also lacked confidence, as we see in a letter he wrote to Professor Monk in Trinity College in July 1820. After his first spell of fieldwork he told Monk "I have several times thought of getting up a geological article for the *Quarterly* [*Journal of the Geological Society of London*]. ... My health is never to be depended on; I have no facility of composition; what is more I am much engaged; still I think that I might be able to bring together some remarks not entirely undeserving of insertion in that *Journal*." Others would dispute Adam's lack of "facility of composition". Colin Speakman (1982) describes him as having "a vivid literary style and an ability to use metaphor with stunning force and clarity, qualities that made his lectures famous."

There's little doubt that Adam was a procrastinator. Clark and Hughes tell us that Adam "could never shut his eyes and ears to what was going on around him ... [and as a result] geological memoranda which ought to have been arranged when the subject was fresh in his mind were laid aside; specimens remained for months – sometimes for years – undetermined [not identified and named], or even not unpacked; promised papers were not finished – perhaps not begun." *The Times* described Adam in July 1890, in a review of *Life and Letters*, as "more active in the field than in the study." We'll see in Part Three how this would often cause friction with geological collaborators, particularly Roderick Murchison, over the writing up of joint fieldwork.

As Adam's geological career progressed, particularly between 1838 and 1851, he spent more time in his papers "engaged chiefly in filling in details, in defending the positions he had formerly taken up, and in correcting errors into which he had fallen, either from generalising on insufficient data, or from having too hastily accepted the incorrect sections of others", as Clark and Hughes point out.

Books
Although Adam described his geological work in his academic papers, he never got around to writing a geology book that would bring together his various studies, set them into context alongside the work of others, and provide an over-arching framework or narrative about his views on the state of geological thinking in his day. Colin Speakman (1982) regretted Adam's "chronic inability to produce a sustained geological text, an equivalent to Lyell's *Principles of Geology* or Murchison's *Silurian System*; a brilliant and self-publicising major work that would have become a standard student text-book."

Early in his Professorial career Adam showed signs of having the ambition to write such a book with fellow geologist William Conybeare, an Oxford graduate who was ordained and ended up as Dean of Llandaff (1845) in Wales. Conybeare was a keen amateur geologist and an early member of the Geological Society of London, who guided William Buckland (of which more in Chapter 10) and Adam Sedgwick in their early days as geologists. Conybeare and William Phillips had published *Outlines of the Geology of England and Wales* in 1822, and six years later Adam and Conybeare exchanged letters about jointly writing "a continuation" of that book. Although "for some years Sedgwick was always intending to begin it, and we believe that the needful preparation determined the direction of several of his geological tours," Clark and Hughes regret that "it was never really begun." In a letter he sent to Ainger in March 1832, Adam mentions his hope that, within months, "I shall begin to write a book with which I have been pregnant for seven or eight years."

Though the book with Conybeare was not to be, Adam still held out hope that one day he would be able to get down to writing a book on geology. We read of his undiminished ambition in a letter he sent to Murchison in January 1843, in which he talks of his hope of publishing "as a large pamphlet or little book, my synopsis of the classification of the old rocks of England and Wales etc., with a few sections and plates of fossils", which would be "an introduction to my larger work, should I ever have health and courage to go through it, which I trust I shall." He dreamed of retiring to Germany for a year, where he would "hire lodgings at some of the watering-places" to get the writing done. That trip, like the book ambition, never materialized.

Colin Speakman (1982) believes that Adam's "failure to produce a glittering opus on a sufficiently grand scale has resulted in his achievements [in geology] being eclipsed by gifted rivals."

Although it did not compensate for the lack of a major geological text, Adam did invest time writing a number of other books that greatly help us to understand his priorities and wider concerns. We've already encountered his *Syllabus of a Course on Geology* earlier in this chapter. In Chapter 8 we'll consider his *Discourse on the Studies of the University*, and in Chapter 18 we'll look at *Memorial by the Trustees of Cowgill Chapel*.

Promoting geology
During his time as Professor Adam worked hard to help establish geology as a serious field of study within the natural sciences in Universities, and to promote it more widely to the general public. To further both aims he played active roles in the leading scientific bodies of the day.

Cambridge Philosophical Society
During a brief trip to the Isle of Wight in 1819 in the company of Henslow, who was teaching Adam the rudiments of field geology, the pair discussed the idea of creating a society where scientists and others interested in natural science could meet, share ideas, and learn about developments elsewhere. By then Cambridge University had developed a strong reputation within Natural Science (then referred to as Natural Philosophy), and Sedgwick and Henslow persuaded some like-minded colleagues to join them in establishing the Cambridge Philosophical Society. The Society held its first meeting in the Museum of the Botanical Gardens in December 1819, where its purpose was agreed: "That this Society be instituted for the purpose of promoting Scientific Enquiries, and of facilitating the communication of facts connected with the advancement of [Natural] Philosophy." Adam was appointed one of its two

Secretaries at that first meeting, and he read his very first geological paper, on the geological structure of the ancient rocks of Devon and Cornwall, to the Society in March 1820.

Senior members of the University had a range of reactions to the setting up of this new Society. Adam told his fellow scientist William Herschel by letter in late February 1820, "some laugh at us; others shrug up their shoulders and think our whole proceedings subversive of good discipline; a much larger number look on us, as they do on every other external object, with philosophic indifference; and a small number are among our warm friends."

Geological Society of London
The Geological Society of London was founded in October 1807 at a tavern in Great Queen Street in the Covent Garden district. It moved to Burlington House in Piccadilly in 1874, and today is the oldest national geological society in the world.

Adam was naturally keen to join the Society that was composed, as he described it, "of robust, joyous, and independent spirits, who toiled well in the field, and who did battle and cuffed opinions with much spirit and great good will. For they had one great object before them, the promotion of true knowledge; and not one of them was deeply committed to any system of opinions." By "any system of opinions" he meant the members were committed to seeking "true knowledge" by collecting and interpreting facts, not by debating ideas, particularly Theories of the Earth. As we'll see in Chapter 15, Adam was deeply committed to that approach (the so-called inductive method), so he was naturally drawn to the Society.

He was admitted to the Society as a Fellow in 1818, shortly after being elected Professor of Geology. Although in the early years he was not able to attend meetings regularly, he soon felt at home there and enjoyed engaging with its activities and members. As Clark and Hughes point out, "in such an assemblage Sedgwick was sure to take a foremost place, and we are not surprised to learn that some of his 'most honoured and cherished' friendships originated in the Society."

He was an active member for decades and soon rose through the ranks. He was elected to the Society's governing body, its Council, in 1824 and three years later was elected Vice-President. That post offered much work but no pay, and in March 1827, shortly after taking up the office, he wrote to advise his friend Ainger that "this honour brings no grist. There is no manger in my stall, so that notwithstanding my V.P.G.S. at the tail of my signature, I may die of hunger."

The following year he was invited to succeed William Henry Fitton as President. Fitton had trained in medicine, married "a lady of means", and devoted himself to Geology. He was aware of Adam's many responsibilities and packed diary, so he sought help from Whewell (who would serve as President 1837-39) to persuade him to accept the invitation. Whewell wrote to his colleague Adam – both were then Fellows at Trinity College, Cambridge – in October 1828, urging him not to turn down the invitation but to "make it possible, somehow or other, for the thing is every way in the highest way desirable." Presumably he meant desirable to the Society rather than particularly desirable to Adam. The trick worked, and in February 1829 Adam was formally installed as President of the Geological Society, a post he would occupy for two years.

The President is required to deliver an annual Address to the Society; Adam's two Presidential Addresses, in 1830 and 1832, were published in the Society's *Journal*. We'll pick up some themes from his Addresses in Part Three, but for now simply quote from what he said in 1830, to underline his firm belief in the inductive method. He told the assembled members "No opinion can be heretical, but that which is not true ... Conflicting falsehoods we can comprehend; but truths can never war against each other. I affirm, therefore, that we have nothing to fear from the results of our enquiries, provided they be followed in the laborious but secure road of honest induction. In this way, we may rest assured that we shall never arrive at conclusions opposed to any truth, either physical or moral, from whatever source that truth may be derived."

The year before Adam became President, Thomas Hyde Wollaston had donated £1,000 to the Society, on condition that the interest earned on it be used "in promoting researches concerning the mineral structure of the earth, or in rewarding those by whom such researches may hereafter be made." A commemorative gold medal was designed and Council agreed to make one each year to be awarded to the geologist whose work best met Wollaston's criteria.

Early in 1831 Council agreed unanimously that the first Wollaston Medal should be awarded to William Smith, "in consideration of his being a great original discoverer in English Geology; and especially for his having been the first, in this country, to discover and to teach the identification of strata, and to determine their succession, by means of their imbedded fossils." Adam Sedgwick was delighted to confer the medal, as President, on the man he referred to as "the Father of English Geology",

commenting on the debt of gratitude he owed him for "the practical lessons I have received from Mr Smith". We'll look at William Smith's
contribution to geology in Chapter 10.

Twenty years later, in February 1851, Adam switched roles and
found himself the recipient of the Wollaston Medal. It was presented to
him at the February meeting of the Society by Charles Lyell, then President, "for his important and original researches in Geology, more
especially for his Memoirs inserted in the *Transactions* of the Geological
Society of London and Philosophical Society of Cambridge, developing
[an understanding of] the structure of the British Isles, the Alps, and
Rhenish Provinces [Rhineland, then a province within the Kingdom of
Prussia]."

Despite the many highs during Adam's time as an active member of
the Geological Society, it ended with a low in 1863, as a result of the
fallout between Adam and his co-worker Roderick Murchison during the
co-called Cambrian Controversy, which we'll look at in more detail in
Chapter 12.

Royal Society
The Royal Society is a learned society for science, the equivalent in the
UK of an Academy of Sciences. Its origins can be traced back to a group
of polymaths that started meeting in November 1660 after a lecture at
Gresham College by Christopher Wren. The group soon received royal
approval, and from 1663 it was known as The Royal Society of London
for Improving Natural Knowledge. Its Fellows – distinguished scientists
and engineers – share a determination "to withstand the domination of
authority and to verify all statements by an appeal to facts determined by
experiment". This commitment is captured in the Society's motto *'Nullius
in verba'* "take nobody's word for it").

To be elected a Fellow of the Royal Society (FRS) was in Adam's
day the highest honour available to scientists. Adam was nominated for
that honour by twelve existing Fellows, including Sir John Herschel, in
February 1821. To be nominated at all is a measure of how highly his
scientific peers regarded him, but to be nominated within three years of
being appointed Professor of Geology shows their trust that Adam had a
very promising future ahead of him amongst the finest scientific minds in
the country.

Life and Letters is relatively silent on the matter of Adam's engagement with the Royal Society and its Fellows. Whilst his other
commitments must have made it difficult for him to attend most of their

regular meetings, the Fellows were clearly aware of and appreciated the contributions he was making to geology. This is reflected in their decision to award Adam the Copley Medal, the highest honour in their power to confer for outstanding achievements in any branch of science, in November 1863. He was awarded it "for his observations and discoveries in the Geology of the Palaeozoic Series of Rocks, and more especially for his determination of the characters of the Devonian System, by observations of the order and superposition of the Killas Rocks and their fossils, in Devonshire."

Adam, then 78 years old, was surprised and pleased to receive the "very agreeable" news. He wrote to his friend Hugh Falconer that month admitting "[for] years I have considered myself on the retired list. The pressure of advancing years and the alarming attacks of giddiness ... drove me from all exciting field-labours, and still more made me incapable of any labour ... requiring continued thought." He also wrote to his friend Professor Clark, wistfully reflecting on the fact that "our sand is nearly run out; I trust that God will forgive and bless us both; and allow us to slide gently out of the world, whenever He may in His secret counsels resolve to call us away."

Adam enjoyed the special dinner given by the Society to celebrate his award, particularly because "some honoured friends of mine were there", but he was saddened not to be "greeted by my dear old friends and fellow-labourers. Hardly one was there. They had been called to their account [died] before me."

British Association
The British Association for the Advancement of Science is usually referred to as the British Association, and is now called the British Science Association. It was founded in 1831 to help promote science in Britain in the aftermath of the French Wars, and during a period of economic decline and political instability, which together had drained the country of money, energy and resolve.

It was formed at a meeting held in York in September 1831, which agreed its objectives as "to give a stronger impulse and more systematic direction to scientific inquiry, to obtain a greater degree of national attention to the objects of science, and a removal of those disadvantages which impede its progress, and to promote the intercourse of the cultivators of science with one another, and with foreign philosophers". This was the first of a series of annual meetings that has continued almost unbroken since then.

Adam Sedgwick and fellow geologist William Buckland were among the founder members of the Association. Although Adam was unable to attend the inaugural meeting in York, he was an active member over many years and occasional President of its Geology Section, and served as President of the Association at its third annual meeting in Cambridge in 1833. He regularly gave presentations on his current geological work at the annual meetings, as a way of promoting public understanding of geology.

The 1844 meeting in York was the scene of a serious clash between Adam and the Dean of York on the topic of the Biblical creation narrative, which we'll look at further in Chapter 14.

Leaving geology
The first hint we get in *Life and Letters* that Adam was considering retirement from his professorial post comes in a letter he wrote to fellow geologist Rev Peter Brodie at the end of December 1858. He told Brodie that he had recently given his 40th and final series of lectures, because "I cannot now do the exploring field-work. 'Tis poor work to be retailing other men's adventures". He added that the only reason he was not resigning straight away was because he still had important work to finish sorting and cataloguing rocks in the Geology Museum, which he would do with the help of his trusted and dedicated assistants.

Adam finally retired as Woodwardian Professor of Geology in 1871, having been in post for 53 years. He was succeeded by Thomas McKenny Hughes, who held it for 44 years before retiring in 1917. He had worked for the Geological Survey between 1861 and 1873, and later helped keep Adam's memory alive as co-editor of *Life and Letters*, which was published in 1890.

Reflections
By the time he reached his mid-sixties, Adam was aware that he would not be able to continue doing geological field-work for many more years, and without that his lectures would be impoverished. In 1852 he wrote "my period of service is nearly over, and I am now becoming unfit for the robuster duties of an office which I hope soon to resign to more youthful and vigorous hands."

He wrote that as part of the evidence he gave to the Royal Commission of Inquiry (that we'll look at in Chapter 8), about his endowed chair and geological museum. His submission included a history of the rock collection up to that year, details of the many benefactors who had supported that work, and a series of recommendations designed to promote the continued development of geology at Cambridge.

His thoughts and suggestions were informed by his 5 decades of personal experience as Professor of Geology; he knew what he was talking about. He recommended that the terms of reference for the post should be broadened to include three or four months of geological fieldwork during the summer vacation, "either in the British Isles or on the Continent". He urged the University to appoint two additional part-time Inspectors, "at least one good naturalist and geologist", and "some scientific inspector, who was not a member of the University", to "inspect and report upon the new collections" and ensure that "the collection will not stagnate". He also urged the University to appoint an Assistant Curator to assist the Professor "in making catalogues, in mounting and labelling specimens, and (while the Professor is absent) in daily explaining to visitors and students the nature and arrangements of the collection", and to rehouse the Geology Collection adjacent to the Comparative Anatomy Collection, that would thereby "gain continual interest by an appeal to analogous organic structures derived from the Old World." He also recommended that College reserves should be used to help fund the teaching of geology within the University.

8. Reformer and Activist

"He took pride in having consistently voted on the side of civil and religious liberty since becoming a member of the Senate House."
Eric Ashby and Mary Anderson (1969)

Although Adam Sedgwick's main focus as an adult was on geology, he was committed to and actively supported a number of causes close to his heart, within and beyond politics. In terms of political leanings, he was a Whig (Liberal), although in later years he felt drawn more towards conservativism.

Adam also played an active role in university politics and administration, particularly after being appointed Vice-Master of Trinity College in 1845. He served on committees that reformed the administration of university education and the academic programmes offered by the university. As we'll see in the next chapter, he also played a key role in the Parliamentary Commission into Cambridge University in 1858.

Adam's most lasting contribution to higher education was his 1833 book *Discourse on the Studies of the University*, that helped lead Cambridge to become a modern university, by changing the undergraduate curriculum.

Anti-slavery

Adam's father Richard found the slave trade abhorrent, as we saw in Chapter 1, and that rubbed off on Adam. He and his brother Richard followed their father in campaigning for the abolition of the slave trade, and they were strong supporters of William Wilberforce.

The abolition of slavery was a dominant theme in the 1806 General Election. In those days, Cambridge University was represented in Westminster by two Members of Parliament. Both seats were won by Whigs – Lord Henry Petty and the Earl of Euston. Petty, who would later serve as Chancellor of the Exchequer, campaigned as an abolitionist at the suggestion of Wilberforce, who personally canvassed on his behalf.

The Abolition of Slavery Bill that Wilberforce had championed received Royal Assent in 1807. Forty years later, in July 1848, Adam wrote to Bishop Wilberforce that "The earliest pictures shown to me by my father when I was a child were ugly pictures of the horrors of slavery. As soon as I had learnt to scrawl my name in child's characters I remember asking leave to sign a petition against the slave-trade. Leave was granted, and I felt proud of the first political act of my life, when my dear father patted me on the head."

Anti-Catholic

In his youth, Sedgwick had also acquired from his father "a wholesome horror of the Church of Rome" (the Roman Catholic Church and its people), and that coloured many of his attitudes and some of his behaviour during the early stages of his academic career.

The so-called "Catholic Question" was very prominent in national politics at the start of the nineteenth century. The 1807 General Election was called after the King had dismissed the Government "on a point connected with the relief of the Roman Catholics" and Parliament had been dissolved, making the relief or emancipation of Roman Catholics a core theme in debate, canvassing and voting. Adam was at that time doggedly Anti-Catholic, and his sympathies were on the side of maintaining the status quo. The two MPs elected to represent Cambridge University were the Earl of Euston (Whig, liberal), who had served as MP several times before, and Sir Vicary Gibbs (Tory, conservative).

Early in 1812, both Houses of Parliament had debated "making some concessions to the Roman Catholics, in connection with the peace and good government of Ireland" and the setting up of "a committee on the state [condition] of Ireland". Ireland was then still part of the United Kingdom, and did not become a separate State until 1916. The vote on setting up a committee was lost. A proposal to support Catholic Emancipation was also debated by the Senate in Cambridge. Adam campaigned and voted against it, but the proposal won by a very small majority.

Further into his career, with greater confidence in his own liberal political views, he was to radically change his attitudes towards Roman Catholics. He woke up to "the justice of removing the civic disabilities of Roman Catholics", and supported local and national campaigns for Catholic Emancipation. He was then out of step with the majority view in Cambridge University, where most senior members were Anglican clergymen and, like many clergymen across the country, feared that "the Church and the Protestant ascendancy were both in danger" from Catholics. We see this clearly in the outcome of the 1822 Cambridge University by-election, and the 1826, 1829 and 1834 General Elections.

8. Reformer and Activist

The death of MP John Henry Smyth (Whig) in October 1822 triggered a by-election, at a time when Catholic Emancipation was the pressing national issue of the day. Viscount Palmerston (the sitting MP) and the three candidates who came forward were all in favour of Emancipation. But the University was then petitioning the House of Commons every year against the Catholic claims, and it was keen to have someone on the ballot who would represent their views. William John Bankes, a man of independent means and "as determined an opponent of concession [against Catholics] as could be desired", was willing to stand. Bankes was elected and Palmerston continued; both were Tories. Sedgwick and his friends had supported James Scarlett, a Whig, who came last.

Seven years later, in the 1826 General Election, most Fellows in Cambridge hoped that Anti-Catholic Bankes would be re-elected and pro-Catholic Palmerston defeated. A writer in *The Times* was horrified at the prospect, writing how "this once liberal University is seized at this moment with such a violent horror of the Pope that in its panic it forgets the services of an old and tried member ...". Sedgwick was a strong supporter of Palmerston and an active member of his campaign committee. Palmerston held onto his seat but Bankes lost his to Attorney General Sir John Simpleton Copley, who declared himself to be "decidedly adverse to the claims of the Catholics". So, once again, the University had one pro-Catholic MP (Palmerston) and one anti (Copley).

Another by-election in Cambridge was called in 1829 after MP Sir Nicholas Conyngham Tindal was made Chief Justice of the Court of Common Pleas. Two men contested the seat – George Bankes (Tory), whose views on Catholics were widely regarded as fluid, and William Cavendish (Whig), a wealthy landowner for whom Adam Sedgwick worked hard to marshal support. Cavendish beat Bankes and joined Palmerston as MP; the ideal team in Adam's eyes.

Adam was also active in the run-up to the 1832 General Election. Sir Walter Scott (Tory) was continuing, but Adam and his friends tried hard to persuade the voters that John William Lubbock (Vice-President of the Royal Society), "a man distinguished for his literary and scientific attainments", would be a more suitable representative than a career politician for a learned body. Adam chaired Lubbock's election committee, but Lubbock withdrew after ten days when it became clear that he had little support across the University. Two Tory career politicians – Charles Manners Sutton (former Speaker of the House of Commons) and Henry Goulburn (inheritor of a slave plantation in Jamaica, and former

Chancellor of the Exchequer) – were duly elected to serve as Members of Parliament for Cambridge University.

Parliamentary Reform
1832 Reform Bill
As Adam Sedgwick approached the end of his term as President of the Geological Society, he was looking forward to having more time for his geological fieldwork and for writing up a growing back-log of academic papers. But, only two weeks after he had delivered his farewell address at the Society's annual meeting in 1832, his time and attention were captured by a national debate about reforming the electoral system in England and Wales.

Lord John Russell (Paymaster General in Earl Grey's Whig government) had introduced a Reform Bill into the House of Commons that was designed, according to its preamble, to "take effectual Measures for corrective diverse Abuses that have long prevailed in the Choice of Members to serve in the Commons House of Parliament". The "diverse Abuses" included the radically varying size of constituencies ("boroughs"), some having as few as 20 people while others had up to 12,000; the effective control of many boroughs by one powerful and typically wealthy patron; variations between boroughs in the criteria for defining who was eligible to vote (men only, these in pre-suffragette times); the power that the monarch could exercise in deciding which of the new towns and cities that had grown up during the Industrial Revolution would be allowed to be declared "boroughs" and thereby have their own MPs; and differences in the number of MPs a borough could elect, 2 was the norm but a few could only elect 1.

The Bill was strongly opposed, particularly among wealthy landowners and members of the House of Lords, but it was passed, mainly as a result of public pressure. After receiving Royal Assent, the Bill became an Act of Parliament – The Representation of the People Act 1832. The Act enfranchised many more people, giving them the right to vote. As a result, the total electorate in England and Wales grew from about 500,000 to 813,000, accounting for about 1 in 5 adult males. But the Act did not address some major issues – it still denied women the right to vote; the enlarged electorate still only amounted to about 6 percent (roughly 1 in 17) of the total population; and most working class men were not enfranchised because voters were required to possess property worth £10, that was a large amount at that time.

8. Reformer and Activist

The Act was deeply unpopular in Cambridge University, where most of the Fellows favoured the status quo. Soon after it was introduced, the University sent a petition against it to the House of Commons. The University was a very privileged borough, and would remain a separate constituency until 1950. It had 2 seats in the House of Commons and the electorate included all graduates of the university, no matter where they lived. Cambridge town had its own 2 MPs, but many local people had no vote at all in Adam's day.

Adam was very much in favour of the Act, despite the strong opposition to it within the University. That might have put him in a rather difficult position with his colleagues, but as Clark and Hughes point out, "his high personal character, his great popularity, and his uniform kindliness and good humour towards those who differed from him, enabled him to pass through the ordeal unscathed."

1867 Reform Bill

In 1866, Prime Minister Lord Russell introduced a new Reform Bill into the House of Commons. Amongst other things, it proposed giving the vote to "respectable" working men (defined as those with a household worth at least £7) but not to unskilled workers and the so-called "residuum" (men who MPs looked upon as the "feckless and criminal" poor). The Bill was defeated, and Russell's Liberal government resigned and was replaced by a new Conservative Government led by Lord Derby.

There was still strong public support for further reform of the House of Commons. A new Reform Bill was proposed, and in mid-July 1867 a new Representation of the People Act was passed. Amongst other things it created some new boroughs with their own MPs, and effectively gave working class men over the age of 21 the right to vote. Women would not win the right to vote for a further six decades, until the Representation of the People Act of 1928.

Adam's views had changed a great deal over the three decades between the first two Reform Acts. He had been very much in favour of the 1832 Act but was deeply troubled by the 1867 Act, that he described in a letter to his cousin Mrs Norton as "a most dangerous leap in the dark", as a result of which "the sky is putting on mourning".

In late August he admitted to his cousin "All my long life I have been called a liberal; all my votes since I came to manhood have been called liberal till now. But now I am a stiff-backed Tory, and I think that our liberals are turned raving mad, and that a good-hearted old man [he was then 82] should not sail in the same boat with them."

Studies of the University

One of the things for which Adam is best known outside of geology is his book *Discourse on the Studies of the University*, the first edition of which was published in 1833. It would have a significant impact on reforming the curriculum at Cambridge, and helped it become a modern university with a global reputation.

But it all started in a rather low key way, as a sermon that Adam delivered in the Chapel of Trinity College on the 17th of December 1832.

Commemoration Service (December 1832)

Each December the Master, Fellows and students of Trinity College gathered in the Chapel for an annual service to commemorate their benefactors over the ages. It was Adam's turn to preach, as an ordained Fellow of the College.

The usual theme of the sermon was a retrospective focussing on "the founders, benefactors, distinguished members of the college, and those who have passed away since the last occasion, with the obvious lessons to be drawn from such occurrences", as Clark and Hughes tell us. But Adam had a different idea in mind. He wanted those gathered before him to consider what the students were being taught at the University, and to reflect on what this told them about the nature of God and how it challenged them to see God in every aspect of their learning. Given the customary focus his choice of theme was provocative, and not by accident.

Adam had no doubt been thinking through those themes for some time but he only started writing the sermon on the Thursday, three days before he was to deliver it. It was written in a hurry.

The Cambridge curriculum

To understand how provocative Adam's theme would inevitably be seen at the time, it is helpful to know how the Cambridge curriculum was then structured.

Two groups of male students were admitted as undergraduates – Honours men (the brighter students who would be studying for honours degrees) and Pollmen (who would be studying for an unclassified ordinary degree). Both groups studied compulsory courses in three areas – Natural Philosophy, Theology & Moral Philosophy, and the Belles Lettres [Great Literature]. This sounds like an intellectually stimulating syllabus but, in reality, each subject was taught in a dry, strictly didactic fashion, with no scope for independent thought or critical engagement. As Eric Ashby and Mary Anderson (1969) put it, "it seems that each subject was taught with the attitude one would expect from an unimaginative gym instructor: to discipline the mind rather than to enrich or inform it; toughening intellectual muscles, but to no evident purpose."

The Pollmen were much the larger group. They were assessed in two public examinations. The first, called the Previous, was taken in the second term of the second year. It was "a perfunctory test in Theology and Moral Philosophy and the Belles Lettres – one of the four Gospels or the Acts [of the Apostles] in Greek; Paley's *Evidences*; and one Greek and one Latin classic". The second, called the Final, was taken in the third term of the fourth undergraduate year. It was a longer and more searching test, which also covered Locke's *Essay on the Human Understanding*, Paley's *Moral Philosophy* and other classic works, and papers in Natural Philosophy (that included the earlier propositions of Euclid, along with elementary arithmetic and algebra).

The Honours student had to pass the Previous and then proceed to major in mathematics, no matter where his academic interests lay. He had to make the honours list in the Mathematical Tripos to qualify him for sitting the Classical Tripos, which was the only other examination open to him. The Mathematics examination was a serious ordeal for all of the honours students. For men like Adam, who were aiming for the distinction of being a Wrangler, the requirements were particularly tough.

At that time in Cambridge, as Ashby and Anderson (1969) note, "the undergraduate who was ambitious for a Fellowship or other academic preferment had therefore to become a slave to the examination system, and this severely limited his intellectual horizon. The curriculum in the early decades of the nineteenth century was excessively circumscribed and artificial ..."

Discourse on the Studies of the University (1833)

Six days after Adam delivered his sermon in the Chapel at Trinity College, his friend and colleague William Whewell, then Senior Tutor, wrote to encourage him to publish it. A number of undergraduates who had listened to the sermon were impressed with what Sedgwick had said and they were eager to have it printed so they could re-read it, study it, and discuss it amongst themselves. Whewell told Adam "the rising generation ... declare that their intellectual culture requires that you print and publish your sermon." He added "I thought your sermon full of notions, as the Americans speak, which it will be very useful and beneficial to put in their heads; I hope you will be able to extract from some abysmal recess your manuscript, and to place it before the astonished eyes of the compositor [get it printed]."

Adam agreed to the request and started work on the book without delay. But, as often happened with him, progress was delayed by ill health and the pull of other interests. The book finally appeared in November 1833, almost a year after he had delivered the sermon.

The sermon is believed to have taken several hours to deliver, which would not have been unusual for church sermons in those days. But Adam thought it only proper that the book should provide more detailed coverage of many of the themes he had sketched out in the sermon. As a result, the book is a great deal longer and more detailed than the sermon. The first edition is twice the size of the sermon (later editions were longer still), and it contains 27 pages of appendices to support the main narrative.

The books remained a work in progress for many years. It went through four editions between 1833 and 1835, with the fifth and final edition being published in 1850.

Even Adam's close colleagues were disappointed with the style of his writing in *Discourse*. Clark and Hughes described the first edition as "heavy and laboured, and there are none of those eloquent passages which made his speeches so animated and so delightful." They were equally disappointed with later editions and thought "the style of writing was turgid and in the dropsical fifth edition ideas are jumbled together like objects in a boutique of curios."

Structure and content

Adam structured his sermon and book in three parts, each one dealing with a different aspect of the Cambridge syllabus. Two overarching themes tied the three parts together – the search for order in everything we see in the world around us, and the search for causes, with a particular emphasis on divine action.

As Ashby and Anderson (1969) point out, "to some undergraduates it must have come as a reassurance from Sedgwick to learn that the arid puzzle in probability theory, the treacherous question in geometry, the speculations of philosophers and the assertions of theologians, were, if one only understood it, all manifestations of a tidy and relevant universe."

Part 1 focussed on The Laws of Nature. In terms of the search for order, Adam talked and wrote about Newton's three laws of motion (the Law of Inertia; the relationship between force, mass and acceleration; every action has an equal and opposite reaction) that govern the relations between non-living objects, and about the "laws" governing how living creatures operate, that scientists were then starting to work out. Adam and other scientists at that time recognised that both sets of "laws" are fixed and unchangeable, and that they describe what Aristotle called "efficient causes", by which he meant agents that bring things into being or cause things to happen.

Adam viewed The Laws of Nature through the eyes of an ordained intellectual with a deep personal Christian faith. He looked upon natural science and its findings as a window on God's handiwork in creating all things in the universe; today this perspective is called the Argument from Design. As Clark and Hughes put it, Adam believed that natural science should be subject to "a reverent study", and that "its various branches, Astronomy, Anatomy, Geology, minister to natural religion, and [in Adam's words] 'teach us to see the finger of God in all things animate and inanimate.'" He was unshakeable in his belief that the Laws of Nature were proof of an intelligent final cause (God), that explains why the efficient causes do what they do. This, he argued, was how the undergraduates at Cambridge should look upon the scientific parts of their education.

Part 2 focussed on Ancient Literature and Language, and it was much shorter than Part 1. Adam had studied Classics as part of his own undergraduate degree, as an adult he liked reading books by Greek and Latin authors, and he was a strong supporter of continuing to include ancient languages and ancient history in the Cambridge syllabus. But he was in favour of making the links between classical studies and Christian beliefs more explicit. For example, he approved of including works by Greek and Latin authors but "with certain limitations", and he argued for greater study of philosophical and ethical works by such authors, alongside their historical writings. To support this proposal, he pointed out that "the argument for the being of a God, derived from final causes, is as well stated in the *Conversations* of Socrates, as in the *Natural Theology* of Paley."

In Part 3 Adam moved on to Ethics and Metaphysics. His focus was on where and how humans get the capacity to distinguish between right and wrong. He was very critical of two leading English philosophers – John Locke (1632-1704) and William Paley (1743-1805) – whose books were then required reading for students at Cambridge.

Locke formulated a "theory of mind" that he described in his 1690 book *An Essay Concerning Human Understanding*. His theory was that, at birth, our mind is like a blank slate, a *tabula rasa*. Descartes (1596-

1650) had earlier proposed that we are born with minds that contain pre-existing ideas, like a modern-day computer pre-loaded with digital information. Locke disputed that view and argued that we are born without any inherent or instinctive ideas and our initially empty mind is then shaped by our experiences, through sensations (experiencing things) and reflections (thinking about things).

Adam Sedgwick, insistent that God would not create humans with empty minds to start with, argued that Locke was simply wrong. He asked rhetorically if, as Locke believed, "the mind be without innate knowledge, is it also to be considered as without innate feelings and capacities – a piece of blank paper, the mere passive recipient of impressions from without? The whole history of man shows this hypothesis to be an outrage on his moral nature. Naked he comes from his mother's womb; endowed with limbs and senses indeed, well fitted to the material world, yet powerless from want of use; and as for knowledge, his soul is one unvaried blank: yet has this blank been already touched by a celestial hand [God] ..." We'll return to this idea of the mind as an initially blank slate mind in Chapter 15.

Adam attacked Paley for promoting utilitarianism, a doctrine first proposed by Jeremy Bentham (1748-1832) and strongly promoted by John Stuart Mill (1806-1873). Using happiness as a measure of usefulness or utility, the "utilitarian theory of morals" argued that an action is right in so far as it promotes happiness, and that the guiding principle of conduct should be the greatest happiness of the greatest number of people.

Adam was critical of Paley's view, developed in his 1785 book *Principles of Moral and Political Philosophy*, that "utility is the touchstone of right and wrong", that was then required reading at Cambridge. Adam disagreed. and insisted that "God implants into human consciousness an innate realisation of the distinction between good and evil, and he implied that the distinction was absolute, unchanged by time or place", as Ashby and Anderson (1969) put it. He firmly believed that using expediency as a way of judging between right and wrong, rather than having an absolute God-given definition of right and wrong, would make virtue "a matter of profit and loss", and would have a "degrading effect on temper and conduct". As a result, he argued that "undergraduates must reject such a notion, and, with it, they must reject utilitarian philosophy, which has no common bond with Christian ethics."

In his more charitable moments Adam dismissed Paley's support for utilitarianism as a lapse of judgment. Like many other scientists and churchmen at that time, he was a big fan of Paley's 1802 book *Natural Theology or Evidences of the Existence and Attributes of the Deity*, and acknowledged that its author had done "more for the cause of revealed truth than any other writer in this country."

Reception and reactions
Discourse was well received, both inside and beyond Cambridge. By the time the first edition appeared in 1833, it's author had developed a reputation as an engaging and charismatic speaker, a distinguished scientist, a fearless campaigner, and a respected and influential senior member of Cambridge University.

The theme of university reform also had great appeal at that time, partly because only eighteen months before Adam delivered his sermon in Trinity College Chapel William Hamilton, an Oxford graduate, had launched a very public attack on Oxford University. Hamilton compared Oxford to a poorly run school, and described it as "of all the academical institutions at once the most imperfect and the most perfectible". In two influential articles he wrote in *The Edinburgh Review* in June and December 1831, he criticised the Oxford colleges as private foundations that held far too much power and influence within the university, and called for a Royal or Parliamentary Commission to restore the English universities to their right status, "controlled and privileged by public authority, for the advantage of the state."

Some readers of *Discourse*, perhaps attracted by its provocative title, might have been disappointed with its content. They would have found that Adam Sedgwick had little to say about Hamilton's ideas and suggestions, and rather than discussing the deficiencies of the existing curriculum at Cambridge, he focussed on its potential as the foundation of a sound Christian education. Ashby and Anderson (1969) describe the book as "more of an apologia than a critique."

Most reviews of *Discourse* were very positive. The month after it was published, *The Times* called it "a work of great and varied excellence", and the following year the *Quarterly Review* described it as "perhaps the most remarkable pamphlet that has appeared in England since Burke's *Reflections*".

The book also had its detractors, the most prominent of which was philosopher John Stuart Mill, who panned it in a caustic article in *London Review* in April 1835 that was subsequently reprinted in his *Dissertations and Discussions* (1859).

Fifth edition (1850)
It is a measure of the pace of change in both geology and philosophy during the first half of the nineteenth century that Adam felt obliged to significantly expand his book to bring it fully up to date in the fifth edition, that was published in 1850, 18 years after the first edition. Most of the new material appears in the weighty Preface (442 pages) and Appendix (228 pages); the *Discourse* itself remained relatively succinct at 94 pages. Adam described it as "a grain of wheat between two millstones". Overall, the 1850 edition that Adam described as "a fat volume of nearly 800 pages" was more than four times the 190 pages of the original 1833 edition.

Part 1 was updated to include Adam's response to Robert Chambers' *Vestiges of the Natural History of Creation* which had caused quite a stir when it was published in 1844, as we'll see in Chapters 10 and 14. Adam had felt the need to expose "the mischief of modern pantheistic doctrines when applied to physical, moral, and religious questions."

There were a few small updates to Part 2, but Adam substantially revised Part 3 because recent academic changes at Cambridge had made the original narrative redundant.

By 1850 he was keen to combat the rising popularity of two schools of thought within philosophy. One was materialism (the theory that the only thing that can be truly proven to exist is physical matter) that, he argued, promoted "conditions of the mind that have led men to deny a Personal Creator". We'll return to this theme in Chapters 14 and 15. Adam was also critical of Locke's ideas on idealism, the theory that the only thing actually knowable is consciousness or the contents of consciousness. He argued that this perspective, which allows no room for divine revelation or inspiration, also denied God.

Adam also mentions the new theory of physiophilosophy (a natural philosophy concerning natural history and relationships) that had been proposed by German naturalist Lorenz Oken in his 1847 book *Elements of Physiophilosophy*. Adam admitted "I have read his Work and I have striven to perceive some glimmerings of steady light among the mists of his first sixty or seventy pages". But he must have been sympathetic to Oken's claim that "Physio-philosophy has to show how, and in accordance indeed with what laws, the Material took its origin; and, therefore, how something derived its existence from nothing. It has to portray the first periods of the world's development from nothing; how the elements and heavenly bodies originated; in what method by self-evolution into higher and manifold forms, they separated into minerals, became finally organic, and in Man attained self-consciousness." Oken was hinting that nature was a work of God, created to serve humans, or as Clark and Hughes put it, that nature exhibited "evidence of a scheme conceived in the Divine Mind from the beginning, and adapted to the wants of His creatures in successive acts of creation". As we'll see in Chapters 14 and 15, Adam Sedgwick would agree with that perspective.

In the Preface to the 1850 edition of *Discourse*, Adam also reasserts the argument for final causes, discusses the credibility of miracles, and declares induction to be "the fountain of all material truth". Induction and the search for truth were central themes in much of his geological thinking and writing, and key aspects of his *modus operandi* throughout his adult years. They would also be central pillars in his very public debates about geology, transmutation, and theology, as we'll see in Chapters 14 and 15.

Adam also discusses the current state of the University, including the introduction of new triposes which he approved of. He also gives an update on the Cambridge Philosophical Society and the development of the University's museums, including his own Museum of Geology.

Like the four earlier editions, the 1850 edition was generally well received. Clark and Hughes, admittedly not disinterested observers, describe it as "a storehouse of arguments against transmutation [evolution] of species; and further, against the tendencies of modem speculation towards materialism." But they were not blind to its weaknesses, particularly the structure which they describe as "unfortunate". Some of Adam's friends were disappointed with the weighty volume. Lord Brougham, for example, spoke of "the somewhat amorphous – at least oddly-proportioned – book", and Professor Owen wrote "I hope you may be spared to expand it into a form agreeable with its true nature and importance ..."

University reform
Abolition of religious qualifying tests
In 1834 Adam Sedgwick led a campaign to make it possible for students who were not members of the Church of England to study at Cambridge University, by removing strict religious tests that had been in place for more than 200 years to identify and keep out Dissenters and Roman Catholics. The campaign was unsuccessful at that time, but momentum gathered and the tests were subsequently abolished in 1869.

The 1834 campaign had begun five years earlier, when the University decided to petition Parliament against a Bill that the Duke of

Wellington intended to introduce promoting Catholic emancipation. The opposition of Liberal members of the Senate to such a move had failed on several previous occasions, but this time it was successful; 43 members voted in favour of the petition and 52 voted against. Despite his earlier Anti-Catholic sentiments, Adam Sedgwick was by then a strong supporter of Catholic emancipation, and he played a prominent role in promoting the vote against the petition within the University.

In the following month, Wellington's Bill was accepted in both the House of Commons and the House of Lords. The Roman Catholic Relief Act 1829 received Royal assent in April that year.

Adam continued to campaign within the University for the abolition of qualifying tests at Cambridge. In 1834 he chaired a meeting in St John's College of like-minded Fellows, who agreed that a Petition in favour of it should be drawn up and sent to both Houses of Parliament. The key clause in the Petition was the proposition that "no corporate body like the University of Cambridge can exist in a free country in honour or in safety unless its benefits be communicated to all classes as widely as is compatible with the Christian principles of its foundation." To that end, the signatories suggested that legislation be introduced to remove "every religious test exacted from members of the University before they proceed to degrees, whether of bachelor, master, or doctor, in Arts, Law, and Physic."

Adam pointed out, in a letter to Lord Blomfield in April 1834, that any Nonconformist student admitted to the university must have the same rights and responsibilities as all other students. including keeping all college and university rules and regulations. He also argued that "moderate, well-informed Dissenters" should be welcomed. He pointed out that "we have had amongst us during the last twenty years Roman Catholics, Methodists, Presbyterians, Quakers, Congregationalists of every shade, and they all attended lectures, and never, I believe, made a single objection to a lecture given in College."

Adam and fellow supporters of the abolition of religious entry tests were eager to ensure that Cambridge's reputation as a seat of learning was not undermined by outdated and unnecessary restrictions on the type of students who could be admitted. Most of the 180 members of the Senate were sympathetic to the position that Adam articulated; 62 of them signed the Petition and a further 101 signed the accompanying Declaration.

However, not everyone at Cambridge was in favour of the abolition of religious tests. Thomas Turton, Regius Professor of Divinity at Cambridge and Dean of Peterborough, was strongly opposed and put his views down in writing in an 1834 pamphlet entitled *Thoughts on the Admission of Persons, without regard to their Religious Opinions, to certain degrees in the Universities of England* that was very widely read and talked about.

Turton's views incensed Connop Thirlwall, an Assistant Tutor in Trinity College and one of Adam Sedgwick's closest friends. He wrote a stinging reply to Turton, in which he pointed out that the only provision for theological instruction made by the colleges was compulsory attendance at chapel, which he denounced as "a positive evil". The Master of Trinity, Christopher Wordsworth, thought Thirlwall had gone too far in attacking a well-established part of college discipline, and demanded that he resign as Assistant Tutor, which he did without delay. Thirlwall subsequently devoted himself to parish duties, and in 1840 was appointed Bishop of St David's in Wales.

The matter of abolishing religious tests would not be fully resolved for a further three decades. In late November 1869 Adam was invited to attend a meeting in St John's College of like-minded Fellows to discuss the most appropriate way of drawing their views to the notice of the Government. His views were unchanged since 1834 and he was keen to lend his support to the initiative. His attendance at the meeting was to be his last appearance on a public occasion in Cambridge; he was then 84 years old, and would die less than 4 years later.

The 1869 Cambridge resolution formed part of a wider campaign that gathered momentum and resulted in The Universities Tests Act 1871. The Act abolished the communion 'Tests' and allowed Roman Catholics, non-conformists and non-Christians to take up fellowships at the Universities of Oxford, Cambridge, London and Durham.

Royal Commission of Inquiry (1850-1852)

The first half of the nineteenth century was a time of great social, political and economic change in England. During the preceding century, the Universities of Oxford and Cambridge had both faced calls for reform, but by the mid 1850s the calls were getting louder and more persistent. Critics called for reform in a number of areas, including their constitutions, entrenched religious exclusivity, financial inefficiency, and increasingly outmoded traditional attitudes, practices and programmes of study.

There was widespread opposition in Cambridge to many of the changes being called for. This is reflected, for example, in the resistance shown by the University in the long struggle to remove religious tests, and in its reluctance to adopt proposals made by its own members to update the teaching programmes. These included proposals that Sedgwick had made in *Discourse* (1832), a suggestion made by Trinity College Fellow Benjamin Walsh for the establishment of five new triposes (1837), and William Whewell's proposal for a General Tripos in the Inductive Sciences (1840).

The movement for reform in Cambridge was boosted by the election in 1847 of Queen Victoria's Prince Consort, Albert, as Chancellor of the University. We'll look at Albert's influence on the University, and Adam Sedgwick's influence on Albert, in Chapter 9. The movement also gained momentum when a petition signed mostly by Cambridge graduates was presented to the Prime Minister, Lord John Russell, declaring that both Oxford and Cambridge Universities were failing in their duty to promote the advancement of learning.

The new Chancellor was a keen supporter of reform at Cambridge. Within a year, with his encouragement, two new Honour Triposes were introduced, in the Natural Sciences and the Moral Sciences in 1848. The following year the University appointed a committee to revise its statutes.

While the University was starting to make progress in reforming itself, external calls for change continued, and critics argued that the reform was too little too late. Proposals had been made in 1837 and 1844 to set up a Royal Commission to examine both Oxford and Cambridge Universities. Both proposals were rejected, but the issue did not go away. It sprang to life again in December 1847, when Prime Minister Lord John Russell told Prince Albert that he was in favour of advising the Crown to "appoint a Commission to inquire into the state of Schools and Colleges of Royal Foundation." The Chancellor wrote back defending what was already being done at Cambridge, and expressing the hope that Russell would "pause with the recommendation of a Royal Commission of Inquiry till we have seen whether any good can be effected in the way now proposed to be followed."

Many graduates and former members of both Universities, along with some Fellows of the Royal Society, were keen to promote the cause of reform. They circulated a *Memorial* urging the Prime Minister to advise Queen Victoria "to issue Her Royal Commission of Inquiry into the best methods of securing the improvement of the Universities of Oxford and Cambridge." More than 200 graduates of Cambridge (133) and Oxford (62), and Fellows of the Royal Society (29), signed what was affectively a petition for change.

8. Reformer and Activist

The *Memorial* was presented to the Prime Minister in July 1848, and although he doubtless gave it serious thought he took no action, probably out of a desire not to offend Prince Albert. The matter was raised again in a motion to the House of Commons two years later, in April 1850. Lord Russell again declined to support the motion, but he told MPs "it is certainly our intention to advise the Crown to issue a Royal Commission to inquire into the state of the two Universities of Oxford and Cambridge." Many senior people in Cambridge – Heads of Colleges, Professors, Tutors and Lecturers – were horrified at the prospect of external interference in their affairs; 156 of them urged the Vice-Chancellor "to take such steps as the emergency may appear to require, and to consider especially whether it may not be proper to represent to His Royal Highness our Chancellor the interference with our freedom, rights, statutes, possessions, and usages, which appears to be threatened."

The Cambridge opposition failed, and in April 1850 a Royal Commission of Inquiry was appointed "to inquire into the state, discipline, studies, and revenues, of the University and the Colleges at Cambridge". A similar one was set up for Oxford.

The Prime Minister wrote to Adam Sedgwick the following month inviting him to become a Member of the Commission, as a "distinguished Professor". Adam had very mixed feelings about accepting the invitation. He wrote to Prince Albert's Private Secretary, Lieutenant-Colonel Grey, advising that he would personally prefer not to serve as a Commissioner, but was willing to do it if that was what the Chancellor wanted. He also doubted his suitability, but recognised that he would bring relevant experience and insight to the task. Adam listed numerous reasons why he felt unsuitable, including long spells of ill health, increasing age, lack of business experience, lack of time, a growing backlog of geological work to complete and publish, and the real risk of losing the support of many of his close friends. Besides which, he added, he had "contracted very solemn obligations both to the University and Trinity College, under the sanction of an oath", which might compromise his ability to serve as a Commissioner and create conflicts of interest for him. Furthermore, a key condition of his Woodwardian Professorship was that he would not undertake other work that would take him away from a strict focus on geology.

Despite Adam's reservations, Prince Albert wanted him to accept the invitation and argued that it was "most essential that the Commission should be formed of the friends of the University ...". When the list of Commissioners was announced in August 1850, it contained the name

Adam Sedgwick alongside John Graham (Bishop of Chester), George Peacock (Dean of Ely), Sir William Herschel (astronomer) and Sir John Romilly (Solicitor General). William Henry Bateson (theologian of St John's College, later Master) was appointed Secretary to the Commission.

The Commission started work in the Michaelmas term of 1850, and it occupied a great deal of Adam's time and energy over the next two years. He often had to travel to London on Commission business, and also had many meetings in Cambridge. As a result, his geological work suffered and his backlog of unfinished papers grew ever longer. Adam ended up spending much of 1852 drafting major sections of the 200-page *Report* of the Commission.

By July 1852 the Cambridge Commissioners were able to read a draft of the *Report* of the Oxford Commissioners. Not surprisingly, Prince Albert (sponsor of both Commissions) was eager to know what it said. He summoned Adam to Osborne House, the royal residence on the Isle of Wight (of which more in Chapter 9), to brief him about the likely recommendations in both *Reports*.

Highlights from the Oxford *Report* included removing the limit on the number of undergraduates that would be admitted, and creating a new category of student (not necessarily belonging to a particular college, bound by regulations of the University, to be called Town-men) as well as the existing College Men. Albert admired the *Report* and was sympathetic to these new ideas, which mixed elements of the current English system and more progressive Edinburgh and foreign University systems. Adam strongly advised Albert against that way forward, arguing that it was unnecessary because "Cambridge has been far in advance of Oxford in everything regarding internal administration, and we have not half so much to reform as they have."

The Cambridge Commissioners submitted their *Report* at the end of August 1852. It recommended many reforms, including making the University Senate more democratic; abolishing archaic privileges; reforming examinations to allow a preliminary examination in the second year, after which students would be allowed to transfer to study a subject of their choice; creating Boards of Studies for departments that award honours degrees; awarding scholarships and fellowships by merit only; making colleges contribute to the salaries of Public Lecturers and Professors (who depended on student lecture fees); reviving the ancient system of hostels affiliated to colleges; and building new Museums of Science.

8. Reformer and Activist

Parliamentary Commission (1855)
The recommendations of the *Report* of the Royal Commissioners (1852) made good sense to many well-informed people across England, who were keen to see the two ancient Universities maintain their reputation as world-class institutions of higher learning. But Cambridge once again showed stubborn resistance to external influences and pressures, and failed to act on the recommendations.

In April 1855 the Government agreed to introduce into Parliament a Bill for the reform of the University of Cambridge, which would appoint a Parliamentary Commission with the aim of enacting into law many of the reforms proposed three years earlier by the Royal Commissioners. Adam Sedgwick was one of seven Commissioners appointed to the Parliamentary Commission, along with William Cavendish (Earl of Burlington), Thomas Sprint Rice (Lord Monteagle), John Graham (Bishop of Chester), Sir Edward Alderson (Baron of the Exchequer), John Cowling (barrister), and John Lefevre ("a Gentleman who was distinguished at Cambridge") as Clerk.

The Bill was passed by the House of Lords but rejected by the House of Commons, after the men who promoted it discovered, as Clark and Hughes put it, "that they had misunderstood the state of public opinion at Cambridge, where their proposals encountered determined opposition." Although he had been an active member of the Commission, Adam Sedgwick disliked some of the changes it proposed. A series of amendments were introduced to remedy some of the most serious problems in the draft legislation, but the Bill was so flawed that it had to be abandoned.

A new measure was introduced in 1856, and a different set of Parliamentary Commissioners were nominated to smooth its passage through the system. Adam Sedgwick was at last free to campaign openly for what he believed in, rather than being compromised by the cabinet responsibility of being a Commissioner. He now found himself outside looking in, rather than inside looking out.

He wrote to Dean Peacock in February 1858 spelling out what his views were on the priorities for reform at Cambridge – "to make the Professorships worth having" and require the Professors to live in College and provide "ample teaching"; "to make the Colleges pay for new endowments, each out of its own funds, and in proportion to its net income"; "to encourage goodwill study" by allowing students to choose what subject to study from those on offer, "but these not to be counted as Honours", which should only be given by new Triposes, such as the recently introduced Natural Sciences Tripos. He was also very keen on the construction of new buildings in the old Botanical Garden at Cambridge, that would include lecture rooms, laboratories, and one or more new Museums.

By late 1858 the Parliamentary Commissioners, as part of their remit, had produced proposals to revise the statutes of the Cambridge Colleges. Amongst other changes, they had suggested that "any Fellow should vacate his Fellowship at the end of ten years after attaining the full standing of Master of Arts, except in certain specified cases." Adam seconded a motion against this that was put forward by the Master of St John's College, because he "looked upon his Fellowship as a freehold ... and he could not conceive anything more degrading than to make it a terminable annuity." He also believed that the proposal "would tend to the moral degradation of the different societies; it would encourage favouritism, and all those points which lowered the moral standard of academic bodies."

During 1858 and 1859 Adam had to sit through many long meetings of the governing body of Trinity College, where the Commissioners' proposals were debated. By then he was an old man of 74, and felt his reforming days were over. But he still made his feelings known; he told a college meeting about the proposals "I hate the sight of them; ... I think their provisions may take away all future glory from the noble society where have lived such men as Newton, and Bacon ... and thousands of good and true men. ... the Commissioners ... have done that which will tend, I verily believe, to degrade the moral character and independent loyalty of the College."

9. Royal Connections

"He performed his duties zealously, but without either subserviency or affectation; and in all his relations with the Court he maintained the same simplicity of manner, and the same plainness of speech, by which his whole life had been distinguished."
Clark and Hughes (1890) on Adam Sedgwick

We have already caught a glimpse, in Chapter 8, of the close working relationship that Adam enjoyed with Prince Albert, Queen Victoria's Consort, after Albert was elected Chancellor of Cambridge University in 1847. Adam was a staunch supporter of the monarchy, by temperament and family background, and he took great delight in meeting them and making himself available to serve them.

Queen Victoria

In June 1837 Victoria succeeded to the throne, at the age of eighteen, on the death of her father William IV. Three years later she would marry her first cousin, Prince Albert of Saxe-Coburg and Gotha, who she affectionately called Bertie, and who would stand close by her side as Prince Consort.

Coronation (June 1838)

Adam was first introduced to Victoria when she paid a visit to Cambridge University, one week before her Coronation. In a letter to his niece Emma, three weeks later, he described how "It was a splendid show, as all the foreign ambassadors, who had come to grace the Coronation, were present. When it was over, a party of the Royal Society [of which Adam was a Fellow] were introduced to the Queen in her private closet [room]. We had an excellent opportunity of seeing her, and hearing her speak, as she received the Duke of Sussex [her uncle] without any of the formality of a Court … He afterwards presented us all in turn, and we had a most gracious reception."

Like many other people, Adam was keen to witness at first hand the Queen's Coronation in Westminster Abbey. He travelled to London by train, and through some well-connected acquaintances – the Queen's Equerry and his wife, a Lady of the Bedchamber – was given a grandstand seat in the Abbey, "the best place in the whole Abbey, just on one side of and overlooking the two thrones", as he wrote to Emma. He added "I certainly never saw before so grand, dazzling, and solemn a ceremonial ... The little Queen performed her part with grace, dignity, and good feeling; and all hearts seemed to swell with delight. In the evening there was in the parks the finest display of fireworks I ever beheld."

The following Sunday Adam was privileged to gain entry to the service in the Royal Chapel, courtesy of the Sub-Dean with whom he was acquainted. He told Emma that "the Bishop of London preached a good plain sermon; and the young Queen, the Queen Dowager, and the Duchess of Kent sat in front of the Royal pew. They were all dressed as plain as plain could be, stopped to receive the Sacrament [Holy Communion] together, and seemed anxious to throw away all the pomp and pride of greatness as much as they could."

Royal visit to Trinity College (October 1843)
Five years would pass before Adam had another opportunity to meet the Queen. In June 1843 he was visiting family and friends in Dent when he was summoned back to Cambridge by William Whewell (his Trinity College colleague then serving a 1-year term as Vice-Chancellor of the University) to help prepare for a royal visit planned for late October.

Adam rushed back to Cambridge without delay. One of the first things he did when he got back to College was order some new clothes fitting for a royal encounter; he asked his tailor to make him "a pair of shorts and a silk cassock", noting that "pantaloons ... are an abomination in the eyes of Kings and Queens." Next, he tidied up the Museum of Geology, putting it "in royal order" with the help of his College manservant John and three or four assistants.

The "big day" for the royal visit to Trinity College was Wednesday the 25th of October. The weather was good, after overnight strong winds and light rain. The royal party arrived in Cambridge by train just after mid-day. They were taken by horse-drawn carriages to the Great Court in Trinity, where at two o'clock they were welcomed by more than 2,000 members of the University who had assembled there. In a letter to Miss Kate Stanley, sent five days after the event, Adam described how, "while the Queen was refreshing the inner woman, and preparing her dress", the great and the good – Noblemen, Heads of Colleges, Doctors, and Professors – processed into the College Hall to be presented to the Queen. Adam had a good view as she passed by, and he thought Prince Albert

9. Royal Connections

"was looking well and happy. … it is plain that the royal pair love one another." After the formalities were completed, the party walked along to the Chapel in King's College, where Adam had a seat in the Choir, which gave him another clear view of the Queen.

The plan had been for the Queen to then return to Trinity College and visit the Library, but instead she "retired to rest, and slept soundly in the state-bed" in the college. Adam had offered the Master the use of his rooms during the royal visit, which were adjacent to the State Apartments in the College Lodge. His dining room was used by the Queen's ladies-in-waiting to store her clothes, and as a result his "walls, walls, floor, chairs, and tables were covered with the gorgeous and costly trappings of royalty" during the royal visit. Everything was later "returned to its old place", and he found himself "in solitude, among ill-arranged papers, sometimes listening to the [ticking of the] clock, at other times turning my ear to the melancholy murmuring of my dirty tea kettle."

Astronomer Royal Sir George Airey visited Adam on the Thursday morning, and they had a chat about the alignment of the stars. Shortly afterwards Adam was told that Prince Albert hoped to visit the Museum of Geology straight after a ceremony at which he would be awarded an Honorary Degree. The museum visit was unexpected, so Adam hurried to clear the route to it of clutter before "a goodly red carpet" was put down. He checked that the inside of the museum was tidy, before running to the Senate House in time to see the Prince receive his degree, then racing back to the museum to greet the Queen on her arrival. He was pleased with how the visit went; he described to Kate Stanley how "the Queen seemed happy and well-pleased … The subject [geology] was new to her, but the Prince evidently had a good general knowledge of the old world [earth history]; and not only asked good questions, and listened with great courtesy to all I had to say …".

Prince Albert

Tory politician and British aristocrat Hugh Percy, the 3rd Duke of Northumberland, was elected Chancellor of the University of Cambridge in 1840. The Chancellor is the non-residential ceremonial head and works closely with the Vice-Chancellor who is the executive head. The Duke served with distinction but his death seven years later, at the age of 61, created a vacancy which had to be filled.

William Whewell, Master of Trinity College, was in London on business at the time of the death in early February 1847, leaving Adam Sedgwick responsible for overseeing matters within the College in his role as Vice-Master. Many senior figures in the University hoped that Prince Albert could be persuaded to allow his name to go forward for the post, and to be elected unopposed. Their first wish came true but not the second one – the Prince was reluctant but willing to stand, with much encouragement from Sedgwick, but members of St John's College encouraged the Earl of Powys to stand against him, making an election necessary. Adam was a strong supporter of Prince Albert but knew that, as Vice-Master, he would have to act with strict neutrality. Polling took place over a three-day period, and the Prince won the election and accepted the post.

Secretary to Prince Albert
Shortly after his election as Chancellor, Albert invited Adam to be his Secretary at Cambridge. The two men saw eye to eye on many things and realised they should be able to work effectively together, for the benefit of the University.

Adam accepted the invitation, which marked the beginning of a close and successful working relationship between himself and both the Queen and her Prince Consort. As Clark and Hughes put it, in rather gushing language, Adam "was animated by a chivalrous loyalty to the throne and the person of the Queen; and it gave him infinite pleasure, in the evening of his life, to feel that he could in any way make himself of use to her husband."

Adam saw serving the monarch as a privilege rather than a chore. The workload turned out to be much higher than he had imagined, and it left him with little time to pursue his geological interests, but that was a price he was willing to pay.

By early May 1847 we find Adam hard at work on his new duties as Secretary to the University Chancellor, visiting the Prince in London to help with the preparations for "the Public Commencement" at which he was to preside. Two months later Adam accompanied Prince Albert and his guest Charles Frederick, Grand Duke of Saxe-Weimar-Eisenach, at the Oxford meeting of the British Association.

Installation as Chancellor
At the start of July Adam was called to London with the Vice-Chancellor to finalise arrangements for the installation of Prince Albert as Chancellor. They met in Buckingham Palace, and as well as explaining "matters of Academic form – degrees etc." to Prince Albert, Adam had to write numerous letters on behalf of the Chancellor, including one inviting Sir

Harry Smith to attend the Installation ceremony in Cambridge, where the Queen wished to present him with an honorary degree.

Smith was a well-known English soldier and military commander in the British army, who had a long history of distinguished service in war zones, including the Napoleon Wars and wars in North and South America, South Africa and India. After receiving the degree, he returned to South Africa to serve as Governor of Cape Colony and High Commissioner in South Africa, a post he was to hold until 1852.

The Prince was formally installed as Chancellor of the University of Cambridge on the 6th of July 1847. The previous day he had presided over the ceremony in the Senate House at which Sir Harry Smith was awarded his honorary degree. Adam was looking after the Prince throughout, and sat directly behind him. After the ceremony the pair visited several colleges. The Senate House was packed for the Prince's Installation Ceremony where, after singing God Save the Queen, the assembled crowd gave three very hearty cheers. The Royal couple were guests of honour at a formal dinner that evening in Trinity College, at which Adam Sedgwick sat at one end of Top Table beside the Duke of Wellington. He was able to enjoy the honour of a brief conversation with Queen Victoria in the drawing room after dinner.

Visits to Royal residences

After Adam was appointed Secretary to Prince Albert at Cambridge, he enjoyed numerous visits to the Royal residences to spend time with him on official university business.

His first visit to Osborne House on the Isle of Wight came in December 1847, six months after the Installation Ceremony. He was invited there by the Queen who hoped he would be able to offer them advice on the prospect of being able to secure a good supply of fresh water by boring a well into the rocks below the estate. The Queen had only purchased Osborne a few years earlier, but the house had already been enlarged and greatly improved.

Adam was struck by how informal the visit was, and how comfortable Queen Victoria seemed to be in her island retreat. He wrote to his niece Isabella about how amused he was "at seeing carts, toys, and other signs of young children, scattered about the hall in considerable confusion." He noted how "the Queen in public life is the most punctual of womankind; but here, in private, she is more irregular. She drives [in a horse-drawn coach] about the grounds in all weathers and sometimes returns late. ... We had a very good, but not an ostentatious, dinner. ...The conversation was general and cheerful, without the shadow of any formality either seen or felt." He told Isabella how, the following day, he and Prince Albert walked through the estate and looked at some quarries, before returning to Albert's study where they poured over a geological map of the island and discussed possible sites for a well. The conversation then turned to the studies of the University, which convinced Adam that Prince Albert had "the deepest interest in the wellbeing of Cambridge." He described him as "a well-read man, whose mind is admirably cultivated in many departments of learning little studied by our young noblemen .... Our discussions lasted nearly two hours." The Prince's understanding of the university was doubtless enhanced by reading the fifth (1850) edition of Adam's *Discourse*, which Adam had instructed his London bookseller to send to the Prince at Balmoral.

Adam also spent time with Victoria and Albert at Windsor Castle, in early February 1851. He wrote to Isabella that "everything went off as smooth as silk; everybody seemed perfectly comfortable and at his ease and the Queen seemed the merriest and happiest of the whole party. She looks the picture of good health ...".

He returned to Osborne House in July 1852 to discuss the *Report of the Commissioners for Oxford* with Prince Albert. Again, we hear of the trip through his letter to Isabella the same month. He described for her a walk he had taken in the park, where he played ball with Victoria's young son Prince Arthur, "a very fine merry child". He told her how much he loved the Isle of Wight "because I have worked through all corners of it, hammer in hand; and because I have spent in it some of the happiest days of my life. ... Everything here is unostentatious – no bands of music, no soldiers. There is a policeman at the gate of the Park, and at the landing-place; with this exception there is nothing here that much differs from a private gentleman's house. ... We had a good dinner, but not by any means an ostentatious one. The wines I never tasted, as I found at my elbow a bottle of seltzer water with a little brandy in it, which you know is my best beverage. I acted as chaplain. The Queen is in excellent health, and in joyous spirits."

One trip that particularly impressed Adam was one he took to Balmoral in September 1859. He described it in some detail in a letter to Mrs Richard Sedgwick (wife of his nephew Richard) later that month; "The Castle is new, but in excellent taste. It stands in a beautiful park surrounded by wild Highland mountains. The Prince wore the full Highland costume, bare knees and kilt; so did the Prince of Wales and Prince Arthur. The Queen did look happy and well. She and her three daughters wore the Stuart tartan, and each had the Highland scarf with the buckle on the left shoulder. ... We had a muster of the clans, each coming in full costume, headed by its chieftain, and attended by its bag-piper. The sight was beautiful and striking, but the skirling pipes were a dire ear-torment ... When all was ready the Queen took her place upon a terrace, and then a succession of games began: foot-races; tossing the sledge-hammer; tossing the bar etc.; ending with Highland reels. Then we had a lunch in the ballroom. Everything was beautifully and amply prepared. For my share I secured a very large basin of plain Scotch broth ... and I then had the wing of a chicken and a glass of sherry."

Death of Prince Albert (1861)
Adam's closeness to the royal family came to an end in December 1861 with the unexpected death of Prince Albert, from typhoid fever, at the age of 42, at Windsor Castle. He was buried nine days later in St George's Chapel in the Castle. A year later his body was reinterred a mile away, in the Royal Mausoleum at Frogmore House. The death of her beloved Albert plunged Victoria into deep mourning which lasted until she died 40 years later, in 1901.

In early February 1862 Adam wrote to his niece Isabella to tell her that the Queen had sent him two large lithographic drawings of herself and Prince Albert, and a note saying "By Command of Her Majesty the Queen. *In Memoriam*. Osborne, January, 1862."

It triggered a sincere reflection by Adam of the royal charge he was honoured to serve. He wrote "what a glorious example the Prince set to all right-minded Englishmen! He was a man of an astonishing range of information. On the subjects he had handled (and there were few subjects of literary, scientific, artistic, and economical interest which he had not studied well) he was never superficial. His knowledge was not merely extensive, but profound. He had almost incredible industry; ... great benevolence, and wisdom, and love of truth. ... sweet manners and a noble presence. ... He always treated me as if I were his equal; and encouraged me to speak frankly to him, just as if he had been my personal friend and equal ...".

PART THREE. ROCK MAN

When Adam Sedgwick was appointed Woodwardian Professor of Geology at Cambridge in 1818 "a general notion prevailed – agreeing closely with old Dr. Woodward's theory, who founded the chair – that all fossils were the result of a universal Deluge which had once swept over the whole earth, and to the agency of which all the strata owed their origin. For notwithstanding the writings of Werner, Hutton, and Playfair, William Smith, and others, already in existence, only the key-notes of geological science had as yet been touched, and it was needful that the patient labours of many such men should accumulate for years before the full chord of geological harmonies could be evoked."
Anonymous biography of Adam Sedgwick in the *Geological Magazine* (1870)

10. Geology before Sedgwick

"When Adam Sedgwick first assumed the Professorial gown, little was known in England of geology as a science."
Obituary to Adam Sedgwick in *The Times* (28 January 1873)

In this chapter, we'll review the state of geological thinking at the start of Adam's career as Professor of Geology, and consider some important ways in which it informed and shaped much of the work he did in the subject.

Birth of geology

Whilst humans have had an interest in the lie of the land and been puzzled about what lay beneath it since time immemorial, it is only in recent centuries that serious thought has been given to how best to find out. As Alan Smith (2001) points out, before about 1800 "in many areas of Britain and Europe, collecting rock and mineral specimens, recording of fossil remains, portraying the rock outcrops and their structures and extolling the scenic wonders of the area had long been pursued." This reflected an interest in natural history and was usually done by enthusiastic amateurs.

The Age of Reason
The term "geology", derived from the Greek *geo* (meaning earth) and *logia* (the study of), was first used by an English writer in 1661.

Modern geology emerged as a branch of science in the seventeenth century, as science emerged from Natural Philosophy during the Enlightenment. The Age of Reason brought new ways of looking at and thinking about the world around us. As scientists began to study and understand the Earth, they collected hard facts and measurements, and collated their observations into a structured system of knowledge. In this way, modern astronomy emerged at roughly the same time as modern geology and modern biology.

But those early scientists went further than just collecting and collating facts. In interpreting what they were seeing, measuring and collecting, they abandoned speculation based on faith – the approach used by their predecessors – and insisted upon reasoning based on observation. Doug-las Robson (1986) notes how, "in the earlier decades of the eighteenth century, men were just beginning to record the fact that some of the rocks which outcrop on the earth's surface present a succession of alternating layers of varying types of material. ... it was only towards the close of that century that evidence began to be linked with the fossils such rocks contain."

Scriptural geology
In the period before the emergence of modern science, a number of men proposed *Theories of the Earth* in attempts to explain how the earth and its rocks had been formed. These early *Theories* were informed more by the Biblical narrative about creation and the Great Flood, as described in Genesis, than by what could be seen in the field. The most famous of the early theorists was Nils Steenson, better known as Nicolaus Steno (1638-1686) or simply Steno.

Steno was born in Copenhagen in 1638. He studied medicine and became physician to the Grand Duke of Tuscany in Florence. But he was very keen on walking through the countryside, hiking over hills, and vis-iting quarries throughout the region. He wrote a geological history of Tuscany, the first geological history of its kind, which he thought would apply across the whole earth. His interpretations were heavily influenced by a firm belief that all rocks everywhere had been formed, and were still being formed, by settling out from fluids. Without speculating on when or how it all started, he identified six phases or epochs in the formation of the earth:

1. Sea covered the surface of the earth and rocks were deposited without any trace of life;
2. Land was raised above the sea, and dry land appeared;
3. Mountains and hills appeared on the plain, after valleys were "eaten out by the force of fires or waters";
4. Sea level continued to rise, and filled the valleys with sandy sed-iments that contained many different types of fossil;
5. Sea level rose and land re-appeared, across which ran rivers that deposited mud, that progressively built up deltas and the plains, forcing the sea to retreat back again;
6. The plains were then lifted up and worn down, while rock strata were destroyed by subterranean fires, allowing the rocks at the surface to break up and in turn create new hills and valleys.

Steno was a devout Lutheran who later converted to Catholicism, and his geological interpretations were informed by and consistent with the Biblical account of creation, as told in Genesis. He looked on his work as his Christian responsibility to investigate the wonders of God's creation. He subsequently lost interest in geology and medicine, took holy orders, and was made a Bishop.

In 1650 James Ussher, Archbishop of Armagh, used the genealogy of people listed in the Old Testament to calculate when the earth had been created; he reckoned it was on the 23rd of October, 4004 BC. Nearly five decades later, in 1696, William Whiston calculated that Noah's Flood had started on the 18th of November 2349 BC. He believed it was caused by a great downpour triggered by the passage of a comet's tail across the equator, at the same time that an "abyss of internal waters" broke out and swept over the surface of the land.

In 1695 John Woodward, benefactor of the Professorship of Geology to which Adam Sedgwick was appointed in 1818 (who we looked at in Chapter 7), published *An Essay toward a Natural History of the Earth and Terrestrial Bodies, especially Minerals*. Like Steno and other early geologists, Woodward is silent on the question of how and when the earth had formed, but the initial part of his explanation conforms to the biblical creation narrative. He imagined the centre of the earth to be a spherical cavity filled with water, which burst out onto the surface at the time of Noah's flood. Whilst the creation narrative leaves things there, Woodward imagined the impact the flood would have had on the surface of the earth. First, he suggested that "the whole Terrestrial Globe was taken all to pieces and dissolved" by the floodwaters. Then "Stone, and all other solid Minerals, lost their solidity, and … the sever'd Particles thereof, together with those of the Earth, Chalk, and the rest, as also Shells, and all other Animal and Vegetable Bodies, were taken up into, and sustained in, the Water;". Finally, he imagined that "all these [materials] subsided again promiscuously" – they settled to the bottom of the water – "and without any other order than that of the different specific Gravity of the several Bodies in this confused Mass, those which had the greatest degree of Gravity sinking down first, and so settling lowest; then those Bodies which had a lesser degree of Gravity fell next, and settled so as to make a Stratum upon the former; and so on, in their several turns, to the lightest of all, which subsiding last, settled at the Surface, and covered all the rest."

Put simply, he believed that the heaviest material settled out of suspension in the water first, then progressively finer material settled out, leaving distinct layers (strata) of rock beneath the water. Woodward believed that all of the rocks on and below the earth's surface had been formed straight after the Flood, as a result of it. He rejected any suggestion that there might even have been "Changes and Alterations in the Terraqueous Glob" since "the Deluge", except minor ones caused by human activity, like mining or quarrying.

In 1756, a century after Steno published his *Theory of the Earth,* a similar *Theory* was proposed by German scientist Johann Lehmann, who became Director of the Imperial Museum in Moscow from 1761 to his death six years later. Lehmann believed that the earth had begun as a vast drop of water in which muddy particles were uniformly dispersed, without speculating about when and how it had formed. Like Steno and Woodward, he adopted a Biblical framework for explaining what happened next. At the point of creation the mud settled, creating a shell around the water, the high parts of which became islands and continents, as the remaining water drained into an abyss within the shell. At a much later date a universal flood – the Deluge of Noah – covered the whole surface of the earth, washed sediments from the mountains, and deposited them along the shoreline. Other rock formations appeared later, some deposited by later floods and others having flowed out from the earth's interior as lava flows, or been thrown out by volcanic eruptions.

These early ways of describing and accounting for rocks and landscapes were all consistent with the Biblical creation narrative, and they neither challenged nor were challenged by theologians of the time. The early explanations were based on a Biblical timescale and the unquestioned assumption of divine creation. That was, after all, God-given truth against which all else would have to be judged. The Genesis account was to be accepted literally – a young earth (probably less than 5 or 6,000 years old), created instantly (over a 7-day period), in its final form (with no change since then), by divine instruction. It was all God's handiwork.

By the late eighteenth century, as a result of more "scientific" research by many people in many places, geology was starting to move beyond the Biblical creation narrative, and it seemed poised to embrace new ways of interpreting what geologists were finding. Old interpretations of fossils as living things buried by Noah's Flood were being discredited, evidence of order in the rock layers and the fossils within them was accumulating from many areas, as was evidence that rocks are generally found in distinct groups or assemblages. It was also becoming clear that some parts of the earth's crust had been lifted up by earthquakes, that volcanoes had been active in the past, and that basalts were the result of volcanic eruptions. Evidence was also emerging that the rocks of the Alps appeared to have been compressed and altered. A better understanding of the importance of erosion in shaping the landscape was also emerging, along with a growing awareness of the importance of time in understanding the processes and results of geological change.

A more systematic approach to the study of earth history was emerging towards the end of the eighteenth century and into the early years of the nineteenth century. As Alan Smith (2001) notes, "gradually it was being realized that within the rocks themselves, the minerals, the fossils and the nature of the landscape was a coherent record of earth events awaiting to be deciphered."

In the decades leading up to Adam Sedgwick's appointment as Professor of Geology at Cambridge, two major schools of thought emerged within the subject – Catastrophism and Uniformitarianism. Each had its own distinctive *Theory of the Earth*, and each helped to shape Sedgwick's own thinking, approach to research, and ways of explaining what he saw, found and read.

Catastrophism

Catastrophism is the theory that the Earth has been affected in the past by sudden, short-lived, violent events – catastrophic natural disasters that were possibly global in scale. The term was coined by William Whewell in his book *History of the Inductive Sciences* (1837).

Abraham Gottlob Werner (1787)

One of the first modern *Theories of the Earth*, which strongly influenced Sedgwick's early understanding of geology, was proposed by Abraham Gottlob Werner in 1787.

Werner (1749-1817) was born in Russian Silesia (now Poland), the son of an iron works inspector. He studied law and mining in Freiberg (in Saxony, Germany) and Leipzig, and returned to Freiberg in 1775 at the age of 25 to work as an inspector of mines and teacher of mining and mineralogy. For a number of decades he was the most influential geologist in Europe, a towering figure at a time when the subject (in common with the other natural sciences) was beginning to replace speculation with knowledge.

He was confident and assertive in all he did, to the extent of even refusing to use the term *geology* (meaning literally 'earth discourse') which, as Fenton and Fenton (1952) explain, he dismissed as "a pretentious structure of speculation about the origin and early history of our planet. Such nonsense was anathema to … [a man] whose goal was order and good, solid fact without trace of theory or guesswork." Instead, he referred to his subject as *geognosy*, meaning 'earth knowledge'.

Werner never described his work as a *Theory of the Earth* because he insisted that he dealt only with facts, and his work was not theoretical. His objective was to create an earth science that could be taught as fact, based on definite knowledge that involved no speculation and was beyond debate – hence his insistence on *geognosy* rather than *geology*.

Despite his insistence in dealing with *knowledge* rather than *discourse*, the roots of Werner's ideas can clearly be traced to Lehmann's *Theory*. He accepted without question Lehmann's assumption that, somehow, the earth had started as a giant water-covered ball on which solid material was deposited while the liquid disappeared. Werner's school of thought was called Neptunism, after Neptune the Roman god of the sea, because he was convinced that all rocks had settled out of waters that at one time had flooded the surface of the whole earth.

Werner was not short of ambition. At the age of thirty-eight, having travelled little beyond his home town and having read little about developments across the natural sciences, he boldly claimed to be able to tell the story of the whole earth from its very beginning, based only on his observations around Freiberg. There he identified four formations (mappable units, that he called *Gebirge*) of rocks. He assumed, rather rashly and arrogantly, that the formations and his interpretation of their geological history would be universal and apply to all places everywhere.

The first and oldest formation was what he called the Primitive (*Uranfängliche Gebirge*) or Primary Series, which forms the core of mountain ranges and is found below the other series. These are the densest kinds of rock on Earth, and include granites, slates, basalts, some marbles, and schist. Werner assumed they had formed when the heaviest particles settled first on the bed of the deep sea, where they solidified, during the earliest times before dry land appeared after the global flood. He concluded that these rocks, which contain metallic ores but bear no trace of life, date back to the very creation of the Earth. Geologists today would explain some of them (granite and basalt) as igneous rocks, formed by the cooling and solidification of lava or magma, and others (slate, marble and schist) as metamorphic rocks, formed by the transformation of existing rocks by great heat and pressure.

Above the Primitive formation, and younger than the Primary rocks, lay the Secondary rocks. Werner called this the *Flötz Gebirge*, meaning literally 'flood-deposited formations'. These included limestones, sandstones, conglomerates, chalk, gypsum, shale and coal. Many of these stratified (layered) rocks contained fossils, but Werner was unable to say what they were. He believed that, like the Primary rocks, much of this material had settled in the ancient sea, but coarse fragments within it had been worn from the Primitive mountain ranges. In this way, he looked on the secondary rocks as preserving evidence of more than one phase of deposition, not just the original act of creation.

Above the Secondary formation, and even younger than it, lay what Werner called the *Aufgeschwemmte Gebirge*, literally the '*swept-together*' formation. It comprised sedimentary deposits including gravel, sand, clay and soil that now cover much of the land surface. Some historians of geology refer to this as the Alluvial formation.

A few other geologists had described another separate group of volcanic rocks (ash and lavas), but Werner included them as part of his 'Alluvial' formation under the heading *Vulkanische Gebirge*. He believed that volcanic strata were neither common nor extensive, and he explained them as the result of coal beds deposited in the *Flötz Gebirge*, that had somehow burst into flames underground. He thought of them all as young rocks.

Later he named, in his teachings but not in print, a new formation that he called the Transition rocks (*Übergangs Gebirge*). These consisted of greywackes (dark, coarse-grained sandstones), limestone and trap rocks (basalts) that sat on top of the Primitive rocks. Werner believed that, once these rocks started to appear above the receding waters of the flood, the Earth became habitable and the first life appeared, as shown in the fossils found in these rocks.

He thought that, after the Primitive and Transition rocks were formed, the water suddenly rose over them again to a great height; when it subsided again, it left them covered in many places with a new formation of rocks, consisting of sandstone, conglomerates, limestone, gypsum, chalk and rock salt ... the *Flötz Gebirge*. Since then, the wearing down of the rocks by the activity of weather and other natural processes, and the washing away of the worn materials by rain and streams, have formed soil, gravel, sand, peat and other beds ... the *Aufgeschwemmte Gebirge*.

Werner had no doubt that his explanations were the right ones, even though 'facts' appeared that did not fit his 'model'. Rather than change the model he looked for ways of explaining away the discrepancies. This is why he inserted a Transition Formation between the Primitive and *Flötz* Formations. It also explains why he moved columnar basalt from the Primitive into the *Flötz*, and why, when young granites and porphyries were discovered which could not be Primitive, he had to squeeze them into the *Flötz*. It's why he insisted that what we now know are great faults in the Alps were in fact relatively small cracks caused by pressure differences at or near the surface of the Earth.

Perhaps Werner's *pièce de résistance* was his supposition, when challenged by other geologists to explain how the deep ocean in Primitive times had mysteriously drained away, that much of the atmosphere and water on the early Earth had been captured by some other celestial body. It didn't seem to trouble him, either, when some of his contemporary disciples reintroduced water across the surface of the Earth to explain how basalt had been deposited in *Flötz* times on the young mountains made of sandstone, limestone and shale.

Werner's ambition to free natural science from speculation by replacing theories with facts was well intended but ultimately beyond his means The only way he could convince himself, and for a time many other geologists, that he was dealing only with facts and not with theories (even theories of his own making) was through what Fenton and Fenton (1952) describe rather generously as "intellectual evasions".

Werner's debt to Johann Lehmann, who had earlier suggested the Primary, Secondary and Alluvial formations, is very clear. His interpretation of earth history was consistent with what the Bible said – the earth was relatively young (no more than thousands of years old), all rocks had been deposited in a flood that had once covered the whole earth, and the earth's surface had changed relatively little since then – although Werner made no attempt to correlate his history of the rocks with Biblical chronology.

Unlike other leading natural scientists of his time, he never wrote a major book to promote his ideas. Instead, he outlined them in a 28-page booklet that was published in 1787. As well as the lectures he gave to his own students, he gave informal lectures over a 26-year period that attracted the attention of many natural scientists, but he never wrote his ideas down in detail. Nonetheless, he influenced the thinking of a generation of geologists, including Adam Sedgwick in his early years as a Professor of Geology.

Georges Cuvier (1813)

Many early nineteenth century geologists were also influenced by the work of Georges Cuvier (1769-1832). Leopold Chrétien Fréderic Dagobert Cuvier was the son of a lieutenant in the Swiss Guard. After being home-schooled by his mother, he excelled in secondary school and at the Caroline Academy in Stuttgart. He had a long-standing interest in natural history, became a leading French naturalist and zoologist, and was elected a member of the French Academy of Sciences in 1796.

Through his work in comparing living animals with fossils, he is sometimes referred to as the "father of palaeontology", the scientific study of fossil animals and plants. He played a key role in developing the use of fossils in unravelling geological history.

As part of a wide body of work in natural history, he wrote two very influential papers in 1796 that changed the way scientists understood the importance of fossils and how they interpreted them. One was about the skeletal remains of Indian and African elephants, and mammoth fossils. The other was about a large skeleton found in Paraguay, which he named *Megatherium*. He believed that it represented an extinct animal and, by comparing its skull with those of living species of tree-dwelling sloths, he concluded that it was a kind of ground-dwelling giant sloth. This was a ground-breaking discovery, because at that time it was generally believed that no species of animal had ever become extinct.

Cuvier's research had confirmed, for the first time, the reality of extinction. But he went further, because his fossil findings led him to conclude that at least some species had become extinct in response to abrupt changes on the Earth's surface over very long periods of time. This would add to the growing challenge to scriptural geology that was by then building across Europe.

Cuvier's theory on extinction was not universally welcomed at the time. Other natural scientists, most notably Charles Darwin and Charles Lyell, believed in extinction but thought of it as a gradual rather than a sudden process. They believed that, like the Earth itself, animals progressively change as a species, over a very long period of geological time.

As an active proponent of the Catastrophism school of geology, Cuvier favoured more dramatic changes over much shorter timescales. He explained many of the geological features of the Earth, and the history of life on Earth, as the result of catastrophic events that had caused the extinction of many species of animals. Whilst he was convinced about extinction, he strongly opposed the theories of evolution – or transmutation, as it was then called – being proposed by his French contemporaries the naturalists Jean-Baptiste de Lamarck (1744-1829) and Geoffroy Saint-Hilaire (1771-1844). Cuvier believed there was no evidence for evolution; he could find no evidence in the geological record of one fossil form gradually changing into a different fossil form. Instead, as he suggested in his *Essay on the Theory of the Earth* (1813), new species appear to have been created after periodic catastrophic events such as global floods.

As a result of his detailed scientific studies of fossils, Cuvier concluded that the Earth had not been shaped by just one catastrophe (such as the Biblical Flood) but by several major ones, each resulting in a different group of animal species. Working with his colleague Alexandre Brognant on the different rock strata in the Paris Basin, Cuvier established the basic principles of biostratigraphy (the use of fossils in dating rock formations), based on identifying distinct and characteristic fossil shell remains in individual beds of limestone. This approach would prove invaluable in helping subsequent geologists, including Adam Sedgwick, to correlate rock strata within and between areas, and to unravel the geological history of those areas.

William Buckland (1823)
Another man who left an indelible mark on geological thinking in the early nineteenth century was William Buckland (1784-1846). He was born in Axminster, Devon, the son of the Rector of Templeton and Trusham, and after being schooled in Tiverton and Winchester, in 1801 he won a scholarship to Corpus Christi College, Oxford. He was a model student and graduated with the degree of Bachelor of Arts in 1804. Four years later he was elected to a college Fellowship and ordained priest.

Buckland had been interested in natural history since childhood, and he developed it further during his Fellowship years when he travelled widely on horseback throughout England, Scotland, Ireland, and Wales studying the landscapes and rocks. He was also an enthusiastic collector of rocks. In 1813 he was appointed Reader of Mineralogy at Oxford, where his duties included giving lectures and developing the collections in the geology museum. From 1816 onwards he undertook a number of geological excursions in Europe, including visits to Germany, Poland, Austria, Italy, Switzerland, and France. As well as providing opportunities to add to the rock collections, these trips allowed him to meet leading scientists and natural historians in different countries, greatly broadening his intellectual horizons as well as his social network.

Buckland's experience and reputation as a geologist continued to grow, and in 1819 he was appointed Reader in Geology (as well as Reader in Mineralogy) in Oxford. The following year he published his inaugural lecture as a book – *Vindiciae Geologiae; or the Connexion of Geology with Religion explained* – in which he demonstrated the compatibility of geological evidence with Biblical accounts of creation and No-ah's Flood. The book cemented Buckland's reputation as a leading scriptural geologist of his day.

His reputation was further enhanced by a detailed study he made in 1821 of a collection of old animal bones that had been discovered in a cave near Kirkdale in the Yorkshire Dales. He visited the cave, studied its contents, and identified what animals the bones belonged to. He listed 23 species, including elephant, rhinoceros, hippopotamus, horse, ox, deer, hyena, tiger, bear, wolf, fox, rodents and birds ... some of which lived in tropical areas, others in much colder places.

Caves containing bone collections had previously been discovered in other places, that were assumed to be the remains of animals that had been drowned in the Flood and carried from their original homes in the tropics by the floodwaters. Buckland challenged this interpretation. He noted that many of the bones in Kirkdale were from hyenas, and a great number of the other bones were very splintered and bore the teeth-marks of hyenas. This led him to conclude that hyenas had lived in the cave be-fore the Flood; they had dragged the carcasses of their victims into the cave and eaten them there; the Flood had subsequently covered the bones, where they lay, with a layer of mud. The evidence from Kirkdale cave figured prominently in Buckland's 1823 book *Reliquiae Diluvianae; or Observations on the Organic Remains attesting to the Action of a Univer-sal Deluge*, in which he argued that such evidence threw light on the character of the Earth and the creatures that lived on it before the Flood, as described in Genesis.

Buckland was elected President of the Geological Society in 1824. At his very first meeting in the chair he announced the discovery at Stonesfield, near Oxford, of the bones of a giant reptile that he named *Megalosaurus*, meaning "great lizard". His paper about it, published that year, is the first detailed account of what would later be called a dinosaur, after Richard Owen gave the name "terrible lizards" (*Dinosauria*) in 1842 to a group of animal remains then being unearthed in the South of Eng-land, that he believed formed a distinct taxonomic group.

Buckland resigned his college fellowship in 1825 when he was ap-pointed Canon of Christ Church in Oxford. But he still found time to continue much of his geological work, including giving his annual course of lectures in geology and palaeontology, which were very popular amongst students and senior members of the University. He also contin-ued to promote scriptural geology, expanding his 1820 *Vindiciae Geologiae* into a book in 1836 with the more mundane title *Geology and*

Mineralogy considered with reference to Natural Theology. It was part of the eight-volume Bridgewater Treatise that was published between 1833 and 1840, having been commissioned by the Earl of Bridgewater, a gentleman naturalist, to explore "the Power, Wisdom, and Goodness of God, as manifested in the Creation."

To the end, Buckland was committed to the belief – shared with Adam Sedgwick, William Conybeare and others – that geology should confirm the biblical texts. But, as we'll explore further in Chapter 14, as the nineteenth century progressed he increasingly found himself swimming against the tide of geological thinking. Some called him the "last great diluvialist", because he was convinced that a series of global floods, particularly Noah's Flood, could account for the extinction and emergence of species, and for most of the rocks and landforms on Earth.

Whilst Buckland was confident in his Biblically-based interpretation of geological features, in his later years he showed a willingness to embrace new ideas when the evidence was strong enough. This is clearly demonstrated in a trip he made to Switzerland in 1838 to meet Louis Agassiz, the well-respected innovative Professor of Natural History at University of Neuchâtel. The previous year, Agassiz had been the first scientist to propose that the Earth had been subject to a great Ice Age. Agassiz argued that, at some time in the relatively recent geological past, glaciers had flowed outward from the Alps and large ice sheets had simultaneously grown southward across the plains and mountains of Europe, Asia and North America, covering the entire northern hemisphere in thick ice for a long period of time.

Buckland travelled to Switzerland to examine for himself the polished and striated (scratched) rocks and deposits that Agassiz believed were the product of ancient glaciers. He started out sceptical of the whole idea, but soon found the evidence convincing, and became an enthusiastic supporter of the Ice Age theory. But he realized it was more than just a theory, and started to see great similarities between the evidence of glaciation in Switzerland and what he had observed in Scotland, Wales and Northern England.

In 1840 Agassiz was invited to attend the annual meeting of the British Association, held that year in Glasgow, where he read a paper about the action of glaciers and the deposits associate with them. He then joined Buckland on a field excursion to look at the evidence for former glaciation in Scotland, after which they returned to London and presented their findings to the Geological Society, of which Buckland was once again President. Few members of the Society were convinced about the arguments or the evidence put forward by Agassiz and Buckland, but Buckland was convinced that glaciers were the real origin of many of the surface deposits covering Britain. This was despite his earlier insistence that there were only two types of recent deposits – 'alluvium', the product of local river floods, and 'diluvium', the material deposited by the Great Flood – which he took to be material proof of the scriptural story of the destruction of life by Noah's Flood, as he had argued seventeen years earlier in *Reliquae diluviana*.

Buckland was appointed Dean of Westminster in 1845 and died in 1856.

Uniformitarianism

Uniformitarianism is the theory that all of the geological features on and beneath the surface of the earth have been created by natural processes (such as erosion and deposition), operating slowly and progressively over very long periods of time. William Whewell coined the term, as well as Catastrophism, in his book *History of the Inductive Sciences* (1837).

James Hutton (1785) Theory of the Earth

The Uniformitarian school of thinking within geology was started by James Hutton (1726-1797), who is widely regarded as the founder of modern geology.

Hutton was born in Edinburgh in 1726. His father, a successful merchant and treasurer of the city, died when James was young. But the family was financially secure and James was well educated. He trained in medicine and, after a brief career as a doctor, turned his hand to running the family farm he inherited. When he was about forty years old, he rented out the farm and established himself in Edinburgh as a gentleman of leisure, looked after by his three maiden sisters. He had plenty of time to discuss ideas with and learn from leading Scottish scientists such as geologist John Playfair, and mathematician and chemist Joseph Black.

As a young man Hutton was drawn to natural history, noting how soils were related to the rocks beneath them, and observing how the growth of crops was related to minerals in the soils and rocks.

As he toured around Scotland, he saw rocks that appeared to be slowly being dissolved by water seeping through them, and observed how rain falling on bare ground washed soils into rivers and wore deep gullies in hillsides. In Edinburgh, he was intrigued by Castle Rock that appeared to have been formed from molten rock that solidified underground, and by Arthur's Seat and Salisbury Crag that appeared to be remnants of a sheet of volcanic lava that had flowed out over the land surface. He was struck by the power of the Water of Leith (a major river that flowed westwards from Edinburgh) to wear down the land, exposing sections of tilted strata of great age. Further afield, he examined salt mines in Cheshire and iron mines near Birmingham, and studied basalts and granites in different parts of the country.

With time on his hands, Hutton was well-read in the geological thinking of his day, and was familiar with the work of many pioneers in the field, including de Saussure's studies of the rocks and glaciers in the Alps, and Desmarest's description of volcanic flows in the Auvergne region. His approach to everything he did was based on careful observation and rational thought, and he was particularly critical of Werner's speculation. Unlike many of his scientific peers, he felt no obligation to make his interpretations consistent with Biblical teaching. His observations in the field, coupled with an imaginative and deep-thinking mind, led him to develop geological interpretations that would have seriously offended disciples of Werner. However, unlike some of his peers, he did not rush into print but instead took his time forming and developing his own *Theory of the Earth.*

Hutton was one of the founding members in 1783 of the Royal Society of Edinburgh, and he read a summary of his ideas at one of its early meetings. It was more an essay than a full-blown paper, but its title – *Theory of the Earth; or an Investigation into the Laws Observable in the Composition, Dissolution, and Restoration of Land upon the Globe* – was clearly designed to attract attention. It was published in 1788 in the first volume of the society's *Transactions*, and won attention but received mixed responses. The most serious criticism came from Professor Richard Kirwan, a scriptural geologist from Dublin who accused Hutton of atheism. He argued that Hutton "had denied our earth a beginning ... and had made himself ridiculous by describing forces operating at the centre of our planet." He also dismissed as absurd Hutton's claim that coal was nothing more than a mass of plant remains, when it was obviously formed by the decay of granite and basalt which produced grains of bitumen and carbon that settled on the sea bed, from where they worked their way through the soft clay and gathered together in beds of coal.

Soon after his paper was published, and criticised by Kirwan, Hutton began to write a full-length *Theory of the Earth*, as friends had for years been urging him do. He was approaching seventy years old when the book appeared in 1795, in 2 volumes. It effectively launched the Uniformitarian school of geology. He spells out his central message in an early passage attacking Werner's ideas, where he writes "when a geologist shall indulge his fancy in framing, without evidence, that which had preceded the present order of things, then he either misleads himself, or writes a fable for the amusement of his reader. A theory of the earth ... can have no retrospect to that which had preceded the present order of the world; for this order alone is what we have to reason upon; and to reason without data is nothing but delusion."

The key words in that passage are "present order of the world" and "this order alone is what we have to reason upon". Hutton's central thesis – and the oft-repeated mantra of Uniformitarianism – is that "the present is the key to the past", meaning that in geology we can only understand the past by understanding present day processes. In a direct challenge to the Catastrophist idea that all rocks and surface features are the result of periodic large-scale catastrophic events, Hutton proposed a model based on natural processes operating slowly but progressively over long periods of time. As he put it "the natural operations of this globe, by which the size and shape of our land are changed, are so slow as to be altogether imperceptible to men", but given enough time they are capable of producing all of the rocks and landscapes we see in the world around us.

The principle of Uniformitarianism is based on three important things –

1. Natural processes that we see at work today (such as rain, rivers, waves, wind, volcanoes, earthquakes), with no need for divine intervention;
2. Very long time scales, much longer than the few thousands of years that scriptural geologists had assumed; and
3. Progressive development, the result of relatively slow processes operating over geological time, rather than one-off creation, with changes continuing to occur today. In essence, what we see today is a snap-shot from a continuous film of geological change.

Douglas Robson (1986) has suggested that Hutton's medical training might have given him the idea that "the earth, like the body of an animal, is wasted at the same time as it is repaired." Hutton's *Theory* assumes a continuous process of erosion and deposition of sediment, a constantly recycling Earth, in which rocks and deposits are weathered, material is washed away by rivers, deposits build up in the oceans, heat within the Earth promotes the uplift of new land and lateral movement of (what we now know as) crustal plates. Hutton identified three main sources of energy that drive this cyclical system – the internal heat of the earth, heat from the sun, and the force of gravity.

Hutton knew that the idea of progressive change over a vast period of time would be seriously challenged by other geologists, and he spent a great deal of time and effort searching for ways of proving it. A breakthrough moment came one day in 1787, when he was walking along the north shore of the Isle of Arran, off the west coast of Scotland. There, in the cliffs, he found an unusual pattern of rocks – the remnants of strata from one period of geological activity had clearly been lifted, folded, and heated (to form schist), then eroded over a long period of time (to create a flat, horizontal surface) and then overlain by strata from another period (horizontal beds of Red Sandstone). Geologists would later call this eroded surface an unconformity. Hutton would subsequently search for and find other examples of unconformities, in cliffs near Jedburgh in southeast Scotland, and more famously at Siccar Point on the Berwickshire coast east of Edinburgh. The evidence in each case pointed to a very old Earth, multiple cycles, and natural processes.

As well as replacing global catastrophes with natural processes, and removing the need to invoke divine intervention, Hutton's *Theory* avoids speculating about when or how the Earth began. He insisted that there was no way of telling how many cycles of change the Earth had gone through, or of knowing how old the Earth is, or predicting when it might end. As he wrote in the last sentence of his paper to the Royal Society of Edinburgh in 1788, "we find no vestige of a beginning, no prospect of an end", a catchy phrase that has become another mantra of Uniformitarianism.

Hutton died in 1797, two years after his *Theory of the Earth* was published. The book was not particularly well received, partly because many people found his writing style heavy going and his arguments difficult to follow. Hutton's ideas were new and controversial and, although admired by his friends, they were attacked by supporters of Werner and were not widely accepted in his day.

In many ways the book was ahead of its time, full of progressive thinking. But it appeared in a political climate marked by fear of revolution, soon after the American Revolution (1765-1783) and while the French Revolution (1789-1799) was still under way. It was ahead of its time in another way, too. As Caruthers and Clinton (2001) point out, "in the eighteenth century, not many people knew anything about geology. Although a few schools taught practical courses in mining, none offered geology classes. Geology was a pursuit for gentlemen-scholars, men with the intelligence, the leisure [time], and the resources to follow their interests in a serious way."

10. Geology before Sedgwick

Despite the lack of support for his ideas and interest in his book, Hutton opened up a new way of thinking about the history of the Earth that was to bear fruit in the decades after his death. His central thesis of progressive change by natural processes over vastly long periods of time would in turn inspire Charles Darwin's theory of the evolution of species by natural succession, as described in his 1859 *Origin of Species*.

But, before that could happen, Hutton's ideas had to be explained in a more accessible way and more engaging style. The challenge of doing that fell initially on the shoulders of one of his close acquaintances and supporters in Edinburgh.

John Playfair (1802) Illustrations of the Huttonian Theory of the Earth
John Playfair (1748-1819) was the son of a Scottish preacher, who from childhood had shown great ability in mathematics. He graduated from St Andrews University, was ordained, and in 1773 became vicar of two parishes made vacant by the death of his father. He continued to study mathematics and natural philosophy. In 1782 resigned his church post and was engaged as a tutor to Adam Ferguson, who became a noted Scottish philosopher and historian of the Scottish Enlightenment. That gave him time to make regular visits to Edinburgh and immerse himself fully in the literary and scientific society that was blossoming there at that time.

In 1785 Playfair was appointed Professor of Mathematics at the University of Edinburgh, switching in 1805 to become Professor of Natural Philosophy. His credentials for being offered that post included writing the book *Illustrations of the Huttonian Theory of the Earth*, which had been well received when it appeared in 1802.

After moving back to Edinburgh, he had spent much time walking and talking about geology with his friend James Hutton, and he devoted his holidays to geological excursions across Great Britain, Ireland, and parts of Europe. In fact, he appears to have travelled much more widely than Hutton, who seems never to have set foot outside mainland Britain. Extensive travel and skillful observation enabled Playfair to explain and extend Hutton's ideas, and illustrate them with suitable examples. Amongst other things, he gave better descriptions of what unconformities reveal about Earth history. He also described the uplift and folding of strata, the intrusive (sub-surface) origin of granites, and the process of erosion along lake shores. He was probably the first geologist to realise that large erratic boulders, found far away from their original sources, might have been transported by glaciers that have since melted away.

Through his *Illustrations* Playfair not only supported Hutton's Uniformitarian ideas, he clarified and developed them, and made them accessible to a wider audience. It is likely that, had Playfair not championed Hutton's work, it might well have languished in the dusty recesses of specialist libraries and become little more than a footnote in the history of modern geology.

If this story was a relay race, in which Hutton ran the first leg and then Playfair took over, he in turn handed the baton on to another Scottish scientist called Charles Lyell.

Charles Lyell (1830) Principles of Geology
The context within which geology operated changed a great deal in the decades after Playfair's *Illustrations* was published. By the 1820s there were more geologists working in the field, literally, including Adam Sedgwick, mapping, studying and collecting rocks in many different places across Britain and Europe. As a result, the volume of field evidence continued to rise, as did the need for a fresh synthesis of the new evidence, ideas and interpretations. The climate within which geology operated had also changed; suspicion of revolutionary ideas had been replaced by a new intellectual and political openness, and more liberal attitudes were developing about the interpretation of the biblical narrative of creation and the Flood. The great controversy concerning the origin of species in general, and of humans in particular, was then still three decades in the future.

The stage was set for the emergence of a new intellectual giant within geology, who could inject enthusiasm and imagination, along with objectivity and rationality, into the subject. Step forward Charles Lyell (1797-1875).

Lyell was born in 1797 in Kinnordy, north of Dundee in Scotland. His father, also called Charles, was a gentleman of means, a member of the landed gentry in Scotland whose income and home (Kinnordy Manor) were derived by inheritance. Charles junior was a bright youngster, but his schooling was often interrupted by poor health. He was admitted to Exeter College in Oxford in 1816, and graduated with the degree of Bachelor of Arts in Classics in 1819, and Master of Arts in 1821.

He had long been interested in natural history, was a keen observer and collector, and had attended a course in geology at Oxford given by William Buckland. He spent the summer vacation of 1817 examining volcanic rocks in Scotland, climbing the lava cliffs near Edinburgh with two friends, crossing the Grampian Mountains, and taking a boat ride to see for himself the newly discovered basalt columns in Fingal's Cave, a sea cave on the uninhabited Scottish island of Staffa. The following summer – at the same time that Adam Sedgwick was appointed Professor of Geology at Cambridge – Lyell joined his family on a three-month tour of Europe. While his parents and sisters enjoyed easy tourist trips, the budding geologist took full advantage of the opportunities to climb some mountains, walk across the Mer de Glace (a glacier near Chamonix), see at close quarters how water had soaked into the soil and caused an avalanche that buried fields and a village under tons of rock, and study the flood damage caused by alpine rivers swollen by ice melt.

After graduating he trained as a lawyer, entering Lincoln's Inn in London in 1820. He qualified as a barrister five years later. He spent half his time practicing law, but had a lot of time to pursue his geological interests, including studying rocks and fossils and attending meetings of the Geological Society of London. By 1827 he had abandoned a career in law and committed himself full-time to geology, made possible by the private means he inherited from his prosperous family.

His ambition was to write a book that would build on Hutton's ideas but go much further and offer a new synthesis of the fast-growing science of geology. To achieve that he would have to collect new information, include previously unstudied areas, and carefully review regions that had already been described. With that in mind in 1828 he took a trip to Europe with family friends the Murchisons (who we'll see more about in Chapter 11). The group left Paris in May and travelled by coach and on horseback, accompanied by Mrs Murchison's maid and Lyell's secretary. They worked long days, stayed in wayside inns, and by all accounts ate heartily. They returned to England early in 1829, and Lyell set to work on his book.

Lyell re-imagined Hutton's ideas for a more receptive audience, and he built on Playfair's *Illustrations of the Huttonian Theory of the Earth.* Through all his geological writing, he convinced scientists that Uniformitarianism was the proper way to study the Earth. Following Hutton's lead, he emphasised the present as the key to understanding the past, the cumulative effects of everyday processes operating over long periods of time, and the misguided thinking of the Catastrophists.

His first book *Principles of Geology* was published in three volumes, that appeared in 1830, 1832 and 1833. It opened with a historical outline of the progress of geology, continued with descriptions of all the processes that can be seen at work changing the surface of the Earth today, and closed with a summary of the distribution of plant and animal life on

Earth and a description of the sequence of organic forms revealed in the fossil record. By 1834 the first two volumes had been updated and the complete work appeared in a new edition with four volumes.

In 1838 the fourth volume of *Principles* was enlarged and published as a separate book *Elements of Geology*. In 1851 it was restructured as the *Manual of Elementary Geology*. *Elements* described the three groups of rocks (sedimentary, igneous and metamorphic), summarised the order in which the sedimentary rocks and their fossils had been deposited, discussed the age of the igneous (volcanic) rocks as determined from the strata with which they are generally associated, and discussed the varying ages of the metamorphic rocks in areas where they are associated with sedimentary rocks that could be dated by their fossil content.

Lyell's books influenced the thinking of many scientists, both at the time and subsequently. Not least of these was Charles Darwin, who was given a copy of Volume 1 of the first edition of *Principles* just before he set sail as naturalist on *The Beagle's* five-year expedition to South America in 1831, by the ship's captain Robert Fitzroy. Successive volumes were sent out to him, and he enthusiastically read them all. The book, as well as some field teaching in geology that Darwin had earlier received from Adam Sedgwick in Wales (as we will see in Chapter 11), helped him understand the geology and geological history of the places he visited on the voyage. He sent letters back to England describing some of the things he saw, and the ways in which he interpreted them.

From 1830 onwards Lyell was effectively a full-time writer; his reputation and main source of income both came from his books, each of which was regularly revised and updated. Whilst *Principles* was well-received, sold well, and influenced the thinking of many scientists of the time, it did have its critics. Werner, the high priest of Catastrophism, was by then dead but his many disciples – including Adam Sedgwick initially – were determined to keep his intellectual legacy alive. Buckland was still promoting Noah's Flood but adding two other global floods that carved valleys, floated huge boulders over great distances, and deposited 'diluvial' gravel over low-lying areas. Others, including the influential French geologist Jean-Baptiste Élie de Beaumont (1798-1874), continued to write about massive upheavals that raised whole mountain ranges virtually overnight. Others described catastrophic events, including violent volcanic eruptions and earthquakes.

Lyell's work definitely put Uniformitarian thinking on the map, but it was still competing with modern versions of traditional geological ideas. By the 1830s scriptural geology was on the decline, but it was still alive and kicking. The consensus in that school then was that periodic global catastrophes remodelled the Earth, wiping out all living things and preparing a stage for new divine creations to act upon. The end result was a series of geological periods separated by cataclysms and identified by groups of plants and animals that appeared when each period began and disappeared when it came to an end.

In 1831 Lyell was appointed Professor of Geology at King's College, London. The lectures he gave there were well prepared and attracted students as well as scientists, lawyers and gentlemen of leisure, often accompanied by their wives and sisters. He resigned from the chair in 1833 when the numbers registered for his classes dropped significantly, after the College closed them to women.

Charles Lyell received a knighthood in 1848, died on 22 Feb 1875 (2 years after Adam Sedgwick), and was buried in Westminster Abbey.

Field geology – mapping and stratigraphy
During the first three decades of the nineteenth century geology was a battleground between competing claims within the Catastrophism school (between the so-called Neptunists, who attributed large-scale changes to flooding, and the so-called Vulcanists, who argued that volcanic activity was more important), and between Catastrophism and the emerging Uniformitarianism. While these debates raged, and theoretical geology was pulled in different directions, great advances were being made in field geology.

Werner and Hutton – champions of Catastrophism and Uniformitarianism respectively – both divided Earth history into a series of periods, each one represented by a distinctive series of rocks that overlay others in the order in which they had formed. But neither of them had any reliable way of determining the actual age of individual strata, other than by their positions in a sequence; for rocks in their original positions this would provide a relative age – oldest at the bottom and youngest at the top. Neither were Hutton's followers able to arrange formations scattered across a region into one continuous series, which made it impossible to build a reliable picture of the geological history of that region from discontinuous evidence.

But a way of building up such a picture had already been worked out, by an industrious country surveyor and engineer who had been commissioned to plan the routes for the canals then being constructed in parts of England.

William Smith (1815)

William Smith (1769-1839) was born in Churchill, Oxfordshire, the son of a blacksmith called John Smith who died when William was eight years old. He was raised by his uncle, also called William Smith, and was largely self-taught but highly intelligent and observant. He became a surveyor's assistant at the age of eighteen, and four years later moved to Somerset. Part of his work there involved inspecting coal mines, where he first observed and recorded the layers of rock through which the mines had been sunk. He found that certain rocks were always found in a definite order, but the miners themselves disagreed with his finding.

At the age of twenty-five Smith was appointed surveyor and engineer for the Somerset Coal Canal. His work centred on surveying the land and choosing the best (cheapest) routes for the canal as it wound its way through hilly country. As he walked and rode on horseback over a wide area, exploring possible routes, he paid close attention to the underlying rocks as well as the land surface. Although he could only study rocks exposed at the surface, he noticed that all the strata (beds) he saw in that area appeared in the same sequence everywhere, and without exception they were not horizontal but tilted towards the south-east.

Parliament approved the building of the Somerset Canal in 1794, after which Smith was commissioned by the Directors of the company to study the construction and management of other inland waterways across England. He travelled more than nine hundred miles in a light horse-drawn carriage, noting how different rock formations reached the surface as they moved northwards, and learning to predict the rocks below from the surface conditions. For example, he noted that rolling meadows in that area were often underlain by chalk, and that damp pastures with willow trees were often underlain by clay. As he travelled around inspecting the canals, he stopped to examine bridges, locks and retaining walls, which also gave him opportunities to take a close look at the underlying rocks. He was employed for six years as engineer for the canal, carefully surveying its entire course and supervising the construction work.

Unlike the mainstream geologists of the day, Smith had little interest in developing a *Theory of the Earth* or speculating about when and how the rocks he was finding might have been formed. He was interested only in applied matters, and his focus was on collecting information in the field in a systematic way that could be put to practical uses. Smith's studies down the coal mines and along the canal routes gave him a unique set of vantage points showing how rocks are often found in recurring sequences, that were instrumental in shaping his theories of stratigraphy, the study of rock layers (strata) and layering (stratification).

His extensive field studies helped him to identify four important patterns –

1. The rock layers (strata) across an area were usually arranged in a predictable sequence;
2. The various strata could always be found in the same relative positions;
3. Each particular stratum could be identified by the fossils it contained; and
4. The same succession of fossil groups from older to younger rocks could be found in many parts of England.

Using the language of today's geologists, Smith's work focussed on the stratigraphic column, allowing him to build up an overlapping sequence of rocks across the country, and thus to correlate strata in different places. This suggested to him a Law of Superposition – sedimentary layers become progressively younger upwards through an undisturbed stratigraphic sequence.

In addition to the four general stratigraphic patterns outlined above, Smith's other major contribution to the development of modern geology was his new way of assigning relative dates to rock strata on the basis of the fossils they contained. He recognised that different layers of rock contained different sets of fossils and, more importantly, that these characteristic fossils occur in a regular series of layers. Smith accounted for this pattern as the result of all rock layers containing the same kinds of fossil having been deposited in the same period of time, when those particular creatures had lived. This new understanding opened up a very useful new way of correlating rock strata in outcrops scattered across a large area, even between different parts of the country, by their fossil content.

Smith realised how useful his method would be to other scientists, and in 1796 he planned to write a book about it. But life got in the way – he got married, and had little spare time as the work on his Coal Canal progressed. He was also discouraged by not being able to interest other people in his discoveries.

By the early 1800s, having made little progress on the book, he abandoned it. Instead, he turned his attention to producing the first geological map of England and Wales. He started work on that in 1813, and completed it two years later. The ground-breaking map bore the rather wordy title *A Delineation of the Strata of England Wales, with part of*

*Scotland; exhibiting the Collieries and Mines, the Marshes and Fen
Lands originally overflowed by the Sea, and the Varieties of Soil, according to the Variations in the Sub-strata; illustrated by the most descriptive
names.* The map was a work of art; it was huge (six feet by eight feet six
inches), highly detailed, and well engraved, with twenty colours applied
by hand. This made it very expensive, and put it beyond the means of
most individual people. In the end only 450 copies were sold, producing
little financial reward for either the writer or the publisher.

Despite the lack of a book, and the limited commercial success of
the map, Smith's contribution to scientific geology was widely recognised. In 1831 the Geological Society awarded him the first Wollaston
Medal, which (as we saw in Chapter 7) was presented to him by Adam
Sedgwick, who referred to him at the time as "the Father of British geology." Sedgwick adopted Smith's field methods in his own work, as we'll
see in Chapter 11.

The state of geological understanding in 1818
Before we look at Adam Sedgwick's own geological work, it is useful to
reflect on the state of geological understanding at the time he was appointed Professor of Geology in 1818. Pulling together the main points
arising from the work of other geologists before Sedgwick, it is fair to say
that when Sedgwick began his geological studies –

• There was no geological timescale. Indeed, the huge span of geological time had not yet been recognised and the Earth was generally
thought to be no more than 5,000 to 6,000 years old.
• There were no geological periods; what geologists observed was
simply described in relative terms (X is older or younger than Y), not
in absolute terms.
• Only rarely had individual layers of rock (strata) been grouped into
formations, each was typically described and explained separately.
• No systematic correlation of strata between countries had yet been
attempted, so there were no continental or world-wide interpretations
or models.
• The uppermost layers of gravel and pebbles were regularly attributed
to the Great Flood described in the book of Genesis in the Bible.
• Other changes of strata and most landforms were explained as the
result of catastrophic events, although the nature of the catastrophe
was often left unspecified; almost all geological changes were assumed to be rapid, short-term, violent and devastating.

- Scriptural geology, that accounted for everything in ways that were consistent with the biblical narrative of creation by God, was being seriously challenged by the emerging Uniformitarian school of geological thinking, but had yet to be generally replaced by it.
- It was generally accepted that fossils represented forms of past life, and that each rock layer contained characteristic and often unique fossils.
- The extinction of species was generally accepted but rarely emphasised, but there was no widely accepted theory of how or why extinction occurred.
- It was not clear how species originated, although the general idea that one kind of plant or animal could evolve into another (by 'transmutation') was almost universally rejected. It was generally believed that plants and animals had no ancestors, and humans had no predecessors.
- Most fossils then known were shells, assumed to have been buried by the Great Flood.
- Little was known about other invertebrate fossils (of animals without backbones); the fossil remains of only a few recently-extinct large mammals and a few Jurassic reptiles had by then been uncovered, and there were no generally agreed interpretations of either; no fossil dinosaurs or amphibians (aquatic vertebrates) had been discovered, and few fossil fish had yet been studied in detail.
- Almost nothing was known about rocks or fossils older than what geologists now call the Mesozoic Era (between 252 and 66 million years ago).
- Many of the important discoveries in geology still lay a century or more in the future, including the earth's core (1906) and inner core (1930s); continental drift (1911), sea-floor spreading (1950s and 60s), and plate tectonics (1960s); and periodic ice ages (1930s).

11. Mapping the Rocks

"There are no bad countries for geology – change your tools with your ground – keep your eyes wide open – and you may find a harvest everywhere – there are no barren fields to a true lover of nature."
Adam Sedgwick letter to Rev Brodie (May 1842)

Adam Sedgwick loved few things more than having the freedom to roam across the countryside looking at the rocks. His main focus as a geologist was on field mapping, using the stratigraphic approach that William Smith developed for correlating rock strata across areas and regions.

He worked in many parts of Britain and some parts of continental Europe, and often worked in more than one area in the same year or period of time.

Most of the areas that attracted his attention had one thing in common – they had complex geologies dominated by ancient sedimentary rocks that Sedgwick, a disciple of Werner (who we looked at in Chapter 10), described as Primary, Intermediate and Secondary. Today those rocks are described as belonging to the periods of geologic time (outlined in Appendix 1) from the Cambrian (541 to 485 million years ago), the Ordovician (485 to 444 million years ago), the Silurian (444 to 419 million years ago), the Devonian (419 to 359 million years ago) and the Carboniferous (359 to 299 million years ago) Periods or Systems.

This chapter is structured thematically rather than chronologically, in order to describe the main areas in which Adam pursued in fieldwork and to help us understand why he chose them. The main themes within the chapter are introduced in chronological order.

Field mapping
Adam's main responsibilities as Woodwardian Professor of Geology at Cambridge were to give lectures and to maintain and build the rock collection (as we saw in Chapter 7). He knew from the outset that, in order to do both properly, he would have to invest a great deal of time and effort in geological fieldwork. But, as a lover of fresh air and the great outdoors who enjoyed freedom to roam and was happy in his own company; for him that was a bonus not a chore. He described in a letter to his

friend Ainger in August 1825 how "after rambling about in the open air one always sets very reluctantly to work in a dull college room."

Recall (from Chapter 7) that during the contest for the post in 1818 Adam is said to have admitted "Hitherto I have never turned a stone; henceforth I will leave no stone unturned". He may not have literally achieved that, but he certainly threw himself into geological fieldwork with great enthusiasm, and enjoyed long spells between 1818 and 1845 mapping and interpreting rocks in many places in Britain and Europe.

His field research involved extensive travel around Britain and Europe, initially by horse and carriage but after 1830 increasingly by train. If he kept a diary or journal no trace has survived, but his letters give a flavour of just how widely he travelled. For example, he was away from Cambridge on fieldwork between May and October 1837; his journey took him from Cambridge to London, northwards to Westmoreland, south to Cornwall, back north to Cumberland, south to Liverpool, east to the Warwickshire and Leicestershire coal-fields, then back to base in Cambridge.

His primary objectives in fieldwork were to map outcrops and boundaries for major rock series, and work out the stratigraphic order, using the approach developed by William Smith. With growing experience, he also recognized the importance of fossil evidence, although he had to rely on reputable palaeontologists like Cuvier to identify specimens he sent them. But for Adam the rocks always came first; as Thomas McKenny Hughes (1883), his successor as Woodwardian Professor, put it "while he appealed to paleontological evidence, wherever he could, he recognised that the first thing was to get the rocks into the right order in the field."

Adam was clearly one to accept a challenge, and preferred to study the geology of places where little if any systematic fieldwork had previously been undertaken. Much of his work was based on mapping and interpreting complex old rocks and geological structures, particularly in the Lake District, Wales, and Devon and Cornwall. In the field he often worked alone, but he sometimes had the company of a field assistant or a local expert, and in Roderick Murchison he found an inspiring and enthusiastic co-worker.

Adam was dedicated to observing, describing, recording and mapping what he found in the field. As we'll see in Chapter 15, his approach was explicitly inductive, and he was heavily critical of the deductive approach that a growing number of his scientific peers were adopting.

His approach was innovative in that, rather than just focussing on local detail in specific locations, he sought to map the geology of particular regions by building up local detail. He quickly developed the ability to understand the regional significance of local details, and through this he played a significant role in developing ideas on stratigraphic continuity that showed links between rock formations, vertically in particular places and horizontally in different places. Over the years since Adam's time, this led to the development of the Geologic Timescale (Appendix 1) that is an essential resource for today's geologists.

The editors of *Life and Letters* throw a little light on how Adam tackled fieldwork in new areas. They tell us that "he constantly wrote long letters when out on such excursions, put down his first impressions, and discussed all his difficulties. ... He very often made a rough sketch of what he saw, sometimes to amuse a child, sometimes to explain a point to a scientific friend, and, though he much decried his own sections, they always give a very good notion of the really important features in the structure of the country. ... From peak to peak, in traverse after traverse, he always sought some more easily recognised strata as base lines on which to build up the succession, and with which to correlate adjoining sections." (Clark and Hughes 1890a)

Starting out (1818-20)
Shortly after he was elected Professor of Geology in 1818, and after receiving some initial guidance from Cuvier, Sedgwick set out on a few geological excursions to learn the tricks of the trade.

As soon as the Easter Term of 1818 had finished in Cambridge, he headed to Derbyshire and Cheshire to get some first-hand experience of rocks beneath the Earth's surface, by going underground down mines. The trip lasted 5 weeks. He does not mention it in any of his scientific papers, but he touched upon it in a letter to Ainger in late October 1818, where he writes about "following the strata of the different rocks, collecting specimens, and driving into mines". That trip might have been a steep learning curve for the aspiring geologist, and he may have returned to Cambridge with more questions than answers but, as the editors of *Life and Letters* suggest, it probably "convinced Sedgwick that in selecting geology as the work of his life he had made a wise choice."

The following Easter (1819) he followed that initial exploratory trip with a geological excursion to the Isle of Wight, this time with John Stevens Henslow (1796-1861), a colleague. Little did Adam then know that, many years later (in 1847 and 1852, as we saw in Chapter 9), he would return to the Isle of Wight to visit Osborne House as the guest of Queen Victoria and Prince Albert. Like on his first trip to Derbyshire and Cheshire, his objective was for this to be a learning experience rather than an opportunity to make his name, although he did collect rock specimens for the Geology Museum.

Henslow had graduated from St John's College Cambridge the year before. He was ten years younger than Sedgwick, ,who was then 34, and seized on the opportunity to learn from him. By all accounts they were very different characters with different personalities, but they got on well together and subsequently became close friends as well as academic colleagues.

Both men regarded the trip as a success. Henslow learnt enough from Sedgwick to start work on his own the following summer, looking at the geology of the Isle of Man and parts of Anglesey. As well as acquiring "a very large collection" of geological specimens, Henslow shared his knowledge of mineralogy with Sedgwick. He would go on to achieve great things himself, becoming Professor of Geology (1822), Professor of Botany (1827) and founder of the School of Natural Sciences at Cambridge. In 1829 Charles Darwin took Henslow's botany course in 1829, and in the summer of 1831, after Henslow had to turn down an invitation to join the *Beagle* as naturalist on its two-year voyage to survey South America, he recommended Darwin to Captain Robert Fitzroy, and the rest is history.

Although Sedgwick viewed the Isle of Wight fieldwork as a training exercise, he was keen not to waste the fruit of his effort. In 1822 he published a paper *On the geology of the Isle of Wight* in the journal *Annals of Philosophy*, that was published monthly between 1813 and 1827.

Adam's geological career got off to a good start. Within the first two years he had created a lecture series (by June 1820 he had given 22 public lectures at the university), started to enlarge the museum collection and open it to the general public, and at his own expense carried out fieldwork in Derbyshire and Cheshire and on the Isle of Wight. With Henslow and others he had also helped to found the Cambridge Philosophical Society in November 1819, and he was writing one paper for it based on his summer 1820 fieldwork in Devon.

His workload was increasing, but he put time aside for his annual excursion to Dent each summer to visit family and friends, take the fresh air, enjoy the freedom to roam across the hills and dales, and escape from the routines of life in college.

11. Mapping the Rocks

Fieldwork in South West England (1819-20)

The first major geological challenge that Sedgwick set himself after the two exploratory field excursions was to work out the complex stratigraphy of South West England.

In late summer 1819 he travelled to Somerset, and on foot explored the Mendip and Quantock Hills and most of the cliffs along the north-west coast of the county. He chose that area because it contains many examples of what geologists call greywacké, from the German *grauwacke* meaning a grey, earthy rock, a term first used by Werner. Greywacké is a hard, dark, coarse-grained sandstone made of angular mineral grains (quartz and feldspar) and small rock fragments, bound together in a clay matrix.

On that geological excursion Adam received assistance in the field from John Conybeare (1779-1824), Vicar of a church near Bath, who knew the area well. After the trip he wrote to thank John for his help and guidance, because "If I had not been under your tuition for three weeks, I should, I fear, never have been able to disentangle the difficulties of this neighbourhood." Conybeare later became Professor of Anglo-Saxon then Professor of Poetry at Oxford. His younger brother William (1787-1857) was Dean of Llandaff, and also became an eminent geologist; Adam described him as "an Oxford Professor and stone-eater" and "one of my dearest friends, and one of my earliest teachers in geology." William also taught geology to Buckland.

Adam wrote two papers based on the 1819 fieldwork, that show that it also covered much of Cornwall, particularly around the Lizard. Both papers were read before the Cambridge Philosophical Society. The first, *On the physical structure of those formations which are intimately associated with the Primitive Ridge of Devonshire and Cornwall*, was read in March 1820 and published in the *Transactions* of the Society later that year. He drew some important conclusions from his field observations. He believed that the New Red Sandstone in Devon was not the same as that below the Mountain Limestone below the River Avon; some of the Devon sandstones that appear to be equivalent to the Upper Old Red Sandstone; fossils found within limestones in Devon suggest they belong to a different and older formation from the Carboniferous (Mountain) Limestone.

He also wrote about the granite landscapes in Cornwall. He described the surface of the granite moors as covered "by granite boulders, the remains of larger masses of the same kind which have gradually disappeared, through the corrosive action of the elements", and 'logan

167

stones' [large, exposed boulders, balanced so that they are easily rocked] as "spheroidally-weathered masses". He described the granite as "a crystalline aggregate of quartz, feldspar, and mica", described how 'elvans' [a Cornish mining term for a dyke cutting through granite] "often resemble outwardly a fine sandstone", and challenged the suggestion by Swiss geologist Jean-André De Luc (1727-1817) that divisional planes [planes of separation between rock masses] represent lines of bedding [the strata found in sandstones and other sedimentary rocks]. He concluded that the granite of Cornwall "is a true granite, the oldest primitive rock of the Wernerian series". He saw the granite as the most ancient rock, because the killas and other rocks lie on top of it and appear to have been deposited there.

These conclusions offer persuasive evidence of Sedgwick's keen ability to see and record evidence in the field, and his judgment in drawing such conclusions, many of which were decades ahead of their time. As the editors of *Life and Letters* emphasise, this first paper "proves that by steady application a man of talent may be able to make observations of the first order in the field two years after commencing the study of the subject."

Adam's second paper, *On the Physical Structure of the Lizard District*, was read to the Cambridge Philosophical Society at two meetings in April and May 1821. Amongst other things, it discusses the relation of serpentine to the rocks surrounding it. Serpentine is a group of minerals that can appear in green snake-like bands (hence the name) within other rocks. He hinted that it might be metamorphic in origin, caused by intense heating and pressure below ground. Geologists now know that to be the case, but for more than sixty years after Adam's paper it had remained a matter of debate amongst geologists.

After the success of his 1819 field season in the South West, Adam returned the following summer to continue his research in Wiltshire, Somerset and Dorset. He was particularly interested in the sedimentary rocks, and told Ainger by letter in September 1820 that the Mendips were made of the same Carboniferous Limestone as the area around Sedbergh that he was familiar with. He said that the strata there were steeply inclined, in some places almost vertical, and above them (above what geologists now call an unconformity) newer strata are horizontal. Two months later he wrote to Ainger about the South Devon coast around Sidmouth, where "cliffs are on a most magnificent scale, abound in organic remains, and are of great geological interest." Writing about the Dorset coast, he also pointed out that "the geological map of that district is so erroneous that I resolved to rectify it as far as my time would allow, and I succeeded almost to the extent of my wishes."

Adam's early focus on the greywacké sandstone rocks reflected the strong influence of Werner on his understanding of geological history at that time. Werner grouped all of the sandstones, slates, quartzites and schists together, and assigned them to what he called the Transition Group. He believed that group was formed between the Primary Rocks and the Secondary Rocks, in an age during which animals first appeared in the sea, and when sediment worn from land was beginning to replace the earliest rock material that had settled in the Great Flood. But, over the next five years or so, he discovered that the greywacké rocks were much more varied than Werner had thought, and it became clear that they were not one simple group. He found evidence of volcanic lava sheets within greywacké in some areas; some but not all greywacké were stratified (arranged in strata); some contained fossils; and in many the strata were not flat but inclined, or were cut through by faults.

Adam started to think that, although the greywacké seemed to be distinct from other rock formations, they might better be assigned to several series of vastly different ages. This tempting prospect inspired much of Adam's subsequent geological work, both in the field and in his written papers.

Fieldwork in Yorkshire, Durham and Teesdale (1821)
During the summer of 1821 Adam spent nearly three months engaged in fieldwork along the coast of North East England.

He wrote to Ainger in early September, describing Holderness as "well cultivated and well inhabited, but as dull as the fens", and noting that "the sea is making terrible encroachments on the whole district." North of Bridlington he described the different landscape underlain by chalk, with vertical cliffs more than 300 feet high and taller than the chalk cliffs he has seen on the Isle of Wight. At Scarborough he was impressed by the "fine mass of perpendicular rock, which is crowned with the ruins of the Castle", but he described Whitby as "a dirty, stinking, town in a very picturesque situation ... The entrance to the harbour of Whitby is by a narrow opening in the cliff. ... The ruins of the abbey are still very imposing, and in a very beautiful style of architecture." At Robin Hood's Bay he nearly lost the sight of one eye hammering a piece of rock.

He continued northwards, mostly on foot, up the coast of Durham, which "in a picturesque point of view, is very inferior to the north-east cliff of Yorkshire". The dominant rocks were Magnesian Limestone which, as he put it, "performs more freaks in its mode of aggregation than any mineral substance I have yet examined." The field trip ended with a two-day excursion along Teesdale, the higher part of which he described as "perhaps more beautiful than any valley in the North of England."

As well as mapping the rocks, Adam collected specimens for the Geological Museum and sent them off to Cambridge from Whitby, Sunderland, and Newcastle in four large wooden packing-cases.

Adam read the first of four papers based on the 1821 fieldwork, *On the phenomena connected with some trap dykes in Yorkshire and Durham,* to the Cambridge Philosophical Society in May 1822. It was published in the Society's *Transactions* later that year.

The second paper, *On the association of trap rocks with the Mountain Limestone formation in High Teesdale,* was published in the *Transactions* the following year. Trap rocks are dark, fine-grained igneous (volcanic) rocks, such as basalt (but not granite). Adam found vertical dykes (veins) of them within the Magnesian Limestone in Upper Teesdale, displaying features we see today at the Giant's Causeway in Northern Ireland, particularly a columnar structure and distinctive forms of weathering. He noted that some dykes extend more than fifty miles and appear to be of different ages, and concluded that they are the result of underground volcanic activity.

This paper is the first sign that, within a few years of being appointed Professor of Geology, Sedgwick was starting to question Werner's ideas because, if Werner's interpretation of the greywacké rocks was correct, we should not see evidence of volcanic activity within them.

Adam's next two papers focussed on the Magnesian Limestone and New Red Sandstone rocks he had mapped.

The third of the papers based on the 1821 fieldwork, *On the classification of the strata which appear on the Yorkshire coast,* was published in *Annals of Philosophy* in 1826. In it Adam tried to correlate the strata he had mapped along the Yorkshire coast with those he had observed in other parts of England, particularly along the Weymouth area of the Dorset coast.

The fourth paper was a detailed monograph, *On the Magnesian Limestone and lower portions of the New Red Sandstone series,* that was read to the Geological Society in several meetings between November 1826 and March 1828. It was published in *Transactions of the Geological Society* between 1826 and 1828.

That paper is a classic of its time. It was then generally assumed that the New Red Sandstone, and the Magnesian Limestone below it, were

170

both deposited during the same period of time, but Adam found evidence of a clear discontinuity between the two series of rocks. That 'discontinuity' (geologists would today call it an unconformity) represented a long stretch of time during which the lower rocks were eroded and worn down. As Adam put it, "After the production of the [limestone] rocks of the Carboniferous order, the earth's surface appears to have been acted upon by powerful disturbing forces, which, not only in the British Isles, but throughout the greater part of the European basis, produced a series of formations of very great extent and complexity of structure."

Although the discontinuity may have great local importance, Adam argued that it was not necessarily global. As he put it, "'We have no right to assume, nor is there any reason to believe, that such disturbing forces either acted uniformly or simultaneously throughout the world. Formations which in one country are unconformable, may in another be parallel to each other, and so intimately connected as to appear the production of one epoch."

Already, at this early stage in his geological career, he recognised the challenge of unravelling the geological history within any particular area, and of collating evidence between areas. Ever one for a challenge, in the fourth paper Adam correlated the rocks he had studied in Yorkshire with their equivalents in Germany. He found that the deposits above the discontinuity, which in Britain were then called the New Red Sandstone (a term no longer used) and Red Marl, comprising all of the rock formations between the so-called Coal Measures (now described as the coal-bearing part of the Upper Carboniferous System) and the Lias (marine limestones and shales, then regarded as Lower Jurassic), "have several characters in common, which enables us to connect them together, and, for general purposes of comparison, to regard them as one group."

He also reported finding different fossils in the Upper and Lower Limestones below the discontinuity. He referred to the Upper Limestone as the Muschelkalk (German for *mussel chalk*), the first reported finding of this rock in Britain. It consists of a series of limestone and doloritic beds, and today is dated to the Middle Triassic period (Appendix 1). The Lower Limestone (which is mostly dolomite, and now dated to the Permian period) was at that time described in Britain as Magnesian Limestone, but that term is no longer used by geologists.

Fieldwork in the Lake District (1822-1833)
The Lake District (then comprising the counties of Westmorland in the south and Cumberland in the north) was to provide the setting for much

of Adam Sedgwick's geological fieldwork over many years. He never used the term Lake District in his writing, but described the region as the Cumbrian Mountains or Lake Mountains. It was his home territory, much of which he knew well and loved a great deal; unravelling its complex geology provided him with serious intellectual and practical challenges, but he relished them.

As well as feeding his geological curiosity, the area also provided Adam with some great friendships, including with some distinguished men he met during his excursions. In 1822 he met and befriended the poet William Wordsworth (1770-1844), describing him as "so far a man of leisure as to make every natural object around him subservient to the habitual workings of his own mind; and he was ready for any good occasion that carried him among his well-loved mountains." Adam would subsequently write three letters to Wordsworth about the geology of the Lake District which he included in his *Complete guide to the Lakes, comprising minute directions for the tourist* (1843); a further two letters were included in later editions of the *Complete guide*.

On another occasion, whilst out on a "geological ramble", Adam met the poet Robert Southey (1774-1843), with whom he "sometimes shared in the simple intellectual pleasures of his household, and profited by his boundless stores of knowledge. He was, to himself, a very hard taskmaster: but on rare occasions (as I learnt by happy experience) he could relax the labours of his study, and plan some joyful excursion among his neighbouring mountains." Adam was out walking near the summit of Helvellyn one day when he met the chemist John Dalton (1766-1844), "a truth-loving man of rare simplicity of manners; who, with humble instruments and very humble means, ministered, without flinching, in the service of high philosophy ..."

Adam started fieldwork in the Lake District in the summer of 1822, before he had written up the results of his fieldwork in Yorkshire. He spent the next two summers working there, during which he made "a detailed geological map of that rugged region, including a considerable portion of Westmoreland and Cumberland, and a small portion of Lancashire." He returned to the area to do more fieldwork in 1832, 1835, 1845, 1851, and 1857, but his most important was done between 1822 and 1824 when he continued to explore "the most intricate portions of Cumberland, Westmoreland, and Lancashire", although he did not commit any of his conclusions to paper until 1831.

Adam later regretted not looking for fossils during his 1822-24 fieldwork in the Lake District, after having realized that was a mistake.

11. Mapping the Rocks

Thirty years later, in August 1856, he wrote to Robert Harkness (1816-1878), Professor of Geology at Queen's College in Cork, advising him to "hammer well the gritty rocks which appear in the several deep ravines which run up the mountains on the left side of the road from Scale Inn to Buttermere; they promise well for fossils. I never examined them for fossils in 1823 and 1824, because I foolishly thought that they were all below the region of animal life [older than the earliest fossils]. At that time I had not quite learned to shake off the Wernerian nonsense I had been taught."

After three busy summer field seasons in the Lake District, and given his heavy workload in Trinity College during term times, the following summer (1825) he restricted his geological outings to a brief excursion to the south coast. In August he studied the rocks along the coast between Canterbury (Kent) and Bognor (Sussex), with Dr Fitton, and paid a quick visit to the Isle of Wight before returning to Cambridge. He spent much of 1825 and 1826 sorting and interpreting the material he had gathered during the 1822-24 field season in the Lake District, and writing papers for the Cambridge Philosophical Society, the Geological Society, or *Annals of Philosophy*.

Adam's papers on Lake District geology based on the 1822-24 fieldwork started to appear in 1831. He read the first, *Introduction to the General Structure of the Lake Mountains of the North of England*, to the Geological Society in January 1831, and it was published in *Transactions* later that year. It included a brief description of the oldest rocks in the heart of the Lake District, but its main focus was the Carboniferous rocks surrounding them, and what he called "the great dislocations" (unconformity) separating the one from the other. The challenge of describing and accounting for the relationship between ancient rocks and adjacent younger rocks, was to exercise Adam through much of the rest of his geological career.

He read his second Lake District paper, *Description of a series of longitudinal and transverse sections through a portion of the Carboniferous Chain between Penigent and Kirkby Stephen*, to the Geological Society two months after the first, in March 1831, and it too was published in *Transactions* that same year. It described results from some fieldwork he had done straight after reading the first paper, aiming to correlate the younger rocks in the Lake District with those in adjacent parts of North West Yorkshire, based on a series of transects running out in different directions from the central mass. He did this to establish the character and succession of the newer rocks, and their relationships with the central rocks. The transects ran across the highest mountains in the western Yorkshire Dales, running out over Penigent (now usually spelled Penyghent) to the Craven district that includes the area around Malham, and over the Pennines into the Eden Valley near Kirkby Stephen.

Adam followed up the Penigent paper with a third paper, *On the New Red Sandstone series in the basin of the Eden, and North-West coasts of Cumberland and Lancashire*, that he read to the Geological Society in February 1832 and was published later that year in *Transactions*. It describes the evidence he had found in the Eden valley of another great "interruption in the continuity of deposit" (unconformity), like the one between the ancient rocks and the Carboniferous rocks above them that he had observed in the Lake District off to the west.

The evidence in the Eden valley suggested that the Carboniferous rocks had somehow, and at some time, been uplifted then worn down by rain and rivers into "an irregular land-surface", on top of which other sedimentary rocks, "the debris of wasted land", had been deposited. Adam described these upper deposits as "the shingle-beach made up of pebbles from the coast, and the sand and mud with drifted plants which we see along the river-cliffs and hillsides of the beautiful Eden Valley." Geologists today recognize the "pebbles from the coast" as Millstone Grit, and the coarse-grained sandstones – deposited in the delta of a huge ancient river system in Carboniferous times that form the cap rock on the Three Peaks (Ingleborough, Whernside and Pen-y-Ghent) – and the "sand and mud" as the Yoredale Series deposited in Carboniferous times. Adam believed these rocks to be equivalent to the Lower New Red Sandstone rocks he had described six months earlier, much further east on the Yorkshire coast.

Adam read his fourth paper, *On the geological relations of the stratified and unstratified groups of rocks composing the Cumbrian Mountains*, to the Geological Society in May 1832; it was published in *Transactions* that year. In it he describes the sequence of rocks in and around the Lake District, as a more detailed follow-up to his 1831 paper *Introduction to the general structure of the Cumbrian Mountains*. He acknowledges the help he received in the field from local guide and fossil collector Jonathan Otley (1766-1856). Otley knew the area around Grasmere and Keswick in the centre of the Lake District very well, and has since been called "the father of Lakeland geology". Adam pursued an increasingly familiar theme, describing the dislocation (unconformity) between the old rocks at the centre of the area, and the younger Carboniferous rocks surrounding them.

11. Mapping the Rocks

After several seasons studying the rocks in the central Lake District and the younger rocks to the east of them, Sedgwick switched his attention for a short while during the early 1830s onto the Carboniferous rocks in the north-west Lake District, encouraged by a friendship with John Peile. Between 1811 and 1847 Peile was manager of a series of collieries around Whitehaven that were owned by Lord Lonsdale; although he had a sound knowledge of practical geology, he learned a great deal about geological mapping and interpretation while assisting Sedgwick in local fieldwork. He and Sedgwick read a joint paper, *On the range of the Carboniferous Limestone flanking the primary Cumbrian Mountains; and on the coal-fields of the N.W. coast of Cumberland*, to the Geological Society in September 1833, that was published in *Transactions* in 1835.

They read another joint paper to the Geological Society, *On the coal-fields of the North-Western coast of Cumberland*, in June 1836, that was published in the same year. In 1837 Sedgwick read a brief *Notice of an Incursion of the Sea into the collieries at Workington* at the British Association meeting in Liverpool, in which he described the flooding by sea water of a submarine coal mine at Workington on the west coast of Cumberland.

Debate over evidence of an Ice Age in Britain (1825-1855)

When Sedgwick began work as a geologist, no-one had suggested that Britain (in fact, most of the Northern Hemisphere) might at some time in the past have been covered with glaciers and ice sheets, as is now known to have happened. Most geologists at that time explained the surface deposits they called drift (that we now call till or boulder clay) as having been deposited by flood water. But, even in Adam's early days, evidence was being described in some places that suggested that ice might have been involved in some way, most probably as ice-bergs rather than glaciers or ice sheets. The evidence included boulders (now called erratics) found in drift long distances away from where the rock outcrops are found, indicative of long-distance transport, and scratch marks (now called striations) on rock outcrops and boulders, suggesting heavy abrasion during transport.

Adam was intrigued by this possibility. In July 1825 he published two papers in *Annals of Philosophy*, *On the Origin of Alluvial and Diluvial Formations* and *On diluvial formations*, in which he outlined his evidence and thoughts on the matter. Informed by his own fieldwork in the fenland near Cambridge, and around the Humber estuary in Yorkshire, along with observations from other geologists elsewhere, he distinguished between older sediments that he called diluvium (drift) and generally younger alluvial deposits, and described examples of boulders (erratics) in anomalous positions and with irregular distributions.

He was convinced that "the facts brought to light by the combined labours of the modern school of geologists ... demonstrate the reality of a great diluvial catastrophe during a comparatively recent period in the natural history of the earth" and he noted that "many parts of the north of Europe seem to have been swept over by a great current which set in from the north. In some parts of Scotland there has been a great rush of water from the north-west." He concluded that the floods that deposited the diluvium had "swept over every part of England – that they were put in motion by no powers of nature with which we are acquainted – and that they took place during an epoch which was posterior to [after] the deposition of all the regular strata of the earth."

Looking back on those papers more than six decades later, Clark and Hughes (1890a) point out "there is still much difference of opinion as to whether the 'drift' of certain districts is due to land-ice, or to icebergs". They note that the direction of the currents that Adam believed had distributed the diluvium was consistent with much more recent findings, and excused Adam's inability to "recognize the exact mode of transport" on the grounds of his lack of familiarity with glaciated districts in his day.

Ten years after his 1825 papers on "diluvial formations", Adam was still turning over in his mind the question of whether Britain might once have been affected by icebergs and glaciers. Charles Lyell (who we met in Chapter 10) had proposed his Ice Theory in the first edition of *Principles of Geology*, published in 1833. He argued that icebergs could have transported erratics, assuming that during periods of global warming icebergs would break off ice sheets at the poles, float across submerged land masses carrying sediment, that would then be deposited on the land when the icebergs melted.

Adam was far from convinced by Lyell's theory, and wrote to him in September 1835 advising "Your ice theory will, I think, only let you slip into the water, and give you a good ducking. Erratic blocks are diffused in latitudes where there are no icebergs, and never were. How do you get your icebergs to shove the Shap Granite over Stainmoor to the Yorkshire coast; or the Wastdale Granite across Morecambe Bay, over the plains of Cheshire, to the Derbyshire hills, and the outskirts of the Welsh mountains?"

Louis Agassiz, who had first-hand experience of glaciers in his native Switzerland (and we met in Chapter 10), had also given the matter a

11. Mapping the Rocks

great deal of thought. In March 1838, Sedgwick wrote to tell him how much he was looking forward to his forthcoming memoir "on the erratic blocks of the Alps". He told Agassiz that "on the subject of the erratic blocks of Switzerland it strikes me that no one can possibly account for them without the aid of the carrying power of ice", assuming transport by icebergs rather than glaciers. He pointed out that, by then, "a great deal of evidence, both positive and negative, has been advanced in favour of the iceberg theory", including Charles Darwin's evidence "that throughout South America erratic blocks are found within the limits of latitude where glaciers are, or may have been, down to the level of the sea; and that they are wanting in the tropical latitudes, where ice could never have existed near the sea level." He told Agassiz that in England "we have a most interesting series of erratic blocks. I don't think the iceberg theory can be applied to them, because they go in almost all directions, and not towards any prevailing point of the compass, and because they follow the exact line of water-worn detritus and comminuted gravel. Such blocks I attribute to currents produced during periods of elevation and unusual violence." He added that "there are many instances of rocks grooved deeply [striated], and partially rubbed down, by the currents of what we formerly called diluvium ... There are very fine examples of this kind near Edinburgh. Stones transported in this way are always rounded by attrition, and in every question about the origin of erratic blocks we ought to regard their condition (viz. whether rounded or not), as well as their geographical relation to the parent rock."

This letter to Agassiz reveals Adam's growing belief that transport by ice might well explain the distribution of erratic rocks and the striation of rocks, but also his continuing uncertainty, shared by many geologists over at least the following five decades, about whether this would have been by icebergs or glaciers.

In October 1840 Agassiz read a paper *On Glaciers, and the evidence of their having once existed in Scotland, Ireland, and England* to the Geological Society, which generated a long discussion to which Sedgwick contributed. Adam was not persuaded by Agassiz's line of argument, either about the likely existence of glaciers in Britain or glaciers as the mode of transport of till and erratics and the cause of striations. Having recently read Agassiz's book *Études sur les glaciers* (*Studies on glaciers*), then just published, Adam told Murchison by letter in late November 1840 "it is excellent, but in the last chapter he loses his balance, and runs away with the bit in his mouth."

Eight years later, we find Adam still engaged in discussions about the process or processes that gave rise to till and erratics, this time with self-taught Scottish geologist Hugh Miller (1802-1856). He wrote to tell Miller in December 1848 "your remarks on the stones [erratics] imbedded in your Drift Clay, and grooved [striated] parallel to their longer axis, were quite new to me, and I think very instructive, though I was not quite satisfied with your mechanical reasons for the phenomenon. I have seen nothing like it in the Drift Clay (almost exactly like your Till) of the flat southern countries of England. I believe our Till ... was formed exclusively by water – by waves of translation – and not by ice; and I by no means agree with what Lyell has written about it."

The last we hear from Sedgwick about icebergs and glaciers was in October 1855, when he delivered a lecture to the then newly-formed Natural History Society of Kendal in the Lake District. He spoke, as its President, on the geology of the Lake District with particular reference to the influence of the Gulf Stream and the scattering of granite boulders from Wastdale over Northern England by glaciers. By then, Adam, at the age of 70 and after 37 years of geological work, had accepted the evidence for glaciation across Northern England in the geologically recent past, and embraced the implications of that for the formation of the deposits he had long called diluvium and assumed to have been caused by infrequent catastrophic floods.

Sedgwick's first decade (1818-27)
The first decade of Sedgwick's career as a geologist was both formative and productive. These were learning years for him, an apprenticeship during which he scoped and framed the subject that was initially very new to him. His first *Syllabus of a course of lectures on geology*, published in 1821, clearly shows how, within three years of starting his Professorship, he realised the most important problems to be solved, to which he would commit himself.

It was a critical time for learning, discussing, exploring, gaining experience, growing in confidence, and networking. Over those first ten years he travelled extensively around Britain, including the Isle of Wight, the coast of Yorkshire and Durham, Teesdale, Devon and Cornwall, and the Lake District. He had examined for himself the areas in which many of the pioneers of British geology had worked; discussed with leading geologists of the day the best ways of interpreting many different geological structures and outcrops; and engaged in field excursions with Conybeare, Murchison, Peile and others. He had read the books and papers of leading geologists in Britain and Europe, and had launched his own publishing career with some papers that brought his work to the attention of other geologists, and laid the foundations for what would grow into a distinguished and influential career. All of these experiences gave him an excellent grounding, and very valuable experiences and skills for his subsequent work.

Sedgwick's joint work with Murchison

In the late 1820s, after nearly a decade of working in the field mostly on his own, Adam joined forces with Roderick Murchison to do joint field-work in different parts of Britain and continental Europe. Their first two projects took them to Scotland, starting in 1827, and to Europe in 1829. Next, they worked on the complex geology of Wales, starting in 1831 and culminating in the so-called Cambrian-Silurian Controversy, that we'll look in Chapter 12. As if one major controversy were not enough, the pair embarked on fieldwork in South-West England in 1836 that led to the so-called Great Devonian Controversy, that we'll look at in Chapter 13.

Roderick Impey Murchison (1792-1871)
Sedgwick described Murchison, in a letter he wrote to him in July 1851, as "my dear friend in the hammer". For a number of years they worked closely together and appear to have enjoyed each other's company, despite the fact that in terms of family background, education and personality they were as different as chalk and cheese.

Murchison was born into a wealthy aristocratic family in the Highlands of Scotland. He was seven years younger than Sedgwick, who was 43 when they met. Murchison had not gone to university, but pursued a career in the army. He joined up at fifteen, was commissioned a captain at twenty, had served in the Peninsular War (1808-14) against France, and married the daughter of a General who persuaded him to resign after any real prospects of promotion in the military faded with the defeat of Napoleon. His wife planned a comfortable life dedicated to art and literature, and the former soldier became obsessed with fox hunting until he was encouraged by leading scientist Sir Humphrey Davy to try his hand at science. After attending lectures on geology and chemistry in London in 1824, he sat in on Buckland's geology lectures in Oxford, heard Charles Lyell read his first paper on geology, and later accompanied him on some fieldwork in France. He travelled widely and was a great supporter of the views of German geologist von Buch (1774-1853). Despite his lack of formal education, he was accepted by the geological establishment and became an active member of the Geological Society, to whom he read his first scientific paper in 1825.

Murchison was drawn to Sedgwick because of the skill he had already displayed in understanding the complex structure of older rocks, having been challenged by some fieldwork he had recently done in parts of Scotland, including the Isle of Arran in the Firth of Clyde. He contacted Sedgwick shortly after returning from Arran, and suggested they do some joint fieldwork there, which Sedgwick agreed to. On that first excursion, in 1827, Murchison gained a tutor and mentor and Sedgwick gained a companion. For many years the two men enjoyed a harmonious and fruitful partnership, working together and separately to unravel Werner's vague groupings of the Transition Rocks, or as they later referred to it, the "interminable Greywacké". As we'll see in Chapter 13, their friendship was severely tested by a bitter controversy that grew up between them over the Silurian System.

In later years Murchison grew increasingly conservative in his geological thinking, leading him to retreat from the Uniformitarian ideas he and Lyell had developed in 1828 and revert to Catastrophism. His mind closed to ideas opposed to his own, so with von Buch he strenuously denied and protested against the theory of great glaciations. He also insisted that his interpretation on the Silurian Controversy had been the right one. He rejected Darwin's ideas on the evolution of species, and felt slighted when Lyell failed to mention his work in his 1863 book *Antiquity of Man*.

Murchison was knighted in 1846 and in 1854 was appointed Director of the Geological Survey and its School of Mines and Museum of Practical Geology. He died in 1871.

Joint fieldwork in Scotland (1827)

Sedgwick agreed to Murchison's request to join him on a geological excursion in Scotland in 1827. It would be his first fieldwork in Scotland.

The objective of the trip was "to ascertain, if possible, the true relations of the [Old] Red Sandstones [ORS] of Scotland", which geologists then thought were part of the Carboniferous System; but today they are known to belong to the older Devonian System. As well as mapping the distribution of the ORS in Scotland, Sedgwick and Murchison were keen to learn more about the unconformity that Hutton had described at Siccar Point, north of Berwick-upon-Tweed on the east coast, between Greywacké (now known to be Silurian) and the Old Red Sandstone (now known to be Devonian) above. They used the approach to field mapping that William Smith had developed some decades earlier, that by then was

180

11. Mapping the Rocks

Sedgwick's standard mode of working. Working out the order in which strata had been deposited in different places was a great challenge, but it was made easier by Sedgwick's ability to distinguish between stratification (the layering of rocks in strata), jointing (the formation of natural fractures in rocks), and slaty cleavage (the thin, parallel planes of weakness that give a rock like slate its ability to split into very thin plates or layers). No other geologist had previously been able to do that.

The trip began with a close look at the geology of the Isle of Arran. The two men then made their way north, via the islands of Mull and Skye, to Caithness in the North-East tip of Scotland, before heading south to York via Aberdeen, Edinburgh, Carlisle, and Newcastle.

They completed the fieldwork by October 1827, and decided to write two papers based on it for the Geological Society, one on the structure of Arran and the other on the Old Red Sandstone of the north of Scotland. Their first joint paper, *On the geological relations of the secondary strata in the Isle of Arran*, was read to the Society in January 1828 and published in *Transactions* the following year. Their second paper, *On the structure and relations of the deposits contained between the Primary Rocks and the Oolitic Series in the north of Scotland*, was also published in 1829.

Murchison had already had two short papers on Scotland published in *Transactions*, was ambitious, and was eager to see these two joint papers in print without delay. The delay annoyed him greatly, particularly because he was planning a geological excursion to France and was eager to get started. Murchison had plenty of time to commit to the writing, but Sedgwick was as ever weighed down with College, Museum and lecturing responsibilities in Cambridge. His College workload was then heavier than usual because, as Senior Proctor, he had to deal with some difficult student disciplinary cases, including one in which three male students were expelled from Trinity as a result of "ungentlemanly profligacy" (as we saw in Chapter 6). He was also laid low by poor health, including a heavy cold and eye problems (a continued consequence of his hammer incident during fieldwork on the Yorkshire coast some years earlier), and he was struggling to complete the writing of his paper on the Magnesian Limestone, that he had begun two years earlier. In addition, he was anxious that the joint paper on Arran contained theories as well as facts. Recall that he insisted that 'truth' can only be arrived at through induction not theory, so he wrote to advise Murchison that the paper "is cram-full of hypotheses, and truly may want defending; but you must stand up for me."

Sedgwick and Murchison thought that their work would "not only assist in complèting the natural history of Arran ... [but also help] to fix the true epoch of all those interrupted fragments of secondary formations" that are found along the West and North of Scotland. The Arran paper followed Sedgwick's usual three-part format, opening with a detailed description of the sequence of rocks they observed in the field, followed by descriptions and interpretations by leading palaeontologists of the various fossils they had collected, and ending with their attempt to correlate these rocks with those in other areas that had previously been described and published.

In Arran, they identified the three series of rocks they were expecting to find there, and described them in Wernerian terms. The oldest rocks, the so-called Primary Rocks, were mostly "great masses of crystalline schist of unknown age". Above them were the intermediate Transition Rocks, that included a series that Sedgwick and Murchison would later describe as Cambrian and Silurian (see Chapter 12). On top of the heavily folded Transition Rocks, and separated from them by a clear unconformity, were the Secondary Rocks, with Old Red Sandstone at the base.

They wrote about the unconformity in interesting terms, that reveal their allegiance to Catastrophism and rejection of Uniformitarianism. They recognized the usefulness of unconformities as indicators of missing time, but were convinced that they had only local importance, for purposes of classification. Because they believed each unconformity was effectively a local feature that extended only over a relatively small area, they wrote that they "do not think that a want of conformity [the presence of an unconformity] is one of the elements which will much assist us in grouping together or in separating contemporaneous deposits in distant parts of the earth." Later geologists would have exactly the opposite view of the importance and value of unconformities!

In their second joint paper, *On the structure and relations of the deposits contained between the Primary Rocks and the Oolitic Series in the north of Scotland*, Sedgwick and Murchison described what they called the Lower Secondary Rocks, comprising the Old Red Sandstone and overlying deposits, all of which were what geologists today call conglomerates – coarse-grained sedimentary rock composed of rounded fragments cemented together. Above the Lower Secondary Rocks they describe "a middle flaggy stage, with fish remains [fossils]", that they wrongly thought might be correlated with rocks of the Carboniferous System they were familiar with further south in Northern England. As they visited sites around Scotland they found the fish fossils, whose identification was confirmed by Cuvier, more widespread than other geologists had assumed; they could trace the fish-bearing strata across the country, extending as far north as the Orkneys.

Whilst they added useful information and interpretations on the geology of the areas they visited, Sedgwick and Murchison were not the first geologists to study those areas. Most of where they worked had already been mapped by Scottish geologist John MacCulloch (1773-1835), a disciple of Werner, who in 1819 had published *Description of the Western Islands of Scotland*. By the late 1820s he had made good progress in compiling a geological map of Scotland, that would eventually be published shortly after his death in 1835. MacCulloch was by all accounts a rather impatient man who disliked criticism and took it personally. Little wonder, then, that he was not impressed by Sedgwick and Murchison's joint papers on Scotland; he attacked their interpretations, and denounced their trespassing on what he had come to regard as his own geological territory.

Joint fieldwork in Europe (1829)
During 1828 Roderick Murchison and his wife Charlotte took a geological excursion in France and Northern Italy, in the company of Charles Lyell. They set out from Paris in May, and travelled through the Massif Central and on towards the Auvergne region and beyond. The trip lasted several months, and Murchison later referred to it as their geological "Grand Tour". It marked the end of Lyell's short legal career and the start of his geological career. For Murchison it offered an opportunity to stretch his geological wings and the prospect of enhancing his already growing reputation.

Murchison was keen to build on the success of his joint fieldwork with Sedgwick in Scotland in 1827, and to continue the work he had begun on the continent, so he urged Adam to join him in another excursion in Europe in 1829. His invitation was direct but challenging; he told Adam "not to let another year elapse without endeavouring to add to the stock of your British Geology some of the continental materials. Pray do it before you marry and settle for life …" The intention was to leave England in late June and explore the northern side of the Alps and central parts of Germany, Bohemia (now the western Czech Republic) and Saxony (now part of eastern Germany). Sedgwick took the bait and agreed to go as soon as he had finished preparing for publication three papers he had read to the Geological Society the previous year.

The intrepid travellers set themselves three objectives for the trip – they would interpret and correlate the rocks they found on the Alpine ridges between the Rhine and the Danube; they would aim to give a broad overview of the geology of that area, rather than detailed descriptions of particular sites; and they hoped to raise awareness of the areas and its geological challenges amongst English geologists, few of whom had yet visited the Alps.

They left England towards the end of June, took a steam-boat over to Rotterdam, then went by boat up the Rhine to Bonn. After consulting with some German Professors they travelled on to Andernach, where on foot they explored "some very interesting extinct volcanoes", as Adam wrote in a letter to Ainger in mid-September. He described how they "traced lava-currents to their craters, and travelled for miles upon pumice, scoria, and ashes. I was bewildered and confounded at the sight, for these fires have never smoked within the records of mankind."

They continued further up the Rhine to Mainz and crossed to Frankfurt, where they bought a horse-drawn carriage to use in the rest of their trip. After stopping to look at the rocks around several places, including Cassel, Gottingen, the Hartz Mountains, Eisleben and Halle, they moved on to Berlin, where they rested for four days. Then they continued on through the Bohemian Mountains to Prague, "one of the most magnificent cities I ever beheld", through southern Bohemia and Moravia, "a dull and dismal long journey", to Vienna. From there they crossed the eastern edge of the Alps and spent about ten days in lower Styria (now a state in south-east Austria), before crossing "the desolate mountains" of Carinthia (also in south-east Austria) to reach the Adriatic. After spending a day at Trieste, which offered "dull geology, but the finest caverns in the world", they crossed the plains of northern Italy, "among olive-groves and vineyards".

After spending several days exploring the southern side of the Alps, they crossed over the high Tauern Pass on their way to Salzburg. Adam was struck by the great thickness of Tertiary deposits in that region; he described to Ainger how "the Tertiary deposits resting on the outskirts of this calcareous zone are thicker than all our secondary formations [in Britain] put together. For scores of miles they are in a vertical position. In many places the Alps, in rising through them, have lifted great rags of them into the regions of snow. Some of these rags are 3000 or 4000 feet thick …". In Salzburg they visited the glacier and waterfalls at Nassfeld, then quickly explored the Salzkammergut (the Austrian Lake District) before heading west to Innsbruck, then travelling north to Munich and

11. Mapping the Rocks

Strasburg. They passed through what is now central-eastern Germany, which Adam described to Ainger as "the focus of Wernerian geology, and to my infinite surprise it is the most decidedly volcanic secondary country I ever saw. The granite bursts through on one side, sends out veins, and along the whole eastern flank the secondaries are highly inclined and often absolutely vertical." From Munich, they returned home via Lake Constance, down the Danube, via Stuttgart to Heidelberg, and on via Paris.

The trip was a great inspiration for Sedgwick and Murchison. As Clark and Hughes (1890a) put it, "it was not a new and unexplored district, such as Sedgwick loved, and yet it was an area where great problems were suggested, and it formed a fine field for a holiday tour."

It was also a very productive time for the two dedicated geologists. Within weeks of their return they read their first joint paper, *On the Tertiary Deposits of the Vale of Gosau, in the Salzburg Alps*, to the Geological Society; it was published in the *Proceedings of the Geological Society* in 1829. Other joint papers quickly followed, including *A sketch of the structure of the Austrian Alps* that was read to the Geological Society in November 1829 and published in *Proceedings* of the Society the following year; and *On the Tertiary Formations which range along the Flanks of the Salzburg and Bavarian Alps*, read to the Society in November and December.

Amongst other findings, Sedgwick and Murchison were able to correlate the rock series along two transects running out from the centre of the Alps, one in a north-west direction along the Upper Danube, the other running south towards northern Italy. On both fringes of the Alps they observed lower Tertiary strata, "always highly inclined, sometimes vertical, and occasionally conformable to the beds of the older system". This led them to believe that "this remarkable symmetry confirms the hypothesis of a recent elevation of the Eastern Alps; and makes it probable ... that the Tertiary deposits of the Sub-Apennine regions and of the basin of the Upper Danube belong to one period of formation. ... Such a disjunction of corresponding strata is inexplicable on any hypothesis which rejects the theory of elevation." Fossil evidence led them to conclude that unconformable beds of limestone at Gosau are more recent than the chalk, and that thick deposits of lignite (brown coal) in the valley of the River Inn, that contain freshwater and marine shells, are probably of the same age as the London Clay that outcrops in the south-east of England. In the Upper Danube they found two or three deposits of lignite separated by thick sedimentary deposits.

They also showed that "enormous masses of sandstone and conglomerate many thousand feet in thickness, stretching from the base of
the Alps to the plains of the Danube, are chiefly derived from the degradation of the neighbouring chain – that many of these masses cannot be
distinguished from the newest detritus which lies scattered on the surface
of the earth – that in their prolongation into Switzerland they sometimes
contain bones of mammalia that they are regularly stratified, and alternate
with beds containing marine shells – and that they cannot have been
caused by any transient inundation." [Clark and Hughes 1890a]

Sedgwick and Murchison's initial summary of some of their findings, particularly those relating to the area around Gosau in the
Salzkammergut area of Austria, were published as abstracts in the *Proceedings of the Geological Society*. Some of their interpretations and
conclusions were criticised by English and European geologists, so they
decided to test their conclusions by taking a second look at the areas in
question. Sedgwick was too busy with College work to just drop everything at short notice, so Murchison returned on his own to do further
fieldwork during the summer of 1830.

Shortly after he got back Murchison read a paper to the Society,
*Supplementary observations on the structure of the Austrian and Bavari-
an Alps*, that confirmed their original findings and strengthened their
conclusions with additional field evidence. That solo paper by Murchison
was published in *Transactions*. Sedgwick and Murchison subsequently
wrote a joint paper on the geology of the Eastern Alps, *On the Tertiary
Deposits of the Vale of Gosau in the Salzburg Alps*, that brought together
findings from Murchison's 1830 fieldwork and their joint fieldwork in
1829. The paper was read to the Geological Society in January and February 1831 and published in *Transactions* in 1832.

Sedgwick's work during the 1830s

We noted earlier that, in the first edition of his *Syllabus of a course of
lectures on geology* (1821), Adam sketched out some of the challenges
facing geologists at that time. The second edition was published eleven
years later, in 1832, by which time he had been making his own observations in the field, publishing papers detailing his findings and
conclusions, and debating with other leading geologists.

Already, within his second decade as a geologist, Sedgwick had developed a reputation as a serious, active, well-informed and influential
natural scientist. He was taken seriously by his peers, and by the early

11. Mapping the Rocks

1830s was serving as President of the Geological Society of London, then the hub of serious geological discourse and debate in Britain.

Presidential Addresses to the Geological Society (1830 and 1831)
The two Presidential Addresses that Adam delivered to the Society in 1830 and 1831 throw light on what he regarded as the most important developments and challenges within the new but rapidly growing science.

In 1830 he highlighted important recent papers by Charles Lyell and Roderick Murchison, Murchison and himself, and William Fitton. He also discussed new ideas about river currents, sub-divisions of the Tertiary rocks, and the importance of studying fossils. His review of the year closed with a serious critique of a new book by Andrew Ure, *A New System of Geology*, that sought to defend scriptural geology (and we'll return to in Chapter 14).

In his 1831 Presidential Address, delivered to the Geological Society on the same day that he presented William Smith with the Wollaston Medal, he reviewed the progress of what he called "stratigraphical geology", in which he emphasised the importance of rocks versus fossils, and the value of induction over deduction (that we will explore further in Chapter 15). He welcomed William Herschel's paper *On the astronomical causes which may influence geological phenomena*, and spoke highly of several papers on the raising of mountain chains that French geologist Élie de Beaumont had published in *Annales des Sciences Naturelles*. Adam was impressed by de Beaumont's, views and heaped praise on his "noble generalisations ... [and] admirable researches" because "his conclusions are not based upon any *a priori* reasoning, but on the evidence of facts; and also, because, in part, they are in accordance with my own observations." Adam saw de Beaumont as a fellow supporter of the inductive approach that he firmly believed was the only way to "truth". Although he admired the first volume of Charles Lyell's newly published *Principles of Geology*, Adam was highly critical of the Uniformitarian thinking that Lyell was promoting, and "could not but regret" Lyell's role as "the champion of a great leading doctrine of the Huttonian hypothesis".

Sedgwick abandons Werner's Diluvial Theory
Inspired and informed by de Beaumont's writing, Sedgwick concluded that "the vast masses of diluvial gravel, scattered almost over the surface of the earth, do not belong to one violent and transitory period." That was

an important change in his thinking, after having previously being convinced that diluvium was the result of the Great Flood.

It was a major turning point for Adam, the start of a process of distancing himself from Werner's Diluvial Theory. In his 1831 Presidential Address, he wrote of how that was "a most unwarranted conclusion, when we assumed the contemporaneity of all the superficial gravel on the earth. We saw the clearest traces of diluvial action, and we had, in our sacred histories, the record of a general deluge." That "double testimony", as he put it, of rocks and revelation, encouraged geologists to tie the two things together, which he now saw as a mistake.

He told the Society "Having been myself a believer, and, to the best of my power, a propagator of what I now regard as a philosophic heresy, and having more than once been quoted for opinions I do not now maintain, I think it right, as one of my last acts before I quit this Chair [as President], thus publicly to read my recantation. We ought, indeed, to have paused before we first adopted the diluvial theory, and referred all our old superficial gravel to the action of the Mosaic flood." The error which he and other scriptural geologists had been making, he said, was "in classing together distant unknown formations under one name; in giving them a simultaneous origin, and in determining their date, not by the organic remains we had discovered, but by those we expected hypothetically hereafter to discover in them." Acknowledging his own role in propagating the error, he closed by describing it as "one more example of the passion with which the mind fastens upon general conclusions, and of the readiness with which it leaves the consideration of unconnected truths!"

Adam did not say so himself, but Charles Lyell believed that Sedgwick's commitment to the Diluvial Theory was challenged during his trip to the continent with Murchison in 1829. Adam saw things differently, writing to Murchison in November 1831 "If I have been converted in part from the diluvian theory … it was... by my own gradual improved experience, and by communicating with those about me. Perhaps I may date my change of mind (at least in part) from our journey in the Highlands, where there are so many indications of local diluvial operations."

Dynamical geology
Sedgwick's reputation as a geologist rests mostly on his field mapping work, and the correlation of rocks within and between areas. But he also published papers on some geological processes, or "dynamical geology"

as he called it, that helped the development of geology as a proper science.

His most important contribution in this area was a paper on the origin and structure of the older stratified rocks. He read *Remarks on the structure of large mineral masses, and especially of the chemical changes produced in the aggregation of stratified rocks during different periods after their deposition* to the Geological Society in March 1835, and it was published in *Transactions* the same year. The paper focussed on diagenesis, which is the physical and chemical changes that occur during the conversion of unconsolidated sediment into sedimentary rock. He described the process of concretion, by which hard, compact masses of matter are formed by the precipitation of mineral cement in the spaces between individual particles.

More importantly, in this paper Sedgwick was the first geologist to distinguish between stratification, jointing, and slaty cleavage, that would subsequently allow others to work out the stratigraphic order in many complex geological structures. Stratification is the formation of layers (strata) in sedimentary rocks, which are marked by well-defined bedding planes. Slaty cleavage is the very closely spaced, parallel planes of weakness that give a rock like slate its ability to split into very thin, platy layers. Cleavage obliterates the evidence of original stratification, and it occurs through the long-term compression of strata. Jointing is the formation of natural fractures or cracks (joints) in rocks, often by shrinkage or as a result of pressure.

He also described the columnar structure of basalt and attributed it to shrinkage (we now know it is caused by cooling), and explained "some of the curious forms produced among the Granite Tors" in terms of "the peeling off of the exposed surfaces", noting that "ancient pillars of granite have been known to exfoliate in cylindrical crusts, parallel to the axes of the pillars."

In his early geological work he had thought that faults and "dislocations" (unconformities) were local features that would have little value in correlating strata across regions. But in his 1831 Presidential Address he urged his fellow geologists to "trace them through whole regions, and to examine their relations to each other."

Despite his insistence on the inductive method as the only "right" way of arriving at geological "truth", Adam was sometimes willing to try to account for what he had seen in fieldwork with the help of some overarching theories. One was de Beaumont's 1829 theory on the rapid raising of mountain ranges to account for the parallelism of many moun-

tain chains. Noting that the main mountain chains in the Southern Uplands of Scotland, the Lake District, Wales, the Isle of Man, and Cornwall
were roughly parallel, Sedgwick concluded that they were probably
formed during the same period of geological time, with the Pennines
(which run north-south) probably formed in a later period. Sedgwick also
wondered whether von Buch's "craters of elevation" theory might apply
to the central Lake District.

Ground-breaking fieldwork
For two decades, from the late 1820s onwards, Adam Sedgwick worked
hard to sort out the stratigraphic order (the order in which the rocks were
formed) in many of the complex geological structures in the Lake District, Wales and the southern uplands of Scotland. This would turn out to
be his most important work in geology although, as we shall see in the
next two chapters, it would place him at the epicentre of some major controversies that would have lasting impacts on the development of modern
geology.

Sedgwick starts fieldwork in Wales, 1831
While Adam was still wrestling with the complex geology of the Lake
District, he turned his attention to North Wales. As he described in the
first edition of his *Syllabus* in 1821, in his early days he decided to focus
on what Werner had called the Transition Rocks or Greywacké. Over the
following decade his experience, confidence and ambition all grew, and
he threw himself into the task of unravelling the heavily folded and contorted rocks in the mountains of North Wales. By the end of his first field
season there, in the summer of 1831, he had completed "an approximate
Geological Map from actual survey of the whole of Caernarvonshire."

For the first two or three weeks of that fieldwork Sedgwick had the
company of Charles Darwin, then aged twenty-two. Darwin had abandoned the study of medicine in Edinburgh and moved to Cambridge
University where, instead of training to become a Minister in the Church
of England as his father had hoped, he developed a strong interest in natural history. Months later, in December 1831, he set sail on *HMS Beagle*,
under Captain Robert Fitzroy, as the ship's naturalist. The main objective
of the second voyage of *The Beagle's*, between 1831 and 1836, was to
survey parts of the coast of South America, but Darwin used the opportunity to study the rocks, species, and people of the places they visited.
This subsequently led him to propose his theory of evolution as described
in his ground-breaking 1859 book *On the origin of species by means of*

natural selection, or the preservation of favoured races in the struggle for life. We'll look at *Origin*, and Sedgwick's critical reaction to it, in Chapter 14.

Henslow had asked Sedgwick to allow Darwin to accompany him on the 1831 fieldwork in North Wales to teach him the basics of field geology, including how to identify and describe different types of rocks and fossils, how to work out the sequence of strata in a particular place, how to correlate strata between places, and how to tie the different strands of evidence together to make sense of the geological history of the area. Darwin was a quick learner and Sedgwick saw in him great promise as a natural scientist. In 1835, while Darwin was still away at sea, Sedgwick wrote about him to Dr Butler of Shrewsbury, noting "It was the best thing in the world for him that he went out on the voyage of discovery. There was some risk of his turning out an idle man, but his character will be now fixed, and if God spares his life he will have a great name among the naturalists of Europe."

In 1875 Darwin wrote to Professor Hughes, Sedgwick's successor as Woodwardian Professor and co-editor of *Life and Letters*, explaining how, during the 1831 fieldwork, he and Sedgwick "spent nearly a whole day in Cwm Idwal (in north Snowdonia) examining the rocks carefully, as he was very desirous to find fossils. I have often thought of this day as a good instance of how easy it is for anyone to overlook new phenomena, however conspicuous they may be. The valley is glaciated in the plainest manner, the rocks being mammillated [covered with rounded bumps], deeply scored [striations], with many perched boulders [erratics], and well-defined moraines; yet none of these phenomena were observed by Professor Sedgwick, nor of course by me. Nevertheless they are so plain, that ... the presence of a glacier filling the valley would have rendered the evidence less distinct."

Major geological controversies

As Sedgwick and Murchison worked together in parts of Britain and continental Europe, their stature within the geological community, and their reputations as natural scientists, grew apace. But from the early 1830s onwards, some of their interpretations and papers started to attract criticism and generate controversy, because they challenged the received wisdom about the limits of the then-known geological periods or systems.

In the second of these controversies, the so-called Great Devonian Controversy (that we'll look at further in Chapter 13) that arose as a result of their joint work on the geology of Devon and Cornwall, they were on the same side, arguing against the received wisdom of the day that had been championed by a high-profile opponent. Ironically, the first controversy, the so-called Cambrian-Silurian Controversy (that we'll look at further in Chapter 12), that arose as a result of their work in Wales, pitted Sedgwick against Murchison and left them estranged after many years of working successfully together.

Sedgwick on the geology of the neighbourhood of Cambridge (1845)
It is clear from the second edition of Sedgwick's *Syllabus* (1832) that he had kept a close eye on some engineering projects then being undertaken to drain parts of the Fens, a low-lying naturally marshy area around Cambridge. An artificial drainage system involving banks and pumps was being created to reclaim the land for farming, and in some places groundwater was pumped from the Gault, a thick, heavy clay formation beneath the Fens. Both of these operations exposed geological structures, which gave Sedgwick an interesting focus for fieldwork on his doorstep. He seized the opportunity, and in May 1845 he read a paper *On the Geology of the neighbourhood of Cambridge, including the formations between the chalk escarpment and the great Bedford Level* at the annual meeting of the British Association in Cambridge.

Sedgwick book on the Palaeozoic rocks of England and Wales (1841-1855)
Almost all of the fieldwork that Adam Sedgwick did throughout his long career, in many different areas, was based on rocks of Palaeozoic age. In his day, these were thought to be the oldest rocks on Earth, and during his early years in the field he (along with most other geologists at the time, based on Werner's ideas) was sorting out evidence within them of three main groups – Primary, Transition and Secondary.

Today we know a great deal more about the Palaeozoic period and its rocks than Sedgwick and his contemporaries did. The Palaeozoic era ran from 542 to 241 million years ago and is subdivided into six geologic periods – from oldest to youngest, the Cambrian, Ordovician, Silurian, Devonian, Carboniferous, and Permian. During that time plants became widespread, and the first vertebrate animals colonized land. The Palaeozoic ended with the largest mass extinction in the history of Earth, that wiped out roughly 90% of all marine animal species.

But Sedgwick was drawn to work on these complex old rocks as far back as the 1830's, and he spent most of his geological career trying to sort out their relationships and history. These rocks underlie much of

11. Mapping the Rocks

Britain, particularly the high mountain areas in the north and west, and they were the types of rocks that Adam collected as a youngster during his rambles on the hills around Dentdale.

Some time before 1841, with more than two decades of first-hand experience of studying and mapping them in different places, he had set himself the task of writing "a general work" (book) on the Palaeozoic rocks of England and Wales. His aim was to bring together all of his own work, and set it into context alongside what was then known about this intriguing period in geological history. Writing it would turn out to be a major exercise and take much effort over many years.

As we've already seen, with the examples of his many geological papers, Sedgwick was not a quick writer. He was careful, meticulous, thoughtful and at times cautious in his writing, and was determined to marshal all of his evidence properly and avoid making grand sweeping statements without supporting evidence. We've also seen how, on numerous occasions, ill-health and over-work slowed down his progress, particularly on many writing projects. What's more, as we'll see in Chapter 14, during the 1840's and 1850s Adam's attention was often diverted away from his primary task of fieldwork by the continuing tension between scriptural geology and 'modern' geology, and the emerging debate about creation versus evolution. An added factor was Adam's age; by 1840 he was in his mid-50s and the responsibilities of his college and university work in Cambridge and his cathedral work in Norwich (described in Chapter 17) were taking their toll.

Nonetheless, always one to accept a challenge, in 1841 he started work pulling together all the evidence he could find on the Palaeozoic rocks of England and Wales. This included his own work in the Lake District, joint work with Murchison in Wales (described in Chapter 12), Devon and Cornwall (Chapter 13), and Scotland.

Over the next ten years we find him engaging in fieldwork in Ireland (1841), Wales (1841, 1842, 1843,1846), the Lake District (1845, 1851), Scotland (1841, 1848), and Devon and Cornwall (1851). Some excursions were designed to fill in gaps in his first-hand knowledge of particular areas, but others were to review and where necessary update his understanding of areas he had previously worked in.

Sedgwick fieldwork in Ireland (1841) and Scotland (1841, 1848)
There are many areas of Palaeozoic rocks in southern Ireland, then still part of the United Kingdom, but Sedgwick had never been there so he made a visit in 1841 to see them for himself. From Cambridge he trav-

elled to Dartmoor, where he spent a week doing fieldwork, then on to Plymouth where he attended the annual meeting of the British Association and met up with Richard Griffith, who would be his guide in Ireland. After sailing over to Dublin, they worked their way south through Wicklow and Wexford, then headed west to Waterford and Cork, then on to Killarney, where he admitted the lakes were even more beautiful than those in his native Lake District.

Their destination was Dingle Bay, in the south-west tip of Ireland, where they wanted to see "the great promontories that stand out from the ... coast ... [and] are composed of ridges of finely peaked mountains; and the bays that run up for thirty or forty miles between these ridges are most magnificent, when the weather permits you to see them." Adam was impressed by the high cliffs, and the mountains that "rise directly out of the sea ... as high as Scawfell" [Scafell in the Lake District], but not by the local people, noting "you never saw anything so wild as the country and the people, or so miserable as the cabins many of them contrive to live in." They then travelled north to Limerick, then cross-country to Dublin and up the east coast, stopping for a day to climb the Mourne Mountains, a granite mountain range. After crossing the Irish Sea, Sedgwick and Griffith spent three weeks studying rocks and visiting friends in Ayr, Kilmarnock and Glasgow, across "the wild chains of Galloway", before returning to Dent.

Adam returned to southern Scotland in the summer of 1848, to review and revise the findings of his 1841 work along "the southern chain of Scotland that runs from St Abb's Head to the Mull of Galloway." In August 1850 he read a paper to the annual meeting of the British Association in Edinburgh, *On the Geological Structure and Relations of the Frontier Chain of Scotland*, that summarised the findings of those two trips, and the results of the fieldwork done in 1849 by Lake District geologist John Ruthven. He described "the chain" as "essentially composed of a peculiar form of greywacké" that was often coarse, and occasionally passed into "a very coarse conglomerate" that included beds of soft shale that in many places "has undergone such compression and induration that it passes into an earthy flag-stone, and, more rarely, into a pretty good roofing-slate." He noted that, throughout the chain, the beds are "highly inclined" and "thrown into contortions and undulations", and although he saw no "great protruding granitic masses", in many places granite had changed local rock structures, and in a few places he saw mineral veins. After the meeting he took a short geological tour in Scotland with Murchison.

11. Mapping the Rocks

Sedgwick's work on the Lake District (1845, 1851)
Adam spend the summer of 1845 engaged in fieldwork in the Lake District, reviewing his earlier work there and trying to establish where the rocks above the Coniston Limestone (now known as the Dent Group), that he correlated with the Bala Limestone in north Wales, fit into the Silurian system. Several months earlier, in March 1845, he had read a paper *On the Classification of the Fossiliferous Slates of Cumberland, Westmoreland and Lancashire* to the Geological Society, and the following January he read an updated paper that included results from the summer fieldwork.

Between 1851 and 1855 Sedgwick's focus sharpened on the Cambrian-Silurian rocks in the Lake District, North Wales and Southern Scotland. He was fitting together the pieces of his complex geological jigsaw, having recognised that the Silurian rocks in North and South Wales were of different types, and that the rocks he had studied in the Lake District and the south of Scotland were very similar to those in North Wales. Over that period he also did further fieldwork in the hills of southern Scotland, to recheck his earlier conclusions.

Sedgwick finishes the book on the British Palaeozoic Rocks and Fossils (1855)
As the editors of *Life and Letters* put it, "Sedgwick's ... whole geological life was dominated by his intention to write a general work upon the Palaeozoic rocks of England and Wales. ... Material was accumulated year by year, but the leisure for making use of it never came, and at last, as he sadly admitted at the close of his life, 'the infirmities of old age had gathered round me before I had put my work in order.'"

Whilst his ambition had long been to write a whole book about the Palaeozoic rocks, in the end he had to be satisfied with writing a substantial Introduction to a catalogue of the Palaeozoic fossils in the Museum of Geology that Frederick McCoy, his former Museum Assistant (who we met in Chapter 8), had compiled. Sedgwick and McCoy had worked on *A Synopsis of the classification of the British Palaeozoic Rocks: with a systematic description of the British Palaeozoic Fossils in the Geological Museum of the University of Cambridge* for nearly six years, and it was published in 1855.

When McCoy had finished describing the fossil collection, Sedgwick promised to "draw up a Synopsis of the British Palaeozoic System, so far as it appeared to have been made out on good physical evidence", and to locate the fossils and his own geological findings in their right places within the British Palaeozoic series. But ill-health and old age prevented him from completing that task to the standard he had hoped for, and what eventually appeared was a broad overview of the rocks embedded in a rather bitter account of Murchison's role in the Cambrian-Silurian Controversy (Chapter 13) and a spirited defence of his own work in Wales.

Adam's 98-page Introduction to the *Synopsis* was not his finest writing, and it represents a rather melancholy final testimony to his long geological career.

12. The Great Devonian Controversy

"We had a grand battle at the Geological Society last night, in which I bore the brunt on our side; but, though well banged, I was not beaten."
Adam Sedgwick to Canon Wodehouse (June 1837)

The first serious fieldwork that Adam Sedgwick did, in his early days as Professor of Geology in 1819 and 1820, was based in South West England (as we saw in Chapter 11). After that he worked in various parts of Britain, particularly in his home patch the Lake District.

A decade and a half after publishing his first papers on the geology of the South West, he returned to that area in 1836 to study the Culm Measures – the Greywacké, the "older rocks" as he called them – of Central Devon. Murchison also began field mapping in Devon around the same time. Although by then the two men had worked together on numerous occasions, this time they set off working separately, starting from different places. They also used slightly different approaches; Sedgwick was committed to distinguishing different rocks on the basis of stratigraphy (rock structures, strata and mineral content), whereas Murchison put greater emphasis on palaeontology (fossil content).

These investigations, separately and together, brought them into a serious debate with prominent English geologist and palaeontologist Henry de la Beche (1796-1855) over the significance of rock strata in Devon that contained coal plants. That dispute grew into what became known as The Great Devonian Controversy and ended in the recognition of a new system – the Devonian System – within the Palaeozoic Era, between the older Silurian and the younger Carboniferous Systems.

In this chapter, we'll trace the background to the controversy, and explore how it developed and was eventually resolved. The story is described in much greater detail in Martin Rudwick's monumental 1985 book *The Great Devonian Controversy*.

Origin (1834)

By the early 1830s geologists had only a rather basic understanding of the complex stratigraphy of Devon and Cornwall; it consisted largely of indistinct and highly contorted formations of ancient rocks broadly termed Greywacké, after Werner. Sedgwick and Murchison had begun to sort out the Greywacké in North and South Wales (as we'll see in Chapter 13), confirming its geological antiquity. It was then the oldest-known rock, and appeared to be virtually fossil-free.

In December 1834 De la Beche caused a storm, in a letter *On the anthracite found near Bideford in North Devon* that was read to the Geological Society and published in *Proceedings*. He claimed that the Culm strata, that covered much of North Devon and contained fossil plants, belonged to these Greywacké formations. If the claim was true these rocks would be as old as the Greywacké in Wales. More importantly, it would challenge one of the key principles of stratigraphy, that the age and relative position of strata could be determined simply by the fossils they contained. De la Beche argued that finding Carboniferous (coal) fossils deep within the Greywacké strata showed this method of dating rocks to be unreliable, because the strata we see today may not be in their original positions because of geological changes since they were deposited.

Development (1835-1839)

The stakes were high, and de la Beche's bold and controversial claim had to be either verified or withdrawn.

Initial debate

Murchison criticised de la Beche for persisting with a Wernerian approach to describing and dating rocks, that had by then been discredited and largely abandoned. More importantly, he disagreed strongly with de la Beche's interpretation, arguing that he had misread his own field evidence that showed fossils near the top of the strata but not further down. As Murchison pointed out, the fossil plants indicated Coal Measures (Carboniferous), implying that de la Beche must have overlooked a major unconformity between younger Carboniferous rocks and older Greywacké rocks beneath them.

Lyell agreed with Murchison, but de la Beche dismissed both men as armchair geologists who had never even visited the area he was describing. He was enraged by Murchison's attack on his integrity and ability, and looked to Sedgwick for support against the heavyweight opposition of Lyell and Murchison.

Apparently, Sedgwick initially had some sympathy with the position de la Beche found himself in. He reminded Murchison by letter that his argument was based on negative evidence – the lack of any evidence of an unconformity. Besides which, no one had any idea what plants might have existed during the Greywacké era.

Within months de la Beche was appointed head of the newly-created geological branch of the Ordnance Survey, and by mid-1835 he had been promoted to become first Director of the Geological Survey. He now represented the establishment – he held a high-profile post, his views were taken seriously, and he could exert great influence over the ways in which geology would develop. The days of the enthusiastic amateur geologist tramping around the country at will with a hammer and map were coming to an end, certainly as far as serious geological mapping and interpretation were concerned. Opportunities for paid employment and career development in geology were starting to open up.

Despite being initially sympathetic to de la Beche, after giving the matter further thought, Sedgwick realised that Murchison was probably right. What convinced him to switch his allegiance was that, on a geological map de la Beche had produced of Pembrokeshire in south west Wales, some rocks that were Culm-like and contained fossil plants, like the ones Adam had described in Devon, were coloured as Greywacké. But, below and to the north of these rocks were Greywacké rocks that Sedgwick knew looked to be part of a continuous series, but actually had a different strike (they were tilted at a different angle). This suggested to Sedgwick that Murchison was right about the hidden unconformity between the two series of rocks.

Sedgwick-Murchison joint fieldwork in Devon (1836)
After several seasons working separately on the older rocks in Wales, towards the end of June 1836 Sedgwick and Murchison turned their attention to Devon and Cornwall. Their aim was to test de la Beche's claims, and quite literally get to the bottom of the rocks there. They believed that the Greywacké might be anything from relatively young Carboniferous in age to truly ancient pre-Cambrian. This would mark the start of two years of joint fieldwork in which they measured and described geological sections, mapped strata, and collected fossils which they sent to experienced palaeontologists for detailed study and classification. The story became more convincing as the evidence slowly mounted.

They started work in North Devon, where they accepted the older rocks as Lower Silurian. Above them was the Culm – a series of shales and thin sandstones, with slate, limestone and chert in some places; named after the Devon term for soft, sooty coal – that at that time was thought to be Carboniferous in age. Between the Silurian and the Culm they expected to find evidence of a major unconformity, but failed to do so. Within the main body of the Culm they found black limestones containing a fossil bivalve called *Posidonia*, and higher up they found thin layers of coal. De la Beche had reported finding slaty cleavage in some Culm rocks, but Sedgwick and Murchison found none. The evidence indicated to them that the Culm sat on top of the Greywacké, and not within it.

The two men then moved to South Devon to look at the rocks there, where some areas of fossil-rich limestones – around Plymouth, for example – were believed to belong to the Cambrian. They quickly surveyed along a line running north-south through central Devon, and found evidence of a broad underground depression containing Culm rocks, where in places the rock series looked equivalent to the Coal Measures within the Upper Carboniferous Series. The depression was bounded to the north by Cambrian and some Lower Silurian rocks, and to the south by thick Cambrian strata. This reinforced their belief that somewhere beneath Devon there must be an extensive unconformity beneath the Culm, which had yet to be found.

Sedgwick and Murchison reported the findings from their two summer field seasons in Devon in a joint paper, *A classification of the old slate rocks of Devonshire, and on the true position of the Culm Deposits in the central portion of that county*, that was read to the Geological Section of the British Association meeting in Bristol in August 1836. They showed that the Culm Measures lay at the top of the rocks they subsequently named Devonian, and that they belonged to the Carboniferous System.

By all accounts, de la Beche responded badly to "having a paper sprung on him without warning, something he considered ungentlemanly", as Hallam (1989) put it. He accepted that the Culm must lie at the top of the rock sequence, but would not accept that it might be Carboniferous. He clung to the belief that all of the rocks in Devon were older than Carboniferous, reminding critics that no trace of an unconformity had been found anywhere in the county.

Other geologists sprang to support Sedgwick and Murchison's view that de la Beche was wrong and the Culm really was Carboniferous. Yorkshire geologist John Phillips (1800-1874) pointed out that *Posidonia* was a fossil characteristic of the Mountain (Carboniferous) Limestone of Yorkshire, and the Culm could be pre-Carboniferous because he had found the Mountain Limestone passing laterally into coal-bearing deposits in Scotland. The support was welcome, but Murchison was not yet on totally firm ground, because fossil plants had been found in some of the strata that he had assigned to the Lower Silurian, even though he insisted that there were no authentic records of land plants that old. This gave de la Beche some wiggle room to continue insisting that strata containing fossil plants could be traced upwards into the Culm without a break.

Sedgwick-Murchison On the Physical Structure of Devonshire (1837)
In December 1836 Sedgwick and Murchison read their *Description of the raised beach in Barnstaple or Bideford Bay, on the north-west coast of Devonshire* to the Geological Society; it was published in *Transactions* that month. They put forward some unorthodox views that were quite heavily criticised, which made them cautious about stirring up too much opposition just as they were putting the finishing touches to a long-awaited paper dealing with the Culm deposits in Devon.

Through a combination of fatigue, poor health, over-work, and anxiety about taking on de la Beche (who had many friends in high places) in a very public way, both Sedgwick and Murchison were cautious in what they said and how they said it. At the end of May and in mid-June 1837 they read *On the physical structure of Devonshire, and on the subdivisions and geological relations of its older stratified deposits* to the Society. The discussion afterwards was evidently lively. The day after Adam read the second part of the paper, he wrote to tell Rev Philip Wodehouse, a fellow Canon of Norwich Cathedral, "We had a grand battle at the Geological Society last night, in which I bore the brunt on our side; but, though well banged, I was not beaten."

In the paper, they described the Upper Cambrian as well developed in Devon, with Lower Silurian present in the top strata in North Devon, both conclusions based on rock types rather than fossils. They considered the Culm, in which ammonite-like fossils had by then been found, to be equivalent to the Carboniferous Mountain Limestone and Coal Measures.

Sedgwick urged Murchison to avoid personal controversy with de la Beche, particularly after he became Director of the Geological Survey in July 1835. Still anxious about the possible fallout from their 1837 paper, he shared his thoughts in a letter to Charles Lyell. He wrote of how, in his view, de la Beche had "published a map of Devon bad in its details ... and destitute of any principles of classification", despite warnings from Murchison about his errors, and he described how he and Murchison had intended to check out the Culm in Devon for themselves, after a quick excursion to Ireland in the autumn of 1835. He told Lyell that de la

Beche's map "ought to be withdrawn without loss of time. It cannot, by any tinkering, be brought into order. It must start on new principles. Many of the details no doubt may stand, but even the details are very far indeed from what they ought to be." He ended by pointing out that "In our opinion Devonshire is radically wrong, as it is now published" and asking "Are we to shut our mouths, and let the error continue to be propagated?" Sedgwick was clearly feeling the heat at this stage, but not clear about the best way forward.

The debate became even more challenging in 1837, when Devon-based geologist Robert Austen (1808-1884) read his own paper *On the geology of the South-east of Devonshire* to the Geological Society. It was published in *Transactions* in 1842. Austen had studied geology under Buckland at Oxford, helped de la Beche map the area around Newton Abbot in Devon, and assisted Sedgwick in fieldwork in Devon during 1836.

He claimed to have found evidence that, in South Devon, the Culm lay unconformably on top of the Transition rocks that included the Devon limestones, whereas in North Devon there was no sign of any unconformity. His North Devon evidence supported de la Beche's interpretation, but his South Devon evidence (that attributed the Culm to the Carboniferous) supported Sedgwick and Murchison's. He did have one important piece of new evidence – based on the similarity of the fossils he saw in Devon to those in similar strata in the Carboniferous rocks elsewhere, he proposed that the limestone in south east Devon was equivalent to the Mountain Limestone. This finding was a mixed blessing to Sedgwick. Demonstrating distinct differences between fossil faunas in Silurian and Carboniferous rocks challenged the integrity of his Upper Cambrian Series, but it also confirmed the unbroken limestone sequence and the identities of the fossils that he had seen for himself in South Devon.

By this time, Adam Sedgwick was working hard to provide the evidence needed to convince all leading geologists that his interpretation of the geology of Devon was the correct one. Thus, for example, before he started his summer field season in 1838 he prepared and in late March and May read to the Geological Society a very detailed *Synopsis of the English Series of Stratified Rocks inferior to the Old Red Sandstone, with an attempt to determine the successive natural groups and formations* that was published in *Proceedings* later that year. This paper brought together the results of much of his earlier work in the Lake District, Wales, and South West England, and included a table showing how the rocks in different places could be correlated.

12. The Great Devonian Controversy

Sedgwick spent that summer in South Devon, re-surveying the area south of Dartmoor and collecting fossils for palaeontologist John Phillips to classify on his behalf. The results of that work would form part of the joint paper he and Murchison read to the Society the following year, that would generate great excitement and ultimately decide the outcome of The Great Devonian Controversy, at least during their lifetimes.

Breakthrough (1839)

In his eagerly-awaited and comprehensive *Report on the geology of Cornwall, Devon and West Somerset* (1839), de la Beche correlated the Culm with the Upper Greywacké, implying a rough equivalence to Murchison's Silurian, but he interpreted both as essentially local deposits. He continued to insist that all of the older rocks in Devon belonged to the Greywacké Series, but accepted that the Series might continue up to the Old Red Sandstone. But he doggedly hung on to his view that there was still not enough reliable evidence to show that the Culm was not part of the Silurian.

Murchison's book *The Silurian System* (that we'll look at in more detail in Chapter 13) was published in the same year. In it he suggested that all of the ancient rocks in south-west England might be stratigraphically equivalent to the Old Red Sandstone, that he proposed should be treated as a System in its own right rather than being regarded as the base of the Carboniferous System. He emphasised the importance of fossil evidence in correlating rocks within and between areas, and urged geologists to look for transitional fossils that might bridge the sharp divide between the fossils that had already been described in Silurian and Carboniferous rocks. In this, he was still holding out for confirmation of his belief that no unconformity separates the two rock series.

Sedgwick-Murchison propose the Devonian System (1839)

In April and May 1839 Sedgwick and Murchison read to the Geological Society a joint paper *On the physical structure of Devonshire*, that summarised their views on the relative age of the older sedimentary rocks in Devon. Conscious that the debate surrounding de la Beche's proposals was not dying down, they decided to present their paper before setting off for a summer of fieldwork in Europe, despite some reservations from Sedgwick. The paper was published in the Society's *Transactions* later that year.

Their two main conclusions were unambiguous. First, they argued that "the oldest slaty and arenaceous rocks of Devon and Cornwall are the equivalents of the Old Red Sandstone". As Sedgwick's obituary in *The Times* would put it, more than three decades later (28 January 1873), "the bold removal of the whole of the schistose and greywacké rocks of Devon and Cornwall to the Old Red Sandstone is a generalization which could arise only from a long, patient, accurate, and extensive practice in the field, together with a willingness to adopt suggestions from whatever quarter they might be advanced."

Secondly, and even more importantly, Sedgwick and Murchison demonstrated that "there is a group of rocks, characterized by an appropriate group of fossils, in a position, geologically as well as zoologically, intermediate between the Carboniferous and Silurian systems". They named this group of rocks that lay between the Upper Silurian (below) and the Lower Carboniferous (above) groups the Devonian System. The fossil molluscs, corals, brachiopods, and trilobites found in the limestones of South Devon were found to be of mixed Silurian-Carboniferous character, which supported Murchison's earlier claim that no evidence had been found of land plants before the Silurian.

The paper would turn out to be a milestone, not just within The Great Devonian Controversy, but within the development of geology at large. It received mixed reactions at the time. Buckland was sympathetic to their findings, and de la Beche raised no strong objections. George Bellas Greenhough, who had published the first geological map of Devon, was unimpressed that an entirely new stratigraphic system had been proposed, based only on evidence from one particular area. Austen was disappointed not to have his own work in Devon acknowledged more fully.

Sedgwick-Murchison fieldwork in Europe (summer 1839)
Sedgwick and Murchison were keen to find evidence elsewhere that supported their conclusions about the Devonian rocks in Devon so, in the summer of 1839, ten years after their first joint excursion in Europe, they travelled to Germany and Belgium to carry out fieldwork there, guided by local geologists. Their specific challenge was to see if they could find a group of strata between the Carboniferous and Silurian Systems that contained the same fossils as those found in the Devonian rocks in England.

Their observations in the field were not promising. Sedgwick was convinced that rocks in the Ardennes must be Cambrian, and that rocks on both sides of the Rhine that had been thought of as Devonian must be Lower Silurian. He doubted whether any of the rocks they had studied on the continent could be classed as Devonian, and even lost confidence in his Devonian interpretation in south west England. When he got back to Cambridge he wrote that he had told his geology students "that I gave up the Devonian case, and that I considered the whole of the old rocks of Devon and Cornwall (excepting the Culms) as inferior to the Derby limestone; but I added that the matter was still *sub judice*, and that our fossils had not been examined."

Much as Sedgwick had long insisted on the primacy of stratigraphic over palaeontological evidence, he was relieved that Sowerby and Lonsdale subsequently identified Devonian corals in fossils that he and Murchison had collected in the Eifel mountain range in eastern Belgium. That was enough to confirm Devonian strata between the Carboniferous and Silurian Systems in Europe.

Sedgwick and Murchison read a paper describing their findings, *On the distribution and classification of the older or Palaeozoic deposits of the north of Germany and Belgium, and their comparison with formations of the same age in the British Isles*, to the Geological Society in May 1840. The 90-page paper, accompanied by a map, sections and plates of fossils, was published in *Transactions* the same year.

Resolution (1840)

The Great Devonian Controversy had started in 1834 when de la Beche described the Culm Measures in central Devon as Greywacké, defining them in Wernerian terms as Primary rocks. That view had been supported the following year by David Williams at the Dublin meeting of the British Association.

Most other geologists at that time regarded the Culm as Carboniferous, therefore much younger than de la Beche and Williams had thought. When Sedgwick and Murchison started their joint fieldwork in Devon in 1836, their objective was to establish the relative age of the Culm, but they ended up going much further and established an entirely new system of rocks which they named the Devonian System.

The controversy died down after Sedgwick and Murchison found fossil evidence of Devonian rocks in Belgium and Germany in 1839, and Murchison found similar deposits in Russia in 1840. After that, most geologists accepted the Devonian period (that is now dated at 408 to 360 million years ago) as a new Palaeozoic System below the Carboniferous and above the Silurian.

Sedgwick revisited Devon and Cornwall in the summer of 1851, accompanied by his former Museum Assistant (now Professor) McCoy, to check his conclusions about the Culm and Devonian in the light of subsequent work by other geologists. In particular, he wanted to look at some sections along the south coast of Devon that Murchison had coloured Silurian on a geological map of England published in 1850 by the Society for the Diffusion of Useful Knowledge (in Chapter 13 we'll look at the Welsh map by the Society which figures in the Cambrian-Silurian Controversy). Sedgwick described his main findings in a letter to the Duke of Argyll in October 1851, in which he pointed out that "The slate rocks of Cornwall are essentially Devonian – but there is one exception. Part of the promontory running down to the Dodman (between St Austell Bay and Falmouth Bay) is certainly older. I should call it Cambrian; Murchison would call it Lower Silurian. … Last year Murchison put in a colour [on the map] for Upper Silurian rocks through a part of Cornwall and South Devon. He was misled by false information. The parts so coloured are all Devonian." He described the evidence and his interpretations of it in a paper *On the slate rocks of Devon and Cornwall*, that he read to the Geological Society in November 1851 and was published in the *Quarterly Journal* later that year.

13. The Cambrian-Silurian Controversy

"When it came to the test, the bluntness of the Yorkshireman ... and the pride of the Scot, proved incompatible."
Douglas Robson (1986)

In 1831 Adam Sedgwick began fieldwork on the rocks and geological structures of the mountains of North Wales that would form one of his most enduring contributions to the development of modern geology, culminating in the recognition and naming of the Cambrian System. This project would cement his reputation at the forefront of geology during the middle decades of the nineteenth century, but it would also cost him dearly because it led to a serious and lasting fallout with Roderick Murchison.

In this chapter, we look at the background to what became known as The Cambrian-Silurian Controversy, examine how it developed and what form it took, and see how it was ultimately resolved after the death of both men. As we'll see, it overlapped in time with the Great Devonian Controversy, in which Sedgwick and Murchison were on the same winning side, but in this controversy they found themselves on opposing sides, and there could only be one winner.

The story is told in much greater detail in James Secord's (1986) book *Controversy in Victorian Geology: The Cambrian-Silurian Dispute*.

Origin (1834)
Sedgwick and Murchison fieldwork in Wales (1831-1835)
Sedgwick was eager to build a better picture of what were then the oldest-known rocks in Britain, and to see if there was evidence of older rocks beneath them.

By 1831 geologists had pieced together an outline of the sequence and distribution of rocks down to the Old Red Sandstone, that is now known to have been deposited in the Devonian Period between 416 million and 359 million years ago. They had also found and mapped much older rocks below the sandstones in many mountain areas in Britain, which (following Werner) they had called the Transition or Greywacké Series, but they knew very little about them. Sedgwick and others had found fossils in Transition rocks in the Lake District and the Welsh Bor-

207

ders, but no one had yet attempted to correlate the rocks or fossils in Transition rocks between these two areas.

Early in June 1831 Murchison started fieldwork on the "indeterminable greywacké" in Wales. He had invited Sedgwick to join him, which he did after a slight delay caused by ill-health and other work commitments, so Murchison pressed ahead on his own. Although both men had previously done a great deal of fieldwork together, on this occasion they chose to work separately, each mapping the rocks in a different part of Wales but both seeking evidence that they could combine into one cohesive description and interpretation.

The decision to work separately but with a common purpose turned out to be very significant, and it provides the key to understanding why the controversy arose between two experienced field geologists who (as we saw in Chapters 11 and 12) had worked together successfully in other parts of Britain and Europe. As many geologists since then have pointed out, if they had started at the same place and then worked outwards in opposite directions, they would have been much more likely to sort out the sequence of the rocks properly. As it turned out, they had great difficulty and not a little conflict in correlating the rocks series they had mapped in different parts of Wales, with no common "ground zero" to tie everything into.

Murchison's fieldwork and papers

Murchison planned to map the then unknown rocks of the Welsh Borders, starting in South Wales and heading towards the north and the west. As he wrote to a friend after the excursion, his entourage included his "wife and maid, two good grey nags [horses] and a little carriage, saddles being strapped on behind for occasional equestrian use." He traced and recorded the rocks, collecting specimens and fossils along the way. His wife served as field assistant, making sketches of the places and the rocks he worked on.

Luck was on his side, because he found Greywacké (a dark, coarse-grained sandstone) just below Old Red Sandstone, a well-known formation that Sedgwick had described in Devon and named Devonian (as we saw in Chapter 12). Up to that time, the Devonian had been thought to be the oldest rock formation in Britain, and Murchison realised he had found something very special.

The sandstone beds within the Greywacké appeared to in order, unchanged since being deposited, and the uppermost ones contained distinctive fossils that had been described elsewhere and whose stratigraphic limits were known. After tracing them across a wide area, Murchison realised that he could sub-divide the strata on the basis of their fossil content, just as William Smith had done years earlier in many parts of England.

Murchison described what he had found during that first season of fieldwork in Wales at the first meeting of the British Association, held later that year (1831) in York. He also read papers to the Geological Society that were published in *Proceedings* – one *On the sedimentary deposits which occupy the western parts of Shropshire and Herefordshire* (1833) and the other *On the structure and classification of the transition rocks of Shropshire, Herefordshire and part of Wales, and on the lines of disturbance which have affected that series of deposits, including the Valley of Elevation at Woolhope* (1834)

Murchison named this system of rocks the Silurian, after the Silures, a war-like Celtic tribe that lived in the Welsh Borderlands at the time of the Romans, with the Ordovices as their northern neighbours. He divided the rocks into four Groups – the Ludlow, Wenlock, Caradoc, and Llandeilo Groups – naming them after the places where he first identified them. He then described them as two series, the Upper Series comprising the Ludlow Group on top of the Wenlock, and the Lower Series comprising the Caradoc Group on top of the Llandeilo. This was the classification that Murchison described in a paper *On the Silurian System of rocks* that was published in the *Philosophical Magazine* in 1835, and the one he developed four years later in his book *The Silurian System* (1839).

Sedgwick's fieldwork and papers
Sedgwick started his fieldwork in North Wales and planned to work his way southwards, aiming to meet up with Murchison and marry together their two sets of observations. His experience of working on the complex rocks in the rugged mountain terrain of the Lake District prepared him well for work in North-West Wales, including the ancient slates in Snowdonia and the Lleyn Peninsula. He began in August 1831, several months after Murchison had started work further south. He wrote to advise Murchison that, after exploring North Wales, "if I have time, I shall then make a long run towards the south, so as to make one or two long traverses in South Wales. In this way our work will link together."

The 1831 field season took him from Shrewsbury, across the Vale of Clwyd, to Denbigh, north to Conway, and west to Anglesey, that he described as "almost as distinct in structure from Snowdonia, as if they had been separated by the Atlantic sea rather than the straits of Menai." He

Wedded to the Rocks

traced strata across North Wales and mapped faults and displaced rocks, putting most of his time and effort into describing the rocks (the structures, strata and minerals) but paying no attention to fossils, which he later realised had been a big mistake.

Adam described the results of his 1831 fieldwork to the Cambridge Philosophical Society, and presented "a brief synopsis, illustrated by sections" to the meeting of the British Association that met in Oxford in June 1832, with William Buckland in the chair.

He returned to North Wales the following July (1832) when, as well as carrying out his own fieldwork, he gave the young Charles Darwin tuition in identifying, mapping, recording and interpreting rocks and rock structures (as we saw in Chapter 12). Adam later described that field season as "the severest summer's task of my geological life, namely, the interpretation and partial delineation of the order and principal flexures of all the older deposits of the counties of Merioneth, Montgomery, and Denbigh."

Adam studied rocks in Snowdonia and the Berwyn Mountains, mapped folded strata, and described anticlines (folds of stratified rock in which the strata slope downwards from the crest). He was particularly interested in some bands of "black shelly limestone" he found in the rocks at the top of the Berwyns, that he could correlate with rocks he was familiar with in the Lake District. He described them as "absolutely identical with the Transition line which separates the greywacké of Westmoreland from the great system of greenslate and porphyry of the central mountains of Cumberland."

During his 1832 fieldwork in central Wales, Sedgwick found a separate rock formation below and therefore older than the rocks that Murchison had described and later named Silurian. He named it the Cambrian System, after Cambria, the Latin name for Wales. He described it to Murchison and the British Association that same year, ensuring that he would get the credit for finding and naming the oldest rocks then known.

As we shall see, in the years ahead he and Murchison would have serious disagreements over whether what Sedgwick called the Cambrian was just the lower part of Murchison's Silurian, or a completely separate older system. Although Murchison insisted it was the former, the editors of *Life and Letters* were in no doubt that it was the latter. In support of that view, they wrote that "the Geological Survey thirty years afterwards gave no more subdivisions of the stratified rocks of this area than Sedgwick had made in 1832, and ... their principal sections were drawn approximately along the very same lines as Sedgwick had then suggested to Murchison."

Sedgwick-Murchison joint fieldwork
Sedgwick's and Murchison's separate fieldwork in different parts of Wales during 1831 and 1832 had yielded valuable evidence, but it threw up the challenge of marrying together the two sets of findings and interpretations. With that in mind, the two men made a joint trip through parts of Wales and the Welsh Borders in June and July 1834, hoping to establish the relations between their two 'Systems' – Murchison's Silurian and Sedgwick's allegedly older Cambrian.

Six weeks of fieldwork visiting the same sites together allowed them to correlate their findings. Both emerged satisfied that Murchison's Lower Silurian Llandeilo Group sat on top of Sedgwick's Upper Cambrian Bala Limestone, flags and grits, at least in the Berwyn Hills, and that Silurian rocks generally lie above Cambrian rocks. That clarified the order in which the rocks had been deposited, and thus their relative age, but it left open the question of whether the Lower Silurian and the Upper Cambrian were part of the same system or separate systems. This question lay at the epicentre of the subsequent very public dispute between the two geologists.

Development (1835-1851)
Joint paper to the British Association in Oxford (1835)
Sedgwick and Murchison emerged from their joint fieldwork in 1834 comfortable that they had established and agreed the order in which the old sedimentary strata in Wales and the Welsh Borders had been deposited.

They read a joint paper *On the Silurian and Cambrian Systems, exhibiting the order in which the older sedimentary strata succeed each other in England and Wales* to the fifth annual meeting of the British Association in Dublin in 1835, that was published in the Association's *Report* the following year. This was the first time that Sedgwick had used the name Cambrian in public, but he did not refer to it at that time as a System. In the paper, Murchison described his four sub-divisions of the Silurian (Ludlow, Wenlock, Caradoc, and Llandeilo) and Sedgwick described the Upper, Middle, and Lower Cambrian rocks, but said nothing about fossils.

By this stage both men were hopeful that their conclusions would be confirmed in studies elsewhere, but there was much still to play for. Their conclusions were based on rocks exposed in different places, without extensive proof of overlap, and with inference suggesting rather than hard evidence establishing which was the older.

There were other challenges too, because although Murchison had defined his Silurian System on the basis of both rocks and fossils, it was not known how far down those fossils might extend before stopping at some stratigraphic break; the question was, what defined the base of the Silurian rocks? We've already noted that Sedgwick used rock strata and minerals but not fossils to define the three sub-divisions of his Cambrian, and the picture might change radically if the fossil evidence pointed in a different direction.

All seemed well between Sedgwick and Murchison for several years after their joint presentation to the British Association in 1835. In 1838 Sedgwick published *A synopsis of the English series of stratified rocks inferior to the Old Red Sandstone – with an attempt to determine the successive natural groups and formations* in the *Proceedings* of the Geological Society. He believed that paper completed their study of the fossiliferous rocks on the British Isles, but the following year things were to take a turn for the worse, when Murchison published his book *The Silurian System*.

Murchison's book The Silurian System (1839)

Murchison had worked on this book for a long time before it was published early in 1839. It was a major achievement; Clark and Hughes (1890b) described it as a "splendid work ... Carefully worked out, fully illustrated, giving the results of an examination of the fossils by some of the best palaeontologists of the day."

The book ran to eight hundred pages and described the rocks and fossils in Murchison's Upper and Lower Silurian Series. It was accompanied by a supplement containing plates, sections and a coloured map showing the distribution and limits of the Silurian System in South Wales and the Welsh Borders.

Murchison dedicated the book to his friend Adam Sedgwick in gushing terms typical of gentlemanly behaviour of the time – "To you, my dear Sedgwick, a large portion of whose life has been devoted to the arduous study of the older British rocks, I dedicate this work. Having explored with you many a tract, both at home and abroad, I beg you to accept this offering as a memorial of friendship, and of the high sense I entertain of the value of your labours. Yours most sincerely, Roderick Impey Murchison."

13. The Cambrian-Silurian Controversy

He sent one of the first copies of the book to Sedgwick, who was then in Norwich on cathedral duties (that we'll look at further in Chapter 17). Adam's response was apparently favourable; he wrote back to tell Murchison "your book is only a book for geologists. Natives of the country will read and pick out parts of it ... but, as a whole, it is far too good and deep for any but a true geologist." But he turned down a request from Murchison to write a "little article, if only half a column" to promote it in *The Times*, stressing in a friendly note that he was too busy and the book was good enough not to need promoting in that way.

In the book, Murchison attributed all rocks beneath the Llandeilo Group to the Cambrian, but he did not describe any of them in detail. He would subsequently claim that the Cambrian was really part of his Lower Silurian, and that Sedgwick had wrongly thought it a separate system and given it a new name. As Sedgwick's Obituary in *The Times* (28 January 1873) put it bluntly many years later, "the resulting argument ruined their friendship."

Work in Wales by other geologists (1840-1842)
While Sedgwick and Murchison were each trying to defend their position on the Cambrian and Silurian rocks, other geologists carried out field-work in Wales that would have a bearing on the controversy.

In 1840 retired banker and amateur naturalist John Eddowes Bowman studied the boundary between the Cambrian and Silurian rocks in the Vale of Llangollen in North Wales. He reported to the British Association in Glasgow that he was unable to find any natural break in the fossils between the two series of rocks. In 1842 geologist Daniel Sharpe told the Geological Society that, on the basis of both rocks and fossils, the Bala Limestone of Sedgwick's Upper Cambrian should be correlated with part of the Caradoc Sandstone of Murchison's Lower Silurian. In the same year, Geological Survey staff had discovered Lower Silurian fossils in South-West Wales in rocks coloured as Cambrian on the Survey's 1839 map, challenging Murchison's definition of the Silurian-Cambrian boundary.

Murchison defends his Silurian System (1842-1843)
Murchison was by nature both ambitious and defensive. Eager to protect his growing reputation, he seized on the opportunity to clarify his views in Presidential Addresses he made to the Geological Society in 1842 and 1843, both of which were published in the *Proceedings* of the Society the following year.

He offered a robust defence of his Silurian System, reminding readers that he had defined the System, and the groups of rocks within it, in 1839, on the basis of their fossil content, and since then he had found and recorded these rocks and fossils in various places throughout Europe.

To modern minds his logic has a rather circular feel to it. He argued that, if he found rocks anywhere that contained what he defined as Silurian fossils, then obviously they should be classed as Silurian rocks. Everywhere he went, the oldest fossils he found were Silurian ones. He found no fossils in any rocks below these; he called the ancient fossil-free rocks Cambrian, probably as a gesture of goodwill towards Sedgwick. But he remained reluctant to accept that Sedgwick's Cambrian rocks might be both different from and older than his Silurian rocks. He insisted that, if the Bala Limestone contained Silurian fossils, then it must be Silurian, and, because Sedgwick had found Silurian fossils in his Middle Cambrian rocks, then they too must be Silurian.

Murchison continued to insist that most of Wales was underlain by Silurian rocks. That's why a geological map of Wales that he "arranged" in 1843 for the Society for the Diffusion of Useful Knowledge (the English part of which had figured in the Great Devonian Controversy that we looked at in Chapter 12) shows Silurian groups spread across most of the country. The rocks on the map are divided into three groups – Upper Silurian (Ludlow rocks and Wenlock Limestone) at the top; Lower Silurian (Caradoc Sandstone, Llandeilo Flags, and Cambrian Slate) in the middle; and Primary (mica and chlorite slates etc.) at the bottom.

Murchison's views on classifying and naming Silurian rocks changed little after 1843. He used the same classification two years later in his 1845 book *Geology of Russia in Europe and the Ural Mountains* (written after a lengthy geological excursion in Russia guided by two experienced Russian geologists), and an almost identical one ten years after that in his 1854 book *Siluria. The history of the oldest known rocks containing organic remains, with a brief sketch of the distribution of gold over the Earth.*

Sedgwick's fossils and fieldwork (1842-1846)
Sedgwick had collected some fossils during his North Wales fieldwork in 1831 but, without realising how important they might be in supporting his definition of the Cambrian Series, he had left them crated up and collecting dust in the Geology Museum in Cambridge. He finally got around to unpacking them in 1842, and had them identified by Museum Assistant John Salter and English naturalist and illustrator James Sowerby.

13. The Cambrian-Silurian Controversy

As the debate over the Silurian-Cambrian boundary heated up, Sedgwick returned to North Wales in the summer of 1842 to do more fieldwork. He wanted to recheck some geological cross-sections in areas he had studied ten years earlier, including the Bala Limestone and the Berwyn Mountains, but, more importantly, he wanted to collect a set of characteristic fossils from the Cambrian strata. He was accompanied by Irish geologist Richard Griffith and assisted by Salter, who had drawn the plates for Murchison's book *The Silurian System* and was familiar with characteristic Silurian fossils. Adam returned to the same area the following summer. As a result of both field seasons, he was able to confirm that his cross-sections were accurate, but he was surprised by what the fossil evidence pointed to.

Two important things became clear to Sedgwick during these two spells of fieldwork. First, he saw the same fossils in the Cambrian and Lower Silurian rocks, showing that they both belonged to a single system. Secondly, he found that this single system was clearly separated from the Upper Silurian rocks above it (which also contained completely different fossils) by a very clear unconformity. The lower rocks were folded and tilted, and had clearly been buckled into ancient mountains that had then been worn down by natural processes over a vast period of time, before new deposits were laid on top of the unconformity by a late Silurian sea.

The following June Sedgwick read to the Geological Society his eagerly awaited *Outline of the Geological Structure of North Wales*, that was based on the 1842 fieldwork. The paper was published in the Society's *Proceedings* the same year (1843). He described the lower rock unit as "therefore neither Cambrian nor Silurian in the limited sense in which the words were first used; but it represents both systems, inseparable, as they are in nature, from one another."

In following up that conclusion, Murchison asked and received Sedgwick's permission to treat the Cambrian and the Lower Silurian as one System. The request was sent and responded to by both men in good faith, but by all accounts Sedgwick later realised that he had made a serious mistake in agreeing to it. As Fenton and Fenton (1952) point out, "by accepted rules of correlation, this meant that fossil-bearing parts of the Cambrian would be known as Silurian. Sedgwick, however, did not think of that; he gave his consent and then was amazed when Murchison made the transfer."

This further deepened the scientific disagreement between the two former collaborators, but their friendship survived intact, at least for another decade.

Much of Sedgwick's fieldwork in different parts of Britain and continental Europe was designed to enable rocks within and between regions to be correlated (as we saw in Chapter 11), and he continued pursuing this ambition even as the Silurian-Cambrian controversy was under way. We see this, for example, in his attempt to correlate the rocks he was familiar with in the Lake District with those he was mapping in Wales. In 1845 he read a paper to the Geological Society, *On the comparative classification of the Fossiliferous Strata of North Wales with the corresponding deposits of Cumberland, Westmoreland, and Lancashire*, in which he sought to correlate the Lake District rocks with "the three primary divisions of the whole Welsh series" he had described in his 1843 *Outline* paper. In the same year, he published a paper *On the older Palaeozoic (Protozoic) rocks of North Wales* in the Society's *Quarterly Journal*.

Sedgwick did not give up hope of finding distinctive fossils in Cambrian rocks. His hunch was proved to be correct during a ten-day field excursion in Wales in 1846, when he found a group of small and rather insignificant-looking shells in some beds of sandstone that he could confidently assign to the Cambrian System. He was then more convinced than ever that there was an older system of rocks beneath the Silurian System, as he had first suggested four years earlier.

Although Sedgwick and Murchison had discussed and debated their different view on the Cambrian-Silurian boundary through much of the 1840's, by the beginning of 1847 each had established a position on the matter that would subsequently change little.

Further development (1852-1861)

By the late 1840s Sedgwick was growing frustrated that other geologists were increasingly taking Murchison's side in the Cambrian-Silurian Controversy, adopting his definition of the Silurian, supporting his enlarged Silurian System, and describing as Silurian fossil-bearing rocks that Sedgwick would describe as Cambrian.

His frustration grew deeper in 1850 when the Geological Survey, under the direction of Sir Henry de la Beche (Sedgwick's old adversary in The Great Devonian Controversy, as we saw in Chapter 12), published a geological map of North Wales on which many areas that he had already described as Cambrian were coloured as Silurian. The Survey had very clearly adopted Murchison's conclusions; the only rocks shown on the map as Cambrian were the lowest strata Sedgwick had described as Cambrian, none of which contained any fossils.

13. The Cambrian-Silurian Controversy

In the face of growing support for Murchison's ideas about the Silurian, and given that Murchison would neither admit to making any errors in his interpretation of the Silurian rocks nor be willing to allow the lower part of his Silurian to be defined as Cambrian, Sedgwick felt that honour was at stake and he had no alternative but to tackle his former partner head on in an attempt to reclaim recognition of his Cambrian rocks. He did so in a paper he read to the Geological Society in 1852, which signalled the start of a new chapter in the increasingly acrimonious debate.

Sedgwick knew he was playing with fire in launching such a public attack on Murchison, who by then was a well-established figure with a national reputation. He had twice served as President of the Geological Society (between 1831 and 1833, and again between 1841 and 1843), was knighted in 1846, and had been awarded the Copley Medal by the Royal Society in 1849. Anthony Hallam (1989) adds that "his recently purchased home in one of the most fashionable parts of London became a magnet for that City's social and scientific elite", comments on "his already considerable sense of self-importance", and notes Murchison's own view that "the overwhelming mass of evidence accumulated since publication of *The Silurian System* demanded the complete abandonment of the Cambrian as an internationally valid term."

Sedgwick's 1852 paper to the Geological Society
Sedgwick read his paper *On the Classification and Nomenclature of the Lower Palaeozoic Rocks of England and Wales* to the Geological Society in February 1852. It was published in the *Quarterly Journal* later than year.

The paper triggered a lively debate which lasted until midnight. He described it as a continuation of a paper he had read to the Society two months earlier, in December 1851, *On the Lower Palaeozoic rocks at the base of the Carboniferous Chain between Ravenstone and Ribblesdale*, based on fieldwork in North West England, but there was no hiding his real purpose and intention. In the first part of the paper, he finally accepted the Geological Survey's scheme for defining the rock succession in Wales, but continued to dispute the names they had given to some strata and series. In the second part, he launched a bitter attack on Murchison, accusing him of making some serious mistakes and pointing out that "his nomenclature was premature and his base-line was sectionally wrong; and, so far from leading to discovery, it retarded the progress of Palaeozoic geology for, I believe, not less than ten or twenty years."

217

Understandably, Murchison was not best pleased to be on the end of such a critical and public attack by his former partner. The meeting and paper set in train a series of events which led eventually to a permanent estrangement between Sedgwick and Murchison.

Sedgwick's case was strengthened later that year after Frederick McCoy claimed to have found evidence of fossils within the Caradoc rocks that represented two different sets of animal life, one associated with the Upper Silurian and the other with the Lower Silurian Systems. This prompted Sedgwick and McCoy to visit parts of Wales and the Welsh Borders in the summer of 1852 to look for lithological evidence of this difference (that could be accounted for by an unconformity) that they found most clearly at May Hill near Ross-on-Wye. Sedgwick read a paper to the Geological Society early that November, *On a proposed separation of the so-called Caradoc Sandstone into two distinct groups; viz. (1) May Hill Sandstone; (2) Caradoc Sandstone*, that was published in the *Quarterly Journal of the Geological Society* before the end of the year. He proposed dividing the Caradoc into a (lower) Caradoc Formation belonging to the Cambrian Series, and an (upper) May Hill Sandstone belonging to the Silurian.

The unconformity they found at May Hill was nowhere near as distinct and obvious as many other unconformities elsewhere; it was indicated by a slight difference in the angle of the bedding planes in the beds above and below it. Hallam (1989) suggests that "Murchison and the Survey had missed this because they had not sought it, their minds being unprepared."

Further support for Sedgwick's claim of an unconformity within the Caradoc, between the Silurian and the Devonian, would start to appear in the next few years, in reports from Central Europe and North America of discoveries showing important breaks in the fossil sequences through that transition.

Response of the Geological Society

The Council of the Geological Society were eager to avoid the growing controversy between Sedgwick and Murchison getting out of hand, and in particular to make sure that it did not damage their credibility and reputation as a leading scientific institution at a time of rising public interest in science and support for scientific research. Paradoxically, the way they handled the matter triggered the very thing they were trying to avoid.

The Society's objective was commendable – they were trying to achieve clarity and consensus in the naming of rocks, particularly those from the Palaeozoic period. Clarity would not be possible if they allowed geologists to use the same names in different ways, or to use different names for what most other geologists regarded as the same thing. With that in mind, the Society's Publication Committee would, where necessary, revise the names authors used in papers submitted to it, in order to bring them into line with the prevailing consensus among geologists. What's more, the Committee would encourage authors to revise or remove parts of any papers in which the results of observation were not compatible with the theories or principles behind the naming protocol, and it would reserve the right not to publish any papers whose authors refused to do so.

With these 'rules of engagement' in place, Sedgwick's 1852 paper was refereed by peer review on the same day it was read to the Society, following normal procedures. The referee selected by the Publication Committee was Professor John Phillips, a very experienced and distinguished geologist from York who, in 1841, had published the first global geological time scale based on the correlation of fossils in rock strata. Phillips read Sedgwick's paper carefully, then returned it to him with suggestions for how it should be revised. Sedgwick subsequently sent it back to Phillips, although it is not clear that he had taken on board everything that Phillips had required or suggested. The revised paper was reviewed a second time, but the Council was still not happy with it, so they agreed to print only the Abstract and not the whole paper, as Phillips had recommended.

The Council then came under attack for having made what some critics called an uninformed decision, given that no one on the Publication Committee had any first-hand experience of the area in question, or appeared to have a good grasp of the complex issues involved in unravelling the geology of the area. Council seems to have then lost its nerve, and at its meeting on the 19th of May voted to remove the paper from the *Quarterly Journal* and cancel the volume which contained it, encouraged to do so by Murchison.

Not surprisingly, shutting the stable door after the horse had bolted was not a very effective solution; by then the volume had been printed and been in circulation for more than two weeks. So, on the 16th of June, Council withdrew the resolution to cancel the volume and invited Murchison to write a response to Sedgwick's paper that could be read to the Society then published in the *Quarterly Journal*.

Murchison happily accepted the invitation and wrote *On the meaning of the term 'Silurian System' as adopted by geologists in various countries during the last ten years*. It was an overview of his work on the Palaeozoic rocks, and as the editors of *Life and Letters* put it, was "expressed in courteous and considerate language." Just to be on the safe side, three members of Council were asked to read the final draft and reassure Council that it contained nothing that could offend Sedgwick. The paper passed that test, was read to the Society, then refereed and published in the normal way.

Council then rather optimistically hoped that would be the end of the matter, certainly in terms of open warfare in the meetings and publications of the Society. The Society's Secretary wrote to tell Sedgwick that "the Council expressed a strong determination, both parties having said their say, not to allow of any more words from either party." The Society had made its position clear, but that did nothing to ease Sedgwick's sense of being victimised and rejected by a body which he helped to set up, and had long been an active member and keen supporter of. His once-close relationship with the Society was permanently damaged by how it had handled the debate with Murchison.

End of the friendship and working relationship
The Geological Society might have closed the door on further public debate over the Cambrian-Silurian issue, but Sedgwick and Murchison continued their dispute in public. Each attacked the other strongly in *The Literary Gazette*, a weekly literary magazine that had been established in London in 1817 and was widely read and highly influential.

But they also tried to tone down the very personal and public tone of their disagreement, exchanging views through letters. In late February 1853, although Sedgwick was still insisting that he was correct – he wrote "You will find, on mature reflexion [sic], I am persuaded, that there is but one natural history group of life in Cambria and Siluria" – he urged Murchison to remember the good times and keep this dispute in perspective. He wrote "Pray let us wrangle no more about the *vexata quastio*. We have done many a stroke of good work together, and if we had united to describe the whole Principality and the bordering counties of England the lamentable position in which we now stand as apparent antagonists could never have occurred."

The attempt at reconciliation was well intended but failed. By then the friendship was too badly damaged, and it ended abruptly.

It's worth pausing for a moment to reflect on why the dispute between Sedgwick and Murchison, who had previously been happy in each other's company and worked well together on numerous occasions, got so heated. There is no simple answer, but differences in temperament and personality certainly played a part. Both men were serious about their geological work, and both had strong stubborn streaks. Both were ambitious, but Murchison's ambition was legendary. Both strongly defended their ideas, but Murchison was the more protective and flatly refused to admit that he might have made any errors. Both men were well-known and well-regarded in society circles, but when Murchison was appointed as Director of the Geological Survey in 1855 he could 'pull rank' on Sedgwick. In fact, Murchison used that status to influence all subsequent official geological publications, and his reach and influence grew accordingly.

Hallam (1989) puts it more simply, suggesting that Sedgwick's "bitterness towards his former close companion can perhaps most plausible be attributed to the disappointment of an old man who had wished the erection of the Cambrian to be seen as his crowning achievement."

The debate was not helped by the mode of operation both men had adopted when they began their fieldwork in Wales. They worked separately, started mapping the rocks in different places, and Murchison put great store on fossil evidence whereas Sedgwick based his initial conclusions only on stratigraphic evidence.

The fact that they were working on very complex geological structures must not be overlooked either. For a long time both men were blind to the existence of an overlap between the Bala rocks that Sedgwick defined as Upper Cambrian, and the Llandeilo and Caradoc rocks that Murchison defined as Lower Silurian. This was mainly because Murchison had misinterpreted the rock structures around Llandeilo, that led him to believe, at least initially, that the strata he defined as Silurian lie within the Cambrian. But Murchison had also confused the May Hill sandstone (that he defined to be of Wenlock age) with the Caradoc sandstones; they looked alike and were lithologically similar, but they contained very different fossils. That led him to initially mistake the nature and importance of the fossils within the rocks he defined as Lower Silurian.

Sedgwick and McCoy fieldwork in North Wales (summer 1853)
Sedgwick and McCoy returned to North Wales in the summer of 1853 to do further fieldwork, to check their earlier conclusions against what was shown on the Geological Survey map. Bad weather and ill-health thwarted their original plans, but they did find evidence to support their earlier conclusions. Sedgwick wrote up their new findings in a paper for the Geological Society entitled *On the May Hill sandstone and the Palaeozoic*

system of England, in which he also reiterated his views on the limits of the Cambrian and Silurian Systems.

As if to add insult to injury after the fiasco surrounding its treatment of Sedgwick's 1852 paper, the Society also treated him badly in the way it handled this new paper. He had hoped to read the paper to the Society towards the end of 1853 but was unable to do so, and the Society postponed it until spring the following year, when he was unable to attend. Following normal procedures, after the paper was read at a meeting of the Society on behalf of the author, it was refereed and returned to him for revision. But the referee, with the support of Council, recommended major changes that would alter the main line of argument in the paper and, as Clark and Hughes (1890b) put it, "amounted to a resignation [rejection] of his nomenclature and classification". This was a step too far for Sedgwick, who refused to accept the proposed changes and read the Society's treatment as a refusal to print his paper. In response, he submitted the paper to the *Philosophical Magazine*, who published it in 1854. Not surprisingly, Sedgwick's behaviour angered the officers of the Society, and he was seriously criticised by the President at its next meeting. The Society subsequently extended the hand of friendship to Sedgwick and explained their actions, but Sedgwick was not satisfied. He lost confidence in the Society and its officers, and never again attended any of their meetings.

Meetings of the British Association
After this irreconcilable breakdown between Sedgwick and the Geological Society, the final stages of the Cambrian-Silurian Controversy played out at successive annual meetings of the British Association.

Sedgwick was President of the Geological Section when the British Association met at Hull in 1853. He read a paper there *On the Classification and Nomenclature of the older Palaeozoic Rocks of Britain*, in which he defended his position in the controversy. The paper, that he described as "the most important communication he had ever made to the British Association", was printed in the *Report* of the Association.

The following August (1854) Sedgwick and McCoy carried out further fieldwork in South Wales, aiming to complete the work they had started in North Wales the previous summer looking at key sections at the junction of the Cambrian and Silurian rocks. They had found no sites in North Wales where "the characteristic Silurian and Cambrian types are so mixed and confounded as to be inseparable". Although the Geological Survey had claimed to have found some, and called them Middle Silurian, Sedgwick and McCoy disagreed with that interpretation and insisted that the fossil evidence clearly indicated rocks of two distinct systems separated by an unconformity. They confidently claimed that, "If these conclusions be true, there is an end of any legitimate dispute on nomenclature; for we have no example in English geology of two great formations which are, as a general rule, unconformable in their position, yet at the same time belong to a common series, and pass under a common name." Shortly after completing that fieldwork McCoy left Cambridge for Australia, to take up the post of Professor of Natural Sciences in the University of Melbourne (as we saw in Chapter 7).

At the 1854 British Association meeting in Liverpool, Sedgwick defended his conclusions about the May Hill Sandstone that had been rejected by the Geological Society in November 1852 but published in the *Philosophical Magazine*. The session triggered a "spirited discussion" that continued several days later when Murchison read a paper giving his *General observations on the Palaeozoic rocks of Germany*. As Clark and Hughes (1890b) point out, "some of the ablest and most experienced geologists in England were present, and took part in the debate."

Sedgwick and Murchison were brought together again the following year when the British Association met in Glasgow. Murchison read a paper on some Palaeozoic rocks in Sutherland in the Highlands of Scotland, after which Sedgwick rose to speak. The audience expected him to launch a bitter attack on Murchison, but he reassured them *"I am not going to fight him!"*, before proceeding to support what Murchison had talked about.

In 1855 Murchison was appointed Director of the Geological Survey, and according to Sedgwick's obituary in *The Times* (28 January 1873) "then used his powers to have the name Cambrian deleted from all books and maps published by the government." By this time, Murchison was adamant that Silurian rocks covered most of the Highlands and Southern Uplands of Scotland, the Lake District, and north and central Wales, and he was totally unwilling to budge on the matter.

Sedgwick and Murchison both attended the British Association meeting in Cheltenham in 1856, where they heard American geologist Professor Henry Darwin Rogers from Boston read a paper *On the correlation of the North American and British Palaeozoic Strata*, and they discussed it in a friendly manner. As far as the Cambrian-Silurian Controversy is concerned, the most memorable part of the Cheltenham meeting was Murchison admitting to Sedgwick that he had made a mistake in identifying some rocks in South Wales. As Sedgwick wrote in a letter to Lyell in late April 1857, "It was his [Murchison's] policy never to acknowledge a mistake, and on the one matter of fact whether he had made a great mistake, or had adopted it from me, he never spoke out 'till I wrung an answer from him at the last Cheltenham meeting of the British Association. He then, at length, but far too late to save his credit as a fair-dealing man, did acknowledge that the blunder, the actual inversion of the order of super-position from Denbighshire to Carmarthenshire, was his own, and not in any way borrowed from me."

Sedgwick continued to bear a serious grudge against Murchison. When the second edition of Murchison's *Siluria* was published in 1859, he sent a copy to Sedgwick with the hope that, because "time rolls on, and as we passed many a happy day together, I trust you will have some gratification in turning these pages." But Sedgwick's response spoke volumes. He waited a long time to reply, sent a brief note of acceptance which opened "Dear Sir Roderick", then left the book behind in Cambridge, unwrapped, when he took a trip to Dent.

The last time Sedgwick and Murchison met, at least in public, appears to have been in 1861 at the British Association meeting in Manchester. There was to be no reconciliation. Douglas Robson (1986) put it down ultimately to a clash between two different types of character - "When it came to the test, the bluntness of the Yorkshireman ... and the pride of the Scot, proved incompatible."

Resolution (1879)
The Lapworth Solution (1879)
Although the fallout between Sedgwick and Murchison continued to the end of their days, the heat within the controversy slowly died down after the deaths of Murchison, Sedgwick and Lyell in the early 1870s as a new generation of geologists made discoveries that strengthened the evidence in support of the Cambrian System.

The dispute over whether a particular set of rocks in Wales belonged to the Cambrian or the Silurian Period was finally settled in 1879 by geologist Charles Lapworth, then a Professor at St Andrew's in Scotland. Lapworth restudied fossils from the Southern Uplands of Scotland that Murchison had insisted were in Lower Silurian rocks, but he found they were very distinct and certainly not Silurian. He assigned the older rocks to the Cambrian and the newer rocks to the Silurian, and proposed the creation of a new System that he called the Ordovician – after a Romano-British tribe that once lived in the hills in the Bala District of North Wales where the rocks were discovered – for the strata between the two. The

Ordovician, he demonstrated, had its own representative fossils; it comprised Sedgwick's Upper Cambrian and Murchison's Lower Silurian.

The Geological Survey were initially not convinced about Lapworth's Ordovician Series. It would be a further two decades before it adopted the name and definition in 1902, under Sir Jethro Teal, who succeeded Sir Archibald Geikie as Director.

The Ordovician was officially approved by the Stratigraphic Commission of the International Geological Congress in 1960. Since then geologists have used a standard three-fold division of the Lower Palaeozoic into Cambrian (541 to 485 million years ago), Ordovician (485-419 million years), and Silurian (419 to 359 million years).

14. Creation or Evolution?

"The right and true belief, consistent with scripture, was that new species appeared in the fossil record due to successive acts of creation ...; a series of new products from God's workshop, culminating in the production on the celestial drawing board of a design for Man. Not everyone shared this right and true belief."
Eric Ashby and Mary Anderson (1969)

We have focussed up to now in this Part of the book on Adam Sedgwick's work in geology, in which he championed the approach to geological mapping first developed by William Smith. We've seen that much of his work was ground-breaking, and noted how he fought very public campaigns to have recognised two new rock series that he had found convincing evidence of and given names to – the Devonian (Chapter 12) and the Cambrian (Chapter 13).

But, as well as being a leading natural philosopher or scientist of his day, Adam was also a man with a deep Christian faith. He was born into a family of churchmen (as we saw in Chapter 1), and he was ordained in 1814 (as we saw in Chapter 6). As we'll see in Chapters 16 and 17, he held several church appointments alongside his Fellowship and Professorship in Trinity College Cambridge and in 1834 became a Canon of Norwich Cathedral.

This raises an important question – did he ever experience any serious conflict between the two sides of his adult life, as a geologist and as a churchman?

In the history of geology, Sedgwick lived and worked at the point of transition between what has been called Scriptural (or Biblical) Geology, in which all interpretations are informed by and consistent with the Biblical narrative on creation, and modern empirical geology, in which the rocks and fossils are allowed to speak for themselves. This historical context shaped Sedgwick's views, work and interpretations, and it is a key reason why he is such a fascinating character.

In this chapter, we'll focus on his journey through this period, because it throws light on the strength and depth of his personal faith. But it also demonstrates his ability to negotiate what to him was a coherent path between two strongly opposing forces – geology and religious literalism.

Sedgwick on the evidence of rocks and scripture

Adam Sedgwick was a firm believer in divine creation, by "a power I cannot imitate or comprehend - but in which I believe, by a legitimate conclusion of sound reason drawn from the laws of harmonies of nature."

'The waters of a general deluge' (1825)
The earliest thing we hear from him in *Life and Letters* about the interaction between his faith and his science comes in 1825, seven years after he was appointed Professor of Geology. It comes in a paper he wrote *On the origin of alluvial and diluvial formations*, that we looked at briefly in Chapter 11. In the mid-1820s Sedgwick was a supporter of Buckland's interpretation of some particular surface deposits as 'diluvium' that had been laid down by a "great irregular inundation ... [from the] waters of a general deluge", that he believed was Noah's flood as described in the Biblical book of Genesis.

In the paper, he denied that "Professor Buckland, or any other practical geologist of our time, has rashly attempted to unite the speculations of his favourite science with the truths of revelation." The "favourite science" was geology, that provided "the evidence of observation and experiment, by which alone physical truth can ever be established." The "truths of revelation" were "the sacred records" (the Bible), the authority of which "has been established by a great mass of evidence at once conclusive and appropriate." But he acknowledged that it would be "rash and unphilosophical to look to the language of revelation for any direct proof of the truths of physical science."

Although he valued the different forms of evidence that science and revelation could offer, Adam insisted that "truth must at all times be consistent with itself." He was convinced that "the conclusions established on the authority of the sacred records may ... consistently with the soundest philosophy, be compared with the conclusions established on the evidence of observation and experiment; and such conclusions, if fairly deduced, must necessarily be in accordance with each other."

Sedgwick had no difficulty in tying together the evidence of the rocks and the evidence from scripture. As he wrote in that 1825 paper, "The sacred records tell us that a few thousand years ago 'the fountains of the great deep were broken up' and that the earth's surface was submerged by the waters of a general deluge; and the investigations of geology tend to prove that the accumulations of alluvial matter have not been going on many thousand years; and that they were preceded by a great catastrophe which has left traces of its operation in the diluvial detritus which is spread out over all the strata of the earth. Between these conclusions, derived from sources entirely independent of each other, there is, therefore, a general coincidence which it is impossible to overlook, and the importance of which it would be most unreasonable to deny."

Reflecting his unswerving commitment to induction, even at this early point in his geological career, Adam stressed that "The coincidence has not been assumed hypothetically, but has been proved legitimately, by an immense number of direct observations conducted with indefatigable labour, and all tending to the establishment of the same general truth." In Chapter 15 we'll explore his belief in induction as the only way of establishing truth.

Presidential Addresses to the Geological Society (1830 and 1831)
We read more about Sedgwick's views on science and religion in the two Presidential Addressed he gave to the Geological Society.

In his 1830 Address, after reviewing the previous year's most important developments in geology, he turned his guns on a scriptural geologist he believed had done a serious discredit to geology. He severely criticised a recent book entitled *A New System of Geology* by Andrew Ure, a Scottish doctor and fellow member of the Geological Society. Ure claimed to have reconciled "the great revolutions of the earth and of animated nature ... to modern science and to sacred history", insisting on a literal six-day divine creation of the universe that was finished in a perfect form about 6,000 years ago. Dismissing Werner's and Hutton's geological theories (that we looked at in Chapter 10) as inconsistent with what was then known about the mechanical and chemical sciences, Ure devoted the bulk of his book to explaining his views on the year-long global Flood that God had sent as a judgment on the sins of humankind, as recorded in the Old Testament. Sedgwick described the book as a "monument to folly" for promoting views that by then had long been abandoned.

Criticising Ure's book was a side-show compared with the bombshell that Sedgwick dropped in his second Presidential Address that he read to the Society in February 1831. In it he recanted his former belief in Buckland's theory of diluvium as having been deposited by the Biblical Flood, and suggested instead that many of these deposits were dropped by glaciers. Recanting in such a high-profile way was a testimony to his willingness to adapt his views in the light of available evidence, and a very public demonstration of just how much his thinking had changed over a period of less than five years.

Adam was not the first geologists to dismiss the flood theory – Humboldt had shared that idea with him when they had met in Paris, Prevost had lectured against the flood theory, and (as we saw in Chapter 11) Agassiz later (in 1840) argued in favour of Ice Ages. In his 1831, Adam he argued that "Mosaic [scriptural] geologists committed the folly and the sin of dogmatizing matters they had not personally examined." He wrote "If I have been converted in part from the diluvian theory ... it was ... by my own gradual improved experience, and by communicating with those about me."

One thing that helped Adam change his mind on the Flood theory was the lack of any evidence of pre-Flood human activity preserved within the deposits. As he put it, "of man, and the works of his hands, we have not yet found a single trace among the remnants of a former world entombed in these deposits." Having no evidence of human activity before the Flood challenged a literal reading of the Biblical narrative of the Flood as God's response to human sinfulness.

Sedgwick's views on the creation of the Earth
The best source of information about Sedgwick's geological thinking, and about how he reconciled his theology and geology, is his *Discourse on the studies of the university* that (as we saw in Chapter 8) was published in five editions between 1833 and 1850. There we can find his views on the creation of the earth and the history of nature, in his own words.

The key to understanding almost all of Adam's geological thinking was his rock-solid belief that the universe and everything in it is God's handiwork, the result of divine creation. Quite simply, he insisted that "by the discoveries of a new science ... we learn [about] the manifestations of God's power on the earth ...".

Like most believers at the time, and many since, Adam saw in the natural world not just "the hand of God" but clear evidence of "the mind of God". He read the order and pattern that we see in nature as sure signs of intelligent design and divine purpose by a benevolent creator. In this he was strongly influenced by English theologian and clergyman William Paley (1743-1805), particularly his 1802 book *Natural Theology: or, Evidences of the Existence and Attributes of the Deity, collected from the appearances of Nature*, that Charles Darwin also read as a student.

Sedgwick praised *Natural Theology* for its central argument that the more closely we look at nature, the closer we can get to the benevolent mind of God. He firmly believed that the aim of natural sciences such as geology was to decode what God had created, in ways that must be consistent with the Bible, and the only way in which that could be done was through induction (that we will look at further in Chapter 15).

Sedgwick was and remained a member of the Catastrophist school of geology. In this he was in good company alongside other leading geologists of the day, including George Cuvier (1769-1832), William Buckland (1784-1856), Roderick Murchison (1792-1871) and William Conybeare (1787-1857), who we have already met in Chapters 10 to 13. Like them, he was unable to fully embrace the emerging paradigm of Uniformitarianism, first proposed by James Hutton (1726-1797) but then effectively being promoted by Charles Lyell (1797-1875), which took God, creation, the Flood and divinely-controlled catastrophes out of the picture and explained everything in terms of natural processes.

One of Sedgwick's more controversial beliefs, that challenged many churchmen at the time, was that the Earth is much older than the 6,000 years estimated from a literal reading of the Old Testament. Recall (from Chapter 10) that, in 1650, James Ussher had calculated the date of creation as 4004 BC. Based on his own extensive geological fieldwork, Sedgwick was convinced that the Earth must be much older than that. He wrote in *Discourse* that the geologist "counts his time not by celestial cycles, but by an index he has found in the solid framework of the globe itself. He sees a long succession of monuments [different rocks], each of which may have required a thousand ages for its elaboration." He didn't suggest how old the Earth might be – he could place the rocks in sequence by relative age, in terms of which ones were younger or older than others, but no ways had yet been developed for establishing absolute dates or ages of rocks – but he knew it must be much older than 6,000 years.

The early Catastrophists believed that all rocks on and under the surface of the Earth were formed either at the point of creation or as a result of the Great Flood described in Genesis, which is how Werner accounted for his Primary, Intermediate, and Secondary rocks. At the beginning of his geological career Adam Sedgwick followed Werner's teaching and adopted his explanations, but by the 1830s – after he had recanted from holding the views of a Diluvialist like Buckland in 1831 – he became increasingly convinced about the evidence of multiple catastrophes that was then emerging in his own work and the work of other leading geologists.

231

Like others, he still maintained that the evidence pointed to the work of God, but he now saw successive catastrophic episodes as having been timed and driven by God, over a very long period of time.

He wrote in *Discourse* that "the geologist tells us, by the clearest interpretation of the phenomena which his labours have brought to light, that our globe has been subject to vast physical revolutions." The physical evidence in the rocks of these "vast physical revolutions" included unconformities between adjacent rock series in many places, and the existence of different types of fossils in adjacent rock series and of similar types of fossils in the same rocks in different places.

For Catastrophists like Sedgwick the last catastrophe did not have to be the Great Flood of Noah, because they looked on the Book of Genesis as a symbol of Christian faith. To them, interpreting Genesis as theological and moral teaching was more important than accepting it literally word for word.

So, whilst Sedgwick disagreed with Lyell and the Uniformitarian school of geology over the cumulative effects of slow, gradual geological changes over very long periods of time, and instead saw in the rocks evidence of periodic major catastrophes separated by long periods of stability, he at least agreed with the emerging consensus amongst Uniformitarians about an old earth.

Sedgwick's views on the history of nature
Seeing evidence in the rocks of multiple catastrophes spread over a long period of time allowed Sedgwick to visualise how and why different series of rocks contained different sets of distinctive fossils. His explanation was logical and seemed to fit the evidence he had seen with his own eyes.

Creative additions
First, he assumed that divine creation gives rise to particular life-forms (plants and animals) at particular points in history, as God decides, as part of his great over-arching plan for the universe. The next major geological catastrophe kills and wipes out these species, but their remains are preserved as fossils in the rocks deposited during that period of geological history. After that next catastrophe, divine creation populates the earth with a new set of species, different to the earlier ones but fully formed from their first appearance, as and when God decides. Sedgwick referred to these as "creative additions".

This cycle continues through successive catastrophes, leaving different sets of rocks, each with its own distinct set of fossils left behind in the rocks as memorials of what had lived during that period of time. So, not only did the fossil evidence allow similar-looking rocks to be distinguished one from another and particular rocks to be correlated across wide areas, it also preserved within itself the story of the history of nature.

As Adam wrote in *Discourse*, the geologist "arranges [the rocks] in chronological order; observes on them the marks of skill and wisdom [evidence of God's design and handiwork], and finds within them the tombs of the ancient inhabitants of the earth [fossils]. He finds strange and unlooked-for changes in the forms and fashions of organic life during each of the long periods he thus contemplates." As Ashby and Anderson (1969) put it, "the right and true belief, consistent with scripture, was that new species appeared in the fossil record due to successive acts of creation ...; a series of new products from God's workshop ...".

Adam wrote that "The elevation of the fauna of successive periods was not therefore made by transmutation [evolution], but by creative additions; and it is by watching these additions that we get some insight into Nature's true historical progress."

He was highly critical of the suggestion made by Louis Agassiz at the 1835 meeting of the British Association in Dublin that the fossils in successive rock formations had been "brought from some unknown region" by the catastrophe that gave rise to the rocks "and deposited where we find them". He dismissed Agassiz's suggestion as "a long stupid hypothetical dissertation on geology, drawn from the depths of his ignorance."

Order in creation
Sedgwick dismissed emerging ideas about the transmutation of species as misguided and just plain wrong, arguing that there was no evidence of progressive changes between species, within or between rock types and geological periods. He insisted that nature is highly ordered and always had been.

As he put it in *Discourse*, "If Genera, Orders, and Classes be now distinct and separate, they were equally distinct and separate in all periods of the old world. ... if the theory of development [evolution] were true, there must be ... such a blending and penetration of types [intermediate forms] as would blot out and obliterate our lines of separation between [what are now distinct and separate] Genera and Orders and Classes. But we look in vain for any semblance of such obliteration ... The oldest types fall into their place in the general scale, as naturally as the newest. ... They continue as strong and as abruptly marked as they were before."

How did Adam think it all begin? His writing contains no suggestions or speculations about when life first appeared on Earth, but he always insisted that the origin of life on Earth was God's decision and God's handiwork. In *Discourse* he writes of how the geologist "traces these changes backwards and through each successive era, till he reaches a time when the monuments lose all symmetry, and the types of organic life are no longer seen. He has then entered on the dark age of nature's history; and he closes the old chapter of her records." In other words, Adam believed that we simply don't know, and it's quite possible that God never intended for us to know.

Once begun, how did he think it then unfolded? Adam saw clear evidence of an order of creation, following God's grand design, with each type of life-form appearing fully formed and occupying their rightful place "at the head of nature", before being wiped out in the next catastrophic event and then preserved in the fossil record.

He described five phases of "creative additions" in this order of creation, starting with the cephalopods (primitive marine molluscs that today include squid, octopuses and cuttlefish), followed by fish, then reptiles, and then mammals that "seem to have been added suddenly ... [some of which] we now know, only by ransacking the ancient catacombs of Nature, were powerful and gigantic [a reference to dinosaurs, which were first named in 1842 by Richard Owen] ...". The fifth and final phase of "creative addition" saw the creation of humans, as special creatures within God's created order, as a result of which nature "is more exalted than she was before".

Sedgwick's views on the creation of humans

Sedgwick believed that the "creative additions" or "series of new products from God's workshop" culminated in the creation of humans. In the same way that God had created other species in their final form, with distinctly different species in different rocks series, he believed that God had created humans as we see them – ourselves – today, in final form, and distinctly different from other species in creation, as part of his universal grand design.

Adam looked on the creation of humans as the crowning glory of God's creative handiwork. In the fifth edition of *Discourse* (1850) Sedgwick argued that "Man [sic] stands by himself the despotic lord of the living world: not so great in organic strength as many of the despots that went before him in Nature's chronicle, but raised far above them all ...". He looked on humans as "raised far above" other creatures, because God had endowed them with special qualities – "by a higher development of the brain – by a framework that fits him for the operations of mechanical skill – by superadded reason – by a social instinct of combination – by a prescience that tells him to act prospectively – by a conscience that makes him amenable to law – by conceptions that transcend the narrow limits of his vision – by hopes that have no full fruition here – by an inborn capacity of rising from individual facts to the apprehension of general laws – by a conception of a Cause for all the phenomena of sense – and by a consequent belief in a God of Nature."

In his 1868 book *Memorial by the Trustees of Cowgill Chapel* (that we'll return to in Chapter 18), Sedgwick wrote that "man [sic] alone has the high faculty of drawing general truths out of separate instances that have come before his senses— of observing the beautiful order in which the events of the natural world are linked together, and of rising to a conception of material laws, ordained by the prescient, creative power of God for the government of the natural world." Writing about "the glories of creation among the lights of the heavens, and the multitudinous forms of animated nature, and the grand adaptation of the several parts of nature", he asked rhetorically "when we see all this, shall we shut our eyes to the grand lesson, and refuse to accept the fundamental truth, that all nature, moral and material, is an emanation from the sovereign will of the Great First Cause – from the God that created all worlds, and all things therein, whether dead or endowed with life?"

Fighting on two fronts (1844)
Not everyone shared Sedgwick's "right and true belief." His controversial views came under attack from defenders of traditional church teaching on creation, some of whom accused him of heresy. Few churchmen were more annoyed than Rev Henry Cole (1792-1858) who, after reading them in the first edition of *Discourse*, responded by writing a long, detailed and highly critical critique (actually a 136-page book) that was published in 1834, entitled *Popular Geology Subversive of Divine Revelation! A Letter to the Rev. Adam Sedgwick ... Being a Scriptural Refutation of the Geological Positions and Doctrines Promulgated in his Lately Published Commencement Sermon.* In 1844 Sedgwick found himself at the centre of a heated and very public debate with the Dean of York, a staunch defender of the Biblical creation narrative.

But Sedgwick's views also came under attack from the opposite direction, from supporters of the emerging school of geological thinking based on the progressive transformation of one species into another over a long period of geological time – "transmutation" as they called it, or "evolution" as Darwin would subsequently call it. This fuelled an acrimonious series of very public exchanges with Robert Chambers, author of a best-selling book on the natural history of creation, also in 1844.

Clash with the Dean of York (1844)
While he became increasingly Evangelical with age, Sedgwick defended many of the advances being made in geology against attacks from conservative churchmen. His most high-profile clash was with Sir William Cockburn (1773-1858), the Dean of York, at the British Association meeting in York in 1844. Cockburn was a Cambridge graduate, a Fellow of St John's College. As a prominent scriptural geologist and a vocal critic of Buckland and the British Association, he was keen to defend traditional church teaching on creation, that he saw being undermined by the emerging evidence from geology.

Cockburn was particularly concerned that two of the most prominent geologists at that time – William Buckland and Adam Sedgwick – had changed their views on the geological evidence of the Great Flood described in Genesis. Recall (from Chapter 10) that in 1823 Buckland had published an account of his excavations of animal remains in Kirkdale Cave in Yorkshire, which he interpreted as evidence of the flood. Thirteen years later, in 1836, he denounced Diluvialism in his Bridgwater Treatise Geology *and Mineralogy considered with reference to Natural Theology*, in which he openly admitted the futility of trying to reconcile Genesis and geology, and accepted that the Earth must be much older than the six millennia claimed by scriptural geologists. Recall, too, that in 1825 Sedgwick had interpreted diluvial deposits as evidence of the Great Flood, but six years later (in his second Presidential Address to the Geological Society) he recanted and renounced Diluvialism.

Cockburn launched his first public attack on Buckland in 1838, when he published *A letter to Professor Buckland concerning the origin of the world*. In the same year he warned the Duke of Northumberland, President of the British Association at its meeting in Newcastle that year, against what he called "the dangers of peripatetic philosophy". The full title of his paper was *A Remonstrance addressed to his grace the Duke of Northumberland on the dangers of Peripatetic Philosophy*.

14. Creation or Evolution?

When the British Association met in York six years later, Cockburn seized his opportunity to challenge Buckland in a very public way. The Association's officers found themselves in a difficult position; they must have been tempted not to accept the offer of a paper by the Dean of York, to be delivered under the shadow of his own cathedral, but the Dean was an important local dignitary and they recognised that his supporters would accuse them of cowardice if they refused to let him have his say.

So it was that, in September 1844, Cockburn addressed a packed meeting of the Geology Section of the British Association. His views were well known, and the audience expected a heated debate. His talk was entitled "Critical Remarks on certain passages in Dr Buckland's *Bridgewater Treatise*", and in it he repeated his objections to Buckland's account of earth history before presenting his own theory based on Old Testament history. By all accounts, few members of the audience took Cockburn's suggestions seriously and some could not contain their laughter, but the Dean carried on regardless, with a booming voice and a steely determination.

Buckland was unable to be present at York for the meeting, but Sedgwick replied on his behalf. His reply was long – he spoke for an hour and a half – and spirited. He pulled no punches in attacking the Dean's "irrational guesses and absurd hypotheses", and he defended Buckland's *Treatise* as a fair statement of geological knowledge at that time. But Sedgwick also reassured the Association and its audience that there is no inherent incompatibility between science and religion. He told them that "truth could not be opposed to itself, and that the highest discoveries of science would ever be found in perfect harmony and accordance with the language and meaning of revelation."

Cockburn continued his attack on Buckland in a sermon in York Minster the following Sunday. He also demanded that the Association organise a second discussion, face-to-face with Buckland, but the request was refused. Not one to back down, he then published *The Bible defended against the British Association*, which appeared in five editions between 1844 and 1845. It contained his York paper and a *Letter to the Inhabitants of York*, that he insisted represented the feelings of a large majority of people in Britain at that time. Cockburn later explained his own theory of earth history in *A New System of Geology: dedicated to Professor Sedgwick* (1849), that he claimed faithfully agreed with the account given in the Old Testament. The dedication to Sedgwick is intriguing, given how heated the debate at York had been.

The 1844 confrontation between Sedgwick and Cockburn received national publicity, and views about it were polarised. The liberal press applauded Sedgwick's courage in taking on such a high-profile defender of scriptural geology, particularly given that Adam was himself a churchman but of a different persuasion and churchmanship to Cockburn. The established church took the opposite view, and the senior clergy in York Minster refused to sit down with Sedgwick. He was also pilloried by Conservative newspapers including *The Times*.

Vestiges of the Natural History of Creation (1844)
A book was published in the autumn of 1844 that added fuel to the debate over creation and evolution. It had the title *Vestiges of the Natural History of Creation* and, though it was published anonymously, its author was later discovered to be Scottish amateur geologist Robert Chambers (1802-1871), from Edinburgh.

Chambers' objective was to replace the idea of creation as a series of special and arbitrary acts by a theory that he called his "development hypothesis", aiming to establish a scientific law that explained the transmutation of species. He wrote that "a review of the several geological formations indicated a gradual progress; speaking generally, lower forms had preceded higher. Further … an obvious gradation may be observed among existing forms of animal life, and, at the same time, an obvious unity of structure …". In Chambers' mind this pointed to an obvious conclusion – "all animated things are parts of one system, the creation of which must have depended upon one law or decree of the Almighty."

In broad outline Adam Sedgwick would have agreed with this, but then Chambers' argument took a turn he would definitely not agree with, promoting transmutation (the progressive change of one species into another). Chambers argued that it was a simple step to the hypothesis that "the simplest and most primitive type gave birth to the type next above it, that this again produced the next higher, and so on to the very highest, the stages in advance being in all cases very small, namely, from one species only to another."

Chamber's book received mixed reactions when it was published in October 1844. The general public lapped it up. It sold extremely well and became a publishing sensation, passing through four editions in the first six months and eleven editions by 1860. Success on that scale was almost unprecedented for what purported to be a serious science book, but – as Clark and Hughes (1890b) put it – "*Vestiges*, with its agreeable style and reverential tone, was probably regarded by many as a pious compendium of all that had been most recently ascertained respecting the world and its inhabitants." The fact that the book was published anonymously doubt-less added some curiosity value. Many possible authors were talked about, and even the writer's gender was debated. Sedgwick initially thought the book must have been written by a woman; he wrote to Lyell in April 1845 "I cannot but think the work is from a woman's pen, it is so well dressed, and so graceful in its externals. I do not think the 'beast man' could have done this part so well."

Scientists "unanimously condemned [it] ... and held [it] up to scorn and ridicule in the best critical journals," as Clark and Hughes (1890b) point out. They criticised the book for trying to synthesise evidence from multiple branches of study, including chemistry, physics, botany, zoolo-gy, phrenology (study of the shape and size of the human head as a pointer to character and mental abilities, which was then fashionable), comparative anatomy, psychology, language, metaphysics, and philoso-phy. Chambers' lack of scientific training or understanding, and his naïveté in trying to tackle so huge a challenge, were also heavily criti-cized; he was a "man of letters" who was blind to his own limitations and let ambition get the better of him. Adam Sedgwick was among the many eminent scientists who thought the book misguided and ill-conceived. Like them he initially ignored it, referring to it as "the foul book", but when it caught the public imagination he relented and read it carefully if reluctantly.

Many of Adam's friends, aware of his frustration at Chamber's lack of understanding, attention to detail, and scientific naivety, encouraged him to write a response to *Vestiges*. Early in 1845 he turned down an in-vitation by *The Edinburgh Review* to write a review of the book, citing ill-health (a spell of the gout) and work commitments (his course of lec-tures to give in Cambridge) as the main reasons.

In April 1845 he wrote a letter to Charles Lyell about *Vestiges*, de-scribing the book as "base, vulgar in spirit, ... false, shallow, worthless, and, with the garb of philosophy, starting from principles which are at variance with all sober inductive truth." He also wrote scathingly about its author and his "silly philosophy", questioning his "intellectual capaci-ties" and his "morality and his conscience". He bemoaned the consequences of Chambers' conclusions, telling Lyell "if the book be true, the labours of sober induction are in vain; religion is a lie; human law is a mass of folly, and a base injustice; morality is moonshine; our labours for the black people of Africa were works of madmen; and man and woman are only better beasts!"

Sedgwick later changed his mind and wrote a withering review of *Vestiges* for *The Edinburgh Review*, dismissing its "amateurish, material-ist, amoral and faulty views suggesting evolution of the universe ... [as] nothing more than blasphemous speculation." He pointed out some of the many scientific errors in the book, and voiced serious concerns about the moral implications of Chambers' idea of transmutation, predicting "ruin and confusion in such a creed" that would "undermine the whole moral and social fabric" of society." Adam later launched a lengthy attack on *Vestiges* and theories of development in general, in the Preface to the fifth edition of his *Discourse* (1850).

Sedgwick's uncompromising attack on Chambers was a foretaste of how he would respond to the theory of evolution that Charles Darwin described in *Origin of Species*. Many historians of science believe that Chambers' "development hypothesis" paved the way for *Origin* 15 years later, though Darwin was already working on his theory of evolution by 1844. When *Origin* was published in 1859, Darwin rejected Chambers' ideas about the method and cause of evolution, but concluded that *Vestig-es* had "done excellent service ... in calling attention to the subject, in removing prejudice, and in thus preparing the ground for reception" of his own ideas.

Sedgwick returned to the question of transmutation in 1845, after Louis Agassiz had sent him a copy of his new book on fossil fish. Adam wrote to thank him for it, but much of the letter is taken up with a strong critique of the transmutation theory of French naturalist Étienne Geoffrey Saint-Hilaire (1771-1844) who had been Professor of Zoology at the French National Museum of Natural History and then at the University of Paris. Adam wrote that "the opinions of Saint-Hilaire and his dark school seem to be gaining some ground in England. I detest them, because I think them untrue." He dismissed Saint-Hilaire's views because "they shut out all argument from design and all notion of a Creative Provi-dence", and because of the deductive method he had used in arriving at his conclusions. "When men of his school ... talk of spontaneous genera-tion and transmutation of species, they seem to me to try nature by a hypothesis, and not to try their hypothesis by nature. Where are their facts on which to form an inductive truth?", he asked.

Adam was also annoyed by Saint-Hilaire's "turgid mystical bom-bast" and his "cold and irrational materialism", as well as the ease with which he and his followers dismissed the received wisdom of divine crea-

14. Creation or Evolution?

tion. "I deny their starting condition," Adam told Agassiz, adding "if no single fact in actual nature allows us to suppose that the new species and orders were produced successively in the natural way, how did they begin? I reply by a way out of and above common, known, material nature, and this way I call creation."

Some historians of science think that Saint-Hilaire helped create a receptive audience for Darwin's theory of evolution (1859), although Darwin had earlier written to Lyell that Saint-Hilaire's thesis was "a grand piece of argument against mutability of species and I read it with fear and trembling."

On the Origin of Species (1859)

In the summer of 1831 Charles Darwin (1809-1882), then a young Cambridge graduate, accompanied Adam Sedgwick in some geological fieldwork in North Wales (as we saw in Chapter 11). Earlier that year he had attended Sedgwick's geology lectures, and found them fascinating. He was particularly struck by Sedgwick's ideas about the age of the Earth, and later wrote "What a capital hand is Sedgwick for drawing large cheques upon the Bank of Time!", hinting that this might have given him permission to think in terms of long-term changes even before he started his own field studies.

Sedgwick taught Darwin the basics of field geology, including how to recognise and name rocks, draw geological maps, collect and describe fossils. That experience would stand him in good stead over the next five years as naturalist on the round-the-world voyage of HMS *Beagle* (1831-1835). During the voyage, Darwin sent to Sedgwick descriptions of the geology of South America, and specimens of many of the rocks and fossils he collected there.

Sedgwick was greatly impressed by the application and natural curiosity his protégé displayed during the voyage, and by his meticulous recording of field notes and observations. He wrote to Darwin's former schoolmaster Dr Samuel Butler that "It was the best thing in the world for him that he went out on the Voyage of Discovery. There was some risk of his turning out an idle man: but his character will now be fixed, and if God spare his life, he will have a great name among the Naturalists of Europe." Butler passed these compliments from the great geologist on to Darwin's family.

As well as teaching geology to Darwin, Adam also became one of his mentors and benefactors. He introduced Darwin to the Geological Society by reading some of the geological reports he sent back from South

America at meetings of the Society in November 1835. This helped to kick-start Darwin's reputation as a scientist, and he was inducted into the Society in 1836, shortly after his return.

After returning from the voyage Darwin spent many years writing up his notes and observations, and carrying out further research inspired by what he had seen and found in South America. He was determined to mine as much useful information as possible from the unique opportunity he had been given. Over those years he gave much thought to the question of the transmutation of species which, as we have seen, was then a lively topic of scientific debate.

With his ideas well developed by the mid-1850s, and having been encouraged to put them into print before others could beat him to it, Darwin spent the latter part of that decade writing the ground-breaking book that would radically change the creation-evolution debate. *On the origin of species by means of natural selection, or the preservation of favoured races in the struggle for life* was published in November 1859. Darwin could probably have completed the book some years earlier, but he wanted to make his line of reasoning as water-tight as possible, and his supporting evidence as persuasive as possible.

Having witnessed Sedgwick's scathing attack on Robert Chambers' *Vestiges* in 1845, Darwin knew he would have to defend himself against such prominent, articulate and intellectually entrenched critics. He read it correctly – Adam Sedgwick was upset and disappointed by *Origin of Species*, and the theory of evolution that was so central to it, primarily because it had no place for divine creation or intelligent design, indeed no place at all for God. We know about Sedgwick's views on *Origin* mostly through various letters he wrote at that time, that are included in *Life and Letters*.

Darwin sent Sedgwick a copy of his book in November 1859, as soon as it was published. He enclosed a letter assuring Adam that he had sent the book out of respect, noting "as the conclusion at which I have arrived after an amount of work which is not apparent in this condensed sketch, is so diametrically opposed to that which you have often advocated with much force, you might think that I send my volume to you out of a spirit of bravado and with a want of respect, but I assure you that I am actuated [motivated] by quite opposite feelings. Pray believe me, my honoured friend, Your sincerely obliged, Charles Darwin."

Sedgwick wrote back two weeks later, praising "the great knowledge, store of facts, capital views of the correlation of the various parts of organic nature, admirable hints about the diffusions, through wide regions, of nearly related organic beings", but unable to contain his disappointment. He wrote "I have read your book with more pain than pleasure. Parts of it I admired greatly, parts I laughed at till my sides were almost sore; other parts I read with absolute sorrow, because I think them utterly false and grievously mischievous."

Much of Adam's disappointment centred on the deductive approach he claimed Darwin had adopted in arriving at his conclusions about evolution, arguing "you have deserted … the true method of induction … Many of your wild conclusions are based upon assumptions which can neither be proved nor disproved." In an attempt to reconcile their very different views, Adam wrote "you do not deny causation. I call causation the will of God; and I can prove that He acts for the good of His creatures. He also acts by laws which we can study and comprehend. Acting by law, and under what is called final cause, comprehends, I think, your whole principle."

So far so good, but Sedgwick then highlights the gulf between them over the moral implications of their different views, on which he said they were "point-blank at issue". He reminds Darwin that "There is a moral or metaphysical part of nature as well as a physical. A man who denies this is deep in the mire of folly." He adds "Tis the crown and glory of organic science that it does, through final cause, link material to moral." To drive home the point, he writes "Passages in your book … greatly shocked my moral taste. I think, in speculating on organic descent, you over-state the evidence of geology …"

Towards the end of the letter, he criticises Darwin for "the tone of triumphant confidence in which you appeal to the rising generation … and prophesy of things not yet in the womb of time, nor … ever likely to be found anywhere but in the fettle womb of man's imagination." That said, he closes by asking Darwin to "forgive any sentence you happen to dislike; and believe me, [in] spite of our disagreement on some points of the deepest moral interest, your true-hearted old friend, A. Sedgwick."

Darwin wrote back to Sedgwick two days later. He thanked Adam for his "honourable compliment … in expressing freely your strong disapprobation of my book. I fully expected it." He admitted "I daresay I may have written too confidently from feeling so confident of the truth of my main doctrine. I have made already a few converts of good and tried naturalists, and oddly enough two of them compliment me on my cautious mode of expression!" Despite being "grieved … to have encountered your severe disapprobation and ridicule", Darwin defends his theory of evolution by pointing out "I cannot think a false theory would explain so many classes of facts, as the theory seems to me to do."

The trail of letters then goes cold, and the next source we have is a letter Sedgwick sent to a Miss Gerard in January 1860. He tells her that he has read Darwin's book, which is "clever, and calmly written; and therefore, the more mischievous, if its principles be false; and I believe them utterly false. It is the system of the author of the *Vestiges* stripped of his ignorant absurdities." He regrets that the book rejects any notion of final cause and "seems to shut the door upon any view ... of the God of Nature as manifested in His works." He is also annoyed that it promotes materialism (the philosophical theory that nothing exists except matter), declaring that "from first to last it is a dish of rank materialism cleverly cooked and served up", that ignores the available evidence, "the vast treasury of facts that the Author of Nature has, during the past two or three thousand years, revealed to our senses." Reflecting on what Darwin's motivation might have been in formulating his theory and writing the book, he concludes "For no other solid reason, I am sure, except to make us independent of a Creator ...".

Sedgwick touches on some of these criticisms of Darwin's work in a letter to English palaeontologist Richard Owen (1804-1892) three months later, in March 1860. He accuses Darwin of having "deserted utterly the inductive track - the narrow but sure track of physical truth, and taken the broad way of hypothesis, which has led him ([in]spite of his great knowledge) into great delusion; and made him the ... teacher of error instead of the apostle of truth". He also accuses him of being "(whether he intends it or not, or knows it or not) ... a teacher of that which savours of rankest materialism, and of an utter rejection of the highest moral evidence, and the highest moral truth." But Adam also wanted to hear what Owen thought about "creation's law ... [by which] I mean order of succession ...". He told Owen "In that sense I do not believe in any law of creation. The highest point we can, I think, ever reach is a law of succession of forms, each implying a harmonious reference to an archetype, and each having indications of the action of a final cause - i.e. of intelligent causation, or creation."

Four days earlier Adam had written an anonymous review of *Origin of Species* in *The Spectator*. He could not hide his disapproval of Darwin's theory of evolution, ending by writing "I cannot conclude without expressing my detestation of the theory ... because it utterly repudiates final causes and therefore indicates a demoralised understanding on the part of its advocates."

14. Creation or Evolution?

In May 1860 Adam read a paper *On the succession of organic forms during long geological periods; and on certain theories which profess to account for the origin of new species* to a packed meeting of the Cambridge Philosophical Society. Not surprisingly, he was highly critical of Darwin's theory of evolution, dismissing it as "a mere hypothesis, at variance with the true inductive methods of attaining truth." Most people in the audience sided with Sedgwick, and although Darwin's friend and mentor John Stevens Henslow (who had recommended Darwin as naturalist on the voyage of the *Beagle*) agreed with much of what Adam said, he suggested that "the theory ought to be classed among those imperfect inductions which point the way to truth", as Clark and Hughes (1890b) put it. In other words, Henslow believed that Darwin's book should be seen as a stepping-stone towards truth, rather than truth itself.

Sedgwick could not rest easy over the question of evolution, and he seized on the opportunity to make his views clear in the Preface he wrote for Salter's *Catalogue of the Collection of Cambrian and Silurian Fossils contained in the Woodwardian Museum of the University of Cambridge* that was published in 1873. Recall (from Chapter 7) that between 1842 and 1845 Salter had helped Adam arrange the fossils in the Geology Museum, and in 1842 and 1843 accompanied him in geological excursions in North Wales, before being appointed to the staff of the Geological Survey in 1850.

Defending his unshakable belief in God's grand design and humans as the crowning glory of divine creation, Adam wrote in the Preface to Salter's *Catalogue* "We all admit that Nature is governed by law: but can we believe that a being like man is nothing but the final evolution of organic types worked out by the mere action of material causes? How are such organic evolutions to account for our sense of right and wrong, of justice, of law, of cause and effect, and of a thousand other abstractions which separate man [sic] from all the other parts of the animal world; and make him, within the limits of his duty, prescient and responsible."

Sedgwick bitterly opposed Darwin's idea of evolution for the rest of his days, dismissing it as misguided and atheistic. But, despite their profound differences of opinion and interpretation on such important matters, the two men remained friends to the end of their days.

Adam Sedgwick died at the age of 88 in 1873, and Charles Darwin (24 years his junior) died nine years later, in 1882, aged 73.

Wedded to the Rocks

Sedgwick's geological thinking in context

Before we leave Sedgwick's engagement in the creation-evolution debate, it is useful to reflect briefly on how his thinking fitted in with the prevailing scientific views of the day.

Helpfully, *Life and Letters* contains a letter he wrote to a Mrs Cropper in June 1858 in which offers his views on the state of the debate a year before *Origin of Species* was published. He recognised that the debate was far from fully resolved, and there was much to play for and more work still to be done. He told her "I have no fear about the ultimate result, but we have ample work for another half-century before we can be prepared to draw our lines of demarcation correctly, and till that is done I should think it premature to talk of comparing the geological days (or periods) with the Mosaic [scriptural] days." He added "that this will be done one day I have very confident expectation, because we have already done much, though a few blots remain to be removed by the honest scrubbing-brushes of the rising generation of geologists ...".

He spelled out for Mrs Cropper his own thinking on the matter, noting that "It is something to prove against some sturdy infidels (who would scoff at the Bible if it were spoken of) that the world is not eternal. Therefore it was created by a power external to itself, acting with prescient wisdom, and ordaining all laws by which the order of nature is maintained. The same creative power has not been quiescent, but has been employed again and again in replenishing and renovating the earth. Land and sea have changed place. The tops of our highest hills have been under water. Therefore the fact of an historic deluge is not impossible or improbable. Though the world is very old (we have no measure of the epochs of geology, only we are certain that they involve enormously long periods) man [sic] is but a creature of yesterday."

Looking back through the lens of today's understanding of geology, Adam Sedgwick's interpretation of the rocks and the fossil record, and how they were formed, looks both antiquarian and rather fanciful, but we can see it as a coherent attempt to explain things from the vantage point he had at the time. His understanding was heavily influenced by four factors.

The first was his starting assumptions about divine creation and God's grand design, and his unswerving commitment to make sure his geological interpretations were consistent with the Biblical narrative.

The second, which sprang directly from the first, was his blindness to the evidence within the rocks of long-term progressive change as well as periodic catastrophes, and his reluctance to consider that the Uniformi-

246

tarian school of thought might have some merit, although he did concede that the Earth must have been much older than the 6,000 years that theologians had long insisted.

Thirdly, no geologist in his day was able to establish absolute dates for rocks. They could give relative dates (younger or older than) based on position in the stratigraphic sequence, but that was as far as they could go, before the development of modern scientific methods of absolute dating.

Fourthly, but critically, in rejecting emerging ideas about transmutation and subsequently Darwin's theory of evolution, Sedgwick stopped short of being able to identify and account for progressive changes within and between species.

15. Induction and the Search for Truth

*"we have nothing to fear from the results of our enquiries, provided
they be followed in the laborious but secure road of honest induction. In
this way we may rest assured that we shall never arrive at conclusions
opposed to any truth, either physical or moral, from whatever source that
truth may be derived".*
Adam Sedgwick, Presidential Address to the Geological
Society (1830)

Two main threads run through Adam Sedgwick's adult life – his geology
and his Christian faith. We'll look more closely at his faith and churchmanship in Part Four, but before we move on from his geological work
we should pause and reflect on how he tied the two threads together. As
we saw in Chapter 14, this interplay between his faith and his science is
clearly illustrated in the high-profile role he played in the debate on creation versus evolution, during the early decades of the nineteenth century.

Adam's primary concern, in both his faith and his science, was the
search for truth. As he said in his 1830 Presidential Address to the Geological Society, "No opinion can be heretical, but that which is not true.
... Conflicting falsehoods we can comprehend; but truths can never war
against each other."

In his faith he accepted without question the truthfulness of the Bible
and its teachings, but in his science he had to find a reliable and "truthful"
way of judging between alternative (and sometimes contradictory) ways
of explaining observations and findings. He insisted that "we have nothing to fear from the results of our inquiries, provided they be followed in
the laborious but secure road of honest induction", and he looked upon
induction as the only way to establish truth in science.

He often used the term induction in his writing, but he but never explained precisely what he meant by it. In this chapter, we'll explore how
he understood and used the terms *induction* and *truth*, how that shaped
his thinking, and how he judged claims made by other geologists of his
day. As we'll see, he had a very particular way of understanding *induction* and, by the standards of today, a very particular understanding of
truth.

Sedgwick's understanding of truth

The search for truth drove everything Adam Sedgwick did, but what exactly did he mean by *truth*, and how did that shape the way he approached the search for it?

The foundation of Sedgwick's understanding of truth, the basis on which he defined truth, was what he called the "truth of revelation". By that he meant what has been revealed by God and recorded in the "sacred scriptures". To Adam, everything he saw and thought must be consistent with what is written in the Bible, so this means truth as affirmed by the Bible, and truth as affirming what is in the Bible.

For Adam, this traditional Christian understanding of truth was so taken-for-granted that it is rarely mentioned explicitly in *Life and Letters*. But we do catch the odd glimpse. For example, in *Memorial* (1868) he described how his father's "influence ... over the minds of his flock rested on his humble teaching of Gospel truth", and on preaching in Norwich Cathedral in 1855 he later wrote "I preach what I believe to be Christian truth ...". Sedgwick saw everything through the lens of his Christian faith, including the Biblical account of creation, and the ways in which God interacts with the earth and its people.

But, alongside the "truth of revelation", he was a firm believer in what he variously called "true knowledge", "material truth", or "scientific truth". By this he meant truth based on evidence from observation and experiments in the natural world. Thus, for example, he wrote after a spell of field mapping in North Wales with his friend Griffiths in 1854, "We sought the truth, and would have embraced it, to whatever conclusions it might lead us." Nine years earlier he had written to William Whewell, his Master at Trinity College, trusting that "under Providence [the protective care of God] you will be permitted ... to enjoy the happy fruits of your long-continued services in the great cause of scientific truth and sound academic learning."

Adam was insistent that "truth must be consistent with itself", as he argued in his review of William Buckland's 1823 book *Reliquiae Diluvianae*. He meant that what is revealed in the two forms of *truth* must be aligned because "truths can never war against each other". To him it was beyond question that, if the two are not aligned, "Gospel truth" must always take precedent. Thus, as he points out in his review, "The conclusions established on the authority of the sacred records may ... be compared with the conclusions established on the evidence of observation and experiment; and such conclusions, if fairly deduced, must necessarily be in accordance with each other."

He later acknowledged that, in his eagerness to make sure that "the authority of the sacred records" and "the evidence of observation" aligned properly, he had made one or two errors early in his career. We see this, for example, with his insistence in the 1825 paper on diluvium that surface deposits spread across Britain were laid down by the Great Flood described in Genesis, which he recanted five years later. In 1873, at the age of 88, a more mellow and reflective Adam wrote in his Preface to Salter's *Catalogue of the collection of Cambrian and Silurian fossils contained in the Geological Museum of the University of Cambridge* of how "we are led to feel the sanctity and nobility of Truth, under all the forms in which it shows itself, to rejoice in its possession, and to honour it as the gift of God."

Truth, for Adam, was a matter of integrity and fairness. The editors of *Life and Letters* describe how, as a boy, he was "distinguished for undeviating truthfulness in all that he said and did. Among his brothers and sisters and school-fellows, if Adam said a thing was so, there was no further question about the matter."

He also saw truth as a virtue. For example, in 1822 he wrote to William Wordsworth praising the way in which the poet could "teach your fellow-men the pleasant ways of truth and goodness, of nature, and pure feeling." At the 1833 meeting of the British Association he applauded scientist John Dalton (1766-1844), "a man whose whole life has been devoted to the cause of truth … [who had] a beautiful moral simplicity and singleness of heart, which … taught him to do homage to no authority before that of truth." After Prince Albert died in 1862, Adam wrote admiringly of how he had "united great benevolence, and wisdom, and love of truth."

Approaches to truth

Philosophers in Sedgwick's day, when modern science was challenging and starting to displace scriptural geology, recognised two different approaches to establishing truth – a deductive approach and an inductive approach. Both approaches are still in use today, but in more refined forms.

The deductive approach is based on testing a theory or hypothesis. The deductive scientist starts by thinking up a theory about the thing they are interested in, then narrows that down into a more specific hypothesis that can be tested. They then collect evidence (typically specific data collected by observation and experiment) which they use to test the hypothesis, with a view to confirming the hypothesis and the theory. All the early modern geologists, including Woodward and Werner (who we looked at in Chapter 10), used this theory-driven deductive approach. Their "theory" was that God had created the Earth and all the rocks in and on it. By describing their evidence and framing their interpretations in ways that by definition were consistent with the creation narrative, they succeeded (at least to their own satisfaction) in confirming their hypothesis and theory.

The inductive approach works the other way around, and seeks to derive general principles from specific observations. The inductive scientist starts by collecting specific data by observation and experiment, then looks for patterns and regularities in the data. After that they formulate one or more tentative hypotheses, before evaluating how well different hypotheses explain the patterns they find. The ultimate goal of the inductive approach is to develop some general conclusions or theories that should apply universally. William Smith's geological fieldwork based on stratigraphic mapping was ground-breaking in adopting an inductive approach, which is why it appealed so much to Adam Sedgwick when he launched his own geological career.

Whewell on induction
We have already met William Whewell (1794-1866), who (as we saw in Chapter 6) was a colleague of Adam Sedgwick's in Trinity College and served as Master from 1841 until his death in 1866. Whewell was nine years younger than Sedgwick, and was born in Lancaster, thirty miles south of Dent.

Whewell was the ultimate polymath – philosopher, theologian, Anglican priest, scientist, historian of science. Amongst many other things, he coined many of the scientific words that we use today, including scientist (previously "natural philosopher" or "men of science", for men they all were in those days), Catastrophism, Uniformitarianism, and consilience (the building of consensus by convergence of evidence from independent unrelated sources). He was a leading figure in British science at that time – a Fellow of the Royal Society, President of the Geological Society, and co-founder of the British Association for the Advancement of Science.

Of particular interest to us here is the work that Whewell did on the history, philosophy and practical application of the inductive method. He wrote some very influential books on the matter, including *The Philosophy of the Inductive Sciences, Founded upon their History* (1847), *History of the Inductive Sciences* (1857), and *On the Philosophy of Dis-*

252

covery (1860). None of these are easy reads, but American philosopher Laura Snyder has written a more accessible overview of Whewell's ideas about induction in the online *Stanford Encyclopedia of Philosophy* (2012).

The key to understanding Whewell's thinking is his belief that "in every act of knowledge ... there are two opposing elements, which we may call Ideas and Perceptions." Unlike other philosophers, such as Kant who argued that the key element in knowledge was ideas, and Locke who argued it was empiricism, Whewell argued that both are required. So he insisted that, in order to gain knowledge, we must bring together two things – subjective ideas or ideals (our conceptions of what is perfect), and objective or empirical elements (information that we acquire through observation or experience, not from theory or logic) – in what he called the "fundamental antithesis" of knowledge.

Fundamental Ideas and Conceptions
Although Whewell put great store on both ideas and perceptions, he was particularly interested in what he called Fundamental Ideas (such as space, time, cause, and number). He regarded Fundamental Ideas as the most important, essential, and enduring ideas, without which lesser ideas cannot exist or be imagined, and he looked on them as the basic building blocks of knowledge.

He noted that all observation is "idea-laden" and involves "unconscious inference", and argued that Fundamental Ideas help us structure and make sense of the many observations we make and experiences we have. He believed that each science has its own particular Fundamental Idea, that it needs in order to organise the facts it deals with. Example include Cause as the Fundamental Idea in mechanics, and Substance as the Fundamental Idea of chemistry.

He also believed that each Fundamental Idea has particular "conceptions" included within it, that are "special modifications" of the Idea applied to particular circumstances. Snyder gives the example of the conception of force as a modification of the Idea of Cause, applied to the particular case of motion.

Unlike other leading thinkers of the day, including John Stuart Mill and Sir William Herschel who believed that we form ideas based on our observations of the world around us, Whewell believed that Fundamental Ideas are "supplied by the mind itself". He wrote, in his *History of Scientific Ideas* (1858), that they are "not a consequence of experience, but a result of the particular constitution and activity of the mind, which is independent of all experience in its origin, though constantly combined with experience in its exercise." This frames the human mind in a very particular way, as "an active participant in our attempts to gain knowledge of the world, not merely a passive recipient of sense data", as Snyder (2012) points out.

Discoverer's Induction
Whewell coined the term "Discoverer's Induction" to describe the way in which science and scientists operate. He saw it as a two-stage process that starts with examining ideas (a process he called the "explication of conceptions"), then involves putting these ideas together with the available facts (a process he called the "colligation of facts"). He believed that scientific knowledge is built by following these two stages, each of which requires "invention, sagacity, genius", leaving little if any room for discovery in the sense of simply finding or uncovering things that were previously unknown.

Explication is the process of analysing and developing an idea, in order to make it clearer or more understandable. Whewell adopted the term to describe how, in his view, Fundamental Ideas and Conceptions are provided by our minds, although they cannot be used in their natural form so they have to be "explicated" or "unfolded" in order to make them useable. He argued, in *On the Philosophy of Discovery* (1860), that "the Ideas, the germs of them at least, were in the human mind before [experience]; but by the progress of scientific thought they are unfolded into clearness and distinctness."

Using Whewell's language, he believed that a Conception would be successfully explicated if it allowed the available facts to be colligated into a general description, hypothesis, law or principle that would apply to all facts relating to that idea. This is not done, he believed, by guesswork or by observation, but by "a special process in the mind, in addition to the mere observation of facts, which is necessary".

That "special process in the mind" that Whewell refers to is the process of inference. In *The History of Scientific Ideas* (1858) he explained that "We infer more than we see. Typically, finding the appropriate conception with which to colligate a class of phenomena requires a series of inferences ...". He argued that, when inference is not used to select the appropriate conception, the result is not an "induction" but a "hasty and imperfect hypothesis." To him, inference is a "special process" that God puts into our minds from the moment we are born, which gives humans the unique ability to recognise Fundamental Ideas and Conceptions, and to explicate and colligate them.

From this perspective, colligation is an act of thought involving the "special process" of induction, that allows us to combine empirical facts through a Conception. Whewell defined the act of colligation (combination) as "the mental operation of bringing together a number of empirical facts by 'superinducing' upon them a Conception which unites the facts and renders them capable of being expressed by a general law." The Conception is the "true bond of unity" that holds the facts together, by providing a property that is shared by all known members of that class of facts. Whewell calls this process of generalising the shared property or Conception across the whole class, including all known and unknown members, the process of "generalisation".

Necessary Truth
Whewell's philosophy of science included the claim that empirical science can reach necessary truths. His argument starts with his insistence that there are such things as "necessary truths" – truths that by definition must be true, and cannot not be true.

He believed these truths to be innate (unlearned), and he argued that they can be known *a priori*; that is, they are derived not from observation or experience but by reasoning from self-evident propositions. As Laura Snyder (2012) points out, Whewell believed that, "although they follow analytically from the meanings of ideas our minds supply, necessary truths are nevertheless informative statements about the physical world outside us; they have empirical content."

Whewell believed that the "ideas our minds supply" lie behind the "special process" of induction. His theology shaped his philosophy, because he looked upon these "ideas" as ideas that God puts into our minds from the moment we are born. He believed that, not only did God create the universe, but he did so in ways that conform to certain "Divine Ideas" that he had at the outset, so that all things and events in the world were created to conform to these ideas. Snyder gives an example; Whewell believed that "God made the world such that it corresponds to the idea of Cause partially expressed by the axiom 'every event has a cause'. Hence, every event in the universe conforms to this idea, not only by having a cause, but by being such that it could not occur without a cause."

It's then a short step for Whewell to believe that God created our minds with these ideas (or "germs" of the ideas) already embedded within them, so that "they can and must agree with the world", as he argued in *On the Philosophy of Discovery* (1860).

This way of viewing things has two clear implications – first, that God intends for us to have knowledge of the physical world, and secondly that this is only possible if ,in trying to acquire that knowledge, we use ideas that resemble the ones God used in creating the universe. In Whewell's language, once our ideas about the world are properly explicated, we can properly colligate the facts we collect and form true theories; as a result, every "law of nature" is a "necessary truth", because it conforms to some idea that God used when he created the universe.

As Snyder puts it, "since our ideas are 'shadows' of the Divine Ideas, to see a law as a necessary consequence of our ideas is to see it as a consequence of the Divine Ideas exemplified in the world." Whewell found this way of thinking so compelling that, in his 1833 *Bridgewater Treatise*, he insisted that "the more we study the laws of nature the more we will see necessary truths as intelligible results of intentional design and the more convinced we will be of the existence not only of God, but of God the Divine Law-giver."

Looking back from today on Whewell's ideas about necessary truths, it is difficult to avoid the conclusion that there is a good deal of circular thinking embedded within them. He starts with the "necessary truth" that God must exist, and proposes that God must have put that idea in our minds. He then insists that God defines the Fundamental Laws and helps us find appropriate Conceptions by the processes of explication, induction and collocation. He completes the circle by arguing that we use the Conceptions to interpret our experiences and sensations, which in turn point us to God.

It's also worth pointing out that, whilst Whewell's perspective and conclusions were widely discussed and debated at the time, they were neither uncritically accepted or universally adopted. One of his most vociferous critics was John Stuart Mill who, in his 1843 book *System of Logic*, listed many ways in which he disagreed with Whewell's ideas.

Sedgwick on induction
Adam Sedgwick was a firm believer that the only way of establishing truth is through induction. Indeed, in the Preface to the 1850 edition of *Discourse*, he describes induction as "the fountain of all material truth."

As I worked on earlier chapters in this book, I was often puzzled by his insistence that induction is the only pathway to truth, whilst at the same time he often started discussions (such as the debates and critiques we looked at in Chapter 14) with what today we might think of as one or more presuppositions, particularly about divine creation and intelligent design. Adam's deep Christian faith allowed him to view such "facts" as given truths – taken-for-granted facts that are beyond question, debate or doubt – as revealed by God in the Bible.

Nowhere does Adam explain exactly what he means by "induction", presumably taking for granted that his readers will already know, so it doesn't need spelling out. But there's no doubt that his thinking was heavily influenced by his colleague William Whewell. Sedgwick and Whewell were both Fellows and held senior offices in Trinity College at the same time. They enjoyed each other's company and supported each other's academic work and ambitions.

Whewell started formulating his ideas about induction in the 1830s, although he did not commit them to print until the later in that decade, in his *History of the Inductive Sciences* (1837) and *Philosophy of the Inductive Sciences* (1840).

Clark and Hughes, the editors of *Life and Letters* (1890a), point out that "no less an authority than Dr Whewell has admitted that had not Sedgwick's life 'been absorbed in struggling with many of the most difficult problems of a difficult science,' he would have been his own 'fellow-labourer or master' in the work which he was then publishing, *The Philosophy of the Inductive Sciences.*"

It seems possible, or even likely, that Whewell and Sedgwick had discussed induction before Adam recanted diluvialism in 1831. He was already talking about induction in 1830, in his first Presidential Address to the Geological Society, where he argued that "Conflicting falsehoods we can comprehend, but truths can never war against each other. ... we have nothing to fear from the results of our inquiries, provided they be followed in the laborious but secure road of honest induction."

Whewell's biographers, such as Richard Yeo (2008), suggest that his training in mathematics shaped his philosophical thinking about induction. He was steeped in the subject – after displaying great ability and promise in the subject at grammar school in Lancaster and Heversham, in 1812 he won a scholarship to study it at Trinity College, from where he graduated four years later as Second Wrangler, with the second-highest marks at Cambridge that year. Sedgwick also studied mathematics at Trinity College, but recall (from Chapter 8) that in those days there were only two degree schemes or Triposes at Cambridge, in Mathematics and in Classics. The link between his mathematical background, his commitment to induction, and his work in geology is revealing. Clark and

Hughes (1890a) praise the way in which, in his 1830 Presidential Address, Adam "hints at the true method of correlating facts, and establishing a correct induction from them in a manner well worthy of the 'mathematical geologist.'" Later in *Life and Letters* they comment that "throughout his geological life Sedgwick, thanks no doubt to his mathematical training, was no theorist."

Whewell believed that the duty of science was the "idealization of facts", translating empirical facts into mental ideas. Scientists do this, he argued, by the "progressive intuition of necessary truths", through the "colligation" of facts and the "consilience" of inductions. In this way, he argued and Sedgwick believed, the empirical study of nature will lead to necessary truth, not through simply gathering information but through induction, which required an active mind, the search for patterns, and the formation of explanations. Thus Adam told members of the Geological Society in his 1830 Presidential Address, that by following "the laborious but secure road of honest induction ... we may rest assured that we shall never arrive at conclusions opposed to any truth, either physical or moral, from whatsoever source that truth may be derived."

Adam adopted Whewell's thinking about induction, but not all of his language. For example, in none of his published writing does he mention the terms "necessary truths", "explication", "colligation", although he clearly used the concepts.

Adam rounds off his description of natural history in *Discourse* (1850) by declaring that "the history of Creation ... is not the dream of a disordered fancy, but an honest record of successive facts that were stamped by Nature's hand on the chronicle of the material world", facts stamped by the hand of God, in a grand plan devised by the mind of God before the very start of creation. There was no doubt in his mind that "before the creation of all worlds, there was an archetype of Nature (dead as well as living, past as well as present) in the prescient mind of God."

Similarly, Adam never did define or spell out what his Fundamental Ideas and Conceptions were. But it is clear from all he wrote that he took as given – what Whewell would call Necessary Truths – not only the idea of God but the existence of God. He also took as given the idea of "the mind of God" (a divine intelligence, a divine plan, and a grand design) and "the hand of God" (divine creation of the universe and everything within it, including all living things with humans as the crowning glory).

He took these ideas as non-negotiable truths. He saw them as "germs" of ideas that God had planted in the human mind, innate ideas that are nurtured by our experience, sensations and observations. Philoso-

258

phers today would regard them as presuppositions, preconceived ideas that are tacitly assumed; scientists today would view them as hypotheses to be tested.

In support of Whewell's idea that God implants ideas in our mind at birth, in the first edition of his *Discourse* (1832) Sedgwick seriously criticised English philosopher John Locke's (1632-1704) notion of the human mind as a blank slate on which experiences and written and stored as we progress through life. In rather flowery language not untypical of the day, he wrote about the history of humans, noting that "Naked he [sic] comes from his mother's womb; endowed with limbs and senses indeed, well fitted to the material world, yet powerless from want of use; and as for knowledge, his soul is one unvaried blank: yet has this blank been already touched by a celestial hand ."

Induction versus deduction
When, in 1863, the Royal Society awarded Adam Sedgwick its prestigious Copley Medal, for "outstanding achievements in research in any branch of science", Vice-President Hugh Falconer, praised him as "one of the leading minds which shaped geology into an inductive science."

Sedgwick had no doubt that "the laborious but secure road of honest induction" leads to truth. He believed, as he said in his 1830 Presidential Address to the Geological Society, that by following it "we may rest assured that we shall never arrive at conclusions opposed to any truth, either physical or moral, from whatsoever source that truth may be derived …".

Adam allowed for "truth" to be refined as and when "new discoveries" are made, because they will "lend support and illustration to things which are already known, by giving us a larger insight into the universal harmonies of nature." This is well illustrated in the way, in his 1831 Presidential Address, he was willing to recant diluvialism as a "philosophical heresy" and admit that "to seek the light of truth by reasoning of this kind [putting together "the clearest traces of diluvial action" and "in our sacred histories, the record of a general deluge"] … will ever end in erroneous induction." He excused his error by dismissing it as an "example of the passion with which the mind fastens upon general conclusions, and of the readiness with which it leaves the consideration of unconnected truths." That error of judgement did not knock him off course about the truth-affirming promise of induction.

Against this background, we can better understand Sedgwick's strongly critical attacks on other geologists of his day. He was a complex character, with great ambition and confidence in his own judgments and interpretations, but he was also very defensive and had limited patience. But the attacks were driven less by personal ambition and defensiveness than by an unswerving commitment to establishing truth, and here he believed that many contemporary geologists were routinely falling short.

As Adam wrote to his niece Fanny Hicks in December 1848, the "two kinds of truth, embodied in physical history [the focus of science] and revealed religion [the Bible], so far from being conflicting, were entirely in unison and harmony, if we investigated the one, and read the other, in a right spirit." To him, induction was the key to establishing truth, by making sure that the way in which scientific evidence was interpreted, and the way the Bible was read and understood, were always aligned with each other. Failure to do both "in a right spirit" – by which he meant "by induction" – would make it impossible to arrive at truth.

The main criticisms that Adam levelled at other geologists, beyond the very specific geological debates within the Great Devonian Controversy (Chapter 12) and the Cambrian-Silurian Controversy (Chapter 13), fall into two types.

Some of his criticisms reflect his belief that particular geologists were using a type of induction but not "in a right spirit". We've seen some examples in Chapter 14, including his case against Chambers' book *Vestiges*, and his clash with the Dean of York, both in 1844.

Other criticism was directed at geologists he accused of using deduction, that he was convinced could not possibly lead to truth. We've also seen examples of this in Chapter 14, including his attack in 1845 on "the opinions of Geoffroy St Hilaire and his dark school", and his persistent attacks on Charles Lyell and the Uniformitarian school of geology, which he dismissed in his 1831 Presidential Address to the Geological Society as "an unwarrantable hypothesis with no a priori probability ... as far as I have consulted the book of nature ... They may serve to enunciate the propositions of a hypothesis; but they do not describe the true order of nature."

Sedgwick's biggest target for criticism on the grounds of having adopted a deductive approach was the evolutionary ideas that Charles Darwin developed in *On the Origin of Species* (1859). He accused Darwin of having "deserted ... the true method of induction ... Many of your wide conclusions are based upon assumptions which can neither be proved nor disproved" and he wrote in his review of the book in *The Spectator* wrote that "Darwin has deserted utterly the inductive track –

the narrow but sure track of physical truth – and taken the broad way of hypothesis, which has led him into great delusion …"

Sedgwick's criticism is open to challenge, because historians of science today would dispute that Darwin started out with a theory (about transmutation or evolution) then collected evidence in the field to allow him to test that theory. The key reason why Sedgwick disagreed so much with Darwin was that, in his eyes, Darwin's thinking was not constrained by the "necessary truth" of God as creator. By not explicitly adopting the inductive approach, as Sedgwick understood and framed it, he was convinced that Darwin could not possibly have established anything truly truthful.

PART FOUR. CHURCH MAN

"Sedgwick's views as a churchman resembled his views as a politician. He shared the old Whig antipathy to 'Popery' and High Church and the old latitudinarian leaning towards Dissent. He hated the Penal Laws, but he feared 'Papal Aggression,' and he is always girding at the 'unhealthy craving for a priesthood,' the 'coxcombry and Popish apery,' and the 'sacred medieval knick-knacks' of 'the High Church [Anglo-Catholic] party.' In Newman and the chiefs of the Oxford Movement he could see nothing but 'fanaticism, sophistry, and dishonesty,' while the Eastern [Orthodox] Bishops were to him 'a pack of superstitious rascals – quite as bad as the Catholics.' Although not himself wholly satisfied with her liturgy, he never wavered in entire devotion to the [Anglican] Church."
Review of *Life and Letters* in *The Times* (29 July 1890)

16. Ordination

"I wish I had a better motive than I have for beginning these labours. I acknowledge the necessity and importance of them, but I feel an indifference to serious subjects which I shall find it difficult to conquer."
Adam Sedgwick in a letter to Ainger (1810)

At first sight, Adam Sedgwick's decision to take Holy Orders looks slightly curious, certainly to twenty-first century eyes, given his undying interest in rocks and his life-long commitment to the development of geology as a branch of science. Although he was born into family of churchmen, he apparently showed no particular interest in theology or any ambition to be ordained, before he won his College Fellowship in 1810. He never mentions it at all in any of the letters in *Life and Letters* before that date, and mentions it only rarely after 1810.

The letters show that he studied for ordination reluctantly and at best intermittently; he had more interesting things to do with his time. The decision to seek ordination was clearly a pragmatic one, made more out of necessity than any sense of calling or vocation. It would allow him to remain at Cambridge as a College Fellow, if he wished to do so.

Taking Holy Orders
The Statutes of Trinity College in Sedgwick's day required that "all the Fellows save two should be in Priest's Orders [ordained] within seven years from the full completion of the degree of Master of Arts, under pain of forfeiting their Fellowship." So, as we saw in Chapter 6, whether or not they intended to accept a College living, all Fellows were required to train for ordination as a condition of continued employment and residence in the College.

Adam had been awarded his MA in 1811, so the clock was ticking ... he would have to be ordained by 1818 at the latest. The stakes were high, because failure to meet the deadline would mean the loss of his coveted Fellowship. He got his head down, did the required studying, and worked towards ordination.

Theological study
His intentions were good, but he struggled to fulfil them. Year after year he intended to be ordained by the end of summer, and year after year he failed. This was partly because procrastination was in his nature, but also because he found so many other things much more interesting. Studying theology always kept dropping down his "to do" list.

Adam never hid the fact that he found the study of theology tedious. He often mentioned it in letters to his old friend William Ainger, who also got ordained and secured a college living for himself. In 1810 he wrote to tell Ainger that he intended "to begin my theological labours in about a fortnight. I wish I had a better motive than I have for beginning these labours. I acknowledge the necessity and importance of them, but I feel an indifference to serious subjects which I shall find it difficult to conquer." He wrote again the following February, "You will recollect that I made several resolutions to read divinity this vacation. I did begin, but that was all, for I made no progress. Boswell's *Life of Johnson* is the only book I have seen this Christmas." Adam kept promising himself and Ainger that he would soon get down to work; he wrote again in March 1815 advising Ainger that "On Monday I shall begin to read divinity. I have got about twenty folios out of our library."

A curious incident relating to ordination is mentioned in *Life and Letters*. In 1814, three years before he was ordained, Adam was offered the curacy of a small church in Northamptonshire of which Trinity College was patron. He was assured, Clark and Hughes (1890a) tell us, that the church "would not be too much for his lungs; but he had not energy enough to submit to even the small amount of work then required of candidates for ordination, and so the proposal was declined." This raises the question of why he was offered a church post before he had even been ordained. The College clearly thought he was up to the job and worthy of it, so did they perhaps make the offer in order to spur him on with his theological studies?

Ordination (1817)
The formal process of ordination required Adam to take two steps. First, he had to obtain formal permission from a Bishop to be ordained in a different diocese. He received this from the Bishop of Bristol, William Mansell, who had been Master of Trinity College since 1798. Step two was to be ordained deacon, which was done in July 1817 by Henry Bathurst, Bishop of Norwich. A deacon is an ordained minister of a rank just

below that of priest, with similar responsibilities, but is not allowed to preside at Holy Communion. A deacon can normally be "priested" (ordained priest) after a year, effectively having served an apprenticeship in churchmanship.

It seems fitting that Adam first performed the duties of a clergyman in Dent, where he spent most of the summer of 1817, shortly after his ordination. It was here, in the parish church under the watchful eye of the Vicar (his father Richard) that he started to write and preach sermons.

Divinity Act (1829)

In April 1828, twelve years after his ordination, Adam wrote to Roderick Murchison, explaining why he was unable to join him in geological fieldwork: "My hands at present are sufficiently tied. I am in the first place reading the [Desert] Fathers and School Divines by way of preparation for my Divinity Act, which I must keep on the 30th of this month. In the meantime I have a rascally examination to superintend [as part of his College duties] which will nail me down for a whole week."

The Divinity Act was part of the assessment for the postgraduate qualification of Bachelor of Divinity at Cambridge and Oxford. In Cambridge, resident Masters graduates who chose to take the degree were required to preach in the University Church (St Mary the Great), and to keep one Act and two Opponencies, just as Adam had done some years earlier at part of his assessment for the degree of Bachelor of Arts (as we saw in Chapter 5). The Divinity Act required the Respondent (Adam) to propose two Questions then read a thesis (essay) on the first, which would be "criticised" (debated) by three Opponents. The Moderator was normally the Professor of Divinity but sometimes a Doctor of Divinity, and they were allowed to "criticise" the thesis. Acts were public events, open to spectators as silent witnesses, and they often gathered quite large audiences.

Adam had written to Ainger in June 1811, the year he was awarded his MA, "I cannot yet propound to you any difficult questions in divinity, because I have not taken the trouble to look for them." Quite why it took Adam so long to finally complete his Divinity Act is not known, but the long delay is curious since, as Clark and Hughes (1890a) point out, at that time every MA graduate "of four years standing ... was obliged, under rather severe penalties, to be a Respondent".

Adam eventually chose two questions for his Act – The divinity of Christ, and A denial of the millennium. *Life and Letters* is silent on whether or not he was successful, but in the absence of evidence to the contrary it is safe to assume he was.

Churchmanship

In terms of churchmanship, Adam Sedgwick was a Conservative Evangelical. Both he and his father were members of the Protestant evangelical tradition that emphasises salvation by faith in Jesus Christ through personal conversion, as well as the authority of the Bible and the importance of preaching the "good news" of the gospel, rather than emphasising church ritual.

Evangelicals in Adam's day were very critical of the Roman Catholic church, its traditions, theology and teaching. During the 1830s some High Church members of the Church of England formed what became known as the Oxford Movement, that developed into Anglo-Catholicism. The movement campaigned for the reinstatement into Anglican theology and liturgy of some older Catholic traditions and rituals, including the establishment of Anglican religious orders both of men and of women, and the introduction of more explicit emotional symbolism in church services, such as wearing vestments and making the Eucharist a central part of worship.

In October 1845 Adam wrote to Miss Kate Malcolm expressing his great disappointment that John Henry Newman, a popular and prominent Anglican priest in Oxford University, and more than twenty other members of the Oxford Movement "have at length gone over to Rome [become Roman Catholics]. Shame on them that they did not do so long since! ... I pity their delusion, I despise their sophistry, and I hate their dishonesty. ... The sin of idolatry is knitted to the human heart. We may worship a priest, or worship ourselves, or worship our own works, while we are talking of idolatry, and thinking that we are serving our Saviour."

The fallout from the High Church exodus "over to Rome" lapped directly around Sedgwick's feet when, in February 1847, his good friend Charles Wodehouse was offered the post of Archdeacon of Norwich, where Adam had held the post of Canon since 1834 (as we'll see in Chapter 17). Wodehouse must have expressed reservations about accepting the offer because, like Adam, he disagreed with some aspects of the High Church liturgy used in services at the Cathedral. But Adam urged him to take it, stressing "There are no duties of the office you may not do with a good conscience; and you will do them, if God spare your life, with a good conscience. The office may enable you to do the cause of honest scriptural truth much good ... Let not good Evangelical men flinch, and refuse office. Now is the time for them to take the front rank, that the ul-tra-High-Church have gone over to the enemy."

Adam Sedgwick was particularly critical of the Anglo-Catholic High Church, that he as regarded as misguided and wrong. He makes his views on the matter very clear in a letter he wrote to David Livingstone in March 1865: "I greatly dislike the tendency to formal superstitious obser-vances in the present day ... [by] the High Church party in England. The idolatrous element is rife amongst us. We want to lean upon our own works and merits, and count them up as if they gave us the right to draw upon our Redeemer's treasures. We are the slaves of our senses, and too willing to follow their lead ... Many of our ministers and people are in an unhealthy craving for the office and power of a sacrificing Priest, and the dicta of an infallible authority, that may save them ... from all further trouble. This might flatter the pride of the shepherd, and save both shep-herd and flock from the toil of thinking, and the fatigue of further wandering. But it is false to the cause of truth ..."

Sedgwick's church posts
Early in 1825, eight years after being ordained, Adam Sedgwick was of-fered the living of St Mary's Church at Shudy Camps, a small village in south-east Cambridgeshire, fifteen miles from Cambridge. It was close enough to Trinity College to allow him to easily travel between the two and, because the College owned the living and appointed him to it, he could hold it alongside his Fellowship and Professorial post, and receive an income from all three.

He learned of the offer by letter when he stopped off at Dent for a few days on his way back to Cambridge from Edinburgh, and responded without delay. As soon as he got back to Cambridge he went to London to be instituted, the process in which the patron of the church (in this case Trinity College Cambridge) formally presents the prospective vicar to the Bishop of the diocese, who grants authorisation to exercise the spiritual responsibilities of the post. The following day Adam was inducted ("read in") at the church, a process lead by the Archdeacon in which the priest recites a standard passage of text and formally takes possession of the income and assets of the church.

Adam wrote about his appointment to his friend Ainger in February 1825, adding as a Postscript "I have accumulated so many [geological] materials that I must remain at home the greater part of this year to digest and write. I have no less than four memoirs on the stocks. One of these will run out almost into a volume. I fear I shall not have much time for sermons, but I have hired a curate." Before 1838 it was possible for an incumbent to enjoy the income of the living, and appoint and pay for an assistant curate to discharge virtually all the spiritual duties of the office at a lesser salary, leaving him as Vicar to live and work elsewhere.

In March 1832 Adam was offered the much more valuable living of East Farleigh in Kent. The offer was made the church's patron Henry Brougham, who served as Lord Chancellor in Earl Grey's reformist Whig government from 1830 to 1834. The living was worth up to £1,000 a year (twenty times what Shudy Camps was worth), but because it was not a College living he would have to resign as Professor of Geology in order to accept it. As a man of duty and honour, determined "not to break off his work in the middle", he had no hesitation in declining the invitation.

He wrote to Murchison after receiving and declining the offer, and told him "I do not think this would be to my honour, or that it would add to my happiness." Several of his friends and colleagues thought different-ly. For example, Charles Lyell recorded in his diary on the 16th of March that year that, if Sedgwick were to leave Cambridge and marry, "he would be much happier, and would eventually do more for geology". Ad-am wrote to Ainger the following day that some of his friends think "that I am raving mad", although he added that "the Chancellor [Brougham] thinks me in my sober senses, and has promised me one of the very first stalls [cathedral posts] which is vacant – which I can hold both with my Fellowship and Professorship, and make my hammer ring more merrily than ever against the rocks ..."

Lyell recognised that Sedgwick's geological work meant much more to him than church work. In his diary entry for the 18th of March he wrote that Sedgwick "hinted that in a year, when [his long-planned book with Conybeare about the Primary Rocks] is done, he may retire on some liv-ing, and marry. But I know Sedgwick well enough to feel sure that the work won't be done in a year, nor perhaps in two; and then a living, etc. won't be just ready, and he is growing older."

Clark and Hughes (1890a) agreed with Lyell that Adam was wrong to refuse the living at East Farleigh. They knew him well, and thought that although "he would have regretted leaving Cambridge at first ... he had a happy capacity for accepting new surroundings and new occupa-tions. ... Nor would he have found the duties of a parish clergyman ... incompatible with the pursuit of geology. His best geological friends, the brothers Conybeare, were both beneficed clergymen, and we believe that they did not neglect either parish or science."

16. Ordination

His biggest mistake, they felt, was that in declining the living "he cut himself off, irrevocably, from marriage; and that he deliberately chose a bachelor life is evident from what he says about his readiness to accept a stall [a cathedral post] which he could hold with his Professorship and Fellowship [neither of which allowed marriage]. We are not aware that he ever owned to regrets for Farleigh; but in the loneliness which is inseparable from old age within the precincts of a college he not seldom dwelt upon what might have been, had he been blessed with a wife and children."

17. Norwich Cathedral

"he recounts with his usual glee the flutter caused amongst 'the good old Tory inhabitants of the rookery' by the intrusion of 'such a monster as a Whig Prebendary,' who set 'Independents and High Churchmen licking out of the same flesh-pots.'"
Review of *Life and Letters* in *The Times* (29 July 1890)

In October 1834, after a successful summer of fieldwork in the open air, Adam Sedgwick returned to Cambridge to deliver his annual series of geology lectures, restored to good health and refreshed in spirit. Shortly after he got back to Trinity College he was surprised to be offered a post at Norwich Cathedral which, "for a part of each year at least, diverted the current of his thoughts into a new channel", as Clark and Hughes (1890a) put it.

Cathedral post

After Lord Grey resigned as Prime Minister in July 1834, the King (William IV) appointed Whig MP William Lamb, Lord Melbourne (1779-1848), to succeed him. Melbourne only served as Prime Minister for five months before the King dismissed him, and his government collapsed in mid-November.

Henry Brougham, Lord Brougham (1778-1868), had been Lord Chancellor in Grey's government since 1830, and he continued under Melbourne. Brougham was patron of two church posts – a rectory in Yorkshire and a senior clergy post in Norwich Cathedral – which both fell vacant on the death of a man who had held the both simultaneously. On his last day as Chancellor he offered the Norwich post to Adam Sedgwick, who shared his Whig (liberal) political views.

The post was Canon Prebendary. In the Church of England, a Canon is an ordained man with special duties in a cathedral, who is bound by the rules or 'canons' of that cathedral. A Prebendary is a senior member of clergy in a cathedral, who has a role in the administration of the cathedral.

Sedgwick was then forty-nine years old. He had relatively little experience in church leadership, but was well-established as a scientist after sixteen years as Professor of Geology at Cambridge. He was in the prime of his geological career, and the Great Devonian Controversy (Chapter 12) and the Cambrian-Silurian Controversy (Chapter 13) were both starting to gather pace, occupy his time, and raise his profile.

Adam accepts the post

Adam accepted the offer of the post and took office on the 1st of December 1834.

Shortly after taking up residence in Norwich he wrote a long letter to his friend Ainger, explaining that the post fitted in well with his College duties in Cambridge and noting that "There are six Prebendaries, and each resides [in Norwich] two months [each year]. Now December and January just suit me, as the greater part of these two months falls in our Christmas vacation."

He described to Ainger how he wasted no time in completing the formalities surrounding the appointment – "went up to Town [London] without an hour's delay – procured my presentation from the Chancellor's office – took an early coach to Norwich – arrived on Saturday, November 29, in time for the Dean's breakfast – took the oaths and signed the books – presented my deed with the great seal affixed to the Dean after the First Lesson in the morning service – was formally installed in the presence of the congregation – read in [installed] on Sunday the 30th – and commenced Residence in my own house on Monday, the 1st inst."

Adam's willingness to accept the cathedral post in Norwich is slightly curious given his obvious commitment to his work in geology, and his reluctance to commit much of his time and energy to church work. As with his reluctance over the decisions to train for ordination and to accept a college living that would require much work (as we saw in Chapter 16), it is tempting to think that he was attracted to Norwich for pragmatic reasons rather than out of any deep sense of calling or vocation.

He hints as much in his letter to Ainger, writing "If my life be spared the stall [cathedral post] will I doubt not turn out a very comfortable thing. I hope I may count upon its producing me nearly £600 a year. This, together with my Senior Fellowship and Professorship, must surely enable me soon to lift my head above water."

Residence

As a Prebendary Adam was required to be "in Residence" in Norwich for 2 months each year. After many years living frugally but comfortably in his rooms in Trinity College, surrounded by familiar faces and following familiar routines, he found the seasonal relocation to Norwich difficult, particularly in the early years. The workload was high and often unforgiving, and at time he felt imprisoned; he told Ainger that "our Residence while it lasts is severe. We are not permitted to be away from our houses for a single night."

He was provided with a cathedral house that would be his throughout the year. He told Ainger the month he moved in that, after buying his predecessor's "furniture and wines" for around £600, he was "gradually settling down into my proper place." The house itself clearly grew on him. In February 1835 he described it to his old friend Rev Charles Ingle as "a queer, old-fashioned, in-and-out, ugly, old, house", but three years later (in January 1838) he wrote to tell his brother John that "really my new house is quite charming. I have one very good bedroom fit for a married couple; and three spare beds for bachelors."

As a middle-aged bachelor, Adam was not left to look after himself while in Residence in Norwich. He told John that Lady Jane Wodehouse, wife of Canon John Wodehouse, had recommended to him "a housemaid, and a young lass to help her", and "a capital housekeeper who provides and cooks for me". He also had the services of his College servant John, who accompanied him on his trips to Norwich. He told his brother John "My own servant comes and acts as my butler and waiter and factotum; and I have an assistant and occasional waiter to rub down my horse."

His seasonal household in Norwich was completed by the presence, particularly after 1840, of one or more of his nieces. In his January 1838 letter to brother John he wrote "When [your daughters] Isabella and Emma are out, they must come their first winter and keep house for me during a two months' Residence. It will be a good start for them: and I shall be able to show them excellent society. Indeed I have more of it than I like."

Responsibilities and duties

Adam got off to a good start in Norwich. The post allowed him to make new friends, and he was generally content with the duties it involved. He reassured Ainger "My clerical employment here is a good thing, and I mean not to flinch from it."

But he was not always able to maintain that initial enthusiasm. When he started at Norwich he was 49 years old, had lived a sheltered life in Trinity College for three decades, surrounded by close academic friends and colleagues, and a high degree of freedom in how he used his time. All this changed when he was in Residence in Norwich.

He told Ainger that his duties as Prebendary involved "attending service regularly, and preaching generally once each Sunday ... We have also to give certain dinners of ceremony to the officers of the Cathedral. Giving and receiving dinners constitutes a formidable service in a city like this." He told Ingle that while in Norwich he held the position of Vice Dean, and "in the absence of the Dean I was the official representative of the dignity of the Chapter - called upon to practice a series of formal hospitalities ..."

As Clark and Hughes (1890a) point out, "Before long ... as the novelty of the situation [in Norwich] wore off, he became less enthusiastic, and for a while was listless and ill at ease. ... at Norwich he could not call a moment his own. He had to lead an essentially public life; to submit to incessant interruptions; to be at the beck and call of anybody who chose to ring his bell."

It's not surprising, therefore, that Adam was not happy at the prospect of extending his annual Residence from two to three months, as the Dean told him would be necessary after the death of a fellow Canon. He wrote to Canon Wodehouse from Cambridge in November 1836, pointing out that "with my present engagements here such an arrangement would be impossible, at least for this year. It would, I believe, compel me to resign my Professorship – a move I am by no means inclined to take." The following month he wrote to Ingle complaining that his winter Residence that year would stretch from the beginning of December to the third week of February, instead of the last day of January as usual.

Adam's workload in Norwich Cathedral was relatively heavy, but his responsibilities extended beyond the cathedral to include regular duties as chaplain at the County Hospital. He explained to Murchison by letter in January 1837 how, after attending a ninety-minute service in the cathedral, some months he would walk the mile to the hospital to read morning prayers there, before returning for "another long Cathedral service from which I shall come home dog-tired and unfit for work." In October 1847 he wrote to Miss Kate Malcolm to explain how, at the County Hospital, "they have prayers twice a week, and prayers and a sermon on Sundays; so that on Sundays I had to attend three full services. In short I became one of the working clergy."

Adam's days in Norwich were full, certainly compared to the more sedate life he enjoyed in Trinity College. He spelt out his daily routine in a letter to Kate Malcolm in January 1844, telling her "My life is very uniform – I rise early (often between five and six) and do all my work in the mornings, often before anyone is stirring. … At nine I meet my servants – quarter past, breakfast – at ten, morning service at the Cathedral – after service, odds and ends – callings and shoppings and I know not what – lunch at one – then a scamper on horse-back (when I have time) with my niece, who loves a horse … and she now rides a lovely bay thoroughbred creature I have hired for her. … Cathedral service again at four – dinner at six: … We are rather given to dining out; and have many kind friends …".

Services and sermons

Adam found the services in the cathedral dreary and draining. He told Murchison by letter in January 1837 how "These long services cut my time to shreds, and destroy the spirit of labour. We have the shadow of Catholicism without a grain of its substance, for not one of the Chapter thinks himself better for these heartless formalities, or nearer heaven. … And what the congregation? One single old woman in addition to the officials."

But he paints a very different picture in some other letters. For example, he told the Duke of Argyll in October 1857 "You must not think … that our Cathedral congregations are always composed of a few tottering old women. I preached every Sunday during my three months Residence of the past year to a very large congregation. And it went on increasing, for every corner of our large Cathedral choir was at length filled, and I had each Sunday of the summer months a congregation of about 1,200 persons sitting under me …". Adam does nor claim credit for the huge rise in the size of the congregation over those two decades, but he clearly welcomed it.

He told Ainger in December 1834 that "the preaching … is not compulsory; but has been commenced of late years by some of the newcomers." Three months later he told Ingle "I have also been much given to preaching, holding forth twice, and sometimes thrice, on a Sunday." Three years after that, he told his brother John "I have been preaching almost every Friday, and often sitting up very late at night, and rising very early in the morning, to write my sermons. I preached last Sunday week in the Cathedral for the benefit of the County Hospital."

Adam had preached occasionally in Chapel at Trinity College and in his father's parish church in Dent, for both of which he had plenty of time to prepare his sermons. But the preaching load in Norwich was much heavier, and it took its toll on him. Amongst other things, it left him with less time than he needed to write up the geological work he was still heavily engaged in. Thus he wrote to Murchison in January 1836 explaining why he was taking so much time writing up their joint work; "Each Sunday I have to attend three services, and to preach twice. My sermons cost me some trouble, and towards the end of the week I have to rise at six in order to find two or three hours I may call my own."

Canon Wodehouse wrote to tell Adam in October 1837 that some members of the congregation had complained to him about Adam's preaching, particularly his apparent reluctance or inability to prepare proper notes for his sermons. Some had asked "How much good might he do if he would turn his talents this way, and give us every Residence a good course of good sermons?" Adam had earlier promised Wodehouse that he would write a short series of sermons which he would publish and preach at the cathedral, but that had not materialised. Wodehouse told him "I am now most anxious you should give us some good, well-considered Theology from the Prebendal Chair."

Adam responded to Wodehouse two days later, with a robust defence. He told him he was too busy with his geological work, remained unrepentant about the preaching, and added "were I to give myself up to theological studies exclusively no doubt I might do more than I have done. But it is at present impossible for me to do so. And were the alternative given me this day of resigning my Professorship or my stall, because I could not do the duties of both properly, I should instantly give up the latter, and not the former." He reminded Wodehouse that "in my first year's Residence I had during the greater part of the time a double duty in the Cathedral, and during three or four successive Sundays I did duty thrice – which was fair hack work. During my second Residence I worked hard at the [Norwich] Museum lectures, and preached on every occasion on which I was apparently called on. The Dean was away, and I was called on at least six or seven times. Last winter I was direly out of sorts for six or seven weeks, and utterly incapable of much intellectual labour."

In his own defence, Adam did admit to his "procrastinating temper [state of mind]" and long spells of "indisposition" through ill-health, and to often finding it difficult to write down his thoughts. He said that "Some of my friends expect more from me than I can do. Because on some occasions I speak fluently, it by no means follows that I write readily. ... I know that much of my life has been dreamy and worthless; but I am constitutionally incapable of much sedentary exertion. My friends also think me a thousand times better than I am."

Public lectures on geology

Norwich was pleased to have in its midst such a distinguished scientist as Adam Sedgwick. Only a year after his arrival he was invited by Norwich Museum to deliver a course of lectures on geology for the general public.

He accepted the invitation, but knew that he would be treading a fine line in speaking about geology as a churchman, at a time of growing interest in the debate between creation and evolution (that we looked at in Chapter 14). He wrote to Canon Wodehouse towards the end of 1835, acknowledging "I don't know my audience, and therefore I want to feel my way. Geology introduces some tender topics which require delicate handling. I must speak truth, but by all means avoid offence if I can. Above all I must try not to make my lecture a bore, which may be done easily in two ways – by firing over their heads, or by running out to an unwarrantable length."

The lectures were clearly not boring. As he wrote to his brother John in January 1838, they attracted an audience of up to four hundred people, including many educated women (or "blue stockings" as he would often call them, as we saw in Chapter 4). He told Miss Kate Malcolm by letter six years later "I think I had a class of nearly 300, and more than half the number were of the softer sex – at least they wore the outer symbols of womankind …"

Thanks to a letter he sent to his niece Fanny Hicks in March 1841 we catch sight of what he covered in the lectures, which usually lasted about two hours. He tells her "My first was about rain, springs, rivers, bogs, and marshes. My second was about snow, ice, glaciers, boulder-stones, and gravel. My next is to be devoted to the classification of such beasts, birds, fishes, and reptiles as are now living on the face of the earth. And the two following will contain the life-history and adventures of the beasts, birds, fishes, and reptiles which lived before the time of Adam, with many interesting anecdotes of their love adventures."

People

It took time, but Adam gradually developed a wide circle of people he could call friends in Norwich. He told his brother John by letter in January 1838 "My friends here received me with their usual kindness, and I was delighted to come again among them". Three years earlier he had written to Ingle that "Everybody was kind and hospitable; indeed I have been almost killed with kindness …".

He deliberately reached out to build bridges with people outside his normal circle of acquaintances, both politically and church-wise. It is easy to sense the smile on his face and the mischief in his eyes as he wrote to Ingle in February 1835 about how "all the good old Tory inhabitants of the rookery seemed mightily anxious to see how such a monster as a Whig Prebendary would behave at meals; … I did, however, contrive to bring together more heretics and schismatics within my walls than ever had been seen before in a Prebendal house since the foundation of the Cathedral, [including] Independents and High churchmen … and Quakers." He closed by commenting "By the way some of the Quakers are my delight …".

Over time he grew to love Norwich and his role in it, particularly when supported by the nieces he adored and treated as if they were his own daughters. As Clark and Hughes (1890a) put it, "he regarded his old-fashioned house in the [Cathedral] Close, especially after it became filled with his nephew's children, as a second home …". We get a flavour of just how comfortable he was in his "second home" in a letter he wrote to Kate Malcolm in January 1844, in which he described how a few days earlier he "had a good Christmas party of children – blind man's bluff and Hyde Hall romps over again; and a good smattering of grown-up children, who thought themselves young again during the sparkling of fireworks and the boisterous mirth of snap-dragon."

We saw in Chapter 4 how, by today's standards, Adam Sedgwick looked down on women, thought them feeble-minded, and at times viewed marriage as a trap to be avoided at all costs. But we also caught glimpses of some purely platonic but relatively close and satisfying relationships he enjoyed with particular women, and how, when it suited him, he greatly enjoyed the company and companionship of ladies, particularly young ladies, including his two nieces Isabella Sedgwick and Fanny Hicks.

Life and Letters contains numerous letters that Adam sent to Kate Malcolm during his time in Norwich, but her identity otherwise remains a mystery and there is no record of them actually meeting in person.

Clark and Hughes (1890a) mention two ladies whose company Sedgwick particularly enjoyed at Norwich. One was a Miss Clarke, who later married and became Mrs Guthrie, who was "widely known for her beauty, her wit, and her active benevolence". In her Adam "found more congenial relaxation in her natural gaiety than in the more artificial courtesies of the matrons of the Cathedral precincts." She clearly felt comfortable in Adam's presence; Clark and Hughes tell of how, during a visit to his house in the company of others "in the evening she draws caricatures of Sedgwick's figure on horseback; next morning she comes to breakfast with him dressed as a Quakeress, and plays her part admirably, to the 'infinite delight' of her host and his friend; on another occasion she dons a gown and cassock, and [im]personates, first Sedgwick, and then an old shuffling canon."

The other lady who caught his eye in Norwich was Catherine Stanley, daughter of Edward Stanley (1779-1849), the Bishop of Norwich and thus Adam's "boss". Adam wrote to Murchison in April 1839 of how, when he visited the Bishop at home, he found Catherine "all glorious to behold, with a gorgeous plume ... So she is now fairly out, no longer a mere chrysalis, a creature without sensibility, having neither organs of nutrition, nor wings, nor legs. But, on the contrary, she has glorious antennae waving over her head, organs of sense to discourse sweet music, arms for offence and defence, and wings glittering like sunbeams on a May morning. ... I shall hereafter treat her with great deference, now that she is transformed, by the magical touch of the royal hand, into a young lady."

Senior church posts Sedgwick turned down
Bishop of Norwich (1837)
When Adam Sedgwick was first "in Residence" in Norwich, Henry Bathurst (1744-1837) was Bishop, and had been since 1805. In 1834 Bathurst was ninety years old, spent most of his time in London and, as Clark and Hughes (1890a) describe him, was "a Bishop of the old school, a man of letters and a politician rather than a churchman, and a devoted whist-player." His death three years later, in April 1837, created a vacancy which some of Sedgwick's friends were eager for him to fill. Adam was reluctant to allow his name to go forward, and relieved when he heard that Rev Edward Stanley (1779-1849) had accepted the post.

Stanley had been Rector of Alderley in Cheshire, of which his family were patrons, from 1805 to 1837. He was the second son of Sir John Thomas Stanley of Alderley Park, and graduated from St John's College, Cambridge. He had studied geology and was a keen amateur naturalist, and in 1836 published *A Familiar History of Birds, their Nature, Habits, and Instincts*. Clark and Hughes (1890a) tell us that Adam "was not at first quite satisfied with the appointment [of Stanley as Bishop of Norwich]; but, before many months were over, the Bishop and all his family became his most intimate friends, and the [Bishop's] Palace was quite as much his home in Norwich as his own residence." Stanley died in September 1849, at the age of seventy, on a family holiday in Scotland, after "congestion of the brain set in" according to Clark and Hughes (1890a).

Wedded to the Rocks

His son Arthur (1815-1881) wrote a *Memoir* of his father in 1851, and in 1864 was appointed Dean of Westminster, a post he held until his death seventeen years later.

Dean of Peterborough (1853)
Early in May 1853 Adam was offered the post of Dean of Peterborough, but he turned it down. As Clark and Hughes (1890a) put it, he was "deaf to the voices of these charmers [old friends Lords Aberdeen and Fitzwilliam]. Without any hesitation, as it would appear, he refused, in a firm, but most full and courteous, letter to the Prime Minister."

Adam wrote to Lord Fitzwilliam "I have lived too long to be ambitious, so the increased ecclesiastical rank has no temptations for me; and I believe that the remnant of my life would be more usefully and more happily employed in doing the duties of the offices I now fill than in undertaking others arising out of high position in the Church."

As well as lacking ambition for a senior church post, Adam said he was content with his cathedral post in Norwich, his teaching at Cambridge, and his ongoing writing projects, though by then he had finished writing geological papers. He ends the letter to Fitzwilliam "I am very anxious your Lordship should understand my motives, and I should grieve that you should think me a moral coward, or a disloyal son of the Church of England, in declining the dignity you offer me."

18. Cowgill Chapel

*"I trust God will bless the undertaking which begins so
smilingly".*
Adam Sedgwick, letter to Canon Wodehouse (8 July 1837)

Adam Sedgwick was never one to avoid a controversy or dodge a good
fight, as we've seen in Chapters 12 to 14. We find him now, in his seven-
ties, rising to yet another challenge. This one centred on the Dentdale he
had always loved, and it was rooted in a dispute relating to St Andrew's
parish church in Dent where his father Richard and brother John had both
served as Vicar before John's son Richard took over in 1859.

Thankfully Adam left a detailed record of the saga, and what he
thought about it, in A *Memorial by the Trustees of Cowgill Chapel* that he
published privately in 1868, and his *Supplement to the Memorial by the
Trustees of Cowgill Chapel* that was published two years later.

Cowgill Chapel
The story begins thirty years earlier, when Adam's sister-in-law Jane,
wife of his brother John who was then Vicar of Dent, decided to do something to help improve the lot of the people living in and around the village
of Kirkthwaite about 5 miles north of Dent.

Cowgill
The area around Kirkthwaite was then known as Cowgill, having earlier
been called Cogill or Coegill. It was a remote rural area with an economy
dominated by pastoral farming and the hand-knitting of stockings, and in
the early nineteenth century coal was mined in Cowgill Head and marble
was also quarried locally and cut and polished at Stone House. In the
1840s a worsted and cotton mill called Dee Mill was built. The Settle-
Carlisle railway line, that later passed through the area, brought many
itinerant workers and an epidemic of smallpox, and boosted the local
economy during the construction stage, but it was not built until the
1870s.

By the first quarter of the nineteenth century the area had sunk into
"a state of comparative poverty", as we saw in Chapter 3, and Jane was

Wedded to the Rocks

concerned about "the unhappy moral consequences which gradually followed", as Adam put it in *Memorial*. He described in a letter to Mary,
Charles Lyell's wife Mary in October 1837 how "many of the poorer inhabitants of the hamlet, especially those in the remoter parts of it, were
without instruction, of reckless life, and without the common comfort and
guidance of social worship in the house of God."

Recall that a number of the families living in Dentdale at that time
were Non-Conformists (including Methodists and Quakers). Cowgill was
then a Quaker stronghold, a Quaker Meeting House having been built
there after a visit by George Fox. But it seems that Jane Sedgwick was
successful in bringing together an ecumenical group to work together for
a common cause – alleviating the poverty and improving the morality and
quality of life of their fellow Dales people. Adam told Mary Lyell how,
over a number of years, Jane "gradually drew together a united body of
Christians, who were ready to sink out of memory all points of dissent or
difference, and with true hearts to join in common worship, and in prayer
for the erection of a chapel to be lawfully consecrated to the services of
the Church of England."

Building the chapel
Once Jane had set the ball rolling and gathered together a group to support the project, the next step was to find a site for a chapel and churchyard. A local man, Mr Bannister, very generously stepped in and offered
to donate to the trustees (which included Adam Sedgwick) the remains of
an old abandoned Presbyterian chapel on his land, along with some adjacent land that "would form a beautiful and convenient site and burial-
ground for a new chapel, which might become forever a chapel-of-ease to
the old church of Dent", as Adam wrote to Mary Lyell. The people of
Dent gratefully accepted the offer.

It was then July 1836, and the Trustees circulated a letter calling upon "all who had a pious interest in the spiritual and temporal wellbeing of
the valley of Dent, to subscribe for the erection of a chapel, to be called
Cowgill Chapel", as Adam told Mary. The public response was very generous, and within a year sufficient funds were raised by public
subscription to build the chapel and establish an Endowment Fund to pay
for a Curate. Adam pointed out, in *Memorial*, that the chapel also needed
an Endowment Fund "to entitle it to Consecration and to give it a right to
a lawful District [parish]."

The foundation stone was laid on the 30th of June 1837 in a ceremony that Adam clearly enjoyed and describes in *Memorial*. "It was a day to

be remembered", he wrote, "The sun shone with its brightest radiance as the inhabitants of Dent, and the visitors from many of the neighbouring valleys, streamed onwards towards that sweet little plot of ground on which the Chapel now stands. Young and old were generally dressed as for a Sunday or a holiday ...".

He gave more details in a letter to Canon Wodehouse a week later, describing how "about seven hundred mountaineers [local people], including nearly two hundred Sunday-school children and about one hundred strangers, some of whom came from the distance of twenty miles, made a curious mixed procession in the wild glen where the little chapel is now rising from the ground. It is built upon the solid rock which forms the bed of a mountain stream that washes the churchyard side, and over which the waters descend in a long succession of rapids and falls; and it will be surrounded by birch, mountain-ash, and other wild trees of the country. I trust God will bless the undertaking which begins so smilingly."

Adam led the service standing on a rock of limestone. It opened with a reading of Psalm 100, then his brother John read several prayers from the Anglican liturgy and a local worthy – Mr William Carus Wilson (1764-1851), Justice of the Peace, Deputy Lieutenant for Westmorland, Member of Parliament for Cockermouth (1821-1827), who built Casterton Hall – gave a short address. Adam was then handed a trowel, and he laid the Foundation Stone and addressed his "countrymen". The assembled crowd then sang God Save the King, before many of them returned to Dent "and had cold meat and coffee at the parsonage. My sister made thirty-six gallons of coffee in a brewing-vessel."

Adam offers no information in *Memorial* (1868) about who designed or built the chapel. He simply noted that, "after the foundation-stone was laid, the building of Cowgill Chapel went forward without delay, and was completed under the design of a good architect; and before long the interior was properly seated for the reception of a congregation." He did add a small amount of colour in a letter to his friend Ainger in October 1838, in which he described the chapel as "a very pretty, correct, building, and admirably fitted for its purpose."

Consecration and early years

Cowgill Chapel was consecrated (dedicated for use as a church) at the end of October 1838. Adam had hoped to be present for that, but it clashed with a commitment he had made some months earlier to spend a few days near Ingleborough, as a guest of James Farrer who had recently

bought the Old Manor House in Clapham. Farrer's estate included Ingleborough Cave, into which he had recently used gunpowder to blast an
entrance, "and so formed communications between a succession of very
beautiful caverns richly adorned with stalactites, some of which reach the
ground, and form beautiful white pillars", as Adam wrote to Ainger a few
days before the consecration ceremony.

He was disappointed to miss the ceremony, but the opportunity to be
one of the first people to look around inside the cave was simply too good
for him to turn down, particularly at a time when he was doing a lot of
geological fieldwork in Yorkshire and the Lake District (Chapter 11), and
The Great Devonian Controversy (Chapter 12) was in full swing. The
ceremony was blessed with fine weather and a "large and sympathetic"
congregation, and he took some comfort from the fact that many people
said they had missed him.

Three months later, in January 1839, Rev William Matthews arrived
in Dent to serve as Curate in Cowgill Chapel. He was then a newly-
ordained deacon, which allowed him to lead services, preach and look
after the pastoral needs of the congregation, but not to preside at Holy
Communion. Only an ordained priest was allowed to do that, so presumably Adam's brother John Sedgwick presided, in his capacity as Vicar of
Dent.

Matthews took the job seriously, and was well-liked by his parishioners. He was ordained priest in 1841, and was offered the Curacy of
Cowgill by the five Trustees, acting as Patrons. The church records show
that on the 10th of April 1841 he was licensed by the Bishop of Chester
"To perform the office of Curate to the Perpetual Curacy of Cowgill in
the Parochial Chapelry of Dent, in the Parish of Sedbergh, in the County
of York." Matthews served as Curate at Cowgill for more than two decades, before leaving to become Vicar of Hawes in nearby Wensleydale in
1863, where he died in post seven years later.

William Matthew's early days as Curate were well-spent and fruitful. Sedgwick wrote to Canon Wodehouse in late October 1840, a few
years after the Chapel opened, reporting that he [Adam] had preached at
Dent in the morning and Cowgill in the evening, and praising Matthews
for having "done his duty there admirably." He told Wodehouse "I found
the little chapel crowded, and a Sunday school of 80 smiling children, in
a place where, a very few years since, everything had run wild for want of
looking after, and there was hardly to be seen a single Christian blos-
som."

18. Cowgill Chapel

Cowgill Chapel had got off to a good start. It was run by a well-liked and hard-working priest, had grown a stable congregation, and was teaching and guiding many local children. It enjoyed a warm and supportive relationship with Dent parish church, and was overseen by five committed Trustees. It's future looked bright, and Adam and his sister-in-law Jane were comfortable with what they had achieved. Adam wrote to Ainger in October 1938 that "Jane talks of nothing but Cowgill Chapel. I think she has a right to be proud of it." At that stage, neither of them could have imagined what would unfold after Rev Matthews left to take up the post of Vicar of Hawes.

Dispute over the name Cowgill
William Matthews' successor as Curate of Cowgill Chapel was Rev Joseph Sumner, who quickly made his name in the dale but not for the best of reasons. He fell out with the Trustees by committing what local historian David Boulton (1984) called "in Sedgwick's eyes two unforgivable sins."

His first "sin", committed shortly after taking up the post, was to attempt to extend his parish from just the district of Cowgill to the much larger area of the old hamlet of Kirthwaite. To do so would mean taking over part of the traditional parish of St Andrew's in Dent, which was understandably not willing to give it up. Sumner's plot failed, or so it seemed at the time.

Proposed change of name
Undaunted by that failure, Sumner pressed ahead with his ambitious plans. His second "unforgivable sin" was to propose that the name Cowgill be abolished and replaced with the ancient parish name Kirthwaite, and to change the spelling to Kirkthwaite (from Old Norse words meaning "a paddock near the church"). Adam Sedgwick devotes a lot of space in *Memorial* (1868) to the argument about changing the name and the spelling, but Sumner's biggest "crime" was changing the name behind the backs of the Trustees and the Vicar of Dent. David Boulton (1984) describes how the name Kirkthwaite "was endorsed by the Ecclesiastical Commissioners and inscribed in stone over the porch of Sumner's new church school."

The story of how the name change was formally approved is full of intrigue. Clark and Hughes (1890b) tell us that, by the time the chapel was consecrated in October 1838, all of the relevant paperwork (the deeds of the Trust and the Endowment, the title deeds of the freehold land on which the chapel stood, and a map of the "district [parish boundary] of the chapel") had been prepared and approved by the Bishop of Ripon. The documents were then "taken away by the Bishop's secretary for registration." The Trustees were more than disappointed to discover, more than two decades later in 1864, that they had not in fact been registered with the Bishop.

No one now knows why the documents had not been registered as expected, but the consequences were very serious. In legal terms, it mean that the Trustees had no rights of patronage, and the chapel had no rights to its own district [parish]. As a result, the Trustees transferred the patronage to the Bishop and asked the Ecclesiastical Commissioners to designate a district for the chapel. After some negotiation between the Trustees and the Commissioners the boundaries of a parish were agreed, and the award of the parish (confirmed by the Queen, as was standard practice) was published in *The London Gazette* on the 12th of September 1865.

The Trustees assumed that the matter was then settled, but they made the mistake of not getting hold of a copy of the award as printed, which was freely available in the *Gazette*. Six months later, in June 1866, they were shocked to discover that the award granted a name change as well as a district; it's formal name was then The District Chapelry of Kirkthwaite.

Sedgwick fights back

Adam Sedgwick did not take the name change lightly. After all, as Clark and Hughes (1890a) make clear, "by a stroke of the pen the whole history of the chapel was to be erased." Adam wrote in *Memorial* (1868) that the chapel "had been consecrated; it had a name which had become endeared, as a household word, by daily use; and its congregation had attended its sacred services for a quarter of a century."

He decided the fight the name change. David Boulton explains how "the restoration of the proper name of the chapel, Cowgill, and of the proper spelling of the hamlet, Kirthwaite, became a crusade into which he poured all the energy he had earlier given to more famous scientific and theological battles with Roderick Murchison and Charles Darwin."

In December 1866 Adam and the two other surviving Trustees (one of whom was Margaret, daughter of Adam's sister Jane who had worked so hard to build and serve the chapel) submitted a petition to the Ecclesiastical Commissioners. They called it a *Memorial*, which Adam later used as the basis for his much larger and more detailed *Memorial by the Trus-*

18. Cowgill Chapel

tees of Cowgill Chapel (1868). It closed with a "loyal and earnest prayer: (1) that the Award... may be so modified that its verbal contradictions may disappear, and the error in the orthography [conventional spelling] of the word Kirkthwaite may be corrected; (2) that the name of Cowgill Chapel be fully retained; (3) that its District be named (as it was named in the three first successive Presentations) the Chapelry of Cowgill." (Clark and Hughes 1890b)

The Ecclesiastical Commissioners replied in March 1867, reporting that they had no authority to alter "the title under which a District may have been legally created", and advising that the matter was now formally closed.

The matter was certainly not closed in Adam's eyes. In order to raise awareness of what he saw as grave injustice, he decided to strengthen the case laid out in the *Memorial* petition, then print it privately to circulate among "the Statesmen and Inhabitants of the Valley of Dent, and the present Representatives of those kind and generous friends who subscribed to the Building and Endowment Funds of Cowgill Chapel." The book-length *Memorial* details the history of Cowgill Chapel and its district, but it also includes chapters on the climate, history and dialects of Dent.

Adam's campaign quickly gathered pace after he sent a copy of *Memorial* to the Dean of Westminster, Arthur Stanley (son of Edward Stanley, Adam's Bishop in Norwich, who we met in Chapter 17). The Dean's wife, Lady Augusta Stanley, wrote to Adam advising that the Queen would like a copy, and he sent one without delay. Recall (from Chapter 9) that Victoria knew Adam well, through his close working relationship with Prince Albert; she liked him and trusted him. She thanked him for the book, and said she thought his argument just and reasonable.

Adam was delighted to read of the Queen's offer to contact the Archbishop of York and ask for his support in getting the original name restored to Cowgill Chapel. That would require an Act of Parliament. The Archbishop of York (William Thomson) introduced the Bill into the House of Lords and the Prime Minister (William Gladstone) supported it in the House of Commons.

The battle over the Chapel's name was won, and in July 1869 the District Chapelry of Kirkthwaite was renamed the District Chapelry (subsequently the Parish) of Cowgill.

The following year, Sedgwick published his *Supplement to the Memorial of the Trustees of Cowgill Chapel*. As Clark and Hughes (1890b) put it, "the previous work [*Memorial*] was a tale of sorrow, but this is a tale of triumph – sobered a little by the thought of his increasing age – but still a joyful statement of what his Dalesmen owed 'to the love of right and the condescending goodwill of our gracious Sovereign.'"

The impact of the chapel naming dispute on the reputation and career of Rev Joseph Sumner remains unknown.

PART FIVE. OLD MAN

"So one day is now gone out of my 70th year. I once thought it impossible that I should ever be so old; not that I thought I was going to die, but because fifty or sixty years in prospect, seemed a prospect of an eternity. And the time does seem long, even in retrospect, when I trace it back from stage to stage. But when I think of the warm scenes of early life, the past time seems nothing. I seem to be still present with those who are gone from this world – to hear their beloved voices – to see their loving smiles – and I can fancy myself walking with them and talking with them among the pleasant fields of my childhood, or boyhood, or youthful manhood. Many of my beloved friends are gone never to return; but I am to follow them, and may that grace of a redeeming God, who (as I hope and trust) received them in heaven, at length, when it is His good will, receive me also!"

Adam Sedgwick letter to Fanny Hicks (23rd March 1854)

19. Old Age

"even when nearer 90 than 80 years of age, he was as full of humour and anecdote as in middle age. For high moral courage, for honesty and singleness of purpose, for generosity of nature, and for a hatred of all that is mean and base, no name ever stood higher than that of Adam Sedgwick."
Adam Sedgwick Obituary in *The Times* (28th January 1873)

From the mid-1840s onwards, we find Adam Sedgwick entering his sixties and starting to look back on his life and achievements and look forward to the end of his days. As an adult, he had often suffered from ill-health, and although his career in geology had been very fruitful for both him and his subject, it had put him at the centre of some lasting controversies that won him friends and foes alike. He never married and, after a long and busy working life in the public eye, old age brought him recurrent loneliness and spells of melancholy.

After 1855, having reached three score years and ten, Adam gradually withdrew from active public life. As Clark and Hughes (1890b) put it, "though his capacity for the enjoyment of society, of music, and of nature, was undiminished, and he could take as keen an interest as ever in what was going forward in the world and the University, his bodily ailments grew more acute, and allowed him shorter periods in which he could apply himself to serious work."

He was fortunate to be able to keep living in his rooms in Trinity College in Cambridge and in his cathedral house in Norwich, with practical support and a circle of close friends available in each place, until his dying days.

The theme of thankfulness, for both his life and his Christian faith, is touched upon in many of the letters he wrote to family and friends during this season of his life. Typical of many was a letter he wrote to his niece Isabella in March 1845, telling her "I ought, day and night, to thank God for the blessings I enjoy, and have enjoyed, not indeed uniform and uninterrupted, but chequered with some pain and sickness and such afflictions as must sometimes meet us on the way if we are permitted to live to sixty ... My domestic griefs have, in comparison of what are often laid on my neighbours, been few indeed, and slight; and none of them, thank God, without the comfort and consolation of Christian hope."

Adam's geological work had taken him to most parts of Britain, and he had visited continental Europe several times. His love of travel remained undimmed in his later years, and in the autumn of 1854 we find him visiting Paris with his two nieces Isabella and Fanny. He described the trip in a letter to Hugh Miller two years later; they went via Boulogne and Amiens, where they took time to visit "the finest cathedral in the world", then moved on to Paris, which he had visited twenty years earlier, and where he was now "astonished and dazzled" by the sights.

That was the last overseas trip he took, but he later still took a keen interest in trips undertaken by family members. He was particularly to read Isabella's letters about a tour of Italy she took with some close friends in the spring of 1869. He wrote to her in April, while they were in Rome, that "for many a long year I have been dreaming of the Maritime Alps, of the Gulf of Genoa, of Rome, of Naples, etc." but age and ill-health ruled out such a trip, adding poignantly that "God does not permit me to cross the Alps in my old age." He enquired if they had visited the cathedral at Sienna, "said to be one of the finest specimens existing of the old Italian Gothic", and asked her "did not your heart beat higher when you saw the dome of St Peter's, and entered the streets of Rome?"

Reflecting on his achievements

There's no denying the fact that Sedgwick's work in geology helped to move the subject forward at a critical time in its development as a scientific discipline, as we saw in Part Three. As noted in his Obituary in *The Times* in January 1873 "In his declining years he ... had the satisfaction of feeling and knowing that he had not lived in vain", by helping to develop the subject and increase its popularity as a science, and by teaching and training many men who became "first-rate practical geologists".

Adam could never be accused of taking his geological work lightly. In Chapter 7 we saw how committed he was to developing and curating the Geology Museum in Cambridge that he inherited when he was appointed Woodwardian Professor of Geology in 1818. In Chapters 11 to 13 we saw how committed he was to the field mapping of rock sequences and structures across large areas, and to offering carefully thought out and well-supported interpretations and explanations of what he found. We've also seen (in Chapters 14 and 15) how he reconciled his scientific work and his deep religious faith, and how that led him to re-imagine creation as a multi-phase phenomenon (involving multiple catastrophes over a

very long period of time, each involving the wiping out of existing creatures followed by the creation of different ones, fully-formed) rather than
a one-off event (Noah's Flood), by divine action (God's handiwork) directed by a supernatural intelligence (the mind of God) and following a
divine plan (God's grand design) established at the beginning of time.

Despite the importance of his geological work, both to him personally and to the subject as a whole, after more than three decdes of more or
less working non-stop on it, Adam was growing weary and looking forward to a rest. He made this clear in a letter he wrote to fellow Canon
Wodehouse in Norwich in February 1847. He told him "Tomorrow I must
… go to my Museum, which I am putting in its last arrangement, so far,
at least, as my own labours are concerned with it. I wish this work were
over, and then I would emancipate myself from Geology, and set my
house in order for the evening of life [old age]. Such are my day-dreams."

He did manage to reduce his workload in geology a great deal after
that, but he still had his Canon's duties to perform in Norwich Cathedral
(Chapter 17) and he committed a great deal of time and effort to the fight
over Cowgill Chapel (Chapter 18).

Adam might have left the front-line of geological controversy, but he
didn't leave the field of play altogether. Not until 1871, at the age of 86,
did he resign as Professor of Geology at Cambridge, and stop lecturing
and supervising Museum Assistants, who he paid from his own pocket.
He remained a Fellow of Trinity College, and retained rights to college
rooms and the services of a servant and his wife. Only a few months before he died in 1873, Adam was still working on his *Introduction* to
Salter's *Catalogue of the Collection of Cambrian and Silurian Fossils
contained in the Woodwardian Museum of the University of Cambridge*.

Adam doubtless did have "the satisfaction of feeling and knowing
that he had not lived in vain", but it was tinged with disappointment that
he had not achieved more. He said as much in a letter to Isabella in October 1847. He told her "Alas! forty-three long years are gone since I came
up [to Cambridge] a freshman. Would that I could show more fruit for so
long a trust! I seem to myself to have led a useless life, and I am certain
that I have not been a good economist of my own happiness."

Facing the challenges of old age
Throughout his adult life Adam loved to spend time in his beloved Dentdale, surrounded by family, taking brisk walks in the hills, enjoying the
clean air, well away from the stresses and strains of work. Even in his
eighties he was keen to make the journey north from Cambridge, which

by then was quicker, safer and more comfortable than in his younger years, thanks to the advent of the railway. But trips to Dent were not without risks; in July 1868, at the age of 83, Adam fell and injured his knee while walking with some of his grand-nephews and grand-nieces near Hell's Cauldron waterfall on the River Dee.

Declining health

Adam had suffered periods of ill-health all through his adult life, and this continued in his later years. He was often laid low by gout, particularly during spring and early summer, that prevented him from taking the long walks outdoors that he loved so much, partly to help clear his head from feeling over-loaded with work. Gout seriously affected his mind as well as his legs; at the age of 84, in May 1869 he wrote to Miss Kate Malcolm about how it "prevents all kindly emotions; makes me sour and selfish; incapable of labour, yet never at rest; dull as ditch-water, yet abominably irritable and waspish; incapable of continued thought bent to any good purpose; my memory refusing to do its hourly duty, yet stored with gloomy, worthless images; my moral sense perverted."

Over many years Adam had also had to cope with eye problems, which often made it difficult for him to read and write by candlelight in his college rooms during the long, dark winter months. His eyesight declined sharply in his later years, almost to the point of total blindness. He wrote to Mrs Thompson in March 1867 advising that, having outlived most of his friends and colleagues in college, he could "bear solitude" by sitting quietly reading books, but "alas! my old eyes are in an angry state, and hardly permit me to read by candlelight. This is a great trial."

To make matters worse, early in 1865, after returning to Cambridge from a short stay with friends in Fakenham in Norfolk, Adam's doctor gave him "a stethoscopic examination [that] proved what I before suspected, that I had an organic disease of the heart", as he wrote to a Mrs Philpott. He told her "if I ever exert myself in any way (e.g. if I walk up my staircase at the pace I used to do) I soon have a warning throb in the left side of my chest, and am compelled to slacken my pace." He added "This knowledge imposes on me ... the necessity of living very quietly, and of doing my best, God being my helper, to set my house in order."

The years were taking their toll on him, but he dealt with his declining health with a mixture of stoicism, resignation, and thankfulness. As Clark and Hughes (1890b) put it, "the load of years sat lightly upon him, for though he had frequent attacks of severe illness, his mind remained clear and vigorous to the last, and, as he often admitted, he was a strong man for his years, at least till after the severe illness in the spring of 1870." Strong he might well have been, but the heart disease made him slow down, get plenty of rest, and avoid arguments and controversy.

It also brought home to Adam that his days were now numbered. He described himself in October 1865, in a letter to Sir John Herschel, as "a man who is deaf as a post, has a gouty temper, and a heart organically diseased, and who bears upon his back the load of eighty years." He wrote to his cousin Mrs. Norton in July 1867 that he was "more feeble in muscular strength than … last year, though in far better general health; I am more deaf, more dim-sighted, more incapable of any severe and continued mental effort. But I try to thank God for the gift of long life."

Loneliness
As a confirmed bachelor had spent all his adult years living alone, both in Cambridge and Norwich, albeit supported by domestic staff and frequently visited by his nieces Isabella Sedgwick and Fanny Hicks.

But he was no stranger to loneliness, and not only coped with it but made a virtue out of it. He wrote to Fanny in March 1841 that "all persons should learn to live alone, I mean sometimes. But there are many persons who are never happy when by themselves, which shows that they want resources in their own minds, and have had a bad moral training." He pointed out to her that "when you are by yourself you are in God's presence; while you walk out you are in a glorious temple built by His hands; and while you have your eyes and understanding you can live and converse with the holy men, and the Apostles, and the poets, and the historians of all time". He urged her to "acquire this temper, and acquire these habits, while you are young and your mind is plastic … [so that] when a woman you may reap a rich harvest of happiness and usefulness."

Although he sometimes complained of having too many visitors disturbing his attempts to write up his geological work, he also often missed the company of others in college, particularly outside term times when the undergraduates and many of the Fellows left town. In early February 1847 he wrote to Julius Hare, Archdeacon of Lewes and former Assistant Tutor in Trinity College, that "during this melancholy vacation I have been very solitary. The college has been empty, so that for days together, I have seen no faces but my own ugly withered face reflected from my looking-glass while I was a-shaving …", with occasional visits from his man-servant John and his "bed-maker", John's wife.

Victorian writers often mention melancholy (pensive sadness usually with no obvious cause), and the elderly Adam Sedgwick was no exception. He wrote to Isabella in March 1854, at the age of 69, "Oh! that I had the placid, patient, hopeful temper my dear old father had during the last years of his long life! During the dismal spring months I am full of bitterness, which seems quite unchristian ... I fight against this melancholy bitter spirit as well as I can, and some of it may be set down to bodily disease ..."

Adam's increasing deafness, failing eyesight, and heart condition increased his growing isolation. As a result, as Clark and Hughes (1890b) point out, "while at Cambridge, he lived during the last four or five years of his life almost alone." By then, the life of Trinity College was dominated by much younger Fellows, who had little direct contact with him.

The death of many of his old friends and colleagues only made matters worse for him, and rubbed salt into the wound of loneliness. He wrote to Rev Arthur Stanley in December 1863 that "some of the most lasting and pleasurable emotions of my life arise from the thoughts of those who are gone." The following March he wrote to Charles Lyell expressing great sadness at the death of Scottish geologist and past President of the Geological Society Leonard Horner, "the last remaining friend of my early geological life", and in August 1864 he wrote to Lady Bunbury on the death of Joseph Romilly, a senior administrator in Cambridge University, "the oldest friend I had in Cambridge. ... the only one left of those with whom I was on close terms of brotherly love during the early years of my academic life."

Over the next few years Adam was to lose a number of other close friends and colleagues, including William Whewell (whose ideas about induction we looked at in Chapter 15, and who died in March 1866), and Archdeacon Robert Wilson Evans (who, as we saw in Chapter 7, had initially competed against Sedgwick for the post of Woodwardian Professor of Geology). Adam's youngest brother James, step-father to Fanny Hicks, died in 1869.

Although he had no children of his own, Adam took a great interest in his nieces and nephews, and enjoyed their companionship when they were able to spend time with him in Norwich. His favourite was Isabella, the eldest daughter of his brother John, who he often referred to in letters to her and others as his "dear daughter". He told his cousin Mrs Norton by letter in July 1867 that "nearly all the objects of my early love are gone from my sight, and now I am reaping my best social joys among my nephews and nieces, and their merry children. Eight young, happy, merry children are here; and the old parsonage is as noisy and full of glee as it was 70 years since."

19. Old Age

Mortality
By 1871 Adam was fully aware of his own mortality. That November, at the age of 86, and having lived in Trinity College for 67 years, Adam wrote to senior members of Cambridge University that, "with thankfulness to God for the past, I know well that I must soon be called away from all earthly duties ...".

Twelve years earlier he had touched on the same theme, but framed in a more hopeful way, in a conciliatory letter he sent to Charles Darwin in November 1859, having just received a copy of *Origin of Species*. He wrote "I find, by loss of activity and memory, and of all productive powers, that my bodily frame is sinking slowly towards the earth. But I have visions of the future. ... [that will come true in the after-life]. But on one condition only – that I humbly accept God's revelation of Himself both in His works and in His Word, and do my best to act in conformity with that knowledge which He only can give me, and He only can sustain me in doing. If you and I do all this, we shall meet in heaven."

Looking back on the times he lived through
Adam lived through interesting times, and towards the end of his life he looked back on the significant historical events that had occurred during his lifetime. He refers to many of them in letters he sent to his sister-in-law Mary (wife of his brother John) in November 1852, and to Mrs Norton in March 1863.

France was in turmoil throughout Adam's childhood and youth. The French Revolution started in 1789 when he was four years old; French King Louis XVI was murdered when he was eight; the Revolution ended when he was fourteen and attending Dent Grammar School. Napoleon Bonaparte declared himself Emperor of France in 1804, when Adam was nineteen, shortly after he had finished at Sedbergh School and started as a student in Cambridge. Nelson's victory over the French at the Battle of Trafalgar the following November was celebrated on the streets throughout England, while the undergraduate Adam was confined to his rooms in Trinity College, sick with fever. The French invasion of Russia in 1812 was commemorated by Tchaikovsky in his famous *1812 Overture*, written to celebrate Russia's defence of Moscow against the French. Napoleon's Empire collapsed and the Napoleonic Wars in continental Europe ended after the Duke of Wellington's victory at Waterloo in June 1815. Adam brought news of the victory to Dent by riding to Sedbergh to meet the post coach then racing back with the *London Gazette* newspaper, and reading the headlines to a crowd of people gathered in the Market Place.

Victoria was crowned Queen in 1837, when Adam was 52 years old, and her reign stretched well beyond the final three decades of his life. We saw in Chapter 9 how closely Adam worked with Prince Albert when he was Chancellor of Cambridge University, and how well he was regarded and warmly he was accepted by the Queen.

The world changed a great deal during Victoria's reign, due in no small measure to the expansion of the British Empire, which by 1850 included India, large parts of Africa, and many other territories across the globe. Britain effectively controlled the economies of many regions in Asia and Latin America, through its dominance over much of world trade.

Adam had a personal connection with the Crimean War (1853-1856), which claimed the lives of 22,000 soldiers from the British Empire. Part of the cavalry regiment that took part in the infamous Charge of the Light Brigade in October 1854 had been based in Norwich where he served as Canon in the Cathedral, so he "knew personally and intimately very many of the gallant men who have fallen, by pestilence, or the sword. ... Three fine, gallant young men dined with me a day or two before their regiment left Norwich, and all of them fell at the fatal charge", as he described in a letter to Miss Gerard four months later.

Adam also had a personal connection with the American Civil War (1861-1865), through a relative of his called Mrs Norton who lived in North America. He wrote to her in March 1863 pointing out the virtues of "the old, monarchical, mixed, Christian, government of England" and praying that "the same God of truth and love [would] put an end to the desolating war of our transatlantic cousins!". He told her "I dislike the temper of your Northern democrats; it is fierce, ambitious, and I believe incompatible with true civil liberty." Six months later he wrote again to Mrs Norton, telling her "It was a dream of my early life that I might some day settle in North America. I am too old to dream now, and if I were a dreamer I should not feel any longing to be naturalized in a country desolated by civil war." After the Civil War ended he wrote again, in February 1866, to say "I give you joy on the successful end of the terrible war which desolated the Southern States of your Union. The price you have paid has been great – but not too great for the purchase of freedom for your negro fellow-creatures. ... It is delightful to think that whoever walks within the limits of the United States, whatever may be his complexion, may now hold up his head as a free man." Adam and his father had long been strong supporters of the abolition of slavery (as we saw in Chapter 2), so whilst he seriously regretted the loss of life and the hardships the war had caused, he was pleased with the outcome of it.

Adam witnessed much more than just economic expansion and military conflict during Victoria's reign, because this was a period of great progress in science and technology. As he wrote to Mrs Norton in March 1863, "the triumphs of science have gone hand in hand with these great world-wide movements; or perhaps it would be nearer the truth to say that science has been their mainspring, and living strength."

The Industrial Revolution had begun to transform Britain in the early nineteenth century, in the early days of Adam's career in Trinity College. He told Mrs Norton that "gas-light, railroads, steam-boats, electric telegraphs, are in my memory but things of yesterday. Years, well remembered, were past in my early life before such things were so much as heard of; and yet how vastly they seem to have changed the whole outer world of civilized Christendom!" The transformation included a rapid rise in the population and rapid growth of cities in Britain, which in turn gave rise to significant social and economic challenges and problems. These same forces of change drove the continued depression of the economy in Dentdale, and the migration of people from the dale, that we noted in Chapter 2.

20. Death and Remembrance

"My eyes have been filled with tears while the dark shade of thought was passing over my mind – that I might never again be cheered by the sight of my dear native dale, and the home of my childhood."
Adam Sedgwick letter to his niece Isabella (20th June 1872)

Having completed his geological work in geology in 1871, Adam largely retired from public view and spent his final two years quietly in his rooms in Trinity College and his cathedral house in Norwich.

His strength was failing and his health declining, but he was still able to receive friends who called in, and to welcome his favourite nieces who paid short visits. His eyesight continued to deteriorate, so that after 1871 he was unable to read a few pages of a book or leading articles in *The Times*, even wearing strong glasses in bright sunlight. It also restricted his ability to write letters to family and friends, so he dictated them to his servant or a niece.

Final six months

Adam spent the August and September of 1872 "in Residence" at Norwich. He started there on the 1st of August, and Isabella joined him there the same day, having travelled down from Yorkshire to help look after him. She described his condition then in a letter to Kate Vaughan on the 27th of January 1873, shortly after he died; "he was cheerful and seemed well" but was frail and unable to greet her at the door, and found it difficult to go up or down stairs. He didn't have the energy to fulfil any the cathedral duties he had performed dutifully for nearly three decades, although he was usually able to attend afternoon services. Isabella noted that Adam then "felt the close of his life approaching" and knew this would be his last trip to Norwich. She was particularly struck by "how constantly his thoughts seemed to be dwelling upon the life beyond the grave" and how, although he still took an interest in events beyond his home, "whenever he was alone, earthly things seemed to lose their interest ...". He read his Bible with renewed enthusiasm, spoke of the Apostles like personal friends, and prayed earnestly and audibly in his bed at night.

Adam returned to Cambridge at the end of September, to the comfort of the rooms in the Great Court of Trinity College that had been his home since before the Battle of Trafalgar. He sent a letter to his family telling them "I keep up my spirits pretty well by thinking of the past and by cherishing hopes for the future, and by reading the letters of my nieces and grand-nieces … I am not unhappy – I have learnt to feel a pleasure in sitting still in my armchair." As in Norwich, he was not able to attend the daily services in the College Chapel, but he did arrange for the morning and evening lessons to be read to him. His servant John read to him for several hours most days, and kept him informed of what was happening in the world beyond College. Thoughts of a final visit to his beloved Dent often passed through his mind, but he grew resigned to the fact that he would never see the place again.

Final days

Friends brought Adam flowers and game to celebrate the New Year of 1873, and his nieces and their families sent him cards, but they all found him low in spirit and in health. Strong medication helped him cope with some digestive problems, but he was still able to take the occasional short drive, by horse and carriage, and visit friends in Cambridge. Isabella told Kate Vaughan that a visit to the Geology Museum early in January was probably the last time he ventured out of his rooms in college. Her letter to Kate throws much light on Adam's final days.

By mid-January he was clearly failing fast. His colleagues at Norwich Cathedral, including the Dean and several Canons, travelled to Cambridge on about the 20th of January to hold a meeting of the Cathedral Chapter in Sedgwick's rooms, partly to avoid him having to go to Norwich but primarily to support him in his last days and to say their farewells. Canon James Heaviside stayed with Adam after the others left, and reported that "he brightened up considerably in the afternoon … and the depression and weakness may be only temporary …. He talked to me as usual; but evidently is conscious of his weakness, and indeed said to me seriously that he did not think he should live through the spring."

Several days later, on the 22nd of January, Isabella received two letters at her home in Langcliffe (near Settle in North Yorkshire), neither bringing good news. One was dictated by Adam with a postscript by his servant John, who advised that he thought Adam was getting weaker. The other was from Canon Whiteside, who said much the same thing. A few hours later she received a telegram from Doctor Paget (Adam's doctor in Cambridge) telling her that "my uncle had fainted when getting up, and that he thought that I had better come at once to Cambridge", as she later wrote to Kate Vaughan.

Isabella knew that time was of the essence, so she caught the next train south to Cambridge, travelled through the night, and arrived in Cambridge the next morning. Adam was very happy to see her, but he told her "I shall not be long here now, you must stay and be with me to the last." He was confined to bed all that day, weak but not in pain, and chatted with her about his parents, brothers and sisters who had all "gone home before him". He asked her to read to him some Psalms and passages from the Bible, before she left him in the care of his servant John and retired for the night to a nearby guest room in the college. The following day (Friday) he was up and dressed when she arrived at his rooms, and she found him slightly stronger, even though he had not slept much during the night. He was still free from pain, but Dr Paget inspected him and thought him weaker.

Adam slept through much of the Saturday, but he picked up towards evening. He was clearly preparing for his own death, and asked Isabella to read him some passages from the Bible. He asked for Psalm 130, that he had read to his friend Ainger on his death-bed, Psalm 51, that had been his father's favourite, and the 17th chapter of John's Gospel, that he had read to her mother Margaret (his eldest sister) the evening before she died. After that, as Isabella wrote to Kate, "he went on to speak of his own hopes of salvation, alluding to himself in words of the deepest humility, saying that his whole trust was in the atonement which his Saviour had made for him, and in the mercy and love of his Father in Heaven."

Death
Death came quietly and peacefully. Isabella told Kate that Adam had a quiet night and slept through most of Sunday morning. In the afternoon she heard him praying in his room, unaware that she was by the foot of his bed and could hear him. His spoken prayers started out quiet and intermittent, but grew stronger and more earnest. The last words he spoke were "Wash me clean in the blood of the Lamb – Enable me to submit to Thy Holy Will – Sanctify me with Thy Holy Spirit". After that his breathing became gentler, and he slept through the afternoon and into the evening.

Isabella sat quietly keeping watch at his bedside, near the window. She heard the organ playing and the choir singing in evening service in the College Chapel, and told Kate "so unearthly in its beauty was the melody, that it almost seemed as if the golden gates of Heaven were opening, and music not of this world was floating down to that quiet room." Adam slept peacefully, without pain, breathing gently until about midnight, when (quoting from Psalm 23) "we saw the shadow of death come softly over his face, and we knew that he had passed into the dark valley, and that the end was near."

Adam died peacefully in his rooms in Trinity College as the clock in the Great Court outside his windows chimed a quarter past one on the morning of Monday the 27th of January 1873. As Isabella put it, "his spirit returned to God".

The following day *The Times* published his *Obituary*, extracts from which have been quoted in this chapter and the preceding one.

Funeral

Adam was buried the following Saturday in Trinity College Chapel, in the centre of a side chapel, close to William Whewell. The coffin was carried round the Great Court, followed by a large group of Fellows and undergraduates from the College, accompanied by senior representatives of the University, and friends and relatives, many of whom had travelled a long way to be there. Rev William Thompson, Master of Trinity College, led the service and read the prayers of committal. Adam's final resting place is marked by a simple brass plaque on the floor of the chapel, showing only his initials AS.

The following day Rev Arthur Stanley (Dean of Westminster and son of Adam's good friend in Norwich Bishop Stanley) preached a sermon in the College Chapel in his memory. He spoke about Adam's commitment to geology, noting that "he left no stone unturned, he left no depth unexplored, out of which he could extract the secrets of nature or dispel the darkness of ages." He spoke at length about Adam's strong Christian faith, pointing out that he never lost "the conviction that in this bold research he was fulfilling his Creator's will. Never did he cease to see in those marvels the signs of the Creator's goodness." He sketched out Adam's many personal qualities, including his "eloquence … [his] eagle eye … [his] rare union of gracious courtesy and noble independence … [his] pride [of] the glories of his Church and country … the ever ready guide and counsellor of kinsfolk and friends … [his] child-like, simple, yet manly and understanding faith … [his love of reading] in public or in private the stirring passages of Holy Scripture … the overflowing thankfulness with which he would recount the many blessings which had followed him … his calm and peaceful close.

20. Death and Remembrance

Will

Adam never married, have children, or set up home beyond Trinity College and Norwich Cathedral. He had shown little interest in acquiring material possessions, and left nothing other than the contents of his rooms in college.

His will was read on the 3rd of April and reported in *The Times* on the 26th of April 1873, three months after his death. His estate was valued at less than £4,000 and its disposal was overseen by three executors – his niece Isabella Sedgwick, nephew Robert Westall, and friend Canon James Heaviside from Norwich.

To his "honoured friend" William George Clark, Vice-Master of Trinity College, he left his two books by classical scholar Richard Porson, alumnus and Fellow of Trinity College (1759-1808) – *Adversaria: Notae et Emendationes in Poetas Graecos* (1812) *The Frogs of Aristophanes* (1837). He left all his geological maps, sections, and manuscript journals, along with the *Proceedings* and *Quarterly Journal of the Geological Society* and the books published by the Paleontological Society of America, to the library of the Woodwardian Museum. The books and pictures that Queen Victoria and Prince Albert had given him were distributed among his family.

Memorials

Adam's life is both described and celebrated in *The Life and Letters of the Reverend Adam Sedgwick* that was edited by John Willis Clark and Thomas McKenny Hughes and published by the Cambridge University Press in 1890. *The Times* chose it as "the principal book of the ... week" on the 19th of June, and reviewed it on the 29th of July. It noted in the June article that "Adam's "life is ... almost a history of the University of Cambridge in his time and a record of the growth and progress of many branches of scientific, especially geological, inquiry."

The two volumes of *Life and Letters* are a very useful source but they are not an easy read. *The Times* commented in June that "a biography extending over more than a thousand pages is a great deal too long. Sedgwick's letters are very pleasant reading, but many of them are of little intrinsic importance." Six weeks later, in its July review, it added that "they abound in trivialities about Sedgwick and irrelevancies about others." More recently, Colin Speakman (1982) has pointed out that "the very massiveness of *The Life and Letters* is a barrier to an objective understanding of Sedgwick; whilst being a magnificent piece of Victorian scholarship, it remains something of a hagiograph; its detail rather obscures the stubborn, reactionary, lonely hypochondriac that Sedgwick became in his later years."

Adam's life is also remembered in a number of ways and in the places that were important to him – Dent, Norwich, and Cambridge.

Dent

There are two memorials to him in Dent, where he was born and where he insisted his heart had always belonged. Inside St Andrew's Church, where his father, brother and nephew had been successive Vicars, and where Adam was baptised and later preached, he is remembered in a brass plaque on a side wall, close to one commemorating his father Richard. The wording on his plaque captures particularly his love of Dentdale and his strong Christian faith –

> *In Memory of THE REVEREND ADAM SEDGWICK L.L.D. Canon of Norwich Cathedral, Senior Fellow of Trinity College Cambridge, and for fifty years Woodwardian Professor of Geology. Born March 22 1785. Died January 27 1873. His University claimed his life's labour, but though removed for the greatest part of his life from his beloved Dent Dale, his love for it was always fresh, and he ever visited it with increasing affection. As a man of science and a Christian, he loved to dwell on the eternal power and Godhead of the Creator as revealed in nature and the fuller revelation of his love, as made known in the gospel of His Son Jesus Christ. His Christian faith and hope are best told by his own last words "Wash me in the blood of the lamb, enable me to submit to thy holy will, sanctify me with thy Holy Spirit." Baptized in this church. Buried in the Chapel of Trinity College Cambridge.*

Close to the church, in High Street, is a striking memorial fountain, rough cut in Shap Granite, with the simple wording 'Adam Sedgwick 1785-1873' inscribed and highlight in gold paint. The £200 cost was quickly raised by the statesmen, family members, and friends, and the simple design reflected Adam's long-term concern about the quality of the water supply in the town. It is fed by a stream that flows down from one of the hills surrounding Dent.

Adam's contribution to geology, both locally and further afield, is commemorated in a geological trail bearing his name that was opened in 1985 to celebrate the bicentenary of his birth. The well-marked 1.5 km

20. Death and Remembrance

Sedgwick Geological Trail follows the River Clough, a tributary of the Rawthey in Garsdale, and was set up by the Yorkshire Dales National Park and the Sedgwick Museum in Cambridge. As well as exploring the Dent Fault, it focusses on the relationship between the Carboniferous and Silurian rocks in the district that first attracted Adam's attention as a geologist, and played a prominent role in the Cambrian-Silurian Controversy (Chapter 13).

Adam's attachment to Dentdale is also celebrated and remembered in his *Memorial by the Trustees of Cowgill Chapel* (1868) and *Supplement to the Memorial of the Trustees of Cowgill Chapel* (1870), which David Boulton (1984) praises as "a classic of dales life". As well as detailing the fight over Cowgill Chapel it includes information about local history and the local dialect, weather, and rivers.

Norwich
Adam is commemorated in Norwich Cathedral in a brass tablet on the wall of St Luke's Chapel, which bears the following inscription written by the Archbishop of Canterbury in 1873 –

> *In Christ. To ADAM SEDGWICK. A master among philosophers, the friend of princes, the delight of little ones, as one who extended the frontiers of science, and was fired by a right royal love of truth, whose character was a grand simplicity, and whose rock was the faith of Christ. To him, once a Canon of the Church of Norwich, this memorial is raised by the Dean.*
> *1873.*

Cambridge
Given that Adam spent all of his adult life based in Cambridge and living in Trinity College, and that his main focus and his reputation were based on geology, it is no surprise that the University took steps to celebrate and remember his life and work. As we saw earlier, a simple brass plaque bearing his initials marks his final resting place in Trinity College Chapel.

The most obvious and prominent memorial to Adam in Cambridge is the Geological Museum that he worked so hard to build up. When he was appointed Woodwardian Professor of Geology in 1821 he took on responsibility for developing and curating the rock collection that John Woodward had started in the late seventeenth century. That task continued to occupy him for the next five decades. He had managed to get a new museum built in 1840, but by the time he died it was too small to house the ever-growing collection of rocks and fossils.

Not long after he died, friends, colleagues and senior members of the University met and agreed that the most appropriate memorial to him would be a new and larger Geological Museum. They agreed that it should be named in his honour, although the proposal that it should contain a bust of Adam Sedgwick was challenged by Professor of Theology William Selwyn, who insisted on a statue; he argued "Let us have the whole man, as we have been wont to see him. For what is a geologist without the hand to wield the hammer? without the feet to carry him over the mountains?" The Sedgwick Museum of Geology in Cambridge was opened in 1904 and included a statue of Adam by distinguished English sculptor Onslow Ford. The Museum is now part of the Department of Earth Sciences and is called The Sedgwick Museum of Earth Sciences.

Adam had the unusual distinction of having a memorial in his name established during his lifetime. Early in 1865, eight years before he died, Augustus Arthur Vansittart (a close friend and Fellow of Trinity College) made a gift of £500 to Cambridge University "for the purpose of encouraging the study of geology among the resident members of the University, and in honour of the Reverend Adam Sedgwick." He and Adam agreed that the money should be used to establish a prize, called the Sedgwick Prize, to be awarded every third year for the best essay on "some subject in geology or the kindred sciences." The prize was first awarded in 1873, and is now a postgraduate prize awarded every second year.

In 1880, seven years after Adam died, a group of students set up the Sedgwick Club in his honour. It is now the oldest student-run geological society in the world, and its original rules, still followed, state that it "should consist of members only of the University of Cambridge", and its objective is "to promote the study of geology by the reading and discussion of papers thereon", which it does through regular talks and an annual conference.

Appendix 1. The Geologic Timescale

Era	Period	Age (million years ago)	Duration (million years)
Cenozoic		66-0	66
Mesozoic	Cretaceous	145-66	79
	Jurassic	201-145	56
	Triassic	252-201	51
Palaeozoic	Permian	299-252	47
	Carboniferous	359-299	60
	Devonian	419-359	60
	Silurian	444-419	25
	Ordovician	485-444	41
	Cambrian	541-485	56
Pre-Cambrian		4,600 – 541	4,059

Source: simplified from International Commission on Stratigraphy (2016) *International Chronostratigraphic Chart*

Appendix 2. Publications by Adam Sedgwick

Sedgwick, A. (1820) On the physical structure of those formations which are immediately associated with the primitive ridge of Devonshire and Cornwall. *Transactions of the Cambridge Philosophical Society* 1: 89-146 [read 20 March 1820]

Sedgwick, A. (1821a) On the physical structure of the Lizard District in the county of Cornwall. *Transactions of the Cambridge Philosophical Society* 1: 291-330 [read 2 April and 7 May 1821]

Sedgwick, A. (1821b) *A Syllabus of a Course of Lectures on Geology.* Cambridge. 2nd edition 1832; 3rd edition 1837;

Sedgwick, A. (1822a) On the geology of the Isle of Wight. *Annals of Philosophy, New Series* 3: 329-366

Sedgwick, A. (1822b) On the phenomena connected with some trap dykes in Yorkshire and Durham. *Transactions of the Cambridge Philosophical Society* 2: 21-44 [read 20 May 1822]

Sedgwick, A. (1823-4) On the association of trap rocks with the mountain limestone formation in High Teesdale. *Transactions of the Cambridge Philosophical Society* 2: 139-195

Sedgwick, A. (1825a) On the origin of alluvial and diluvial formations. *Annals of Philosophy, New Series* 9: 241-257

Sedgwick, A. (1825b) On diluvial formations. *Annals of Philosophy, New Series* 10: 18-37

Sedgwick, A. (1826) On the classification of the strata which appear on the Yorkshire coast. *Annals of Philosophy, New Series* 11: 339-362

Sedgwick, A. (1826-28) On the Magnesian Limestone and lower portions of the New Red Sandstone Series. *Transactions of the Geological Society of* London (2) 3: 37-124

Sedgwick, A. and Murchison, R.I. (1829a) On the geological relations of the secondary strata in the Isle of Arran. *Transactions of the Geological Society of London* (2) 3: 21-36

Sedgwick, A. and Murchison, R.I. (1829b) On the geological relations and internal structure of the Magnesian Limestone and the lower portions of the New Red Sandstone series in their range through Nottinghamshire, Derbyshire, Yorkshire and Durham, to the southern extremity of Northumberland. *Transactions of the Geological Society of London* (2) 3: 37-124 [read 17 November 1826, 30 April, 18 May 18, 7 March 1828)

Sedgwick, A. and Murchison, R.I. (1829c) On the structure and relations of the deposits contained between the Primary Rocks and the Oolitic Series in the north of Scotland. *Transactions of the Geological Society of London* (2) 3: 125-160 [read 16 May and 6 June 1828]

Sedgwick, A. (1830) Address delivered [as President] at the Anniversary Meeting of the Geological Society of London, 19 February 1830. *Proceedings of the Geological Society of London* 1: 187-212

Sedgwick, A. and Murchison, R.I. (1830a) A sketch of the structure of the Eastern Alps; with sections through the Newer Formations on the northern flank of the chain, and through the Tertiary Deposits of Styria. *Transactions of the Geological Society of London* (2) 3: 301-420

Sedgwick, A. and Murchison, R.I. (1830b) A sketch of the structure of the Austrian Alps. *Proceedings of the Geological Society of London* 1: 227-231

Sedgwick, A. (1831a) Introduction to the general structure of the Cumbrian Mountains; with a description of the great dislocations by which they have been separated from the neighbouring Carboniferous Chains. *Transactions of the Geological Society of London* (2) 4: 47-68 [read 5 January 1831]

Sedgwick, A. (1831b) Address to the Geological Society, delivered on the evening of the 18th of February, 1831. *Proceedings of the Geological Society of London* 1: 281-316

Sedgwick, A. (1831c) Description of a series of longitudinal and transverse sections through a portion of the Carboniferous Chain between Penigent and Kirkby Stephen. *Transactions of the Geological Society of London* (2) 4: 69-101 [read 2 March and 16 March 1831]

Sedgwick, A. (1832a) On the New Red Sandstone Series in the basin of the Eden, and North-western coasts of Cumberland and Lancashire. *Transactions of the Geological Society of London* (2) 4: 383-408 [read 1 February 1832]

Sedgwick, A. (1832b) On the geological relations of the stratified and unstratified groups of rocks composing the Cumbrian Mountains. *Proceedings of the Geological Society of London* 1: 399-401 [read 16 May 1832]

Sedgwick, Adam (1833) *A Discourse on the Studies of the University.* Cambridge. 2nd and 3rd editions 1834; 4th edition 1835; 5th edition 1850

Sedgwick, A. (1835a) Remarks on the structure of large mineral masses, and especially of the chemical changes produced in the aggregation of stratified rocks during different periods after their deposition. *Transactions of the Geological Society of London* (2) 3: 461-486 [read 11 March 1835]

Sedgwick, A. (1835b) Introduction to the general structure of the Cumbrian Mountains; with a description of the great dislocations by which they have been separated from the neighbouring Carboniferous chains. *Proceedings of the Geological Society of London* 2 (58): 675-685

Sedgwick, A. and Peile, W. (1835) On the range of the Carboniferous Limestone flanking the primary Cumbrian Mountains; and on the coal-fields of the N.W. coast of Cumberland, *etc. Proceedings of the Geological Society of London* 2: 198-200 [read 10 June 1835]

Sedgwick, A. and Murchison, R.I. (1835a) On the geological relations of the Secondary strata in the Isle of Arran. *Transactions of the Geological Society of London* (2) 3: 21-36

Sedgwick, A. and Murchison, R.I. (1835b) On the structure and relations of the deposits contained between the Primary rocks and the Oolitic Series in the North of Scotland. *Transactions of the Geological Society of London* (2) 3: 125-160

Sedgwick, A. and Murchison, R.I. (1835c) A sketch of the structure of the Eastern Alps; with sections through the newer formations on the northern flanks of that chain. *Transactions of the Geological Society of London* (2) 3: 302-420

Sedgwick, A. and Murchison, R.I. (1836a) On the Silurian and Cambrian Systems, exhibiting the order in which the older sedimentary strata succeed each other in England and Wales. *Report of the British Association, 1835 Dublin Meeting.* Part 2: 59-61

Sedgwick, A. and Murchison, R.I. (1836b) Description of the raised beach in Barnstaple or Bideford Bay, on the north-west coast of Devonshire. *Transactions of the Geological Society of London* (2) 4: 279-286 [read 14 December 1836]

Sedgwick, A. and Peile, W. (1836) On the coal-fields of the north-western coast of Cumberland. *Proceedings of the Geological Society of London* 2: 419-422 [read 8 June 1836]

Sedgwick, A. and Murchison, R.I. (1837a) A classification of the old slate rocks of the north of Devonshire, and on the true position of the Culm Deposits in the central portion of that county. *Report of the British Association, 1836 Bristol Meeting.* Part 2: 95-96

Sedgwick, A. and Murchison, R.I. (1837b) On the physical structure of Devonshire, and on the subdivisions and geological relations to its older stratified deposits. *Transactions of the Geological Society of London* (2) 5: 556-563 [read 14 June 1837]

Sedgwick, A. (1838) A synopsis of the English series of stratified rocks inferior to the Old Red Sandstone – with an attempt to determine the successive natural groups and formations. *Proceedings of the Geological Society of London* 2: 675-685 [read 21 March and 23 May 1838]

Sedgwick, A. and Murchison, R.I. (1839a) Classification of the older stratified rocks of Devonshire and Cornwall. *Philosophical Magazine, Series III*, 14: 241-260

Sedgwick, A. and Murchison, R.I. (1839b) Supplementary remarks on the "Devonian" system of rocks. *Philosophical Magazine, Series III*, 14: 354-358

Sedgwick, A. and Murchison, R.I. (1839c) On the classification of the older stratified rocks of Devonshire and Cornwall. *Proceedings of the Geological Society of London* 3 (63): 121-123

Sedgwick, A. and Murchison, R.I. (1840a) On the classification and distribution of the older or Palaeozoic deposits of the north of Germany and Belgium, and their comparison with formations of the same age in the British Isles. *Proceedings of the Geological Society of London* 3 (70): 300-311

Sedgwick, A. and Murchison, R.I. (1840b) On the physical structure of Devonshire, and on the subdivisions and geological relations of its older stratified deposits. Part II. *Transactions of the Geological Society of London* (2) 5: 633-704 [read 24 April 1839]

Sedgwick, A. (1841) Supplement to 'Synopsis of the English series of stratified rocks inferior to the Old Red Sandstone', with additional remarks on the relations of the Carboniferous Series and the Old Red Sandstone of the British Isles. *Proceedings of the Geological Society of London* 3 (82): 541-554 [read 3 November and 17 November 1841]

Sedgwick, A. and Murchison, R.I. (1842a) On the distribution and classification of the older or Palaeozoic deposits of the north of Germany and Belgium, and their comparison with formations of the same age in the British Isles. *Transactions of the Geological Society of London* (2) 6: 221-301 [read 13 May and 27 May 1840]

Sedgwick, A. (1842b) Three letters on the geology of the Lake District addressed to W. Wordsworth, Esq. (23 May, 24 May, 30 May). Printed in *A Complete Guide to the Lakes*, by John Hudson (1843). Kendal

Sedgwick, A. (1843) Outline of the geological structure of North Wales. *Proceedings of the Geological Society of London* 4 (96): 212-224 [read 21 June 1843]

Sedgwick, A. (1844) On the Older Palaeozoic (Protozoic) rocks of North Wales. *Proceedings of the Geological Society of London* 4: 251-266

Sedgwick, A. (1845a) On the Older Palaeozoic (Protozoic) rocks of North Wales. *Quarterly Journal of the Geological Society of London* 1: 5-22 [read 15 November and 29 November 1843]

Sedgwick, A. (1845b) On the geology of North Wales. *Quarterly Journal of the Geological Society of London* 1: 214

Sedgwick, A. (1845c) Review of *Vestiges of the Natural History of Creation*. *Edinburgh Review* 82: 1-85

Sedgwick, A. (1845d) On the comparative classification of the fossiliferous strata of North Wales, with the corresponding deposits of Cumberland, Westmoreland, and Lancashire. *Quarterly Journal of the Geological Society of London* 1: 442-450 [read 12 March 1845]

Sedgwick, A. (1845e) On the geology of the neighbourhood of Cambridge, including the formations between the Chalk Escarpment and the Great Bedford Level. *Report of the British Association, Cambridge Meeting.* Part 2: 40-47 [read June 1845]

Sedgwick, A. (1846) On the classification of the fossiliferous slates of Cumberland, Westmoreland, and Lancashire. *Quarterly Journal of the Geological Society of London* 2: 106-131 [read 7 January and 21 January 1846]

Sedgwick, A. (1847) On the classification of the fossiliferous slates of Cumberland, Westmoreland, and Lancashire. *Quarterly Journal of the Geological Society of London* 3: 133-164 [read 16 December 1846]

Sedgwick, A. (1848) On the organic remains found in the Skiddaw Slate, with some remarks on the classification of the older rocks of

Cumberland and Westmoreland, *etc. Quarterly Journal of the Geological Society of London* 4: 216-225

Sedgwick, A. (1851) On the geological structure and relations of the Frontier Chain of Scotland. *Report of the British Association, Edinburgh Meeting.* Part II: 103-107

Sedgwick, A. (1852a) On the slate rocks of Devon and Cornwall. *Quarterly Journal of the Geological Society of London* 8: 1-19 [read 5 November 1851]

Sedgwick, A. (1852b) On the Lower Palaeozoic rocks at the base of the Carboniferous Chain between Ravenstonedale and Ribblesdale. *Quarterly Journal of the Geological Society of London* 8: 35-54 [read 3 December 1851]

Sedgwick, A. (1852c) On the classification and nomenclature of the Lower Palaeozoic rocks of England and Wales. *Quarterly Journal of the Geological Society of London* 8: 136-138 [read 25 February 1852]

Sedgwick, A. (1852d) The Silurian System. *Literary Gazette* 1838: 338-340, 417-419

Sedgwick, A. (1852e) On a proposed separation of the so-called Caradoc Sandstone into two distinct groups; viz (1) May Hill Sandstone; (2) Caradoc Sandstone. *Quarterly Journal of the Geological Society of London* 9: 215-230 [read 3 November 1852]

Sedgwick, A (1854a) On the classification and nomenclature of the older Palaeozoic rocks of Britain. *Report of the British Association, 1853 Hull Meeting.* Part 2: 54-61

Sedgwick, A. (1854b) On the May Hill sandstone and the Palaeozoic system of England. *Philosophical Magazine* (4) 8: 301-317, 359-370, 472-506

Sedgwick, Adam and McCoy, Frederick (1855) *A Synopsis of the classification of the British Palaeozoic Rocks: with a systematic description of the British Palaeozoic Fossils in the Geological Museum of the University of Cambridge.* Cambridge. [https://archive.org/details/synopsisofclassi00sedg]

Sedgwick, Adam (1868) *A Memorial by the Trustees of Cowgill Chapel.* Cambridge

Sedgwick, Adam (1870) *Supplement to the Memorial by the Trustees of Cowgill Chapel.* Cambridge

Sedgwick, A. (1873) Preface to "*A catalogue of the collection of Cambrian and Silurian fossils contained in the Geological Museum of the University of Cambridge, by J.W. Salter, F.G.S.*" Cambridge

Bibliography

Anon (1870) Eminent Living Geologists: 1. Rev Adam Sedgwick. *The Geological Magazine* 7 (70): 145-149

Ashby, E. and Anderson, M. (1969) Introduction to reprint of Adam Sedgwick (1833) *A Discourse on the Studies of the University.* Leicester: Leicester University Press

Austen, Robert (1842) On the geology of the south-east of Devonshire. *Transactions of the Geological Society of London* Series 2 6 (2): 433-489

Bailey, Edward (1952) *The Geological Survey.* London: Thomas Murby.

Baxter, Stephen (2003) *Revolutions in the Earth. James Hutton and the True Age of the World.* London: Phoenix

Bonney, Thomas George (1897) Adam Sedgwick. *Dictionary of National Biography* 25: 179-183

Booth, C.C. (1970) John Dawson 1734-1820. *British Medical Journal* 5728: 171-173

Boulton, David (1984) Introduction to *Adam Sedgwick's Dent.* Facsimile reprint in one volume of Adam Sedgwick's *A Memorial by the Trustees of Cowgill Chapel (1868)* and *Supplement to the memorial (1870).* Sedbergh: R.F.G. Hollett & Son

Boulton, David (1995) *A Thousand Ages. The story of the church in Dentdale.* Dent: Dales Historical Monographs

Bowler, P.J. (1990) *Charles Darwin.* Cambridge: Cambridge University Press

Bowman, J.E. (1841) On the great development of the Upper Silurian formation in the Vale of Llangollen, North Wales; and on a plateau of igneous rocks on the east flank of the Berwyn Range. *Report of the British Association* (1840); 100-102

Browne, J. (1995) *Charles Darwin Voyaging.* Princeton, New Jersey: Princeton University Press

Cannon, W.F. (1976) The Whewell-Darwin controversy. *Journal of the Geological Society of London* 132: 377-384

Carruthers, Margaret W. and Clinton, Susan (2001) *Pioneers of Geology. Discovering Earth's Secrets.* New York: Franklin Watts

Chambers, R. (1844) *Vestiges of the Natural History of Creation.* Edinburgh:

Clark, John Willis and Hughes, Thomas McKenny (eds) (1890a) *The Life and Letters of the Reverend Adam Sedgwick. Volume 1.* Cambridge: Cambridge University Press
Clark, John Willis and Hughes, Thomas McKenny (eds) (1890b) *The Life and Letters of the Reverend Adam Sedgwick. Volume 2.* Cambridge: Cambridge University Press
Darwin, Charles (1859) *On the Origin of the Species by Means of Natural Selection.* London:
De la Beche, Henry T. (1834) On the anthracite found near Bideford in north Devon. *Proceedings of the Geological Society of London* 2 (37): 106-7
De la Beche, Henry T. (1839) *Report on the geology of Cornwall, Devon and West Somerset.* London: Her Majesty's Stationery Office *Report on the geology of Cornwall, Devon and West Somerset*
Fenton, Carroll Lane and Fenton, Mildred Adams (1952) *Giants of Geology.* Garden City: Doubleday and Company
Geikie, Archibald (1905) *The Founders of Geology.* New York: Dover Publications
Hallam, A. (1989) *Great Geological Controversies.* Second edition. Oxford: Oxford University Press
Hartley, Marie and Joan Ingilby (1963) *The Yorkshire Dales.* London: Dent
Hudson, J. (1843) *A Complete Guide to the Lakes ... with Mr Wordsworth's description of the scenery of the country, etc. and three letters on the geology of the Lake District by Professor Sedgwick.* Kendal: (4th edition 1853, 5th edition 1859)
Hughes, T. McKenny (1883) Adam Sedgwick. *Proceedings of the Yorkshire Geological Society* 8: 255-268
Hull, D.L. (1973) *Darwin and his Critics. The Reception of Darwin's Theory of Evolution by the Scientific Community.* Boston: Harvard University Press
Kendall, P. F. and Wroot, H. E. (1924) *The Geology of Yorkshire.* Vienna: Printed for the authors.
Lapworth, C. (1879) On the tripartite classification of the Lower Palaeozoic rocks. *Geological Magazine*, New Series 6: 1-15
Lyell, C. (1830-1833) *Principles of Geology.* 3 volumes. London
Lynch, J.M. (2002) Sedgwick, Adam (Rev) (1785-1873). In *The Dictionary of Nineteenth Century British Philosophers.* Bristol: Thoemmes Press

320

McKenny Hughes, T. (1883) Biographical Notices of Eminent Yorkshire Geologists. II. Adam Sedgwick. *Proceedings of the Yorkshire Geological and Polytechnic Society* 8: 255-268

Milner, R. (1993) *The encyclopedia of evolution: Humanity's search for its origins.* New York: Henry Holt.

Moule, Thomas (1837) *The English Counties Delineated: Or, A Topographical Description of England.* London: George Virtue

Murchison, R.I. (1833) On the sedimentary deposits which occupy the western parts of Shropshire and Herefordshire. *Proceedings of the Geological Society of London* 1: 474-477

Murchison, R.I. (1834) On the structure and classification of the transition rocks of Shropshire, Herefordshire and part of Wales, and on the lines of disturbance which have affected that series of deposits, including the Valley of Elevation at Woolhope. *Proceedings of the Geological Society of London* 2: 13-18

Murchison, R.I. (1835) On the Silurian System of rocks. *Philosophical Magazine* 7; 46-53

Murchison, R.I. (1839) *The Silurian System.* London

Murchison, R.I. (1842) Anniversary Address of the President. *Proceedings of the Geological Society of London* 3: 640-652

Murchison, R.I. (1843a) Anniversary Address of the President. *Proceedings of the Geological Society of London* 4: 70-86

Murchison, R.I. (1843b) *Geological map of England and Wales.* London: Society for the Diffusion of Useful Knowledge

Murchison, R. I. (1852) On the meaning of the term 'Silurian System' as adopted by geologists in various countries during the last ten years. *Quarterly Journal of the Geological Society of London* 3: 173-184.

Murchison, R.I. (1854) *Siluria. The history of the oldest known rocks containing organic remains, with a brief sketch of the distribution of gold over the Earth.* London: John Murray

Olson, R.G. (2004) *Science and Religion 1450-1900.* New York: Johns Hopkins Press

Orange, A. D. (1973) *Philosophers and Provincials.* York: Yorkshire Philosophical Society.

Paley, W. (1802) *Natural Theology.* London:

Porter, Roy (1977) *The Making of Geology.* Cambridge:

Roberts, Michael B. (2009) Adam Sedgwick (1785-1873): geologist and evangelical. in M. Kolb-Ebert (editor) *Geology and Religion: A*

History of Harmony and Hostility. Geological Society of London Special Publications 310: 155-170

Robson, Douglas A. (1986) *Pioneers of Geology*. Newcastle upon Tyne: Natural History Society of Northumbria.

Rowe, David (no date) Adam Sedgwick FRS (1785-1873). Yorkshire Philosophical Society. http://www.ypsyork.org/resources/yorkshire-scientists-and-innovators/adam-sedgwick/

Rudwick, Martin (1985) *The Great Devonian Controversy: The Shaping of Scientific Knowledge among Gentlemen Specialists*. Chicago: University of Chicago Press

Rudwick, Martin (1988) A year in the life of Adam Sedgwick and company, geologists. *Archives of Natural History* 15 (3): 243-268

Rupke, N.A. (1983) *The Great Chain of History*. Oxford: Oxford University Press

Scott, Harry J. (1965) *Portrait of Yorkshire*. London: Robert Hale

Secord, J.E. (1986) *Controversy in Victorian Geology: The Cambrian-Silurian Dispute*. Princeton: Princeton University Press

Secord, J.A. (2000) *Victorian Sensation*. Chicago: University of Chicago Press

Secord, J. A. (2004) Adam Sedgwick (1785-1873). In *Dictionary of National Biography*, Volume 49, 647-649. Oxford: University Press.

Sedgwick, Adam (1833) *A Discourse on the Studies of the University*. Cambridge: Cambridge University

Sedgwick, Adam (1868) *A Memorial by the Trustees of Cowgill Chapel*. Cambridge: Cambridge University

Sedgwick, Adam (1870) *Supplement to the Memorial by the Trustees of Cowgill Chapel*. Cambridge: Cambridge University

Sharpe, D. (1843) On the Bala Limestone. *Proceedings of the Geological Society of London* 4: 10-14

Smith, Alan (editor) (2001) *The Rock Men. Pioneers of Lakeland Geology*. Keswick: Cumberland Geological Society

Snyder, Laura J. (2012) William Whewell. In *Stanford Encyclopedia of Philosophy*. https://plato.stanford.edu/entries/whewell [accessed 2 March 2017]

Speakman, Colin (1982) *Adam Sedgwick: Geologist and Dalesman 1785-1873*. Heathfield: Broadoak Press, The Geological Society of London, Trinity College Cambridge

Thackray, J.C. (1976) The Murchison-Sedgwick controversy. *Journal of the Geological Society of London* 132: 367-372

The Times (1873) Obituary - Professor Sedgwick. 28 January 1873

The Times (1873) Deaths – Adam Sedgwick. 26 April 1873

The Times (1890) Adam Sedgwick. 29 July 1890

The Times (1890) Book of the week – *The Life and letters of the Reverend Adam Sedgwick.* 19 June 1890

The Times (1904) The new buildings at Cambridge. 27 February 1904

Thompson, W. (1892) *Sedbergh, Garsdale and Dent. Peeps at the past history and present condition of some picturesque Yorkshire dales.* Leeds: Richard Jackson

Whewell, William (1833) *Astronomy and General Physics Considered with Reference to Natural Theology. A Bridgewater Treatise.* London: William Pickering

Whewell, William (1847) *The Philosophy of the Inductive Sciences, Founded upon their History.* London: John W. Parker

Whewell, William (1857) *History of the Inductive Sciences.* London: John W. Parker

Whewell, William (1858) *The History of Scientific Ideas.* London: John W. Parker

Whewell, William (1860) *On the Philosophy of Discovery.* London: John W Parker

Winchester, Simon (2001) *The Map that Changed the World: The Tale of William Smith and the Birth of a Science.* London: Viking

Winstanley, D.A. (1940) *Early Victorian Cambridge.* Cambridge

Woodward, H.H. (1907) *The History of the Geological Society of London.* London

Woodward, H.H. (1911) *The Story of Geology.* London

Woodward, J. (1695) *Natural History of the Earth.* London

Yeo, Richard (2008) *Defining science: William Whewell, natural knowledge and public debate in early Victorian Britain.* London: Cambridge University Press

Index

Agassiz, Louis, 148, 149, 176, 177, 230, 233, 240, 241
Age of Reason. *See* Enlightenment
age of the earth, 139, 160, 231
Ainger, William, 11, 44, 52, 54, 55, 64, 65, 67, 68, 69, 70, 71, 86, 89, 98, 100, 164, 165, 168, 169, 184, 185, 265, 266, 267, 269, 270, 274, 275, 276, 277, 285, 286, 287, 305
Albert, Prince, 1, 2, 48, 80, 122, 123, 124, 127, 128, 129, 130, 131, 132, 133, 166, 251, 289, 300, 307
Alluvial formation, 143
Alps, 75, 102, 141, 144, 148, 150, 177, 183, 184, 185, 186, 294
Ansted, David Thomas, 95
Arran, 152, 180, 181, 182
Austen, Robert, 202
Barrett, Lucas, 96
Beaumont, Jean-Baptiste Elie de, 156, 187, 189
Bentham, Jeremy, 116
Biblical Flood. *See* Flood, The
Biblical geology. *See* Scriptural geology
Bishop of Norwich, 281, 289
black marble, 27
Bland, Miles, 11, 61, 74
Bowman, John Eddowes, 213
Bridgewater, Earl of, 148, 237, 256
British Association, 1, 56, 103, 130, 148, 175, 192, 194, 200, 205, 209, 210, 211, 212, 213, 222, 223, 224, 233, 236, 237, 251, 252
Buckland, William, 98, 104, 146, 147, 148, 149, 154, 156, 167, 179, 202, 204, 210, 228, 229, 231, 236, 237, 250
Burton, Margaret, 7, 8
Cambrian System, 210, 227
Cambrian-Silurian Controversy, 179, 180, 192, 196, 206, 207, 216, 222, 223, 260, 274, 309
Cambridge Philosophical Society, 99, 119, 166, 167, 168, 170, 173, 210, 245

Carboniferous, 163, 167, 168, 171, 173, 174, 175, 180, 182, 192, 197, 198, 199, 200, 201, 202, 203, 204, 205, 217, 309
Carboniferous Limestone, 167, 168, 175
Catastrophism, 91, 141, 145, 149, 156, 157, 180, 182, 231, 232, 252
Catholic Emancipation, 108
Chambers, Robert, 118, 236, 238, 239, 240, 242, 260
Chancellor of Cambridge University, 129
Cheshire, 89, 150, 165, 166, 176
cleavage, 181, 189, 200
Coal Measures, 171, 198, 200, 201
Cockburn, Sir William, 236, 237, 238
Cole, Rev Henry, 235
Coleridge, Hartley, 26
Conception, 254
Conybeare, John, 167
Conybeare, William, 98, 148, 167, 178, 231, 270
Copley Medal, 103, 217, 259
Cornwall, 100, 164, 167, 178, 190, 191, 193, 197, 199, 203, 205
Coronation of Queen Victoria, 127
Cowgill, 28, 32, 283, 287, 289
Cowgill Chapel, 3, 17, 20, 33, 284, 285, 286, 287, 289, 295
creation, 93, 104, 119, 138, 139, 140, 142, 143, 147, 151, 154, 161, 193, 224, 227, 228, 229, 230, 231, 232, 233, 234, 235, 236, 238, 241, 242, 244, 245, 246, 249, 250, 252, 257, 258, 279, 294
creative additions, 232, 233, 234
Culm, 197, 198, 199, 200, 201, 202, 203, 205
Culm Measures, 197, 200, 205
Cumberland, 25, 164, 171, 172, 174, 175, 195, 210, 216
Cumbrian Mountains. *See* Lake District
curriculum reform at Cambridge University, 112

324

Index